The United States, Honduras, and the Crisis in Central America

Thematic Studies in Latin America

Gilbert W. Merkx
Series Editor

The United States, Honduras, and the Crisis in Central America, Donald E. Schulz and Deborah Sundloff Schulz

Divine Violence: Spectacle, Psychosexuality, and Radical Christianity in the Argentine "Dirty War," Frank Graziano

Land, Power, and Poverty: Agrarian Transformation and Political Conflict in Central America, Charles D. Brockett

FORTHCOMING

The Women's Movement in Latin America: Participation and Democracy, Second Edition, edited by Jane S. Jaquette

The United States, Honduras, and the Crisis in Central America

Donald E. Schulz and
Deborah Sundloff Schulz

Westview Press
BOULDER • SAN FRANCISCO • OXFORD

Thematic Studies in Latin America

The views expressed in this book are solely those of the authors and do not necessarily reflect the views or policies of the Department of the Army or the U.S. Government.

Published in 1994 in the United States of America by Westview Press, Inc., 5500 Central Avenue, Boulder, Colorado 80301-2877, and in the United Kingdom by Westview Press, 36 Lonsdale Road, Summertown, Oxford OX2 7EW

Library of Congress Cataloging-in-Publication Data
Schulz, Donald E., 1942–
The United States, Honduras, and the crisis in Central America / Donald E. Schulz and Deborah Sundloff Schulz.
p. cm. — (Thematic studies in Latin America)
Includes bibliographical references and index.
ISBN 0-8133-1324-4 (hardcover) — ISBN 0-8133-1323-6 (paperback)
1. Honduras—Politics and government—1982– 2. Honduras—Relations—United States. 3. United States—Relations—Honduras. 4. Central America—Politics and government—1979– I. Schulz, Deborah S. (Deborah Sundloff) II. Title. III. Series.
F1508.3.S34 1994
972.8305'3—dc20 93-45691
CIP

Printed and bound in the United States of America

The paper used in this publication meets the requirements of the American National Standard for Permanence of Paper for Printed Library Materials Z39.48-1984.

10 9 8 7 6 5 4 3 2 1

To Deborah's parents,
Dorislee Nicholls and Fredrick Douglas Sundloff,
who did a fine job of getting her to this point, and to
Méndez and the muchachos at Toncontín

The Fruit Company, Inc.
reserved for itself the most succulent,
the central coast of my own land,
the delicate waist of America.
It rechristened its territories
as the "Banana Republics"
and over the sleeping dead,
over the restless heroes
who brought about the greatness,
the liberty and the flags,
it established the comic opera.

Pablo Neruda
"The United Fruit Company"

Contents

Preface

Much water has flowed under the Guanacaste bridge since this book was first conceived in the summer of 1984. Back then it seemed appropriate to write a short, pithy tale of a small, dependent country corrupted by the overwhelming power and influence of the "Colossus of the North." In the process of researching the study, however, we found a history and society much richer and more interesting than that. Having lived in Honduras for two years and visited it on numerous occasions, we came to love it even as we were appalled by its weaknesses. This affection may not always be apparent in the pages that follow. Inevitably, if one is focusing on the causes of a crisis—whether current or chronic—one must dwell on the negative: poverty, corruption, subservience to foreign interests, and so on. Such realities tend to overshadow the positive traits of a people. Yet we have grown to appreciate the strength and courage of the many ordinary Hondurans who continue to live their lives under the most trying of circumstances: mothers attempting desperately to survive and keep together the remains of their families after fathers have left home, peasants still seeking to eke out a living though the land they work cannot support them, schoolteachers trying to survive on a salary that is not nearly enough to sustain a decent living. There is much here to respect, as well as much to criticize.

Above all, we have come to understand that Honduras is not a one-dimensional society. Though the country is best known to North Americans through stereotypes, it is not simply a "banana republic." (Today, in fact, bananas account for only about one-third to one-half of the value of Honduran exports.) Nor is it quite the "constitutional democracy" that the Reagan administration designated it or the "land-based aircraft carrier" that was the object of so much ridicule from the political left during the 1980s. Although all these images capture part of Honduran reality, they are essentially political cartoons; they oversimplify and distort to the point of caricature. Behind them there is a complex, ambiguous, and often contradictory society that has largely defied North American efforts at classification.

Indeed, Honduran politics often has a surrealistic quality about it: It is a politics of indirection, resembling in some respects the swirling, convoluted back roads of Tegucigalpa, which often lead the unwary traveler in directions not anticipated. (Here the shortest distance between two points is often a semicircle.) And so constitutions and civilian institutions are largely—though not entirely—a facade, masking the source and exercise of more fundamental powers in the armed forces. The normal way of transferring power—*substantive* power—is not by elections but rather by subterranean intrigue and provocation. Nor is this a simple matter of brute force. In Honduras, military hegemony relies as much on the submission of civilians as on the threat or exercise of violence. For all the congratulatory and self-congratulatory rhetoric that attended the restoration of procedural democracy (elections) in the early 1980s, civil-military relations since then have not changed much. The civilians are still subordinate to the armed forces. Perhaps they like it that way; they seem to be comfortable in their position of established inferiority.

Beyond this, perhaps the most striking feature of the political culture is its contradictions. If the society has glaring weaknesses, it also has unexpected strengths. In fact, some of the weaknesses are, paradoxically, *sources* of strength. Thus, the very underdevelopment that would seem, on the surface, to make this country a prime candidate for revolutionary turmoil has contributed to its continuing stability. (In contrast, in the more economically advanced El Salvador, development-generated social and political changes played a major role in plunging the country into civil war.) The armed forces, though repressive and plagued by corruption and incompetence, have also been a source of stability: They have been flexible enough to allow a certain amount of reform and to avoid the kind of massive human rights violations that in El Salvador and Guatemala pushed so many people into the arms of the extreme left. Similarly, socioeconomic and psychological dependency, passivity, inefficiency, and corruption—deadweight on economic development and modernization—have provided much of the glue that has held this society together.

Many people have contributed to this book. Over the years, we have interviewed over a hundred individuals and talked with many more. Some, both North Americans and Hondurans, spoke on a not-for-attribution basis, and we respect their wishes by not listing their names below. Others cannot be recognized for lack of space. Special thanks are due so many people that it is hard to know where to begin, but any list must start with Gary Cook and Víctor Meza. Señor Cook gave huge amounts of time and energy to the project. His insights into Honduran society were invaluable, and his extensive contacts led to numerous interviews. Similarly, Víctor Meza, one of the country's most respected journalists, was the source of an enormous amount of information, both personally and in his capacities as director of the Centro de Documentación de Honduras and publisher of the *Boletín Informativo Honduras*. Beyond this, we are indebted to Mark Ruhl, Steve Ropp, Philip Shepherd, James Morris, Thomas Dodd, John Fishel, Gil Merkx, and Gabriel Marcella for their comments on various parts of the manuscript. (Ruhl, Ropp, and Shepherd were especially gracious in this respect, having read virtually all of it.) Their criticisms and suggestions considerably strengthened the final product. Needless to say, any errors of fact or interpretation are entirely our responsibility.

Others who contributed through interviews or private conversations include, on the North American side, John Negroponte, John Ferch, Cris Arcos, Jack Binns, Everett Briggs, Fred Woerner, Shepard Lowman, Don Johnson, Tom Dodd, William Krehm, Chip Barkley, Joe Eldridge, Clarence and Linda Dunkerley, Roger Norton, Bill Millard, Mark Sullivan, Maynard Parker, Bob Killebrew, Sonny Sloan, Bill Prince, David Andrews, Tom Becker, Jan and Len Brockman, and Rob and Marion Howland. On the Honduran side, we are indebted to, among others, Carlos Flores Facussé, Ubodoro Arriaga, Augusto Suárez Lozano, Gustavo Alvarez Martínez, Jaime Martínez Guzmán, Irma Acosta de Fortín, Elizabeth ("Tita") Mazariegos Zúniga, Ricardo ("Tito") Zúniga, Roberto Martínez Ordóñez, Roberto Martínez Castañeda, Mario Berríos, Armando Suárez, Marco Tulio and Gloria Zepeda, Mario Posas, Leticia Salomón, Ramón Oquelí, Longino Becerra, Mario Argueta, Esther Chicas, Luis Alonso Rogel, Esdras López, David Romero, Leyda Barbieri, Jorge Colindres, and Mauricio Castañeda. In addition, a number of long-time U.S. residents in Honduras provided valuable insights and contacts, in particular Doris Morazán, Becky Myton, Karen Martínez, John Rehill, and Sherry Thorne.

Others helped along the way. With the exception of a one-month research grant from Northeastern Illinois University, the project was funded entirely at our expense. Nevertheless, a number of people encouraged us and did their best to help us in the search for funding, and we would like to thank them: Richard Millett, Penny Lernoux, Wayne Smith, Steve Ropp, James Morris, Mark Rosenberg, and Douglas Graham. We also express our deep appreciation to J. Richard Piper for helping us find employment in the United States when our money was running out and things were getting desperate.

We are thankful for the expertise, guidance, and patience of our editor Barbara Ellington, copyeditor Barbara Metzger, and project editor Shena Redmond, and other members of this important publishing house.

A few other debts should also be acknowledged. In addition to the Centro de Documentación de Honduras, we found much useful information in the National Library, the Congressional and Foreign Ministry archives, the libraries of the Instituto Hondureño de Antropología e Historia and the Banco Central, the "Colección Hondureña" of the Universidad Nacional Autónoma, the Dirección de Estadística y Censos, and the Instituto Nacional Agrario. Particularly helpful in guiding our research was the superb bibliography compiled by Colin Danby and Richard Swedberg, *Honduras Bibliography and Research Guide* (1984). Also indispensable, for us as for every serious student of Central America in the 1980s, was the work of some first-rate reporters for the *New York Times* and *Miami Herald*, especially James LeMoyne, Stephen Kinzer, and Sam Dillon.

One of the problems in conducting research on Honduras concerns the reliability of information. In Tegucigalpa, rumor and gossip (the more scandalous the better) often masquerade as fact. Hondurans love to talk about their political enemies and the gringos. Unfortunately, not everything they say is accurate. Nor are U.S.—especially embassy—sources wedded to the truth. During the course of this research, we have been misled by experts of both nationalities, from the left as well as the right. Partly as a result of these experiences, we have adopted a posture of calculated skepticism in our approach to our subject. Where we had doubts, we tried to check our information with other (preferably several) independent sources. In some cases, this was not possible, and we had to use our best judgment as to the reliability of the evidence in question. On a few occasions, when a sole informant spoke on a not-for-attribution basis, we used the information if the source had established a record of reliability or if we knew him personally and were confident of his (or her) veracity. Of course, questions of judgment and memory can cloud the testimony of even "reliable" respondents. Where doubts or conflicts in evidence remain, we have indicated as much in the text or the notes.

Donald E. Schulz
Deborah Sundloff Schulz

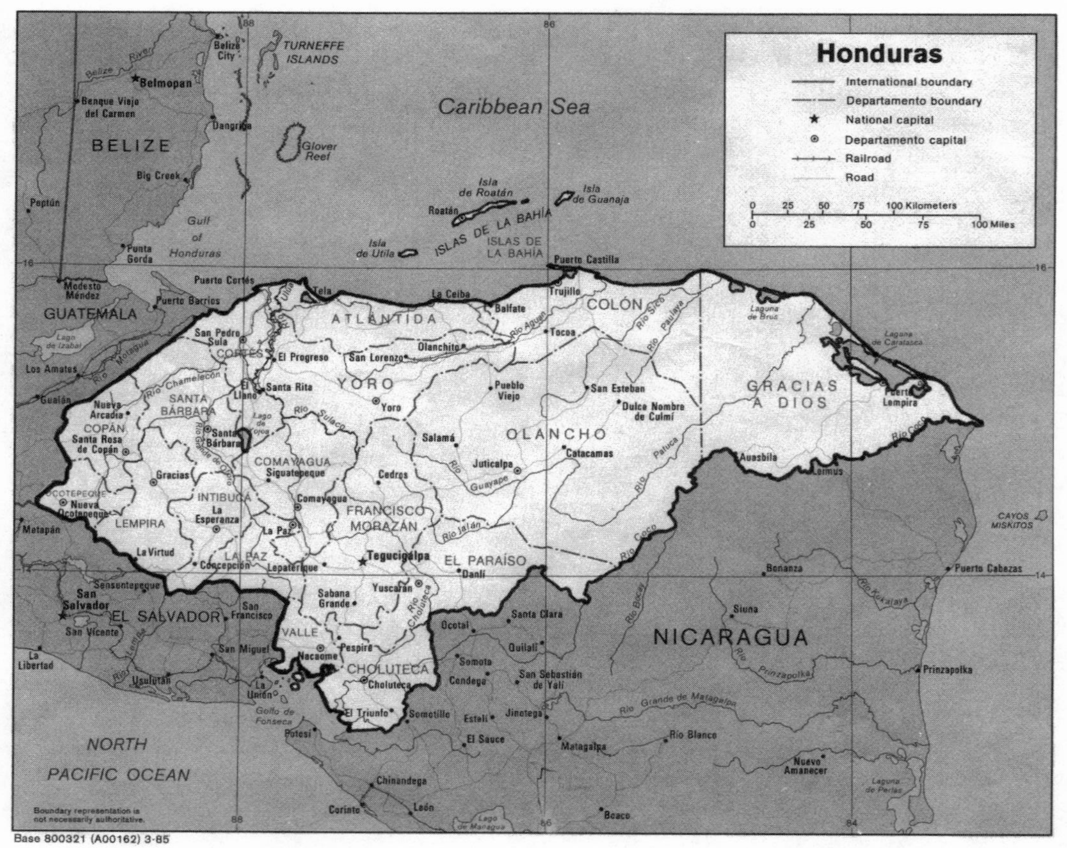

Base 800321 (A00162) 3-85

1

Introduction

Some years ago Thomas Anderson remarked that trying to organize Honduran politicians was like trying to herd mice.[1] We were reminded of his comment in spring 1985, with the start of that year's election campaign, as Honduran political parties began splintering into a blinding array of factions, most of them in rebellion against the administration of President Roberto Suazo Córdova. At one point Congress removed five of the nine members of the Supreme Court, swearing in five new members in their place, in an attempt to prevent the president from manipulating the electoral process for his own benefit. In turn, Suazo charged the new court with treason. The new chief justice was arrested; the others went into hiding. On the president's orders, riot police surrounded the court and Congress. Momentarily, at least, the trappings of Honduran democracy had been stripped away, revealing something far less attractive underneath.

The crisis was finally resolved when the military intervened and a compromise agreement was worked out that allowed all aspiring presidential candidates to run in the forthcoming elections. The campaign that followed bore more resemblance to a Roman Circus than anything. There were no fewer than eleven National Party and five Liberal Party candidates, though these eventually boiled down to four Liberals and three Nationals—plus of course the candidates of the Christian Democratic Party and the Innovation and Unity Party. The campaign was marred by mutual recriminations and petty squabbling. Its most interesting aspects bordered on the bizarre: At one point, the president's supporters in Congress attempted a "technical coup," proposing that the elections be postponed for two years while the legislature transformed itself into a constituent assembly and wrote a new constitution. The debate that followed ended in a fistfight on the floor of Congress—at which point the military once again intervened.

"Why don't they behave like us?" a U.S. official once asked. It seemed at the time that the United States was as culture-bound in Central America as it had been in Vietnam. Honduras is not like the United

States and should not be expected to behave as if it were. Honduran politics is a history of dictatorship, tempered by anarchy and ameliorated by corruption. In the 155 years between independence and 1994, there have been 129 different governments and 14 constitutions. Even today, wags sometimes refer to the capital city of Tegucigalpa as "Tegucigolpe," a pun on the Spanish word for coup.

Moreover, the more one learns about Honduran political culture the more one is struck by its surrealistic qualities. Where but in Tegucigalpa could one find a statue of the national hero, Francisco Morazán, that (so the story goes) is not of Morazán at all but of Napoleon's famous Marshal Ney, having been purchased secondhand in Paris?[2] Where else would a president (Roberto Suazo Córdova) indicate his interest in extending his term in office through the public proclamation of an obscure soothsayer? Or a dictator (Tiburcio Carías) outlaw baseball out of fear that his enemies might use the bats as weapons? (And then rescind the ban after being convinced by his nephew that pitching would be good practice for soldiers learning how to throw hand grenades?)[3]

We use these examples not to ridicule but rather to emphasize the dramatic gap between *el estilo hondureño*—the Honduran political style—and the U.S. style. One cannot understand Honduras through a North American frame of reference. The institutions and constitutions may be similar, but the values and attitudes underlying them more often than not are profoundly different, and this makes for very different political behavior. There is appearance, and there is reality. It is important that the two not be confused.

Unfortunately, illusions sometimes die hard. U.S. misconceptions about Honduras stem from a variety of sources. North Americans have a tendency to project their own values onto others and interpret the unknown in terms of stereotypes. Few U.S. citizens know anything about the country. (Peter Davis's *Where is Nicaragua?* might even more appropriately have been written about Honduras.) Nor have policymakers been much better informed. Until the 1980s, Honduras was a backwater of a backwater, hardly the object of high-level government concern. Until 1981, the U.S. embassy in Tegucigalpa was ranked class four, the lowest class. (It was subsequently promoted to class two.) The last major English-language study of Honduran politics was published in 1950.[4] Even today, experts on the country are scarce. After all, why until recently should anyone have been interested? Central America seemed stable enough until the late 1970s, and even when things began to disintegrate in Nicaragua, El Salvador, and Guatemala, Honduras continued to be an "oasis of peace."

Beneath the surface, however, there were rumblings of discontent. Problems of poverty and social injustice continued to be as serious as anywhere else in the hemisphere—with the exception of Haiti, which was in a class by itself. Social unrest and repression were growing, and U.S. policy seemed aimed more at keeping the lid on the pressure cooker than at addressing the causes of the trouble. Most disturbing, U.S. policies seemed to be aggravating Honduran problems. The push to militarize the country had strengthened the very forces that most threatened democracy and wasted scarce resources that would have been better invested in economic development. Then too, there was the specter of war, either through domestic revolution, invasion or subversion from Nicaragua, or other developments. The creation within Honduras of a veritable state within a state, composed of thousands of armed Nicaraguan exiles was ominous. Increasingly, Hondurans began to worry that the rebels might turn on them should they become frustrated by their inability to overthrow the Sandinistas.

What follows is the story of how Honduras, through a twist of fate, became a staging ground for U.S. Cold War operations in Central America during the Reagan-Bush years. On the one hand, we will examine how Hondurans sought to cope with a massive, multifaceted North American presence. On the other, we will seek to explain how this quintessential "banana republic," the most underdeveloped and seemingly fragile country in the region, managed to avoid the kind of revolutionary turmoil that devastated its neighbors. But first, a bit of history.

Notes

1. Thomas P. Anderson, *The War of the Dispossessed* (Lincoln: University of Nebraska Press, 1981), p. 44.

2. Michel Ney (1769-1815), duke of Elchingen and marshal of France, distinguished himself during Napoleon's Russian campaign. After Waterloo, however, he was shot for treason. When a Honduran commission was sent to Europe to order a statue of Morazán, it is said, it ran out of funds and was reduced to purchasing the Ney monument on the cheap.

3. The Morazán and Carías stories were passed on to us by William Krehm and seem to be myths. A Honduran historian has located in the French National Archives a contract signed by the Honduran government and the sculptor Durini, the creator of the statue of Morazán. We could not disprove the Carías story, but one would think that Mario Argueta, the leading biographer of the dictator, would know of the incident if it occurred, and he does not. Respected Honduran intellectuals such as Víctor Meza, Ramón Oquelí, and Marco Tulio Zepeda are skeptical. We consider the story apocryphal.

4. See William S. Stokes, *Honduras: An Area Study in Government* (Madison: University of Wisconsin Press, 1950). This is not to say that no other books of substance have been published. Particularly noteworthy are James A. Morris' *Honduras: Caudillo Politics and Military Rulers* (Boulder: Westview Press, 1984) and James D. Rudolph's edited volume, *Honduras: A Country Study* (Washington, D.C.: American University Press, 1984).

2

The Land of the Midnight Coup

The history of Honduras can be written on the space of a tear.

—Folk saying

Power abhors a vacuum, and nowhere in Central America is the truth of this maxim more evident than in Honduras. Here internal weakness has time and again tempted more powerful external forces to interfere in domestic affairs. Only rarely have Hondurans been united and strong enough to withstand such incursions. Rather, chaos, confusion, and violence have undermined the Honduran polity from its inception. The structure of Spanish colonialism had been too loosely drawn and too carelessly administered to provide much cohesion once independence was established. Thus, authoritarian centralization quickly degenerated into anarchy. Power struggles between local caudillos, liberal and conservative factions, and the cities of Comayagua and Tegucigalpa took the place of a national political discourse. Indeed, no national consciousness existed. Though Hondurans had a common language and religion, they had no common history. Instead, geographic barriers (mountainous terrain), lack of communications, territorial disintegration, and an absence of national classes and an internal market produced myriad local allegiances, and the fact that there had been no real struggle for independence left Hondurans without the kind of heroic experience that might have created a sense of solidarity and community.

Consequently, there was no agreement on what should replace colonial rule once the Spanish empire collapsed. In 1824 Hondurans opted for membership in a Central American Federation, but the effort was short-lived. The old rivalries continued to undermine domestic tranquility. Moreover, to internal Honduran conflicts were now added the larger struggles of the federation. Turmoil in the provinces led to repeated federal intervention. When civil war broke out, the greatest of all Central American leaders, Francisco Morazán (a Honduran), led the liberals to victory, but, as always, the attempt at unification was only temporarily successful. By 1838, the federation was dead. Nor did matters improve much with the attainment of statehood. Over the next sixty-one years (1839-1900), there would be sixty-two Honduran presidencies and ten *consejos de ministros* (councils of ministers). Anarchy became a way of life. There was no national nucleus, no unifying force that could bring together the various factions vying for power. Under these circumstances, foreign intervention became commonplace. Sharing borders with Guatemala, El Salvador, and Nicaragua, Hondurans found themselves in a geopolitical trap. The liberal-conservative conflicts that consumed the isthmus inevitably spilled over onto Honduran soil. Liberal regimes viewed conservative neighbors as a threat and tried to overthrow them, and vice versa. Exiles gathered in countries run by their political allies and waged war against their homelands. To make matters worse, the British also made demands, intervening from time to time to bombard fortresses, seize coastal cities, or extort money from local governments. Foreign intervention only aggravated and perpetuated domestic instability. Between 1862 and the inauguration of Marco Aurelio Soto in 1876, there were thirty-two transfers of power. One president, José María Medina, was in office on eleven separate occasions.

By the 1860s it had become evident that Honduras could not escape underdevelopment without foreign help. By itself, the country seemed doomed to backwardness. Growth was impeded not only by civil strife and outside intervention but also by lack of transportation, capital, and technology. The various regions were still largely isolated, joined only by primitive mule trails. As late as the first decade of the twentieth century, one observer commented that travel from the north coast to Tegucigalpa was virtually unchanged since the colonial period except that the roads were worse.

Thus it was that Honduras became a country in quest of a railway. Throughout much of this period, many Hondurans saw rail transport as their best chance for opening up the interior and developing the economy. As early as 1853 the Honduran Congress granted the exclusive right to construct such a line to George Squier, a former U.S. chargé in Central America. Two "loans" of US$20,000 each were extended to the Honduran government. Several years later Squier's company failed without having laid a single section of track. His charter was sold to a group of British investors, but they made no more progress. By this time, however, the Honduran government had become psychologically committed to the enterprise. In one of the most dubious transactions in financial history, it contracted a series of British and French loans, totaling some £6 million, for the purpose of constructing the route: "The money stuck to the fingers of politicians and bankers, and to top it all, Honduras made the grievous mistake of paying the contractors by the mile. The railway wriggled imaginatively in the easy lowlands, and got winded before it had penetrated too far inland. By the time fifty miles had been built, the funds had evaporated in the tropical heat."[1]

By 1871, the track extended ninety-two kilometers, from the Atlantic coast past San Pedro Sula. At that point, the British investors withdrew their profits and went home. Subsequent attempts to extend the route led to nothing more than the accumulation of additional debts. By the end of the decade, what tracks had been laid had fallen into disrepair and been abandoned. Although the line to San Pedro was eventually reactivated with the rise of the banana trade in the 1890s, the debts acquired had accumulated to such an extent that Honduras had the highest per capita foreign debt the world had ever known. (By 1909 the total debt amounted to US$120 million. That same year, Honduran government revenues came to only US$1.7 million.) Not until the administration of Juan Manuel Gálvez in 1953—eighty-six years after the first major loan had been contracted—was the obligation finally paid off.[2] As for the dream of opening up the interior by means of a railroad, suffice it to say that even today Tegucigalpa has no links of this kind with the outside world.

Dependency and Development: The Birth of a Banana Republic

The railroad scandal was an omen. Greed, corruption, and incompetence had bankrupted the republic. Yet such was the state of the country's dependency that it had little choice but to continue seeking foreign investments. Neither the state nor the private sector had the resources to build a primary export economy. The society was still in a precapitalist, semifeudal stage. Political chaos and economic stagnation had prevented the formation of a strong national state and a dynamic national bourgeoisie, based in coffee or cattle, that might have responded to the "new demands of the external market" or been able to "form a productive system with significant national participation."[3] Instead, Honduran landowners remained inward-looking and status-quo-oriented, afflicted by the "myopia that resulted from their isolation, insecurity, limited business capacity, [and] scarcity of capital."[4] Lacking the motivation and means of participating in the mining and export agriculture booms that occurred from the 1880s onward, they would be largely irrelevant to the country's economic development. So it was that the Honduran economy "had to link up with the world market . . . as an enclave economy, with the productive sectors of the local economy under direct control of foreign capital."[5]

Before this could occur however, there had to be leaders willing to resurrect the antifeudal revolution begun by Francisco Morazán but aborted after his death. That occasion arose in 1876, when Marco Aurelio Soto came into office. During the administrations of Soto and his successor, Luis Bográn, the state undertook to provide the internal stability and economic incentives needed to attract foreign investment. At first, the primary beneficiary was the New York and Honduras Rosario Mining Company, which was allowed to operate with a minimum of restrictions and a virtual exemption from taxes, and which soon became a major economic and political force. By 1889 the company was shipping over US$700,000 worth of bullion to the United States. Profits were exorbitant. So favorable were the tax exemptions that they were not made public until long after Soto had left office.[6] By the end of the century, however, the mining boom was in decline, and mineral exports had been overtaken by a new competitor. The production and marketing of bananas now became the foundation of the country's prosperity.

Again, it is necessary to stress the juxtaposition of Honduran weakness and foreign strength. Though Soto had made some progress in laying the foundations for modern social and political institutions, Honduras continued to be plagued by chronic instability. A national consciousness was only beginning to develop. Indeed, Honduras at this stage bore more resemblance to a "customs house surrounded by adventurers" than to a coherent nation.[7] Corruption and incompetence were deeply ingrained, and the fruit companies did not hesitate to exploit their hosts' vulnerabilities. Local bosses were given payoffs; desperate governments received loans; presidents and legislators were bribed. This political debility was augmented by the weakness of the Honduran socioeconomic structure. There was no national bourgeoisie capable of resisting and limiting foreign penetration. Native banana producers did not constitute a clearly defined economic group. These small ranchers and independent farmers had little political influence or potential for developing into a "banana oligarchy" comparable to the coffee elites in El Salvador and Guatemala.

Their small production units, dependency on big foreign buyers, lack of capital, and limited capacity for expansion precluded that option. "As a result, the banana companies did not encounter the obstacles usually mounted by a national economic group that has concrete possibilities for its own development. They found no real opposition and were able to present themselves as forerunners of progress and a new civilization."[8]

This explains the ease with which the fruit companies were able to obtain concessions and consolidate an enclave economy on the north coast. In 1899 the Vacarro brothers began to ship tropical fruits from Honduras to New Orleans. A few years later, Samuel Zemurray arrived and set up operations of his own. The Vacarros' business was eventually to be incorporated into the Standard Fruit and Steamship Corporation, with the center of its holdings in La Ceiba. Zemurray's interests would become the Cuyamel Fruit Company, with properties running east of the Guatemalan border to Puerto Cortés. Meanwhile, in 1910, the United Fruit Company (UFCO) entered the country, three years later establishing a subsidiary, the Tela Railroad Company, with its base of operations between the Cuyamel and Vacarro spheres of influence. The companies "bought up lands, built railroads, established their own banking systems, and bribed government officials at a dizzying pace."[9] In 1892 bananas had accounted for only 11 percent of Honduran exports; in 1903 they were 42 percent, in 1913 66 percent, and in 1929 84 percent. Production increased from almost 6 million bunches in 1910 to 29 million in 1930. By 1914 the five main concessionaires held over a million acres of coastal land, much of it the most fertile in the country. Four years later fully 75 percent of the banana lands were owned by UFCO, Cuyamel, and the Vacarro brothers.[10]

In this way was Honduras converted into that quintessential stereotype of monocultural underdevelopment: a banana republic. During the first decade of this century, the country became the world's largest producer, a position it retained for most of the next fifty years. (By 1930 it accounted for one-third of the world's supply.) In the process, the north coast became a foreign-controlled enclave whose wealth was shipped off to New Orleans, New York, and Boston. "Unlike neighboring El Salvador, where a few wealthy families made fortunes in coffee during the nineteenth century then went on to take control of trade and banking, the Hondurans never took that first step of gaining some control over their nation's key product." Instead, the banana plantations, geographically isolated from the rest of the country, became states within the state. Local government representatives were easily bought off, and a "little-governed country became even less governed."[11]

As so often happens, foreign economic penetration was accompanied by political intervention. In 1907 President Manuel Bonilla was overthrown in a revolution that brought Miguel Dávila to power. This provoked the displeasure of Sam "the Banana Man" Zemurray, who had been close to Bonilla and was concerned that the new president might favor his competitors. Zemurray's fears soon proved justified. When the Taft administration moved to substitute U.S. for British control over the Honduran debt structure, matters came to a head. Washington viewed the huge Honduran debt—by now over US$120 million—as a dangerous source of instability. The idea was to refinance it through a customs receivership. A group of New York bankers headed by J. P. Morgan would buy the old bonds at cut-rate prices. The Honduran government would guarantee the bankers' investment out of customs house receipts. The United States would approve future appointments of the customs collector and would gain veto power over Honduran tariff rates. It would also guarantee the country's continued independence. In effect, Honduras would become a U.S. protectorate.

The plan generated considerable opposition, and nowhere was this more determined than in the Cuyamel Fruit Company. Zemurray wanted to expand his operations, and to do so he would have to import railroad equipment and other materials. He wanted them to be duty-free. The customs agreement prohibited such exemptions, but Zemurray was not easily discouraged. He decided to finance an expedition under Bonilla to overthrow the Honduran government and block the still unratified receivership. For a few thousand dollars, Bonilla was able to purchase an armored yacht named the *Hornet.* The story has it that on a cold night in December 1910 Bonilla and his lieutenants—the famous soldier of fortune Lee Christmas and a UFCO "business associate" known as Guy "Machine Gun" Malony—met in a New Orleans brothel. When the Secret Service agent shadowing them grew tired of watching their debauchery and went home, the conspirators escaped. From there they quickly set off for Honduras on the *Hornet,* with a U.S. gunboat on their heels.

During the hostilities that followed, President Dávila tried desperately to get the United States to end the fighting, but the U.S. response was indecisive. The State Department distrusted both Dávila and Bonilla. Since the former headed a legally constituted government, however, the Taft administration initially leaned toward him. U.S. warships were sent into Honduran waters to protect American lives and property. The *Hornet* was captured to prevent it from engaging in hostilities. At this point, it was not clear what the United States would do. On 31 January, however, Dávila attempted to impose the receivership on the Honduran Congress, and a mob invaded the assembly, promising death to anyone who turned the country into an "administrative dependency" of the United States. The president's demand for action only made matters worse. In a rare show of independence, the legislature rejected the plan.

From this moment on, Dávila's days were numbered. The United States now tilted toward the rebels. U.S. naval commanders forced government troops to evacuate Puerto Cortés, a move that made a Bonilla victory almost certain. In the negotiations that ensued, the U.S. arbitrator was given authority to appoint a temporary president from lists submitted by the two sides. He chose one of the candidates proposed by the rebels. Eight months later, elections were held, and Bonilla was returned to the presidency. Lee Christmas became the U.S. consul to Honduras.

Thus was the country saved from the bankers and left free to be conquered by the fruit companies. In the aftermath, Cuyamel and UFCO obtained extraordinary concessions with regard to banana farming and railroad construction, including customs exemptions on all materials required for railways, telephone systems, and irrigation. United received the Tela and Trujillo regions, Cuyamel the western side of the Chamelecón River. These terms had a major impact on the Honduran fiscal system. As late as 1927, the government was losing fully a third of its import duty revenue because of such arrangements.[12]

These concessions, of course, had not been intended as gifts. UFCO had agreed to construct a railroad from Puerto Castilla on the Caribbean coast to Juticalpa, halfway to the capital, and eventually to Tegucigalpa itself. A subsidiary, the Trujillo Railway Company, was to build twelve kilometers of track a year. If it defaulted, an annual fine of US$2,000 would be levied for each kilometer that fell behind schedule. Eventually, either Tegucigalpa would be connected with the north coast or the Honduran government would be rich enough to undertake the construction on its own. Cuyamel made similar pledges, but the companies had agendas of their own. The track laid was little more than what was needed for the operations of the banana industry. That is to say, it ran *parallel* to the sea rather than inland. For each kilometer of rail built, the companies received between 550 and 1,100 acres in lots of 10,000 to 12,000 acres, alternating with similar lots reserved for homesteaders. The idea, of course, was to prevent foreigners from grabbing up the entire north coast. Unfortunately, such legalities tended to be ignored. In addition, the companies, through intermediaries, went in for homesteading; often illegally and at a nominal price, they acquired many of the alternate lots for themselves.

Nor was this the end of the story. In 1920 Cuyamel obtained lease of the national railroad from Puerto Cortés to Potrerillos in return for a million-dollar loan. The latter was intended to improve the rail line, enabling it to haul heavy equipment for Cuyamel's La Lima sugar factory. Once the contracted debt had been repaid out of earnings, the railway was supposed to revert to government control. The route ran through some of the richest banana lands in the world, however, and Cuyamel was in no hurry to give it up. It therefore made sure that the line would not soon return to Honduran hands. In defiance of Honduran law, which prohibited the building of private railways within forty kilometers of the national track, Cuyamel constructed "clandestine lines" in several districts. Eventually, too, it laid a railroad along the Ulúa River, parallel to the national route, to siphon off traffic and profits. Equipment and rolling stock from the national railway were used to build and operate these private lines. In this way, national revenues were kept artificially low. Meanwhile, control over the railroad gave Cuyamel the means of breaking the cooperatives of the independent planters. The entire area became a Cuyamel fiefdom.

The competition between the fruit companies soon led to hostilities. In this, there was no small irony. The assumption had been that the bananas would bring the railways and the railways cohesion and peace. Instead, precisely the opposite occurred: the "traditional strife of rival political bands was now geared to the pitched warfare of the banana barons." Usually, UFCO backed the National Party while Cuyamel favored the Liberals, but both were flexible enough to make whatever moves were required. By the mid-1920s, however, Cuyamel's "clandestine lines" were a hot issue: the president of the republic, Miguel Paz Barahona, was trying to get them legalized, while the president of Congress, Tiburcio Carías Andino, was blocking the motion on orders from UFCO. Cuyamel's control of the national railroad and the lush territories surrounding it depended on the outcome. Zemurray had few compunctions about being blunt. As he told one lobbyist, "We are going to have Congress convoked to grant us a concession legalizing the clandestine lines. Now, I want you to go and tell Carías that either Congress approves the concession, or we will never let him become president."

This was the period in which Zemurray coined his famous phrase "In Honduras, a mule costs more than a deputy." Still, he did not always get his way. The concession was rejected by Congress. Subsequently, Cuyamel threw its weight behind the Liberal Party in the 1928 election. Carías, the National Party candidate, went down to defeat. Once in office, the new president, Vicente Mejía Colindres, dutifully resubmitted the measure but to no avail. At this point, Zemurray sold Cuyamel to the UFCO for three hundred thousand shares of stock, at an estimated value of about US$32 million. He now became an UFCO vice president and the company's largest stockholder, in the process recouping his original Cuyamel investment more than sixfold.

The shape of Honduran politics was transformed almost overnight. Previously the banana companies had often held each other in check in an uneasy balance of power that was reflected in the conflicts between Congress and the executive. Now, however, with the consolidation of the industry, the trend was toward centralized dictatorship and stability. No longer would the legislative and executive branches clash over the issue of company concessions. Mejía Colindres and Carías now found themselves on the same side. The irrigation tax on banana lands could therefore be dramatically lowered. The dispute over the "clandestine lines" could be resolved, the tracks becoming part of the national railway to be operated by UFCO under the terms of the lease. Moreover, in 1932, with the full support of UFCO and Mejía Colindres, Carías was elected president of Honduras. There he remained for the next sixteen years.

Concessions notwithstanding, the 1930s were difficult years for UFCO. In two decades of explosive development, El Pulpo—"The Octopus," as the company came to be known—had bought up most of the best banana lands in Honduras. In 1932, however, its stock plunged precipitously. Company directors began unloading their holdings, and Zemurray could no longer remain on the sidelines. When the UFCO board of directors refused to listen to his ideas for salvaging the enterprise, he quietly began to collect proxies from other disgruntled shareholders. Soon he had enough to take control. Returning to the board a few months later, he reportedly dropped the proxies on the table, declaring, "You gentlemen have been fucking up this business long enough. Now I'm going to straighten it out." And he did. By putting his old Cuyamel team in charge and drastically cutting costs, Zemurray put UFCO back on its feet.[13]

U.S. Policy in the Era of Imperialism

During the early part of this century, the activities of private groups and citizens were more important than those of the U.S. government. Honduras was only sporadically of concern to the policy elites in Washington. Nevertheless, to many observers—especially Latin Americans—the behavior of U.S. political leaders seemed unabashedly imperialistic and exploitative. This was the age of manifest destiny—of gunboat diplomacy, dollar diplomacy, and the "big stick." U.S. forces were sent to the Caribbean and Central America at the drop of a hat. Lengthy occupations were commonplace: the list included Cuba (1898-1902, 1906-1909), Panama (1903-1914), the Dominican Republic (1916-1924), Nicaragua (1912-1925, 1926-1933), and Haiti (1915-1934). Elsewhere, warships or troops were dispatched for short periods. In Honduras, the United States sent in the marines on several occasions (1903, 1907, 1924, 1925) and intervened politically on others.[14] With intervention, moreover, came economic penetration. North American capital flooded the region. Trade flourished. To all appearances, the U.S. government and private enterprise were moving in lockstep.

Yet the relationship was never as simple as that. Economic domination would have occurred even without political and military intervention. Although the U.S. government worked with American investors in Honduras, their relations were not always close; nor were their interests necessarily identical. In 1924, when U.S. troops landed during a rebellion following fraudulent elections, they found themselves pitted against the forces of UFCO's favorite, Tiburcio Carías. By the same token, the United States did not always insist on imposing its will on local authorities, nor did it inevitably side with U.S. investors in their disputes with Hondurans.

The overall thrust of U.S. regional policy is, however, difficult to deny, and Honduras was a part of the whole. Power and profits tended to go hand in hand. The expansion of North American business into neighboring lands was held to be highly desirable, something to be not only encouraged but if necessary defended. Sometimes U.S. political or military intervention was followed by the granting of major concessions to American corporations (e.g., after the ousters of presidents Dávila in 1911 and Francisco Bertrand in 1919). At minimum, Washington's actions helped create the political conditions that made such arrangements possible. Beyond this, U.S. nondecisions were often just as important as decisions. The reluctance to interfere with the fruit companies' activities gave them wide latitude to do as they would, regardless of the consequences for U.S. government or Honduran interests.

Most of the time, however, the direct effects of Washington's actions were limited. Occasionally, troops would be landed to protect American lives and property during the recurrent episodes of civil strife. On such occasions, the danger was usually very real, though it was sometimes exaggerated by embassy paranoia. The following excerpt from a letter from the U.S. chargé says much about the North American attitude toward Hondurans:

> Anti-American feeling in this country is strong and runs throughout all classes of society. It is founded on an inferiority complex coupled with jealousy; and while not always manifest, is likely to show itself at any time when the attitude of the United States Government does not meet with the approval of this government or of an influential faction. . . . The hatred of Americans by individuals is pronounced, especially among the lower classes, and is likely to blaze forth at intervals and manifest itself in the form of riot, assault or even murder. For this reason, it seems to me that the presence of an American warship on the North Coast is eminently desirable at all times. . . . The condition to which I refer is not temporary but will probably continue for some years to come.[15]

Power politics and the Monroe Doctrine were also potent motivators. European intervention in the Western hemisphere was still a concern, and with the Mexican and Bolshevik revolutions, this concern took on new urgency. The specter of communist subversion was raised, and military action seemed a quick and effective way of forestalling such dangers. Then, as now, the "Colossus of the North" had economic and security interests to protect, and then, as now, it often chose to legitimate those interests in terms of more altruistic rationales.

It is hard to say whether U.S. policy was primarily a force for stability or for instability in Honduras. The latter was already so deeply ingrained that it is difficult to sustain the charge that Washington's interventions significantly increased it. They did not, however, do much to reduce it. An extended occupation would probably have been required to stabilize the country, and even then there would have been no guarantees. The history of U.S. occupations in the Caribbean and Central America during this period is not especially encouraging: Without externally imposed discipline, those societies tended either to disintegrate into the chaos that had provoked their occupation or to enforce stability through bloody tyranny.

Honduras never experienced a full-scale or lengthy occupation, and so chaos continued more or less as usual. Washington sometimes supported the regime in power, sometimes the forces of rebellion; it all depended on the circumstances. Although it acted as mediator in the ongoing conflicts within and between Central American states, Washington often ignored the agreements and legal mechanisms that came out of such negotiations. This caused some resentment among Central Americans, who also complained that U.S.-imposed solutions frequently ignored the legitimate interests of the peoples involved and forced on them weak leaders, lacking in legitimacy, who had to rely on North American support to survive.

U.S. leaders rarely listened to Central American voices, and when they did they tended to hear what they were predisposed to hear. There was in North American policy an overweening sense of paternalistic self-righteousness. Washington never seriously questioned its right to intervene wherever and whenever it chose. Only with Franklin Delano Roosevelt's Good Neighbor Policy did this attitude significantly change. By then, however, North American interventionism had reinforced a psychological dependency rooted in two other dimensions of Honduran experience: the Spanish and Indian political, economic, and social heritage that bound Hondurans to each other in relations of dominance and submission and the pattern of dependent capitalist development that turned the country into a raw-material-export economy controlled by North American fruit companies. To this was now added a strong tendency to look to the U.S. government for solutions to Honduran problems.

Carías and the "Blessed Peace"

U.S. policy changed in the 1930s, and so did the pattern of Honduran politics. If the "good neighbor" era witnessed a retreat from North American interventionism, such restraint probably could not have been maintained had not Central Americans found a more effective means of keeping the peace. The 1930s and 1940s were an era of the great dictators: Jorge Ubico in Guatemala, Maximiliano Hernández Martínez in El Salvador, Anastasio Somoza in Nicaragua, and Tiburcio Carías in Honduras. Carías was elected in 1932 for a term of four years under a constitution that prohibited reelection. In 1936, however, Congress extended the presidential term to six years and his own incumbency until 1943, and three years later it gave him a further lease on the Presidential Palace until 1949. Thus was Carías to enjoy the longest period of continuous rule of any president in Honduran history.

One should not be taken in by this record of superficially legitimate extensions. After 1932, there were no more congressional elections. The legislative and judicial branches became mere instruments of the dictatorship. Martial law became a way of life. Internal passports were introduced. The press was gagged, labor organizations destroyed, the jails filled. Carías's victims were never as numerous as those in Martínez's El Salvador, but then, such excesses were unnecessary. Popular organizations were weaker in Honduras; they posed little threat to the regime.

The atmosphere could only be termed medieval. This was an era when members of the opposition were often forbidden to travel in automobiles, the First Lady sold tamales at the Presidential Palace, and the president of Congress justified Carías's long rule by noting that "God, too, continues in power indefinitely."[16] "El Hombre Superior," "Gran Estadista", and "Máximo Conductor de los Destinos de Honduras" were just a few of the titles accorded Carías by sycophantic supporters. The army became a virtual praetorian guard, composed primarily of members of the dictator's National Party. Departmental governors were appointed and removed by the executive, with loyalty to Carías being the main criterion. Many became junior versions of their *patrón*, acquiring considerable autonomy, ruling through intimidation and networks of local informers, operating gambling and prostitution rings, and liquor monopolies, imposing tribute on businessmen, and imprisoning or assassinating political opponents.

It was in this era that the UFCO reached the apex of its power. As early as 1933, a U.S. diplomat could observe that there was not an important government functionary in its north-coast zone who was not under obligation to the company. It paid half the salaries of some local commanders, and those not rating regular payment received frequent tips. Journalists who criticized the banana trust were silenced with bribes or, if that did not work, were "disappeared" into Carías's dungeons. The minister of war, the president of Congress, and the head of the Supreme Court were all UFCO lawyers. Virtually any UFCO petition reaching Congress was favorably received.

Carías was not without his accomplishments. He did bring stability, really the first that the country had seen, and took initial steps—with U.S. assistance—to develop a modern, professional military. At the same time, he extended his National Party apparatus into remote and isolated regions, creating the political infrastructure vital to nation building. In retrospect, Carías provided the national unity and order that made it possible for his successors to accelerate modernization and bring Honduras into the twentieth century. His socioeconomic achievements, however, were modest at best. A favorite Carías dictum was that "en Honduras no hay problemas sociales" (in Honduras there are no social problems)—an extraordinary assessment of a country with an illiteracy rate of over 80 percent and a population very largely rural, isolated, impoverished, and in poor health.

As long as the outcome of the war in Europe remained in doubt, the neofascist regimes of Central America could be justified by the fact that they maintained regional stability. As the war drew to a close, this argument carried less weight. For the United States, these allies had become an embarrassment. For Central Americans, they were far worse. Some argued that the war against tyranny in Europe justified the same sort of struggle at home. Moreover, new voices were calling not merely for democracy but for social justice. In 1944, loose alliances of middle-class professionals, students, and junior military officers led to the overthrow of Hernández Martínez in El Salvador and Ubico in Guatemala. Discontent was also rising in Honduras. In July 1944, dozens of protesters were killed or wounded by government forces in San Pedro Sula. Although the dictator was initially able to ride out the public outrage, he soon came under pressure from the fruit companies, the Honduran elites, and the U.S. State Department, who viewed his rule as a threat to the country's fragile political consensus and an obstacle to modernization. In 1948, Carías was finally persuaded to surrender power. Elections were held. When the opposition Liberal candidate, fearing fraud, pulled out of the race, the way was cleared for Juan Manuel Gálvez to assume the presidency. This he did early the following year.

The Great Banana Strike

Juan Manuel Gálvez, once a lawyer for Cuyamel and UFCO, had been minister of war under Carías and was the man legally responsible for the conduct of Honduran troops during the San Pedro Sula massacre. At first glance, little seemed to have changed. Yet, Gálvez was very different from Carías. He was more urbane and, though conservative, in many respects a progressive. Under his government, considerable press freedom was restored. Opposition political groups and some labor organizations were allowed to operate. Legislation was passed establishing an eight-hour day; workers received paid holidays; regulations were established for the employment of women and children. At the same time, Gálvez promoted institutional modernization and capitalist development. The state apparatus was expanded; infrastructure was built in remote areas; financial and technical assistance was provided. A central bank and a national development bank were created; public works increased. Personal and corporate income taxes were introduced.

In just six years, Gálvez accomplished far more in the socioeconomic realm than Carías had in sixteen. This did not, however, bring political and social peace. The Gálvez era marked another turning point in Honduran history: the end of the traditional oligarchy's domination of politics. Modernization had begun to create new urban-industrial elites that were demanding access to the corridors of power. Belatedly, Honduras was developing a national bourgeoisie. It was primarily these groups that Gálvez sought to promote and to which he looked for political support. At the same time, by easing repression and allowing the working classes greater freedom to organize, he opened up the possibility of significant labor-management conflict. In 1954 the fruit companies would reap the whirlwind as years of pent-up frustration exploded in what is still the most important event in the history of the Honduran working class: the Great Banana Strike.

In the early 1950s UFCO was still by far the most powerful corporation in Honduras. It was "the largest exporter, the largest private employer, the largest capitalist enterprise, . . . the largest private landholder, and the richest entity operating in the country." The economic importance of its subsidiaries in the local economy was "overwhelming, and their available resources were several times greater than those available to the Honduran state." Furthermore, the company served as an important source of "emergency funding for the impoverished public sector. . . . These loans were made to influence . . . government decisions," and they had considerable effect. When UFCO made its wishes known, Hondurans listened.[17]

Whatever their sins, the banana companies brought critical resources to a region that had been economically stagnant throughout the colonial era. In setting up these imperial domains, UFCO and the others built ports, cleared jungle, filled lowlands and swamps, installed spray and irrigation systems, and increased production severalfold. Nor can it be said that Hondurans did not benefit, for in the process population centers were created, along with tens of thousands of jobs. Wages and salaries, though pitifully low by North

American standards, were considerably higher than on Honduran holdings. The companies built hospitals, schools, and sanitary housing, improved water resources, and provided electricity. In 1913 the Vaccaros set up the Banco Atlántida in La Ceiba.

Not all Hondurans, however, appreciated these contributions. Nationalists and leftists were outraged by the companies' interference in Honduran political affairs and by the "giveaway" concessions they had obtained. Between 1925 and 1950 the companies had sent back over US$412 million in profits to their headquarters—an extraordinary average of US$16.5 million a year. From 1912 to 1955 the Honduran government had exempted them from paying some US$121 million. Some estimated that had these exemptions not been granted the state might have increased its income by as much as 50 percent.[18] To such observers, Honduran *soberanía* (sovereignty) and *dignidad* (dignity) were continually being violated. The country was being raped.

Added to resentment over the companies' political and business manipulations were serious grievances over the quality of life on the plantations. True, some things had improved since the early 1930s, when roughly a quarter of the workforce had malaria and a UFCO doctor described the life of the average banana worker as "working under the tropical sun; wading in the mud during the rainy season when frequent showers keep your back well drenched; being ordered by an overseer to move about, while fever, chills and headache are urging you to lie down and die."[19] Although screened-in living compounds, for instance, had reduced the incidence of malaria, other conditions had worsened. Salaries had increased only marginally over the previous twenty years even as the price of consumer goods had soared. Workers on UFCO and Standard Fruit plantations received no severance pay. Housing, health conditions, and medical care were still quite poor. Accidents were frequent, as were labor-related muscular disorders, circulatory diseases, and exhaustion. Though the 1949 labor law had established an eight-hour work day, this was widely ignored on the plantations, where the company foreman alone determined such matters.[20]

In short, the situation was still intolerable. Beneath the surface manifestations of dominance and submission, tensions were building. All that was required was a spark to ignite the flame. On 1 May 1954 dockworkers in Puerto Cortés appeared before a UFCO representative to request double pay for their work the following day, which was a Sunday. They were told that they would receive an answer later. The next day their request was again evaded, and they were ordered back to work. During the mediation that ensued, the workers designated one Luis García to be their spokesman. Having informed the company representative of their demand, they returned to their jobs only to discover that García's time card was missing: He was being denied employment because of his role as an "agitator"—a thinly veiled object lesson to the rest. The dockworkers demanded that García be returned to work. When their request was ignored, they declared themselves on strike. Before long, all of the company's 25,000 workers and 15,000 more at Standard Fruit had joined the protest. The action, which lasted sixty-nine days, spread far beyond the banana plantations to embrace miners, brewers, tobacco and textile employees, and many others. From the north coast to Tegucigalpa, the strike was supported by a broad cross section of Hondurans from all social classes. In the end, the cost to the fruit companies, other foreign businesses, and the Honduran government amounted to millions of dollars. Ironically, that night García would not have earned more than five.

Not surprisingly, the issues quickly became obfuscated by political considerations. This was the height of the Cold War. The paranoia of the McCarthy era was still in the air. In Guatemala, a left-wing nationalist government had instituted major socioeconomic reforms that smelled, to the suspicious, of communism. Accordingly, the Central Intelligence Agency (CIA) was unleashed. With the help of the Gálvez administration, which obligingly allowed Honduran territory to be used as a base of operations, a counterrevolutionary army was created. As had happened so often in the past, Honduras was to become a launching pad for an invasion against one of its neighbors.

Given this climate, it was almost inevitable that charges of "communist subversion" would be raised against the striking workers. At the same time, the U.S. embassy was aware of the danger of being perceived as siding with the companies. The workers had real grievances. UFCO was perfectly capable of using the communism issue to avoid negotiations. Thus, a two-track policy was adopted: The companies would be encouraged to negotiate a fair settlement, and meanwhile the "communists" would be weeded out. The embassy would identify and seek to promote "free" labor leaders who were interested in economic issues (as opposed to political rabble-rousing) and would negotiate in good faith. Behind the scenes, the Americans were prepared to pursue these objectives through tactics ranging from quiet diplomacy to the encouragement of repression.

In fact, communist influence on the strike seems to have been minor. The strike leaders at Standard Fruit were reformers rather than revolutionaries, and although those at the Tela Railroad Company (UFCO) were more militant they appear to have been influenced primarily by the Honduran Revolutionary Democratic Party (Partido Democrático Revolucionario Hondureño—PDRH) rather than the communists.[21] The latter, of course, supported the strike and had some contact with the central strike committee, but that hardly justified charges that the movement was "communist dominated." In any case, the goals of the protest were overwhelmingly economic rather than political. On the whole, the workers behaved with exemplary self-restraint. Incidents of violence were fairly rare.

Standard came around fairly quickly, but the UFCO strike continued. The company also chose a two-track policy. On the one hand, it tried to prolong the conflict indefinitely; on the other, it made efforts to divide and conquer the strikers. Assuming that hunger would soon drive the workers back to their jobs, it refused to negotiate. At the same time, it used intrigue and bribery to subvert the enemy. Largely on the basis of the charge that the committee was being advised by Guatemalan communists, separate talks were opened with the local strike committee from La Lima. From this point on, labor unity was a thing of the past. Eventually, the central strike committee was reconstituted under more conciliatory leadership. New talks were undertaken. It was not until 9 July, however, that an agreement was finally reached, and even then it was only after continuing pressure from the U.S. government and the mediation of the American Federation of Labor (AFL) and the Inter-American Regional Organization of Workers (Organización Regional Inter-americana de Trabajadores—ORIT).

The settlement itself was a disappointment. Few of the strikers' demands were met. Salary increases were minimal. For many, the big incentive was the 40 lempira (US$20) bonus for those who returned to work immediately. Moreover, the final agreement gave UFCO the right to fire workers for economic reasons—a paragraph that would presently be used on a massive scale. By this time, however, the strikers were exhausted. Most of the original leaders were in jail. Their replacements, the so-called free labor leaders, had little commitment to terms they had not formulated themselves. No doubt most workers greeted the settlement with a sigh of relief. "Hunger, political repression, intrigues, and treason" had finally broken their "will to fight."[22]

Still, some gains had been made. The settlement represented an important labor victory in that unions were now at least tacitly accepted as legal. The following year a decree was issued—largely as a consequence of the strike—that guaranteed workers the right to organize, bargain collectively, and strike. Among other things, it recognized that workers had a right to a minimum wage, equal pay for equal work, and regular salary disbursements. It now became illegal for middlemen to discount workers' wages or for management to force employees to patronize company stores. Workers were protected from capricious firings and guaranteed an eight-hour day, paid vacations, additional pay for overtime, and recognition of national holidays. A basis was even provided for a social security law.

If the strike was over, however, the struggle for reform was just beginning. For a brief moment during the spring and summer of 1954, foreign penetration had led to something very rare in Honduras: a widespread sense of shared values and common interests. Nor was this sense of identity confined to the working class. If Hondurans were not yet a nation, they had at least taken an important step in that direction. This collective self-consciousness remained extremely fragile. Even as it was in the process of formation, it began to crumble under the pressure of forces, both native and foreign, in whose interests it was to keep Hondurans divided and weak. Efforts to construct truly national institutions would be systematically undermined. Reform would be counteracted by reaction. Political, social, and economic development would occur, but so would pervasive decay.

The Containment of Labor

Foreign penetration and dependency are themes that reverberate throughout Honduran history. The Great Banana Strike was over. The question remained, however, what kind of union organizations would be created. The U.S. and Honduran governments and the fruit companies were concerned that labor be pro-U.S. and anticommunist, and even before the strike was settled they had begun to mold the movement's leadership. In these and subsequent efforts they were aided enormously by the AFL and the ORIT. When the banana strike finally ended, AFL and ORIT "conciliators" remained in San Pedro Sula to help shape the organization that emerged.

There was, of course, resistance. The PDRH claimed that it had provided the impetus for the strike and therefore had the right to direct the poststrike organization. ORIT efforts were denounced as an attempt to create a "company union." The PDRH's talk was, however, no match for the resources of the Honduran government and the gringos. In August, the Tela Railroad Company Workers' Union (Sindicato de Trabajadores de la Tela Railroad Company—SITRATERCO) was founded, and the following year a union was formed at Standard Fruit (Sindicato de Trabajadores de la Standard Fruit Company—SITRASFRUCO). Both quickly fell under the influence of the ORIT. The latter also succeeded in getting its people into key positions in the labor federations formed in 1957 and 1958. Money flowed freely. Young union leaders were trained in the ideology of "democratic trade unionism" and "anticommunism." If they behaved correctly, they were rewarded with scholarships from the U.S. embassy, paid leaves of absence from the fruit companies, and choice jobs upon their return.

As early as spring 1955 it was apparent that something was going wrong. The previous September, a hurricane had hit the north coast, causing the worst floods in the country's history. The areas under UFCO cultivation had been hit especially hard. Major irrigation and cutting operations had been suspended. It was predicted that as many as 10,000 workers might lose their jobs. Indeed, after surveying the damage, UFCO President Kenneth Raymond had hinted ominously that all company operations might be suspended. The prospect of layoffs, of course, had raised the specter of another strike. Consequently, the company had moved to defuse the crisis with a public relations campaign. Plans were announced for minimizing the storm's impact on the workforce. Significant layoffs were postponed to give the state time to provide jobs for the unemployed. Over 62,000 acres of land were donated for colonization projects. Behind the scenes, the company worked closely with SITRATERCO. In the end, it was agreed that no more than 3,000 workers would be dismissed and then only as they could be hired by the government's public works program.

In fact, public works absorbed only a fraction of the unemployed. UFCO's idle labor force soon rose to almost 12,000. Yet, in spite of its disastrous losses, it did not suspend operations. Indeed, it soon announced that it would *increase* investments by over 19 million lempiras in 1955, 20 million in 1956, and 22 million in 1957.[23]

This was the beginning of something new. Having contained labor unrest, the companies now began to invest in different varieties of bananas more resistant to disease and with a higher yield per acre. Simultaneously, they started a program of "labor rationalization." Work would be intensified and certain areas mechanized. Aerial spraying would be introduced. Bananas would be machine packed in boxes rather than shipped in bunches. In the twenty-year period between the early 1950s and the early 1970s, productivity per hectare would increase almost threefold, while productivity per worker would quadruple. The impact on the labor force would be catastrophic. Between 1954 and 1957 employment at the Tela Railroad Company dropped by almost 50 percent. By 1959 Standard Fruit had fired nearly half of the workers it had employed in 1954. About 19,000 banana workers had lost their jobs, even as production had risen from 9.2 to 12.4 million bunches annually.[24]

Military Hegemony and Liberal Reform

In November 1954 Vice President Julio Lozano Díaz assumed the presidency during a constitutional crisis occasioned by an anarchic election. His ostensible purpose was to save the country from descending into chaos. Once in power, however, he decided to stay there. As time went on and Lozano's popularity waned, the regime was forced to rely increasingly on violence. As it became clear that the president was preparing to maintain himself in power indefinitely, the military decided that it had had enough. On 21 October 1956 it ousted Lozano and set up a junta to govern until new elections could be held.

The coup d'état of 1956 was yet another turning point: It marked the ascendancy of the armed forces as the dominant political force in Honduras. Although some institutionalization and modernization had occurred under Carías, the military on the whole had remained weak and unprofessional. Regional commanders were largely autonomous. Officers placed their loyalty to local superiors above any larger institutional or national allegiance. Soldiers were viewed with a "mixture of repugnance and ridicule." On the one hand, they "evoke[d] a specter of malfeasance and malevolence; on the other, they invite[d] scorn and satire."[25] Starting with the Gálvez administration, however, military "development" rapidly accelerated. In 1952 the Francisco Morazán Military Academy was founded. Two years later an Organic Military Law was issued that defined the army's mission in terms of the defense of national independence and public order. In May 1954, the armed forces' relationship with the United States was formalized by treaty. In return for unlimited access to any "raw and semi-processed materials required . . . as a result of deficiencies or potential deficiencies" in U.S. resources, Washington agreed to supply Honduras with military aid.[26] Schools were set up and scholarships and modern equipment provided. Between 1950 and 1969, 391 officers and 689 enlisted men received training. As a result, skill levels increased considerably. Military institutions became more centralized; regional commanders declined in importance with the creation of five operative field battalions.

Thus were born the modern Honduran armed forces. Prior to the 1950s the military had served as an appendage of whatever political party or faction happened to be in power. Now it was acquiring the organization, cohesion, and strength to act independently.

The other side of the coin was that even as the armed forces were undergoing accelerated development, civilian political institutions were lagging far behind. The traditional parties had never been much more than "semi-institutionalized factional groupings," and by the late 1940s and early 1950s their disarray had reached crisis proportions.[27] The National Party had been largely discredited by its close association with the Carías dictatorship. To make matters worse, it could not agree on a successor to the caudillo. In contrast the Liberals, after a long period of dormancy, had reemerged as a comparatively unified force. Factional conflicts persisted, however, and would deepen in the early 1960s. Most important, the Liberals did not know what to do with the emerging labor movement. Instead of aligning themselves with it, they vacillated, afraid that too close an embrace might leave them open to charges of "communism." Consequently, a golden opportunity to win over this natural constituency was wasted. In short, there was a growing "development gap" between the military and civilian political institutions. The Liberal and National parties had become largely divorced from the emerging issues and power contenders of the day. Given this situation, it was a simple matter for the military to step into the vacuum and establish its hegemony.

At first glance, the coup seemed a benevolent enough intervention. The following year elections were held, and the government was turned over to civilians. Something had changed, however. The new constitution fundamentally altered the relationship between the president and the armed forces. Henceforth, presidential orders to the military had to go through the latter's commander. If a conflict arose between the two, it would be submitted to Congress for decision. Moreover, before assuming his post, the armed forces chief had to take an oath not to carry out orders that violated the spirit or letter of the constitution "even though our superiors command it." Further, promotions from sublieutenant to captain would be bestowed by the president *at the behest* of the chief, and promotions to higher positions would be made by Congress at the *joint* request of the president and the chief.

These stipulations gave the military commander a marked advantage over his civilian "superior." From now on, the president's orders were to be obeyed only if given through the head of the armed forces, who could ignore them if he judged them "unconstitutional." The commander's ability to initiate and (by implication) veto military appointments would enable him to build his own power base within the command structure. New military laws made it almost impossible for the president to remove an incumbent chief or choose a successor. Those decisions were given to a Superior Council of National Defense composed of six active-duty officers, the minister of defense, and the president. Since it took a unanimous vote to remove an incumbent and the commander was himself a voting member, the likelihood of such an eventuality was remote.

In part, the coup and the constitutional changes that followed were an attempt to protect the military from the "ravages of traditional politics." In the past, the chaos and strife of party politics had often spilled over into the armed forces. In the words of one Honduran observer, most previous governments had been "antipathetic" toward the military and "impeded anything that smacked of military progress," rendering it "a small and simple marionette, jiggled at any whim."[28] After October 1956 all that changed. The armed forces had established their autonomy. From there, it would be only a short step to political hegemony. The jiggled would become the jiggler.

First, however, the government would be returned to civilian control. In September 1957, Constituent Assembly elections were held. The Liberals emerged with a working majority. Subsequently, the deputies elected Ramón Villeda Morales constitutional president. Once in office, Villeda lost little time in pledging sweeping reforms. Honduras, he proclaimed, was the "country of the 70s—70 percent illiteracy, 70 percent illegitimacy, 70 percent rural population, and 70 percent avoidable deaths," and he intended to do something about it.

Certainly, Honduras was desperately underdeveloped. Seventy-eight percent of the people still lived in the countryside. Almost two-thirds of the adults were illiterate. Only 30 percent of the population wore shoes, and only a quarter of the peasants farmed with a plow. Infant mortality was among the highest in the world. On top of this, communications remained a major problem. As of 1955, Honduras had only forty kilometers of paved road, and about half of the unpaved roads were impassable in the rainy season. (There were no paved roads between Tegucigalpa and San Pedro Sula.) Furthermore, the country was experiencing an unprecedented population explosion. Since 1930, the population had doubled, and it was continuing to expand at an annual rate of at least 2.8 percent. This placed enormous pressure on Honduras's limited resources. National income had to expand by at least 2.8 percent just to avoid a per capita decline. The domestic resources available to the new administration were woefully inadequate, but Villeda was undaunted. He obtained aid from the World Bank, the International Monetary Fund, and the U.S. government, cut military spending, and embraced a strategy of import-substituting industrialization. In 1960, moreover, Honduras entered the Central American Common Market. The idea was to accelerate regional growth and industrialization by reducing trade barriers among members while protecting Central America's infant industries from outside competition through a common external tariff. Honduran industries producing for the regional market now received preferential financing from the Agency for International Development (AID) and the Inter-American Development Bank. Additional aid came from the Alliance for Progress. The result was rapid economic expansion. Between 1957 and 1964 the gross domestic product (GDP) increased by almost 84 percent.

At the same time, Villeda instituted an ambitious public works program. By 1964 Honduras would have 3,595 kilometers of highway, 382 kilometers would be paved. By 1963 there would be 3,697 primary schools (compared with 2,417 in 1957), and the number of hospitals and clinics would roughly double.[29] In 1959 a new labor code was adopted granting the state broad powers to resolve labor disputes. This same year, a social security law went into effect.

But perhaps Villeda's most significant experiment was agrarian reform. By the late 1950s, conditions in the countryside were becoming critical. As much as 50 percent of the rural population may have been either landless or extremely land-poor, and the situation was rapidly worsening. Several elements were at work here: Natural population increase, the arrival of tens of thousands of land-hungry Salvadoran immigrants, and the return to subsistence farming of many former banana workers meant that more and more people were working less and less land. The soil was overworked, erosion increased, and arability declined.

The most important factor, however, was the explosive growth of export agriculture. Between 1950 and 1965, the amount of land devoted to cotton rose from 1,200 to 18,200 hectares, creating severe land pressure in Choluteca and other parts of southern Honduras, where population density was greatest. Between 1952 and 1965, cattle lands increased by 300,000 hectares. Between 1945 and 1960, coffee production more than doubled. Of these products, the last created the fewest social problems, since it was grown on small and medium-sized holdings. In contrast, the big cotton plantations and cattle ranches tended to expand outward, absorbing neighboring lands by evicting tenants and squatters and fencing in their new acquisitions with barbed wire. In southern Honduras, between 1952 and 1966, two haciendas alone acquired some 54,000 acres through such "competitive exclusion." Moreover, as land grew more scarce, the purchase and rental price of property rose, driving even more people into landlessness.[30]

These developments could not but produce a reaction. As peasant desperation grew, agrarian conflict increased. Campesinos began to resist the encroachments of the big commercial farms. Land invasions and violence became more frequent. Peasant militancy and organization increased. In response, the government set up a colonization program. Between 1958 and 1960, some 75,000 acres of national and *ejidal* (communal) land were distributed. In 1961 a National Agrarian Institute (Instituto Nacional Agrario—INA) was established to oversee the process. A year later Villeda sponsored a new peasant union, the National Association of Honduran Peasants (Asociación Nacional de Campesinos de Honduras—ANACH), to counteract a more radical organization. Like its labor counterparts, ANACH received extensive support from the AFL-CIO and the ORIT.

Villeda's most important contribution was the 1962 agrarian reform law. The legislation that he sponsored had three goals: First, it attempted to promote the efficient use of farmland. Villeda wanted to transform the backward oligarchs into modern entrepreneurs. By introducing the concept that land had "social uses," the law recognized that the interests of society might sometimes outweigh the interests of private property. In effect, the government was telling the large landowners that unless they put their idle and poorly used lands to better use they might lose them. Second, the law tried to create a legal basis for the recovery of national and ejido lands illegally occupied. This meant that an understanding would have to be reached with the fruit companies and that "a whole system of precarious land tenancies which had sprung up . . . had to be systematized."[31] Finally, the measure attempted to provide an escape valve for the anger of an increasingly militant peasantry. Villeda recognized the danger of an explosion. He wanted to defuse the bomb.

The law gave rise to bitter opposition. Though the reform guaranteed private property and set no limit on it, provided that it was properly used, the oligarchs and fruit companies felt threatened. There was an uproar in the U.S. Senate, where angry legislators let it be known that aid to Honduras would be revoked if the measure were not amended. Meanwhile, UFCO had stopped expanding operations, and more jobs were lost. Eventually, Villeda worked out a new version of the law with UFCO negotiators. The result was a mutilated piece of legislation that made it almost impossible to expropriate private land. The episode was significant because it so dramatically demonstrated the limits of change in the system that was emerging. The proponents of reform and reaction were engaged in a protracted conflict over the future. Even when the former seemed to be in the ascendant, the latter were able to frustrate much of the liberal program.

In the final analysis, the Villeda years were a mixture of accomplishments and disappointments. Social programs increased life expectancy and literacy; as the road network expanded, the country became more integrated; industry and services grew rapidly, as did the agro-export and cattle sectors; new labor and social security legislation was enacted. Yet agrarian reform remained frustrated. Landlessness continued to increase. The new labor laws were often ignored or used to restrict union organization. Meanwhile, labor and peasant movements were increasingly penetrated by outside influences. Now, in addition to the Honduran government, the AFL-CIO, and the ORIT, they had to contend with a new organization, the American Institute for Free Labor Development (AIFLD). Even some of Villeda's successes had negative side effects. His development strategy sharply increased foreign economic penetration, deepening the country's dependency on the United States and its relative backwardness vis-à-vis its Central American neighbors.

The Fall of Villeda Morales and the Rise of López Arellano

Throughout his term, Villeda had been under attack by ultraconservative forces bent on destabilizing his administration. The agrarian reform provided those elements with precisely the weapon they needed. An even more serious problem, however, arose from the president's deteriorating relations with the military, which was closely aligned with the National Party. Villeda had replaced the national police, a source of various conspiracies, with a civil guard, responsible to him rather than to the armed forces commander. It was obvious that he was trying to build an institutional counterweight to the military. From the beginning, there were violent clashes between the two.

The straw that broke the camel's back was the impending victory of the Liberal Party's Modesto Rodas Alvarado in the presidential elections scheduled for October 1963. Rodas had a reputation as a radical that was partially attributable to having allegedly made such statements as "Faltarán pinos en Honduras para colgar los nacionalistas." (There are not enough pine trees in Honduras to hang all the Nationalists.) In 1957 he had fought to defeat the constitutional provision granting autonomy to the military. Later he had supported an amendment to restore civilian control. It was small wonder that the armed forces were unwilling to allow this so-called candidate of hatred to take office. On 3 October—ten days before the scheduled balloting—they staged a preemptive coup. Villeda was deposed and the elections canceled. The civil guard was suppressed, Congress dissolved, and the constitution suspended. The president and Rodas were sent into exile.

The U.S. response was instructive. Villeda had been one of John F. Kennedy's favorites: a democrat and a reformer but also a fervent anticommunist who respected private property. He was, moreover, the fourth democratically elected Latin American president to be overthrown since 1962. Such coups undercut one of the basic assumptions of the Alliance for Progress—namely, that the way to prevent Castro-style regimes was to eliminate the conditions that gave rise to them. Revolutionaries thrived on social injustice, poverty, and tyranny. Promoting democratic reformers like Villeda—so the argument went—would pull the rug from under incipient revolutionary movements. Honduras had to be made an object lesson. Accordingly, Washington broke off diplomatic relations.

This did not last long. In November, Kennedy was cut down by an assassin's bullets. His successor, Lyndon Johnson, abruptly changed course. When the new head of the Honduran government, Colonel Oswaldo López Arellano, proved willing to pay the necessary lip service to democracy, relations were restored. Even had Kennedy lived, it is unlikely that things would have turned out differently. U.S. policy was riven with contradictions. Indeed, the coups that were sweeping the hemisphere were in part the *consequence* of that policy. Hand in hand with the Alliance for Progress came a military strategy designed to strengthen the Latin American armies, enabling them to crush any guerrillas that they faced or might have to face.

Under the Kennedy and Johnson administrations, counterinsurgency warfare became the fashion. Military doctrine now acquired political and socioeconomic dimensions. Latin American armies were to become instruments of "development" and "nation building." Military personnel were instructed in the art of "civic action." Troops were taught how to dig wells, build schools, and provide medical services the better to win people's "hearts and minds."

In retrospect, this doctrine seems naive and culture-bound. The U.S. military, in particular, had a "trained incapacity . . . to think about, let alone pursue, questions related to the Latin American military as a political institution."[32] The assumption that Latin American officers shared the values and priorities of their North American advisers ignored the profound social and historical differences between the two cultures. U.S. strategists thought that they were modernizing and professionalizing their Latin American counterparts, and to a degree they were. What they failed to understand was that they were also politicizing them. By giving them a new "mission," defined in socioeconomic and political as well as military terms, U.S. strategists drew the Latin American armies—only a few of which had any strong tradition of obedience to civilian authorities—deeper into politics. By providing them with modern weapons and training, the United States made it easier for them to impose their will on weak civilian institutions. Only belatedly did it occur to some North Americans that their "students" had agendas of their own.

By then, however, the reform component of the strategy had been overwhelmed by pragmatic military and political considerations. The goal of defeating insurgencies had become paramount. Means were of secondary importance. Armed with modern weaponry and a theory of counterinsurgency, Latin American armies crushed one guerrilla movement after another. With every success, democracy and reform became less pressing. With the defeat of the last serious insurgencies in the middle and late 1960s, the Alliance for Progress would evaporate altogether.

As for the new Honduran dictatorship, it quickly repressed the labor and peasant movements. Independent unions were destroyed, as was the radical National Federation of Peasants of Honduras (Federación Nacional de Campesinos de Honduras—FENACH). The agrarian reform was effectively terminated. López Arellano proceeded to develop close ties with the National Party, whose leader, Ricardo Zúniga Agustinus, became secretary for the presidency—in effect the éminence grise of the regime. National Party politicians flocked to the government, which relied heavily on a goon squad, the Mancha Brava, to repress its enemies. To give the regime a facade of popular support, elections for a Constituent Assembly were held in early 1965. The result was a carefully orchestrated fraud. Subsequently, the assembly elected López "constitutional president" for a six-year term.

Development and Decay in the "Living Museum"

If the 1963 coup temporarily ended Honduras's experiment with democracy and reform, economic modernization proceeded apace. This was all in accordance with the rules of what Charles Anderson has called the "living museum": New power contenders could be admitted into the arena of reciprocally recognized elites *provided* that they did not jeopardize the position of established elites.[33] Whereas democracy, independent unions, and agrarian reform constituted clear dangers to the traditional oligarchy, Honduran economic strategy was much less threatening. Import-substituting industrialization focused on the modern rather than on the traditional sector. It thus "avoided the politically explosive issues of agrarian reform and income distribution" and allowed political leaders to "pursue economic development while bolstering the economic and political status quo."[34]

Similarly, the Central American Common Market was an *alternative* to the politically more dangerous strategy of developing an internal market for Honduran manufactured goods. The latter would have required a redistribution of income to enable Hondurans to fuel industrialization by buying the products turned out by their own industries. Such a development had profound implications not only for the economy but for the social and political realms as well. People with income could no longer be treated as peons. They would acquire property and status and sooner or later would demand political power. On the surface, the Common Market appeared to offer elites a way of sidestepping such threats by avoiding income redistribution. Rather than creating internal markets, Central Americans, through a regional common market, would expand their foreign ones.

Although in the short run the Common Market greatly increased regional trade, encouraging economic diversification and fostering modest growth, in the long run it was doomed. The Central American market was not large enough to fuel rapid, sustained growth. Not only was the total population small but its impoverishment meant that relatively few people could afford to buy the goods being produced by the region's industries. There was thus a point of diminishing returns beyond which Central Americans had to look for other ways to stimulate growth.

A more immediate problem, however, was growing dependency. The 1960s witnessed a rapid increase in foreign—mostly U.S.—economic penetration. Between 1961 and 1965, US$200 million in private capital poured into Honduras. Between 1963 and 1967, U.S. investment doubled. Of the sixty-three major companies in the country, thirty-five were set up between 1960 and 1968. One hundred percent of the production of the five largest Honduran firms was controlled by U.S. multinationals; the comparable figures for the twenty and fifty largest companies were 88.7 percent and 82 percent, respectively. By the decade's end, U.S. investments came to over US$200 million—this in a country whose entire gross national product (GNP) was only a little more than US$500 million.[35] This was development of a kind, but the real question was who benefited. U.S. companies took more out of the country than they invested. The net outflow was US$22.4 million in 1968 and US$17.7 million in the following year. The two largest commercial banks, Banco Atlántida and the Banco de Honduras, came under the respective control of Chase Manhattan and the First National City Bank of New York. U.S. interests dominated the banana industry, the largest mining companies, and key elements of the infrastructure, including the two most important railroads.[36]

North American power was taken for granted. Partly as a result, efforts to equalize development and investment among the Common Market countries were abandoned. Foreigners were allowed to invest without any concern for the regional economic balance. Capital poured into the more industrialized economies of El Salvador and Guatemala much faster than it did into Honduras, widening the competitive gap between them. In 1960 Honduras's industrial GNP was 51 percent of El Salvador's; by 1969 it had declined to 32.5 percent. Whereas Salvadoran exports to Honduras in 1968 were more than five times what they had been in 1960, Honduran exports to El Salvador had only doubled. Between 1965 and 1968 the situation became especially acute, as Honduran exports declined and Salvadoran imports almost doubled. In the process, Honduran manufacturers were forced to the wall as the country was flooded with Salvadoran and Guatemalan products.[37] In the face of this, the López regime adopted an increasingly nationalistic stance, demanding preferential treatment because of the country's competitive disadvantages, but little was accomplished. Instead, the economy took a turn for the worse. Unemployment, trade deficits, and corruption grew. Scandals further undercut the government's legitimacy. As political and social tension mounted and opposition increased, the regime responded with more repression.

Meanwhile, in the countryside, land poverty was steadily worsening. Between 1962 and 1966 only a dozen groups had received land under the agrarian reform. Colonization projects were collapsing because of a lack of technical assistance and credit. Yet the economic and demographic pressures that had created the need for reform had in no way lessened. The population explosion continued to swell the ranks of the landless and unemployed. At the same time, the U.S. demand for beef, sugar, and cotton provided large landowners with a powerful incentive to expand their export operations. In the process, the rights of tenants and sharecroppers were often revoked. Growing numbers of peasants were driven off their own and public lands. By mid-decade an estimated 63,120 families—roughly 26 percent of the total rural population—were landless.[38] In turn, this concentration on commercial agriculture at the expense of food crops for domestic consumption aggravated the already serious problems of malnutrition and survival.

It was at this juncture that the Salvadoran immigrants became a major issue. It was a measure of the desperation in the Salvadoran countryside that so many campesinos chose to leave their own country for an even poorer one. As bad as things were in Honduras, they were even worse in El Salvador: There the pressures of population growth and "competitive exclusion" were aggravated by the fact that this was the most densely populated mainland country in the hemisphere. Nor was the oligarchy there willing even to consider agrarian reform. Not only were socioeconomic inequalities greater than in Honduras, but they were rapidly getting worse. Lacking the means of survival in their homeland, the Salvadorans flooded into Honduras. By 1969 they numbered some 300,000. Salvadorans accounted for almost 20 percent of all agriculturalists in the country and occupied over half a million acres of land.[39] To the class conflict between Hondurans was now added growing competition for land between Hondurans and Salvadorans.

In spite of repression, by the mid-1960s Honduran campesinos were fighting back. A new organization, the National Peasant Union (Unión Nacional de Campesinos—UNC), had taken root, inspired by the social Christian doctrines of the Catholic church. After 1964, the UNC took the lead in encouraging peasants to engage in land seizures as a means of recapturing stolen properties and gaining access to others. In turn, this threat of a militant, organized peasantry gave rise to a "cohesive landowning elite which had much in common with the traditional rural oligarchies of Guatemala and El Salvador. The difference was that the Honduran military was not their automatic ally."[40] From 1968 onward, in response to this growing peasant militancy and a wave of land seizures, López Arellano resurrected the agrarian reform. The INA, starved for funds since its inception, was given a meaningful budget. An activist director, Rigoberto Sandoval Corea, was appointed. For the next several years, the agency would play an important though limited role in defense of peasant interests. López was trying to walk a tightrope between peasants and landowners. The question was how to satisfy the demands of the former without alienating the latter. That such an attempt was even made was extraordinary. In El Salvador it would have been unthinkable.

But this was Honduras. Class divisions were neither as deep nor as rigid. As long as there were landowners willing to sell their lands and enough money to compensate them, such a solution was plausible. Even so, this was not always the case. The cattle ranchers, in particular, were uncompromising. By the late 1960s they had begun looking for a scapegoat to divert attention from their own responsibility for the agrarian crisis. The choice was obvious: Salvadorans were already unpopular because of their economic penetration via the Common Market. Some had set up businesses in Tegucigalpa and San Pedro Sula, where with characteristic enterprise—Salvadorans generally being harder workers than Hondurans—they had prospered. These sins, however, seemed minor compared to what was happening in the countryside. There, after all, Salvadoran peasants were occupying territories at the expense of their Honduran neighbors. The landowners now prepared to exploit the resentments inherent in the situation.

In 1966 the large farmers and ranchers had founded the National Federation of Agriculturalists and Cattlemen (Federación Nacional de Agricultores y Ganaderos de Honduras—FENAGH) to "resist peasant demands for land reform and to continue the process of extending the great estates, by means fair or foul."[41] FENAGH now began to incite public opinion, blaming the Salvadorans for the land seizures and the lack of available land. Newspapers began to talk about a Salvadoran "fifth column"; demands were made that the "troublemakers" be expelled. Salvadoran residents were subjected to threats and attack. The following year several incidents along the Salvadoran border added fuel to the fire. For years, this mountainous territory had been the subject of dispute. Not only was the boundary poorly defined but desperadoes of various stripes made the area their home, preying on the populations on both sides. The Salvadoran national guard and vigilantes often crossed into Honduran territory in pursuit of suspected bandidos. As anti-Salvadoran sentiment grew in Honduras, so did the alarm over these incursions.

The Soccer War: Escape Valves and Nation Building

External threats tend to produce internal unity. For that reason, politically endangered elites from time immemorial have tried to divert popular frustrations by magnifying—or even creating—the specter of a foreign enemy. So it was in Central America in the late 1960s. The mistreatment of Salvadorans in Honduras was a means by which the Salvadoran oligarchy could manipulate the peasantry, diverting attention from the need for agrarian reform. Similarly, Honduran landowners could deflect the anger of their own peasants over the growing land shortage by blaming the situation on Salvadoran squatters.

As socioeconomic and political conditions in Honduras deteriorated in spring 1969, the government moved to expel the Salvadorans from the lands on which they were squatting. By early June, some five hundred families, many of which had worked these lands for years, had been dispossessed. Often they lost not only their farms but their other belongings as well. The secret police and the Mancha Brava facilitated the evictions with liberal doses of violence. The Honduran press too was caught up in the fever. A wave of anti-Salvadoran hysteria swept the country. The result was a stampede of Salvadorans back to their homeland. By early July some 20,000 had left, taking with them anything they could carry. Now it became the turn of the Salvadoran press to engage in anti-Honduran histrionics. To make matters worse, in the midst of all this the two countries were facing each other in the World Cup soccer eliminations. The first game of the series had been held in Tegucigalpa in an atmosphere that was, to put it mildly, less than sportsmanlike. When in mid-June the second game was played in San Salvador, the Hondurans were accorded similar treatment. Honduran fans were harassed and sometimes assaulted. The visitors were greeted with water bombs filled with urine. Cars were damaged. Meanwhile, back in Tegucigalpa, the press was magnifying the incident with reports of "violated women and sadistic beatings" and of hungry and thirsty Hondurans "being served urine and manure."

Nothing of the sort had happened, but that hardly mattered. The reports led to a wave of violence against those Salvadorans still in Honduras, and thousands more were expelled. In turn, the Salvadoran government sealed its borders and filed a complaint of genocide with the Inter-American Commission on Human Rights. Diplomatic relations were broken. By early July fighting had broken out on the frontier. On 14 July Salvadoran planes struck targets deep inside Honduras. The army launched an offensive along the main roads connecting the countries. In short order, the Salvadorans captured Nueva Ocotepeque. After that, however, the attack stalled. Salvadoran air strikes proved ineffective. The Honduran air force wreaked havoc on Salvadoran oil storage facilities, accelerating the enemy's growing fuel shortage. The fighting lasted only a hundred hours. There were no victors. By the war's end some 130,000 Salvadorans had been expelled or had fled from Honduras, producing serious economic damage on both sides of the border. Trade between the two countries had been totally disrupted. A devastating blow had been struck at the Central American Common Market. All told, approximately 2,000 people—mostly Honduran civilians—had lost their lives, and thousands more had been left homeless. Airline service between Tegucigalpa and San Salvador would be interrupted for over a decade. Not until 1980 would a peace treaty, formally terminating hostilities, finally be signed.

On the positive side, the war did unite Hondurans as never before. A surge of nationalistic emotion submerged the socioeconomic and political conflicts that had been threatening to tear the country apart. Tens of thousands of workers and peasants set aside the class struggle and begged the government for arms with which to defend *la patria*. In the short run, the tactics of xenophobia worked brilliantly.[42]

The National Unity Pact

The unification of a people under foreign threat is not, however, in itself enough to mold a nation, especially when the danger is short-lived. Once the fighting ended, all the old problems and conflicts reemerged. Even before the war, a broad alliance of north-coast interest groups—including progressive business, labor, and peasant associations—had tried to convince López Arellano of the need for wide-ranging reforms. At the time López and his political adviser, Ricardo Zúniga, had been unreceptive. The latter saw these *fuerzas vivas* (living forces) as a threat to the political dominance of his National Party machine. Similarly, López sensed growing opposition to his continuance in office. He was not yet ready to surrender power.

After the war, however, the fuerzas vivas resurrected their call for change. Over the next year and a half, pressure would be brought on López and Zúniga to step aside so that Hondurans might choose a "national unity" government in the elections scheduled for March 1971. As months passed and sentiment against a Zúniga candidacy grew, the president began to look for a way out. In December 1970, he agreed to a national unity plan that placed responsibility for creating a government of national integration in the hands of the two major parties. A single nonpartisan candidate acceptable to everyone was to be selected. A cabinet was to be formed through the proportional representation of all political and social groups. Elaborate rules were constructed for the composition and leadership of Congress.

Unfortunately, the plan was unworkable. For one thing, the arrangements came as a surprise to most Hondurans. The negotiations had been restricted to elites; the public had not been informed, nor had all of the major interest groups been consulted. Even worse, by shifting the responsibility for implementation to the two major parties the authors of the pact had placed its fate in the hands of those largely responsible for having created the crisis in the first place. The National and Liberal Parties were part of the problem; they could not, by themselves, be trusted to solve it. Bureaucratized, factionalized, riven with corruption and incompetence, they concentrated primarily on self-aggrandizement. Thus, what began as an attempt at purification and reform was soon transformed into a mutual defense pact between traditional elites. Rather than broadening political participation by bringing new groups into the government, it drew the parties together to protect their own interests. In the process, few opportunities for personal gain were missed.

There was one major change in the original agreement: The parties rejected the idea of a common candidate. Rather, the president would be chosen through elections. The Liberals proceeded to nominate Jorge Bueso Arias and the Nationals Ernesto Cruz. Operating on the assumption that the opposition would win an honest balloting, Zúniga contented himself with negotiating the composition of the new administration with the Liberals. The day before the vote a *"pactito"* was reached that divided up the spoils of office.

To the surprise of almost everyone, the Nationalist candidate, Cruz, won. From the beginning, his administration was a disaster.

Ricardo Zúniga was appointed minister of interior, and he proceeded to implement the "pactito" in his own partisan way. There followed a whole series of provocative actions that alienated business, labor, the peasantry, and the Liberal opposition. By spring 1972 the government had isolated itself from all but the most conservative elements in the "living museum." Reforms were ignored even as the economy deteriorated and political strife intensified. Those who had placed their faith in the national unity plan saw their hopes dashed as Zúniga and his cronies ravaged the bureaucracy for their own ends.

The Return of López Arellano

Once again, reform had led to reaction. Hopes and expectations had been raised only to be dashed. Unrest was assuming dangerous proportions. In December 1972 thousands of peasants descended on the capital for a "hunger march." At this point, the military informed President Cruz that his services would no longer be required. López Arellano, who had remained chief of the armed forces, was reinstalled as president.

Whatever else one may think of General López, one must admire his ability to adjust to shifting political winds. In 1963 he had come to power at the head of a coalition of military officers and large landowners whose aim was to purge the government of "communist" influences and terminate the agrarian reform. In 1972 he returned to power with the support of some of the very elements that had previously been branded "subversive." Now he was the champion of agrarian reform.

Much had changed in the preceding decade. A war had been fought and the prestige of the army damaged. A new generation of officers, determined to weed out dead wood and modernize the institution, had come to the fore.[43] Inspired by the military reformers in Peru and Panama, many looked with favor on land reform as a means of defusing the time bomb in the countryside. At the same time, a multiclass alliance of modernizing industrialists, labor unions, and peasants was playing an increasingly important role in national politics. The traditional parties had failed utterly to meet the challenge of modernization. To López, the time seemed right to distance himself from Zúniga and mobilize these diverse forces on behalf of his own ambitions.

Thus, one of the first acts of the new government was the issuance of Decree Law 8, which gave peasants immediate, though temporary, use of disputed national and ejido lands held by the INA. More important in terms of the conflict unleashed, it required private owners either to cultivate or to rent idle holdings. Over the next two years, more than six hundred peasant settlements would be created. Decree Law 8 expired in late 1974, but on 30 December a more comprehensive reform was issued. Decree Law 170 placed a limit of five hundred hectares on the size of most holdings not devoted to export crops. A promise was made to distribute almost 1.5 million acres to 120,000 families over the next five years. Like the previous decree, Law 170 was designed to break up the traditional less productive *latifundio/minifundio* landholding arrangements, replacing them with a more efficient and capital-intensive system of medium-sized and large farms. Simultaneously, it was intended to co-opt the peasantry and contain the land invasions that had become epidemic in the wake of the devastation wrought by Hurricane Fifí in September 1974.

The López reforms provide a clue to Honduran political stability. No other Central American land reform prior to the 1980s accomplished nearly as much. Between 1973 and 1976 over 31,000 peasant families received almost 144,000 hectares of land. This amounted to about two-thirds of all beneficiaries and land distributed from 1962 to 1980. By the end of the decade over 34,000 families, including more than 206,000 people, were still cultivating agrarian reform lands. This was the equivalent of over 22 percent of the landless and desperately land-poor families in the mid-1970s. The reforms served as an important safety valve, diffusing campesino unrest and discouraging independent peasant mobilizations. The plots received may have been small and in distant locations, but they were considerably better than nothing—which was often the only alternative. Many recipients were co-opted into the system, their militancy evaporating as their interest in credit and technical assistance replaced their previous concern for land for those who did not already have it.

The reforms also had important symbolic significance. They raised hopes for the future and suggested that the Honduran government and military might be counted on as allies vis-à-vis the landlords: "The fact that campesinos could win disputes over land titles at the INA and force 'stolen' land to be returned by landlords was extremely significant. Such outcomes would have been almost unimaginable in Guatemala, El Salvador, or Nicaragua." By the same token, the association of the armed forces with the agrarian reform created a "much more progressive image for Honduran soldiers than for their counterparts in neighboring countries."[44] Obviously, this military was not under the thumb of the rural oligarchy. In the final analysis, the López reforms represented a useful, though limited, attempt to contain the country's growing agrarian problem and preserve political stability. They did not solve the problem, but they did buy time.

The other pillar of the López program was state-sponsored industrialization. By the early 1970s, it had become clear that a development strategy based on the Central American Common Market was no longer feasible. A national development plan was drawn up. Although import substitution again served as the basic framework, now the state would accept major responsibility for capital accumulation and investment. Various semiautonomous and autonomous state agencies were set up to help administer the program. Economic diversification was promoted; minimum wage laws were enacted, and controls were placed on foreign-owned mining companies. Honduras joined the banana producers' cartel.

The policies of the second López administration strengthened the peasant and labor movements and bolstered the economy, but this was not enough to save the general from his enemies. By late 1974 the agrarian reform had once more slowed in the face of opposition from FENAGH, the banana companies, conservative politicians and military officers, and the United States. A bitter propaganda campaign was launched against the government. Both Nationalists and Liberals joined in, demanding a return to civilian rule.

Military Politics from *Reformismo* to *Parasitismo*

On 3 February 1975, Eli Black, the chairman of United Brands (formerly the United Fruit Company), tossed his briefcase through the sealed skyscraper window in his Manhattan office and jumped to his death on Park Avenue forty-four stories below. When neither his relatives nor business associates could explain this unexpected behavior, the Securities and Exchange Commission decided to investigate. As it turned out, United was in financial trouble as a result of Black's mismanagement. The value of the company's stocks, bonds, and warrants had declined dramatically, as had its share in the banana market. At the same time, it had acquired an enormous debt and was employing dubious accounting practices. Now it was about to become embroiled in a scandal that would bring down the Honduran government and further damage the company's already dubious image in Latin America. In April, the *Wall Street Journal* published the details.

United Brands had paid a Honduran official US$1.25 million as the initial installment of a US$2.5 million bribe to gain relief from an export tax on bananas. The duty had been levied the previous year. Notwithstanding that this was, in effect, the first price rise in twenty years and that it had immediately been passed on to consumers, the fruit companies had been indignant. Standard had suspended banana exports, but United Brands had had a better idea. It would use *la mordida*. In August, one of its vice presidents had met with the Honduran economics minister, Abraham Bennaton Ramos. After hard bargaining in which the original Honduran demand was reduced by half, it had been decided that the money would be paid into numbered Swiss bank accounts. Shortly thereafter, the banana tax had been reduced by half, saving the company US$7.5 million for 1975 alone.

The scandal could not be ignored. López Arellano had himself been implicated, and although he appointed a commission to investigate the affair, he sabotaged its efforts to determine his own guilt or innocence by refusing to let it examine his Swiss bank account. In this cover-up, the president was aided enormously by Bennaton Ramos, who impeded the commission's attempts to determine from Swiss authorities whether the bribe had gone to anyone other than himself. Subsequently, the former minister was rewarded for his cooperation with a pardon.

The full story may never be known. Even today, some observers believe that López was innocent. United Brands claimed that he had rejected a bribe from Black in a meeting at the Presidential Palace in May 1974. Others say that López's wife had become involved without his knowledge and that this was the reason he had refused access to his records.[45] Whatever the truth, he had a long history of shady involvements. He had begun his career as a poverty-stricken bus driver's assistant. By the time he was forced out of office, he had amassed a fortune of at least US$25 million, much of it through questionable means. Eventually, his holdings would include the national airline, Banco Ficensa, the Flor de Caña rum company, the duty-free stores in Honduran airports, a huge farm in Comayagua, and numerous real estate ventures in Miami.[46]

The president was not, of course, the first Honduran chief of state to abuse his power for personal gain, nor would he be the last. But his involvement in "Bananagate"—as the press dubbed the scandal—gave his enemies the perfect opportunity to remove him. These disclosures were a major source of national humiliation, resurrecting once again the stereotype of Honduras as a banana republic that could be bought or sold for the price of a well-placed bribe. Even López's friends now found him an embarrassment.

In the final analysis, however, Bananagate was more a pretext than a reason for his ouster. This was a period of turmoil within the military. In the aftermath of Hurricane Fifí, corruption had become rampant as officers plundered the relief supplies that flowed into the country. Older, more conservative officers chafed at the reform initiatives of their juniors. In turn, the latter were increasingly impatient with their less well-educated, corruption-prone seniors, who had acquired their rank through bureaucratic intrigue rather than on the battlefield. Not only were they obstructing reforms, but—even more important—they were blocking the younger generation's rise to the top. Nor was López spared criticism: Military modernization could not occur as long as *personalismo* and *caudillismo* prevailed. The moment had come to create a more institutionalized and collegiate command structure.[47]

Caught in the middle of this struggle, López vacillated, alternately trying to placate and contain both sides. In the end, he alienated both. In late January 1975 a major shake-up occurred. A Superior Council of the Armed Forces (Consejo Superior de las Fuerzas Armadas—COSUFFAA), formed mainly of lieutenant colonels, was established in place of the Superior Council of National Defense and the full colonels who had composed it. A limit was put on the term that could be served as military commander. In March, the COSUFFAA ordered that the position of armed forces chief be separated from that of chief of state. López lost his primary power base as Colonel Juan Alberto Melgar Castro became the new military leader. Nor was López the only loser. More than two dozen colonels were retired without pensions. To all appearances, the lieutenant colonels had established their hegemony over the armed forces. Presumably, the political and administrative organs of the state would follow. This was the situation at the time of the *Wall Street Journal* revelations. López would almost certainly have fallen even without Bananagate. The scandal simply accelerated his departure. On 22 April he was removed from his post as chief of state.

At first glance, it was not clear what kind of regime would replace his. True, a new agrarian reform law (Decree 170) had been promulgated a few weeks earlier, and one of the young officers, Mario Maldonado, had been installed as head of the INA. Moreover, the apparent victory of that generation in the military power struggle seemed to bode well for the future. Yet the lieutenant colonels were not monolithic. Politically heterogeneous and ideologically ambiguous, their sole point in common was membership in the same graduating class. Melgar was not one of their own, but a survivor of the older generation. His cabinet appointments caused consternation among those who had hoped for more progressive policies.

The new government was quickly put to the test. As the reactionary right continued to obstruct the agrarian reform, the campesinos once again began to mobilize. The UNC sponsored a wave of occupations followed by a blockade of key bridges around the country. On 25 June the campaign culminated in a nationwide "hunger march" on Tegucigalpa. In the frontier territory of Olancho, marchers were attacked by soldiers and local ranchers. Fourteen people were killed, including two priests who were not even participants in the demonstration. But the campesinos were not intimidated. The massacre only accelerated their radicalization, and within a few weeks the Melgar regime found itself confronted with a movement more united than ever. Land occupations now reached epidemic proportions.

As the crisis deepened, Melgar moved to placate both sides. He named Rigoberto Sandoval Corea head of the INA. This was the same activist director who had instilled life into the institute in the late 1960s. Sandoval would keep the land distribution program on track for almost a year. This time, however, he was no longer serving a president who was interested in reform. By the time he assumed office, the INA was already in the midst of a massive purge. When toward the end of 1976 he tried to expropriate 28,000 acres from United Brands and 58,000 from domestic owners, he was stopped in his tracks. In March 1977 an agrarian policy coordinating commission, stacked with rich landowners, was created, with the power to override the INA director. Seeing the handwriting on the wall, Sandoval resigned. Support for the reform sector now dramatically declined. Aid to cooperatives and other forms of communal ownership was discontinued. Initially, 600,000 hectares were to have been distributed to 120,000 families between 1975 and 1979. Only 15 percent of this area in fact went to just 16 percent of these families; at that rate, the goals would have taken 103 years to achieve. By 1980, almost a third of the families that had received land during 1973-1974 were no longer occupying it.[48]

If the emasculation of the agrarian reform was the most potent symbol of the regime's turn to the right, it was not the only one. Shortly before Sandoval's resignation, the military had occupied Las Isletas, a collective set up with government financial support in October 1975 on lands abandoned by Standard Fruit. The enterprise was run by a board of management elected by the workers. Many of its members had been militants in SUTRASFCO, the Standard Fruit Company union. Their leaders had refused to be bribed or intimidated into selling their produce at artificially low prices. Standard had been hostile to the experiment from the beginning.

Nevertheless, for a while the cooperative had continued to sell its bananas to Standard Fruit, and the enterprise had prospered: Production had increased from 43,000 boxes in 1975 to 1 million in 1976 and 4 million the following year. Wages had risen from US$1 to US$3 a day. In early 1977, however, the collective had considered selling its fruit to COMUNBANA (Comercializadora Multinacional del Banano), the marketing arm of the Union of Banana Exporting Countries. This had been too much for Standard, which would have lost some US$2.5 million a year in freight charges.[49] In February, Honduran army units invaded the cooperative, arresting its leaders on trumped-up charges of embezzlement and "communism." Former employees of Castle and Cook (since 1968 the parent company of Standard Fruit) were brought in to help run the business. One of the new directors' first actions was to sign a ten-year contract to sell all of the collective's bananas to Standard at a price per box of US$1.46 to US$1.19 *below* the price offered by COMUNBANA. While Castle and Cook denied having anything to do with the invasion, its protestations were not very convincing: Company vehicles had been used in the assault, and the commander in charge—Lt. Colonel Gustavo Alvarez—was on the Castle and Cook payroll.[50]

Over the next few years, the new managers would take the enterprise to the verge of bankruptcy. In addition to accepting an embarrassingly low price for their bananas, they agreed to pay freight costs and meet stringent quality controls. Even so, Standard still rejected 20 to 30 percent of their produce. The management also agreed to pay the government banana corporation US$1 million a year for "technical assistance." In return, the collective received the services of "54 sluggards living in air conditioning . . . and developing an expertise in pool." Between 1977 and 1980, the cooperative's debt rose from US$4 million to US$12 million.[51] Nor was Las Isletas an isolated case. In March, Standard broke the militants on its own plantations. Similar measures were taken against other unions. In the process, the north coast became increasingly regimented, with army officers sometimes supervising plantation workers and police agents assuming key government posts.

Requiem for a Reform

How could the political direction of the country have been so easily reversed? In retrospect, it is clear that the military reformers had never had the hegemony suggested by their generation's dominance of the COSUFFAA. The young officers were not politically homogeneous; their ranks contained rightists as well as leftists. This diversity was their Achilles' heel. Their movement could not be sustained solely on generational affiliation. As long as their upward mobility was blocked by their elders, they had a powerful motive for unity. Once that impediment had been removed, their alliance of expediency disintegrated.

The first signs of their weakness were the appointment of Melgar Castro as head of the armed forces and his subsequent move to chief of state, with the even more conservative Policarpo Paz García replacing him as military chief. Though Melgar was of the older generation, he had contacts with the young officers. This initially enabled him to serve as an arbitrator between factions. He was a consensus candidate in a regime that was attempting to restore unity. Too easily, the progressives assumed that he and his conservative colleagues could be contained: After all, the presidency was simply an executive office that would carry out the orders of the COSUFFAA, in which the younger generation had a majority. The new armed forces chief might be ultraconservative, but he was outnumbered. The days of the caudillo were over. From now on, decisions would be made collectively.

The reformers had seriously underestimated their opposition. Politically inexperienced and naive, they did not know how to exercise power. Then too, Melgar had lulled them into complacency. In the beginning, the president had reached out to the left as well as the right. As time went on, however, he began to shift. Economic growth displaced social justice as a priority. Gradually, the advocates of reform were intimidated, bought off, or removed from positions of authority.

It has sometimes been argued that the agrarian reform was doomed by its nature. It was a top-down paternalistic reform, that lacked the stable mass sociopolitical base that might have guaranteed its continuation and radicalization. As long as it was dependent on military politics, it would always be susceptible to sabotage or termination. Still, it is hard to imagine a more substantive program in the Honduras of the 1970s. This was a profoundly conservative society. Revolutionary conditions did not exist. Nor was there support for more radical measures in the higher councils of army and state. Reform had come up against the limitations of the system.

Ironically, Melgar Castro would also soon fall victim to those limits. In late 1977, Mario and Mary Ferrari, who were implicated in the activities of organized crime, were kidnapped and murdered. In the investigation that followed, charges were raised against Juan Angel Barahona, the Honduran Interpol chief, who in turn claimed that high-ranking officers linked to the Mafia were turning the country into a crossroads for Latin American cocaine bound for the United States. Paz García was accused of suppressing evidence of these activities. The military denied the charge and appointed a commission—headed by Paz—to investigate. The situation was further complicated when Manuel Gamero, editor of the liberal daily *El Tiempo*, announced that he had tapes implicating military officers in the drug traffic and the Ferrari case. In June 1978, Gamero was arrested for "withholding evidence." His information was never made public. Shortly thereafter, the military commission released its report, absolving all high-level officers.

General Paz did not appreciate this adverse publicity. As co-owner of a large ranch with Juan Ramón Matta Ballesteros, head of the Honduran Mafia, he had ties with organized crime that could not bear scrutiny. He resented the president's failure to prevent press reports of his involvement in a series of drug and bribery scandals. He was, in addition, displeased with Melgar's political ambitions. The president was trying to form an alliance with the National Party with the aim of perpetuating himself in power.[52] He considered Melgar, who came from humble origins, unworthy of the post. Paz was a war hero and had a comparatively elite military background. He wanted the presidency for himself.

In August 1978, the government was overthrown. As president of the new military junta, Paz García became chief of state. Behind the scenes, financing the move, was Ramón Matta.[53]

Things had come full circle. Reform had been followed by oligarchic restoration. The political system was a homeostatic mechanism. Neither extreme could completely impose its policies; each was strong enough to constrain the other. The result was a dynamic equilibrium, a cyclical process of reform and reaction that, through the 1970s, was sufficient to maintain stability. Whether that would continue to be the case in the 1980s was, of course, another matter.

Notes

1. William Krehm, *Democracies and Tyrannies of the Caribbean* (Westport, Conn.: Lawrence Hill, 1984), p. 81.

2. Alfredo León Gómez, *El Escándalo del Ferrocarril* (Tegucigalpa: n.p., 1978), p. 181; Charles Brand, "Background of Capitalistic Underdevelopment: Honduras to 1913" (Ph.D. diss. University of Pittsburgh, 1972), p. 148; Richard L. Millett, "Historical Setting," in *Honduras, A Country Study*, James D. Rudolph, ed. (Washington, D.C.: American University, 1984), p. 19.

3. Antonio Murga Frassinetti, *Enclave y Sociedad en Honduras* (Tegucigalpa: Editorial Universitaria, 1985), p. 23.

4. Brand, "Background," p. 119.

5. Murga Frassinetti, *Enclave*, p. 25.

6. Eighteen ninety-seven, to be exact. Soto, incidently, was one of Rosario's principal owners. Longino Becerra, *Evolución Histórica de Honduras* (Tegucigalpa: Editorial Baktún, 1988), p. 129; Millett, "Historical Setting," p. 17.

7. Walter LaFeber, *Inevitable Revolutions* (New York: W. W. Norton, 1983), p. 42.

8. Vilma Laínez and Víctor Meza, "El Enclave Bananero en Honduras," in *Historia de Honduras*, Medardo Mejía, ed., Vol. 6 (Tegucigalpa: Editorial Universitaria, 1990), p. 200.

9. LaFeber, *Inevitable Revolutions*, p. 43.

10. Laínez and Meza, "El Enclave," pp. 185, 191; Richard Lapper and James Painter, *Honduras: State for Sale* (London: Latin America Bureau, 1985), p. 22.

11. LaFeber, *Inevitable Revolutions*, p. 43.

12. Unless otherwise noted, the following is based on Krehm, *Democracies*, pp. 83-88. Quoted materials are on pp. 83 and 85.

13. Tom Buckley, *Violent Neighbors* (New York: Times Books, 1984), p. 229.

14. Mario Posas and Rafael del Cid, *La Construcción del Sector Público y del Estado Nacional de Honduras, 1876-1979* (San José: Editorial Universitaria Centroamericana, 1983), p. 80; Marvin Barahona, *La Hegemonía de los Estados Unidos en Honduras, 1907-1932* (Tegucigalpa: Centro de Documentación de Honduras, 1989).

15. Letter from Stokeley W. Morgan to the Secretary of State, 18 December 1924.

16. Krehm, *Democracies*, pp. 90-94.

17. Edward Boatman-Guillan, "The Political Role of the United Fruit Company in Honduras" (Ph.D. diss., draft), quoted in Posas and del Cid, *La Construcción*, p. 69.

18. Marco Virgilio Carías and Víctor Meza, *Las Compañías Bananeras en Honduras: Un Poco de Historia* (Tegucigalpa: Universidad Nacional Autónoma de Honduras, 1975).

19. Charles David Kepner, Jr., *Social Aspects of the Banana Industry* (New York: Columbia University Press, 1936), pp. 160-161.

20. Robert MacCameron, *Bananas, Labor, and Politics in Honduras: 1954-1963* (Syracuse: Syracuse University Press, 1983), pp. 22, 31. The following account of the Great Banana Strike is largely based on this study.

21. The PDRH was a clandestine group that had included many intellectuals opposed to the Carías dictatorship. Once Gálvez eased the repression, some members—most prominent among them president-to-be Ramón Villeda Morales—came in from the cold to join—or rejoin—the Liberal Party. In turn, that shifted the PDRH's constituency more toward the working class and labor radicalism.

22. Becerra, *Evolución Histórica*, p. 167.

23. MacCameron, *Bananas*, p. 83.

24. Daniel Slutzky and Esther Alonso, *Les Transformations Récentes de l'Enclave Bananière au Honduras* (Paris: CETRAL, 1979), p. 32; Posas and del Cid, *La Construcción*, p. 96; Stephen Volk, "Honduras: On the Border of War," *NACLA Report on the Americas*, Vol. 15, No. 6, November-December 1981, p. 8.

25. Louis A. Pérez, "Armies of the Caribbean: Historical Perspectives, Historiographical Trends," *Latin American Perspectives*, Vol. 14, No. 4, Fall 1987, p. 490.

26. John Gerassi, *The Great Fear* (New York: Macmillan, 1963), pp. 413-414.

27. The following is based primarily on Steve C. Ropp, "The Honduran Army in the Sociopolitical Evolution of the Honduran State," *The Americas*, Vol. 30, No. 4, April 1974, pp. 513-517.

28. "Breve Análisis de la Enseñanza Militar en Honduras," *Revista Militar*, Vol. 1, No. 3, July-December 1961, p. 13.

29. Stefanía Natalini de Castro, María de los Angeles Mendoza Saborío, and Joaquín Pagán Solórzano, *Significado Histórico del Gobierno del Dr. Ramón Villeda Morales* (Tegucigalpa: Editorial Universitaria, 1985), p. 63.

30. William H. Durham, *Scarcity and Survival in Central America* (Stanford: Stanford University Press, 1979), p. 122; Lapper and Painter, *Honduras*, p. 52.

31. Volk, "Honduras," p. 9.

32. Robert A. Pastor, *Condemned to Repetition: The United States and Nicaragua* (Princeton: Princeton University Press, 1987), p. 176.

33. Charles Anderson, *Politics and Economic Change in Latin America* (Princeton: D. Van Nostrand, 1967), pp. 104-105.

34. Royce Q. Shaw, *Central America: Regional Integration and National Political Development* (Boulder: Westview Press, 1978), p. 58.

35. Lapper and Painter, *Honduras*, p. 55; Antonio Murga Frassinetti, "Concentración Industrial en Honduras," *Economía Política*, No. 9, April 1975, pp. 70, 85-86; Víctor Meza, "Crisis del Reformismo Militar y Coyuntura Política en Honduras," *ALAI: Servicio Informativo* (Montreal), Vol. 5, No. 3, 9 October 1981, p. 41.

36. LaFeber, *Inevitable Revolutions*, p. 181.

37. Lapper and Painter, *Honduras*, pp. 55-56.

38. United Nations Economic Commission for Latin America, *Tenencia de la Tierra y Desarrollo Rural en Centroamérica* (San José: CEPAL, 1973), p. 70.

39. Durham, *Scarcity and Survival*, p. 125.

40. Lapper and Painter, *Honduras*, p. 59.

41. Thomas P. Anderson, *The War of the Dispossessed* (Lincoln: University of Nebraska Press, 1981), p. 79.

42. Though no doubt neither side had intended that these disputes end in war.

43. The humiliation of the Honduran army by its Salvadoran foe had focused attention on its corrupt and incompetent command structure. The disorganization and confusion during the initial hours of fighting had been scandalous. The high command had not even bothered to visit the front, preferring instead the safety of the basement of the central bank in Tegucigalpa. Ground defenses had been left in the hands of junior officers, rank-and-file soldiers, and civilian volunteers, often poorly armed because of graft and ineptitude in the weapons acquisition process. The air war, of course, had been an entirely different story, with the larger, better-trained, and better-equipped Honduran air force virtually destroying its small Salvadoran counterpart. For details, see Leticia Salomón, *Militarismo y Reformismo en Honduras* (Tegucigalpa: Editorial Guaymuras, 1982), pp. 46-48.

44. J. Mark Ruhl, "Agrarian Structure and Political Stability in Honduras," *Journal of Interamerican Studies and World Affairs*, Vol. 26, No. 1, February 1984, pp. 55-56.

45. Víctor Meza and Manuel Acosta Bonilla, personal communications. Others are skeptical. In Honduras, wives rarely take such initiatives or have such influence on their own. On the Black-López meeting, see "Informe de la Comisión Investigadora al Pueblo Hondureño," in Enrique Flores Valeriano, *La Explotación Bananera en Honduras* (Tegucigalpa: Editorial Universitaria, 1987), pp. 164-165.

46. Interview with Víctor Meza, 15 April 1989; interview with Longino Becerra, 4 February 1989; "Los Tentáculos del Pulpo," *Visión*, No. 15, 15 May 1975.

47. This discussion of military politics is based primarily on Salomón, *Militarismo y Reformismo*, pp. 103-111.

48. Instituto Hondureño de Desarrollo Rural, *84 Meses de Reforma Agraria del Gobierno de las Fuerzas Armadas de Honduras* (Tegucigalpa, 1980), pp. 258-259; Millett, "Historical Setting," p. 45.

49. Lapper and Painter, *Honduras*, p. 70.

50. Roger Burbach, "Honduras: Challenging Castle and Cook," *NACLA Report on the Americas*, Vol. 12, No. 2, March-April 1978, p. 44.

51. In 1990, after another decade of intervention, plunder, and mismanagement, the members of Las Isletas voted to sell the enterprise to Standard Fruit at a fraction of its value. Lapper and Painter, *Honduras*, p. 70; *Boletín Informativo Honduras*, No. 109, May 1990, p. 15.

52. Carlos Flores Facussé and others, personal communications.

53. This from a Honduran who has collected detailed evidence of Matta's relations with Paz and other military officers. This individual showed us some of these materials, including a photograph of Matta posing proudly with Paz and other members of the high command. See also Peter Dale Scott and Jonathan Marshall, *Cocaine Politics* (Berkeley: University of California Press, 1991), pp. 54-55.

3

The Strategy of Conflict

Covert action should not be confused with missionary work.

—Henry Kissinger

In July 1979 an event of unprecedented importance in the history of the independent Central American countries occurred in Nicaragua. After four and a half decades of autocratic rule, the Somoza dynasty crumbled. Into the ensuing power vacuum stepped the Sandinista National Liberation Front. Revolution had come to the isthmus.

The question was whether the contagion could be contained. The preliminary indicators were not good. Civil wars were brewing in El Salvador and Guatemala. The guerrillas there had clearly been encouraged by the developments in Nicaragua. It seemed likely that the Sandinistas would now provide material aid to their Salvadoran and Guatemalan brethren, some of whom had joined them in the struggle against Somoza. The euphoria of revolution was sweeping the region. If the momentum continued, Honduras might soon find itself surrounded by hostile Marxist regimes. Given their vulnerability and their long experience with foreign intervention, Hondurans could not but be concerned that they too might presently have to cope with an externally supported insurgency.

The United States was also worried about that prospect, but its security concerns went far beyond Honduras. Under the Carter administration, an effort was made to woo the Sandinistas—in effect, to buy them off with foreign aid. Subsequently, under Ronald Reagan, a more militant approach was adopted. The carrot was replaced with the stick. The initial goal of containment was superseded by rollback as Washington sought to overthrow the Managua government through the creation of a Nicaraguan counter-revolutionary army. In the process, Honduras would become a launching pad for U.S.-sponsored activities—a kind of "land-based aircraft carrier"[1] from which the contras could carry out their war against the Sandinistas and the United States could conduct intelligence and other operations in Nicaragua and El Salvador. Ongoing U.S.-Honduran military exercises would enormously increase the Pentagon's capacity for intervention while intimidating the Sandinistas and strengthening the Honduran armed forces. Economic and military aid would pour into the country as never before.

Yet U.S. policies would be a mixed blessing for Honduras. On the one hand, they would lead to a restoration of formal democracy, bolster the country's military defenses, and prevent economic collapse. On the other, paradoxically, they would undermine democracy, economic development, and national security: The restoration of electoral democracy would be accompanied by serious human rights violations. The massive buildup of the armed forces would undermine civilian leaders by ensuring that national security policy (broadly defined) would remain in military hands. The perpetuation of the war in El Salvador and the fostering of a new conflict in Nicaragua would make it impossible to attain the regional stability required for socioeconomic development. Meanwhile, the economy deteriorated, unemployment and landlessness grew, and the presence of the contras on Honduran soil raised serious issues of internal stability, sovereignty, human rights, and possible war with Nicaragua.

Hondurans' behavior was in keeping with their political culture and history. In the face of growing danger, Honduran leaders found a foreign protector—a patrón. Lacking a strong sense of national pride and sovereignty and traditionally susceptible to bribery, they opened up the country to massive North American economic, political, military, and cultural penetration. In the process, they tended to overlook the fact that Honduran and U.S. interests, while similar, were not identical.

As time passed, it became apparent that the Reagan administration and the Sandinistas were becoming locked into a fundamentally pathological relationship. Each viewed the other through the distorting lens of an expansionist ideology. Time and again, mutual fear and distrust inhibited constructive initiatives. When such moves were made, they were invariably ignored or misinterpreted. Defensive actions were usually imbued with offensive implications, and offensive actions—including rhetoric—simply confirmed the worst expectations of each. The result was a mutually destructive relationship in which each side repeatedly brought out the worst in the other. In the end, the Reagan administration would become so fixated on the communist "enemy" that it would be blinded to the destructive impact of its policies on Honduras. Indeed, Honduras would be reduced largely to an instrument of U.S. policy, valued not so much for itself as for its usefulness in the crusade against the Sandinistas. The consequence was that the administration's Honduran policy became increasingly counterproductive; a strategy intended to bolster the country's stability had precisely the opposite effect.

The Carter Administration, Honduras, and the Challenge of Revolution

Prior to the Sandinista revolution, U.S. policy toward Honduras was characterized primarily by ignorance and neglect. The country had always been a backwater of a backwater, hardly the object of high-level policy concern. The Embassy in Tegucigalpa was ranked class four, as low as you can get. State Department personnel who were so unfortunate as to be sent to this obscure outpost—a "one-way ticket to oblivion," as one of them called it—endured their stay grudgingly in the hope that the future would bring more exciting and professionally rewarding assignments. Insulated from the larger society in which they were living, few cared about Honduras or Hondurans. Beginning about 1978, however, this pattern of indifference began to change.

A month before the fall of Melgar Castro, the Guatemalan army massacred over a hundred peasants at Panzós, initiating a more intense stage in that country's ongoing civil war. Three days before the Honduran coup, Salvadoran Archbishop Oscar Romero, in an audience with the pope, severely criticized the Salvadoran oligarchy and called for land reform. Two weeks later, Sandinista commandos seized the National Palace in Managua. This growing turmoil could not but spark the concern of Honduran leaders. As the civil war in Nicaragua intensified, Sandinista guerrillas increasingly used Honduran territory as a base for military strikes into their homeland. When the Somoza government protested, Honduran authorities promised to prevent such operations. As early as March 1978 the Honduran and Nicaraguan armies collaborated in an operation designed to wipe out insurgent activities along the border. In the months that followed, a number of raids were made on Sandinista base camps.

Yet these measures were always sporadic and limited. The Honduran military was increasingly divided on the Nicaraguan issue. Most senior officers remained suspicious of, if not hostile to, the Sandinistas. Many of their juniors, however, had become sympathetic to their cause. The rebels' ideological stripes were not yet clear, and Somoza had become hard to swallow: The Nicaraguan dictator had attempted to overthrow the Honduran government; Nicaraguan troops had violated national territory and seized Honduran citizens. As the besieged regime lashed out indiscriminately against its tormenters, thousands of Nicaraguan civilians were killed. International opinion swung sharply against the despot and in favor of the young "freedom fighters." To have taken stronger measures against the insurgents would have given the appearance of siding with Somoza and might have poisoned Honduran relations with a successor government. Besides, it would have embroiled the Honduran military directly in the Nicaraguan civil war. Lives would have been lost in an unpopular cause. It was much easier—not to mention safer—to stay out of the fighting and take advantage of the growing opportunities for profit. The Honduran interior minister, for one, sold his favors to both sides: arms to the guerrillas and intelligence to Somoza.[2]

An intense debate would later be conducted in the United States as to who had "lost" Nicaragua. Georgetown academic Jeane Kirkpatrick would forge a political career out of charges that the Carter administration had "destabilized" Somoza. Although containing a kernel of truth, the claim was much exaggerated. In fact, Somoza destabilized himself. By the time the Sandinistas marched into Managua, the violence of the national guard had alienated so many Nicaraguans that popular support for the dictator was virtually nil. If anything, the Carter administration might be faulted for its timidity in promoting an alternative to Somoza. Had it placed more pressure on the regime in late 1978 and offered the appropriate incentives,[3] the dictator might well have bowed out. Had that occurred, it might have been possible to form a middle-of-the-road transitional government capable of limiting Sandinista influence. In the absence of incentives, Somoza had had little to gain and much to lose from an early departure. Not surprisingly, he chose to stay to the bitter end. By then, the Sandinistas had acquired the military victories and massive popular support that would enable them to assume a hegemonic role in the new political arrangements that emerged.

The collapse of the ancien régime placed the Carter administration in a difficult position. Vacillation and ineffectuality were becoming its hallmarks as it suffered one setback after another during its last year and a half in office. By summer 1979 Arab oil policies were again playing havoc with the economy. A minicrisis arose when in August an alleged Soviet combat brigade was discovered in Cuba. U.S. efforts to pressure Moscow into removing the unit failed to bring the desired result, whereupon the administration was forced to accept what it had publicly deemed unacceptable. In October, forces loyal to the Ayatollah Khomeini seized American hostages in the U.S.

embassy in Tehran, initiating a grueling ordeal that would plague the administration to its final days. In December, the Soviets invaded Afghanistan, sabotaging Carter's efforts to ratify the SALT II arms control agreement. The following spring the Castro regime added to his woes by encouraging a massive exodus of Cubans, some 129,000 of whom promptly headed for the United States. The influx severely strained government resources and caused major socioeconomic disruption in southern Florida—a bitter reward for a president who had initially tried to improve relations with Havana. Later in the year, moreover, an attempt to rescue the hostages in Iran ended in a humiliating fiasco. These tribulations and failures cost Carter dearly in terms of public support.

Although many of Carter's problems were the product of forces beyond his control, the public reaction to them reflected a deep malaise. Nineteen eighty was an election year. The president could not afford any more foreign policy disasters. Faced with a fait accompli in Nicaragua, the administration would try to maintain cordial relations with the Sandinista government while using economic aid to temper its behavior. What Carter could not accept was another Marxist regime in Central America; no more dominoes could be permitted to fall.

This determination had major implications for Honduras. In September 1979, just two months after the Sandinista victory, special envoy William Bowdler was dispatched to Tegucigalpa to meet with General Paz. About the same time, Assistant Secretary of State Viron Vaky delivered a major policy address to the House Subcommittee on Inter-American Affairs, stressing the geopolitical importance of Honduras and its "key role" in preventing guerrilla infiltrations and regional conflicts. The Paz government was praised for the progress it was making toward democracy. By the following March, the general found himself in the White House visiting President Carter amidst much congratulatory chatter. From there he made the rounds of various business groups and lending agencies, including the International Monetary Fund, the Council on the Americas, the Sikorsky helicopter company, and a trade fair in New Orleans. Commenting on this, Jack Anderson noted that "the administration apparently has chosen Honduras to be our new 'Nicaragua'—a dependable satellite, bought and paid for by American military and economic largesse. . . . In secret meetings with the Pentagon's emissary, Major General Robert L. Schweitzer, the Honduran junta was told specifically that it is expected to assume the regional role played for years by . . . Anastasio Somoza—to become a bulwark of anti-communism against the pressures of popular revolt. Guns and dollars will flow if the regime achieves legitimacy in next month's elections."[4]

Democratization was one key to U.S. policy; militarization was the other. These two thrusts, so contradictory in terms of their impact on Honduran politics and society, were in fact strategically complementary. The Honduran military had to be fortified lest revolutionary turmoil in neighboring lands threaten national stability. At minimum, counterinsurgency capabilities had to be strengthened. Beyond that, the Carter administration wanted Honduras to play a more active role in combatting the rapidly escalating insurgency in El Salvador. By early 1980, the two most important Salvadoran guerrilla organizations, the Popular Liberation Forces and the Revolutionary Army of the People, had established camps in the demilitarized pockets (*bolsones*) that had been set up along the Salvadoran-Honduran border as a result of the 1969 war. As the Salvadoran military and security forces stepped up their operations against the guerrillas and suspected sympathizers, thousands of peasants fled into Honduras. At the same time, the rebels began using these sanctuaries to infiltrate men, arms, and ammunition into El Salvador. Increased aid was designed to buy the cooperation of the Honduran armed forces and give them the means of suppressing such activities.

But militarization was not enough. One of the lessons that the Carter administration had drawn from the Central American crisis was the inability of traditional authoritarian institutions to maintain stability in the face of popular pressures for democracy and social reform. With the exception of Costa Rica, Central American societies suffered from a kind of "structural petrification." Political and social institutions were rigid and brittle. Time and again, demands for change had been met with violence that only undermined the legitimacy of the existing order and drove increasing numbers of people into the arms of the extreme left. This "dialectic of revolution" was already well developed in El Salvador and Guatemala, but in Honduras there was still time. "The vital thing," noted one foreign diplomat, "is that no one be able to question the legitimacy of the next government. The political parties must recognize that they have a common interest in making democratic reforms work. Because if they don't, all the parties will be swept away."[5] Then too, the appearance of democracy was crucial if foreign aid was to be obtained. Without it, Congress was unlikely to approve the economic and military assistance necessary to make the strategy work. Dollars would flow for a civilian government in a way that they would not for a dictatorship.

Hondurans did not need much convincing. The traditional politicians had long been clamoring for a return to civilian government—and the opportunities for patronage and graft that went with it. The public was tired of military rule. Corruption and incompetence were rampant. The economy was turning sour. Paz García, while retaining some of his luster as a war hero, was the target of mounting ridicule. "Policarpó the Drunkard," otherwise known as "Inca" Paz (from the Spanish *incapaz*, "incapable"), was hardly the man to lead Honduras into the future. The country needed a massive dose of economic assistance. The armed forces wanted an increase in military aid. Cooperation with the U.S. strategic plan was the obvious (indeed, the only) way to obtain such benefits.

Thus it was that on 20 April 1980, amidst rumors that the National Party was preparing a gigantic fraud (or, alternatively, a coup), elections were held for a Constituent Assembly. The left denounced the balloting and urged its supporters to abstain. In the capital, buses had to be equipped with specially designed brooms placed in front of their tires to prevent punctures from the nails strewn in the streets by saboteurs. Nevertheless, the public response was overwhelmingly supportive. Eighty-one percent of the registered voters went to the polls. To the amazement of most observers, the Liberal Party won a majority of the popular vote and a plurality of seats in the Assembly. The final tally gave the Liberals thirty-five seats to thirty-three for the Nationalists and three for the Party of Innovation and Unity (Partido de Innovación y Unidad, or PINU).

Although these results were widely interpreted as a rejection of the military, they did not lead to an end of military rule. The junta formally turned power over to the Constituent Assembly, but the Liberals, lacking a majority, were unable to form a government. As a way out of the impasse, it was decided that General Paz would stay on as interim chief of state until direct elections for a president could be held. (As one observer commented, this may have been the first time in Latin American history that duly elected civilians voluntarily gave power back to the military.) In the government that emerged, the army dominated almost all of the vital positions, either directly or through its National Party allies: Together, those two forces controlled nine cabinet posts to only five for the "victorious" Liberals. Still, the Liberal leader, Roberto Suazo Córdova, was made president of the Assembly, and his party received a majority of seats on the Supreme Court.

No one was more pleased with these arrangements than General Paz. Even so, things were not quite the same. One had to deal with civilians, and they could be irritating. Paz wanted to legitimate his position by taking an oath of office, but the Liberals and the PINU formulated an oath that was very different from the one taken by regular presidents and that made the provisional president subordinate to the Assembly. The general was insulted. When the time came for the swearing-in ceremony, all the dignitaries were present, but the oath taker was nowhere to be found. Paz was not located until hours later, at which time he told the Assembly what it could do with its oath. A majority of legislators thereupon reversed their position, declaring the oath unnecessary because Paz was only "provisional" president.[6]

This said much about the real sources of political power in the emerging Honduran democracy. Nevertheless, the Carter administration was satisfied that Paz had kept his part of the bargain. The "new" government was quickly rewarded for its cooperation. U.S. economic aid for FY 1980 was almost doubled to US$53.1 million—a full 18 percent of the Latin American total for that year. Military assistance too was increased—from US$2.3 to US$3.9 million. But the official figures told only part of the story. At the administration's urging, Congress agreed to lend ten UH-1H (Huey) gunship helicopters to the Honduran armed forces so that the latter could better patrol the Salvadoran border. U.S. Special Forces personnel were sent to instruct the Hondurans in tactical small-unit and border-guarding operations. By the following year Green Berets, dressed in full camouflage fatigues and carrying M-16 assault rifles, were seen patrolling the area in the company of Honduran soldiers. In the words of their commanding officer: "This dump is the center of the world now."[7]

Meanwhile, there were disturbing reports from the Salvadoran side of the border. The most notorious of these involved an alleged massacre on the Sumpúl River. According to these claims, on 14 May 1980 the Salvadoran and Honduran armies had participated in a joint counterinsurgency operation. As hundreds of fleeing peasants attempted to cross the river into Honduras, they were forced back into El Salvador by Honduran troops and systematically gunned down by the Salvadoran army and national guard. Some six hundred were said to have been killed. The following day a Roman Catholic priest, Father Earl Gallagher, walking on the Honduran side of the border, noticed that the riverbanks were strangely black. As he drew closer, he discovered why: They were covered with buzzards. Gallagher returned to the area with a tape recorder to interview the survivors. Subsequently, his report was published in the press in a joint declaration by the priests of the diocese of Santa Rosa de Copán. The report was denied by the Salvadoran and Honduran governments and the U.S. embassy in Tegucigalpa. Later, the State Department's annual human rights report would dismiss it in a single sentence as having been refuted by "impartial observers" (who, however, remained nameless). Even today, Jack Binns, who was then the U.S. ambassador to Honduras, refers to the incident as the "massacre that never happened."[8]

Although the event has never been fully explained, it seems clear that major violence—either a battle or a massacre or a combination of the two—did occur. For several weeks, reporters and independent observers were barred from the scene. Gradually, however, Salvadoran and Honduran authorities began to concede that something had happened. The Salvadoran defense minister, Colonel José Guillermo García, admitted that people had been killed but not in such "industrial quantities." A Salvadoran cabinet minister told reporters that 135 Salvadorans had died. President José Napoleón Duarte claimed that "about 300 were killed, all of them communist guerrillas." Colonel Rubén Montoya, head of the third Honduran military region, admitted that an incident had occurred but denied that Honduran troops had helped in the "killing of civilians." Even some members of the U.S. embassy were willing to concede that "something did happen," though the "magnitude (massacre) was never confirmed."[9] One other thing can be said with confidence: Salvadoran, Honduran, and U.S. authorities all had a vested interest (psychological as well as tactical) in denying and/or minimizing the significance of such incidents. Conversely, the Salvadoran and Honduran left and Cuba strove to milk these claims for all the propaganda they were worth, sometimes even manufacturing them out of whole cloth. For both sides, disinformation had become a way of life.

Meanwhile, the U.S. strategic plan was developing apace. The next step was to get Honduras and El Salvador to sign a peace treaty formally concluding their 1969 war. Thus it was that on 30 October 1980 the Soccer War finally ended. This was, however, a very odd agreement. Neither border demarcation nor indemnification issues were resolved. Discussions were to continue for five more years, and if they failed the dispute would be submitted to an international tribunal. The only questions that were really decided had to do with joint patrolling of the border and Salvadoran access to the disputed bolsones and the demilitarized zone. From now on, Salvadoran troops would be allowed to cross the border on search-and-destroy missions in cooperation with their Honduran counterparts, who were given the task of policing their own side.

The agreement raised some eyebrows in Tegucigalpa, where critics wondered why the Honduran government had not taken advantage of its seemingly stronger bargaining position to extract more favorable terms. But in fact Honduran bargaining strength was an illusion. The Carter administration wanted an agreement, and the Hondurans were not in a position to say no.

The result of this growing Salvadoran-Honduran military collaboration was more violence: In March 1981 dozens of Salvadoran refugees were killed crossing the Lempa River into Honduras. Salvadoran soldiers now increasingly pursued suspected guerrillas across the border. Salvadoran refugee camps were raided and residents kidnapped or killed. The following year another joint operation led to Honduran occupation of border territory claimed by El Salvador. In retaliation, the Farabundo Martí guerrillas stepped up their operations in Honduras. Little by little, civil strife was being regionalized.

The Reagan Administration and Central America: From Containment to Rollback

In November 1980 the Carter administration was swept out of office on a tidal wave of public discontent. The American people were sick of being humiliated by the likes of the Ayatollah Khomeini. They were tired of a president who talked about "misery indexes" and acted as if the United States were a second-rate power. They wanted to stand tall, restore prosperity, and regain the control their government had once had over foreign affairs. In short, they wanted to believe in themselves and their future. Playing brilliantly on these frustrations, Ronald Reagan was able to parlay them into a landslide victory at the polls. In January 1981 he took office as president of the United States.

The new administration came to power armed with a preconceived doctrine that defined the Central American crisis primarily in Cold War military terms and called for Cold War military solutions. Whereas President Carter and his advisers had tended to see the region's problems in terms of "authoritarian systems eroding under the pressures of demands for reform which they cannot or will not accommodate,"[10] most (though not all) of the Reagan people had a simpler view: To them, the villain was international communism—especially as represented by the Soviet Union and Cuba.

No sooner was the president in office than the State Department released a white paper charging that the crisis in El Salvador was a "textbook case" of international communist aggression. Secretary of State Alexander Haig claimed that the Soviets had a "hit list" in Central America. His deputy announced that the United States would "go to the source" with whatever means were necessary to stop the arms flow to the guerrillas. Underlying this rhetoric was a belief that the world—especially the communist world—needed to be sent a clear and forceful message: No longer would American policy be characterized by vacillation and weakness; rather, resolution and strength would be its hallmarks.

El Salvador provided a convenient opportunity to dramatize this change. Here was a "splendid little war" in which the line could be drawn at minimum risk or cost. The guerrillas were already on the run. Their January offensive had been an embarrassing failure. Accordingly, the administration had little incentive to negotiate. Military and economic aid to El Salvador would be stepped up dramatically in an attempt to apply the coup de grace. Repeated overtures from the Salvadoran opposition would be ignored. The war would drag on indefinitely. Over the next dozen years, billions of dollars in U.S. aid would flow into El Salvador. (By the time Reagan left office, the United States would be giving the Salvadoran government some US$530 million a year. Only Israel and Egypt received more aid.) Though victory proved elusive, American policy did succeed in restoring considerable stability. The guerrillas were denied a victory. Gradually, El Salvador faded from the headlines, and attention began to shift toward Nicaragua.

The Reagan administration's war against the Sandinistas was largely predetermined by the ideological zealotry of both sides. As early as the previous summer, the Republican Party convention had adopted a platform calling for the overthrow of the Nicaraguan government. The president himself was a "true believer," almost totally lacking in substantive knowledge of foreign affairs. (An "amiable dunce" was the way one Democratic Party leader put it.) His world view included a compendium of Cold War stereotypes and slogans, including the notion of rollback—the reversal of Soviet gains in the Third World. Nicaragua would be a test case. Whereas the Carter administration had believed that the best way to prevent the country from "becoming another Cuba was to avoid confronting the new revolutionary regime, Reagan had learned the opposite lesson. Reagan felt the United States must not give Nicaragua time to consolidate its revolution. The time to confront a radical regime was at the beginning."[11]

Over the next few years, both sides would waste numerous chances to avoid the confrontation that was emerging. One opportunity had already been missed when, in autumn 1980, the Sandinista directorate had intervened in the Salvadoran civil war. Whether more restrained behavior would have dissuaded Reagan and his advisers from pursuing the strategy to which they were predisposed may be doubted, but it would certainly have made such a course more difficult. As it was, the Sandinistas' massive effort to arm the Salvadoran insurgents had undermined the Carter policy of accommodation and reinforced the worst fears and suspicions of an increasingly conservative Congress and public. In effect, the Sandinistas gave the Reagan administration the political ammunition it needed to set in motion a "secret war" against Nicaragua.

The Birth of the Contras

On 9 March 1981 the White House sent Congress a presidential finding on Central America authorizing the CIA to increase its clandestine funding of "moderate" opponents of the Sandinistas. In addition, an unspecified covert program was approved to halt the alleged flow of weapons to the guerrillas in El Salvador, Guatemala, and Honduras. These activities were part of a larger proposal that the CIA's director, William Casey, had presented to the president. Casey wanted to rejuvenate the CIA after the demoralization it had experienced during the Carter years. His plan called for the backing of pro-United States forces in Nicaragua, Afghanistan, Cambodia, and a number of other Third World countries. Rollback would now become an operational reality.

The following month, moreover, the CIA station chief in Tegucigalpa informed U.S. Ambassador Jack Binns that the head of the Honduran public security forces, Colonel Gustavo Alvarez Martínez, had requested high-level talks on security cooperation. This was the same Alvarez who, as commander of the Fourth Battalion and while on the payroll of Standard Fruit, had led the attack on Las Isletas. Since early 1980 he had, on his own initiative, been aiding anti-Sandinista rebels in Honduras with arms, medicine, and other materials.[12] A fanatical anticommunist, he believed that "everything you do to destroy a Marxist regime is moral."[13] Among other things, he had proposed to Binns that Honduras launch a preemptive attack on Nicaragua. (The plan was rejected.)[14] Now, unknown to the ambassador, he was contemplating an even more grandiose scheme.

Subsequently, Alvarez journeyed to Washington, where he proposed to Casey that the United States provide covert aid to the former Somoza guardsmen who had been harassing the Sandinistas from Honduras. The idea was to transform these motley bands into a serious fighting force that could move into Nicaragua and create conditions of civil war. Although Alvarez did not have much hope that the insurgents could overthrow the government, he thought that they might be able to provoke it into making a fatal blunder: If the Nicaraguans could be goaded into attacking Honduras or Costa Rica, the United States would have a pretext for intervention. Alvarez argued that the Honduran army could play a crucial role in this struggle and proposed that it be upgraded and equipped. But the goal was the overthrow of the Sandinistas with U.S. help.[15]

Between March and November 1981 the foundations were laid for the CIA's secret war. Shortly after the issuance of the presidential finding, agency operatives initiated contacts with small anti-Sandinista organizations in the United States and Central America. In spite of warnings that the exiles would discredit legitimate opposition within Nicaragua, the agency began channeling money to the rebels. Training camps were set up in Florida, California, and Texas. Former Green Berets and Vietnam veterans gave instruction in military tactics. Though these activities seemed a violation of the 1794 Neutrality Act, law enforcement officials turned a blind eye. By early 1982 between eight hundred and twelve hundred Nicaraguans would be preparing for the coming "war of liberation."

Meanwhile, Argentina had come into the game. Even prior to the "dirty war" of the mid-1970s, the Argentine military had made anticommunism a fanatical religion. In summer 1980 U.S. intelligence discovered an Argentine presence in Honduran military intelligence (G-2). At the time, this had been a source of puzzlement. It did not remain so for long. The following spring Enrique Bermúdez, a former Somoza guardsman who by now was on the CIA payroll, journeyed to Buenos Aires to persuade the Argentines to become more involved. Subsequently, the base of operations of the rebels' 15 September Legion was transferred from Guatemala City to Tegucigalpa. Funds began to flow. In mid-1981 the U.S. embassy detected an upsurge in the number of Argentine agents in the Honduran capital. The visitors soon set up a guerrilla training base and sent several dozen rebels to Buenos Aires for intelligence instruction.

By August a bureaucratic infrastructure was in place. Casey appointed Duane "Dewey" Clarridge chief of the CIA operations directorate's Latin American section. A flamboyant zealot, Clarridge "sported safari suits in the field and at home decorated his jeep with a post-Grenada bumper sticker that read: 'Nicaragua next.'" To his detractors, he seemed a "cowboy, dumb and dangerous." He was, however, a "can-do," "no-problem" activist—precisely the kind of person Casey wanted. Like those of so many other members of the Reagan policy team, his views were uncomplicated by any previous experience in Latin America.[16]

In early August Clarridge was dispatched to Honduras for a secret meeting with Gustavo Alvarez and Policarpo Paz.[17] He told his hosts that President Reagan had sent him to inform them that the United States would support the resistance in its struggle to "liberate" Nicaragua. In fact, the president had apparently not yet given any formal approval for such a program, but Clarridge's word was good enough for Alvarez and Paz. On 11 August, with the encouragement of the Hondurans, the Argentines, and the CIA, the 15 September Legion and the Nicaraguan Democratic Union met in Guatemala City and agreed to form a single organization, to be called the Nicaraguan Democratic Force (Fuerza Democrática Nicaragüense, or FDN), to fight the Sandinistas.

From the start, the military leadership of the FDN was dominated by former members of the national guard. Over the previous year their leader, Enrique Bermúdez, had emerged as the "point man" for the CIA's project. To some, he seemed an unlikely choice. He was a desk officer who had never held a command and had spent the civil war as a military attaché in Washington. He had a "lackluster background—no guts, no charisma, no accomplishments." But then, that was what the agency wanted—not a warrior or a political visionary but a logistics officer, someone who could do the mundane administrative tasks that were needed to keep the operation going. Bermúdez "spoke English and didn't mind following orders. . . . He was malleable, controllable, docile."[18]

Later in August, Clarridge returned to Tegucigalpa, along with the deputy chief of Argentine military intelligence, to firm up the arrangements. The two visitors met with Alvarez, Paz, and the head of Honduran military intelligence, Colonel Leonidas Torres Arias. Again, Clarridge presented himself as speaking for the president. He assured the Hondurans of U.S. support for the project. When Torres Arias expressed his concern that it could become another Bay of Pigs, Clarridge told him that would never happen. Thus was born a quadripartite alliance in which the Americans would supply the money, the Hondurans the territory, the Argentines the cover, and the Nicaraguan rebels the bodies. The Hondurans and Argentines came away with the clear impression that the United States had made a commitment. Not for three months, however, did the Reagan administration formally make a decision and inform Congress, and when it did Congress was told only part of the story.

On 23 November President Reagan gave the formal go-ahead to the CIA to create a five-hundred-man paramilitary exile squad to attack Nicaragua's economic infrastructure. Anticipating resistance to any attempt to overthrow the Sandinistas, Casey, on 1 December, presented Congress with another presidential finding depicting these operations as being aimed at the Cuban presence and the Cuban/Sandinista support system. Their purpose, it was claimed, was merely to interdict arms traffic from Nicaragua to El Salvador.

In fact, the plan was far more ambitious. Even before Casey's congressional appearance, an aggressive new ambassador, John D. Negroponte, had been sent to Tegucigalpa. By early December, the first of dozens of new U.S. intelligence operatives began arriving. The U.S. embassy was upgraded. The CIA station roughly doubled in size. Arms for the contras—as the counterrevolutionaries were called—began to flow in from Miami. Safe houses were set up. A training facility was established a few miles west of the capital. At base camps along the Nicaraguan border, U.S. and Argentine personnel began to train rebel troops in everything from the use of special weapons and explosives to the basic rules of infantry.

These efforts soon led to results. Whereas the counterrevolutionaries had been limited to sporadic and ineffective cross-border attacks, after late 1981 the intensity of their operations increased dramatically. In January and February they raided numerous small villages and outposts in northern Nicaragua. In mid-March they blew up major bridges in Chinandega and Nueva Segovia. In the three months that followed over a hundred incidents occurred, leading the Sandinistas to declare a state of emergency, imposing censorship and limiting the activities of the opposition.

In part, the idea was to provoke the enemy into overreacting—in effect, to foster Sandinista repression. If the regime could be made to lash out indiscriminately against its domestic opponents, moderates might be radicalized. If momentum could be built, the Sandinista government might "fall like a house of cards in the wind."[19] And even if it did not, it would be weakened for any eventual invasion. It was a classic strategy, and its initial results were encouraging: In

January, the Sandinistas had forcibly relocated some 8,500 Miskito Indians who could not otherwise be defended/isolated from contra attacks and political activities. No matter that the provocation had been considerable (in the two months prior to early January, forty-five soldiers and fifteen civilians had been killed in assaults across the Coco River), the Sandinistas reacted as the United States had in Vietnam. "Strategic hamlets" and "free-fire zones" became the order of the day. The results were predictable: Government human rights violations and insensitivity to the cultural and political desires of the indigenous population led to a serious backlash on the east coast—and a propaganda bonanza for the Reagan administration. Here was tangible evidence of the regime's "totalitarian" and "aggressive" nature.

Beyond this, the war would disrupt the economy and force the regime to divert scarce resources to the military. Perhaps the most serious threat posed by the Nicaraguan revolution to U.S. interests was that of emulation. Already other Central American leftists had been inspired to imitate the Sandinistas. If the latter could create a more just and productive society, the attraction of their experiment might prove irresistible. If, instead, they could be forced to divert resources from the socioeconomic sector and bled through a combination of economic and guerrilla warfare, then none of their ambitious development goals would be achieved. The Managua government would have to rely increasingly on coercion to survive. Deprived of their legitimacy and romantic image, the Sandinistas would lose their ability to inspire. Indeed, the failure of their revolution would become a potent object lesson to other Central Americans who might otherwise be tempted to take up arms.

As for the interdiction program, the results were mixed. When the administration failed to take advantage of the opportunity afforded by the decline in weapons shipments following the January 1981 offensive in El Salvador, the flow of arms was resumed. By early 1982 deliveries had reached the highest level in a year as the Salvadoran guerrillas sought to disrupt the elections scheduled for that March. The flow continued throughout that year and into the next, both by sea and overland through Honduras, eventually declining again after the U.S. intervention in Grenada.

Still, the program did have some effect. Occasionally, Honduran authorities would intercept an arms shipment or raid a safe house. Even more successful (Congress was not told about this) were the assassinations by the Hondurans and contras participating in the CIA program. A number of guerrilla groups were broken up in these operations. In Choluteca, strategically located between Nicaragua and El Salvador, Nicaraguans, Salvadorans, and Hondurans detained on suspicion of gunrunning simply disappeared. Although CIA agents reportedly did not directly take part in these activities, limiting themselves to intelligence gathering, training, and funding, they clearly knew about them and looked the other way. The flow of arms declined, and the administration came to regard the program as a major success.[20]

But the killings were not restricted to gunrunners. Between 1981 and 1984 scores of people, most of them suspected leftists, were assassinated or "disappeared" for political reasons. Under the patronage of the Reagan administration, the genial corruption of Honduran military politics was being transformed into something far more sinister.

Military Hegemony and the Crisis of Civilian Leadership: The Making of a "Facade Democracy"

On the surface, Honduras once again seemed to be on the road to democracy. Elections were scheduled for November 1981. Attempts by reactionary elements in the military and the National Party to sabotage the balloting had been thwarted. The most serious incident had occurred in September when the COSUFFAA had decided to postpone the elections and maintain Paz in office. But that move had been strongly opposed by the air force chief, Walter López Reyes. Leaving the meeting, López had returned to the air base in Tegucigalpa, whence he began rounding up support from junior officers and civilians. Army units were called in to defend against attack. The Liberal candidate, Roberto Suazo Córdova, was alerted to the crisis, and he informed the U.S. ambassador. It soon became apparent that the COSUFFAA's scheme had no support among the junior officers, and the plan died. Even so, Paz continued to "bang his tin cup" before anyone who would listen, insisting that the elections would be "fixed" and had to be postponed.[21] Only when news of a land scam involving one of his close associates was leaked to the press, with a strong hint that the scandal could be extended into the Presidential Palace if need be, did the general finally see the writing on the wall and desist.

As is so often the case, however, appearances masked a very different reality. One problem was the weakness of civilian institutions and leadership. Both Liberal and National Parties were oligarchic in their internal structure and functioning. Both had steadfastly resisted attempts to infuse their conservative, clientelistic bureaucracies with new leadership, democratic procedures, or a coherent vision of the future. After the death of Modesto Rodas in 1979, a split had occurred between the traditional leaders of the Liberal Party (the *rodistas*) and a social democratic reform faction (Alianza Liberal del Pueblo—ALIPO) led by the Reina brothers, Carlos Roberto and Jorge Arturo. The rodistas had been able to manipulate the party machine to ensure that their candidate, Roberto Suazo, would become the standard-bearer in November. In the process, the existing election law had been emasculated by provisions that had effectively denied ordinary members any say about the party's candidates. These machinations had created bitterness and for a while threatened the Liberals' chances of winning the presidency. Though the ALIPO was clearly the minority faction, it held the allegiance of perhaps 10 or 15 percent of the rank and file, whose support would in a close race be crucial. Moreover, its "unlikely mix of university leftists, mildly progressive business people, and a strong presence in the national press gave it an influence disproportionate to its size."[22] The problem was that ALIPO had nowhere to go. Initially, some of its members threatened to bolt the Liberal Party and form a coalition with the PINU and the Christian Democrats. But this was a futile enterprise. Neither of those groups had much of a following. Rather, they were parties of protest. Although there was always the possibility that one or a combination of these organizations might become a major force in the future, their chances in 1981 were nil. Under the circumstances, the best that could be hoped for was a coalition that might prevent either of the main parties from acquiring a majority of votes. If that could be done, it might be possible to trade the support of ALIPO and its allies for certain policy and personnel concessions. But for this strategy to be credible there had to be a realistic possibility that the minor parties might throw their support to the National Party or at least abstain and allow it a victory. That prospect was removed when the Nationals, in internal elections every bit as stacked as those in the Liberal Party, chose as their candidate that quintessential ward politician and bureaucrat—the "Tricky Dick" of Honduran politics[23]—Ricardo Zúniga.

Perhaps no single event better symbolized the Honduran crisis than the 1981 election. In contrast to the high hopes raised by the return to democracy were the qualities of the men contending for office: Ricardo Zúniga had been an adviser to López Arellano and Paz García. A counselor to the more reactionary sectors of the military and a former contact man with the Mancha Brava, he was a "corrupt, thieving, wily, manipulative individual"[24] who had always placed political loyalty over competence when staffing the National Party organization.[25]

The Liberal candidate was no better. Roberto Suazo Córdova was a small-town doctor known as "El Brujo de la Paz" because of his reputation for dabbling in *santería*. In the words of one critic, he had "all the defects that Hondurans are supposed to have—he is a libertine, he lies, he conspires, he is incompetent, he plays cards, he is a reformed alcoholic."[26] His amorous adventures would become the talk of Tegucigalpa. On one occasion he would bare his chest—and potbelly—to a national television audience to "prove" that he had not been shot by a jealous mistress. Alas, the skeptics were not persuaded. The aggrieved lover, it was rumored, had been aiming at a more personal part of the anatomy. (Supposedly, he had been shot in the buttocks while running from his attacker.)[27] During his tenure, corruption would become an art form.

In 1981, however, Suazo was largely an unknown. The dominant faction of the Liberal Party had pulled him out of obscurity, leaving the Reinas and their followers with the choice of either backing his candidacy or seeing Zúniga win the presidency. In the end, the rebels backed down, mollified by the promise of cabinet positions should the Liberals win.

The two major candidates assiduously avoided dealing with the grave socioeconomic problems facing the country and instead engaged in a mudslinging contest. Their platforms, long on promises and short on solutions, were barely distinguishable. This was symptomatic. The Liberals and Nationals had rarely been able to rise above the petty squabbling and corruption that had plagued traditional politics, and this campaign was no exception.

Even so, the military was in no mood to take chances. In early October, less than two months before the election, Zúniga, Suazo, and their advisers were summoned to separate meetings in which conditions for a return to "civilian rule" were laid out: Limits were to be placed on the policymaking power of the new government. The armed forces would remain dominant in all matters relating to national security, internal as well as in foreign policy, including border and refugee problems. They would select the defense minister and have veto power over other cabinet appointments. Nor would civilian control over the pay and structure of the armed forces or any challenge to military performance be allowed. This latter was especially important, since it meant that there would be no investigation of the corruption that had accompanied military rule. A civil inquiry was already in progress. The candidates were informed that the commission in charge was "playing into the hands" of the country's enemies. If elections were to proceed, the offending body would have to be reconstituted. (Shortly thereafter, the aggressive minor party members were removed.)[28]

These matters having been settled, on 29 November the elections were held. Seventy-eight percent of the eligible voters went to the polls. Suazo Córdova and the Liberals were swept into office, winning 54 percent of the vote to 42 percent for the National Party and forty-four of the eighty-two seats in Congress. (The Nationals won thirty-four, the PINU three, and the Christian Democrats one.)

Foreign Penetration, Military Hegemony, and Civilian Complicity

In the mountains overlooking downtown Tegucigalpa sits the headquarters of the Honduran security police (Fuerza de Seguridad Pública, or FUSEP). Farther up, overlooking the FUSEP headquarters, is the residence of the U.S. ambassador. By the early 1980s, many Hondurans had come to think of this geographic relationship as symbolic: "The FUSEP watches the city, and the embassy watches the FUSEP" went one popular saying.

In reality, the relationship between the U.S. embassy, the Honduran military (of which the FUSEP is a part), and the civilian government has never been that clear-cut: "While the three claim to co-exist in harmony, in practice the relationship is rather tumultuous. Each seeks greater autonomy, while attempting to reduce the jurisdiction and influence of the other two."[29] The most powerful actors in this trio have been the embassy and the military, but beyond that the relationships have been complex and difficult to define. Although the former can place considerable pressure on the armed forces, rarely can it dictate. Honduran officers remain largely autonomous, with personal and institutional interests of their own, and they often pursue those interests no matter what the United States might say.

This being said, the United States, with its enormous economic and military resources, has usually been able to make it in the interest of the armed forces and the government to see things in Washington's way. Hondurans have always been vulnerable to bribery, and in the years after 1980 the Reagan administration used material incentives in a massive way to obtain cooperation. By FY 1982, more U.S. military aid and sales were being provided Honduras than in the entire period from 1946 to 1980. Between 1980 and 1984, military aid would increase almost twentyfold, from US$4 million to US$78.5 million. Economic support would more than triple, from US$50.7 million to US$168.7 million. This "rain of dollars" strengthened the Honduran armed forces, kept the country's economy from collapsing, and provided a wealth of opportunities for graft.

The key players on the Honduran side were the new president and the powerful head of the armed forces, Gustavo Alvarez. By the late 1970s, Alvarez had established himself as a man to watch. His military training included stints in the United States, the Panama Canal Zone, Peru, and Argentina. In Washington, he had studied police operations under the auspices of the Office of Public Safety before Congress terminated that program because of the brutality of some of its Latin American graduates. He had received advanced training at Fort Benning and the School of the Americas. In addition, he had studied at the Superior War College in Peru and the National Military Academy in Argentina. This last, in particular, had left its mark: It was there that he had fallen under the influence of the neofascist "doctrine of national security," which "like its Nazi predecessor [was] founded upon the concepts of geopolitics and war without quarter, admitting no distinction between combatants and civilians, against domestic and international communist subversion."[30]

By the time of the 1981 elections, Alvarez had held a string of important military positions: head of the Fourth Infantry Battalion in La Ceiba, commander of the Second Military Zone in San Pedro Sula, and, from August 1980 onward, chief of the FUSEP. He was considered by the U.S. embassy to be one of the best officers in the military. He was relatively free from the corruption that plagued so many of his colleagues. Even before the 1980 Constituent Assembly elections, Suazo had begun to court him. In the past, the National Party had always "depended on its open political alliance with the military" to ensure its victories. Now that coalition was "to be ruptured, thanks to both the Liberals' stealth and Alvarez's cunning."[31]

In August 1980—the month in which Alvarez had been appointed head of the FUSEP—a shake-up had occurred in the high command. Twenty-six senior officers, most of them from the more progressive wing of the officer corps, had been forcibly retired. In the months that followed, power gradually coalesced around a group of seven officers, known as the "iron circle." Of these, three eventually emerged as the favorites to replace Policarpo Paz as head of the armed forces. One was Colonel Hubbert Bodden, the commander of the First Infantry Battalion near Tegucigalpa. Another was the head of military intelligence, Colonel Leonidas Torres Arias. The third was Alvarez.

As long as the Carter administration was in office, Bodden was thought to be the U.S. favorite. With the election of Ronald Reagan and the beginning of the contra war, however, the CIA began to favor the more hard-line anticommunist Alvarez. The agency never had so much influence that it could dictate such matters. But the CIA station and the defense attaché let their Honduran counterparts know their preference, and this undoubtedly helped smooth the way.[32] In the final analysis, however, it was the "logic of the Liberals' quest for power" that brought Alvarez to the apex of the Honduran military. Suazo needed him to counter the National Party's influence with the armed forces. In turn, Alvarez needed Suazo if his own ambitions were to be fulfilled. Mutual enmity between the former and Ricardo Zúniga further cemented the alliance. Thus, "independent of U.S. interests, . . . Alvarez and the Liberal Party leaders met each other's needs."[33]

Still, there were problems. The armed forces' rules of promotion stipulated that to occupy the country's highest military post one had to possess the rank of general; they further stated that to become a general an officer had to have completed at least five years as a colonel. Alvarez fulfilled neither requirement. In addition, his arrogance and ambition had earned him enemies. When Suazo named him armed forces commander, there was considerable resistance from within the officer corps. Alvarez had only been second on the list of "nominees" presented to civilian authorities by the COSUFFAA. In the end, the latter consented to the appointment only on the condition that the new chief work closely with Bodden and Torres Arias, among others. Subsequently, in April 1982, Suazo further consolidated his alliance with Alvarez by altering the military code to promote him to brigadier general.

Clearly, this president was no puppet. Equally to the point, he was not living up to his end of the bargain that he and Zúniga had struck with the military the previous October. The COSUFFAA had not been advised of Alvarez's promotion to brigadier general until the last minute. This was blatant civilian interference in internal military affairs and set a bad precedent. So outraged were Bodden and Torres Arias that they and three other members of the high command reportedly confronted Suazo, placing their troops on alert. At about the same time, Torres Arias arranged to have discovered two large "clandestine cemeteries" near the capital in an attempt to undercut Alvarez (who, as head of the FUSEP, had been responsible for a growing number of human rights violations). But it was too late. By this time, Alvarez had acquired enough support to initiate a new purge. Bodden and Torres Arias were sent packing into diplomatic exile.

The third major actor in this drama was the U.S. ambassador. A seasoned diplomat with extensive experience in Southeast Asia, John Negroponte had a reputation as a consummate professional and hard-line anticommunist. As an aide to Henry Kissinger at the Paris peace talks, he had argued that Kissinger, in his rush to reach an agreement, was conceding too much to the North Vietnamese. The penalty for this temerity had been diplomatic exile to Quito. Subsequently, he had become U.S. consul general in Thessaloniki. Now he was in Tegucigalpa, where his primary mission was to keep Alvarez and Suazo on board the Nicaraguan program.

This proved to be more difficult than anticipated. Although Alvarez had secured President Suazo's support for his plan to build up the contras in order to provoke the Sandinistas into an attack (thus providing the United States with a pretext for military intervention), he had not told Negroponte about the scheme. Indeed, in his conversations with the ambassador he took the line that the guerrillas were the "cheapest way" for both Central Americans and the United States to avoid more costly confrontations.[34] Already, there was a major misunderstanding between the Honduran strongman and his North American mentors. As Roy Gutman has noted, Washington was deeply "divided over the purpose of the insurgency, and the competing forces there never could agree on the strategy, structure, and tactics. They certainly could never have agreed among themselves to Alvarez's scheme. With so shaky a basis of understanding, it was only a matter of months before the first crisis developed."[35]

Negroponte's relations with Alvarez and the contras remain the subject of debate. At the time, the U.S. press often portrayed him as the quintessential proconsul: arrogant and ambitious, issuing economic advice to the Suazo administration "in the imperative form of Spanish," meeting with Alvarez on a daily basis to plan the contra war, censoring embassy cables so that his superiors would know only what he wanted them to know. *Newsweek's* sensational November 1982 cover story on the secret war was a classic case in point. Negroponte was so outraged by the piece ("that hatchet job," as he called it) that he sent a letter of protest to the magazine's owner,

Katherine Graham. To no avail. Even today, the editors and reporters who worked on the story support its conclusion that he was "the point man" in the "covert offensive" against the Sandinistas, "a central player" in the operation to arm, train, and direct the contras, and that "many of his suggestions were implemented" by General Alvarez.[36]

Not surprisingly, Negroponte and his deputy, Shepard Lowman, tell a different story. According to the former, he had only seen Alvarez "from time to time" and did not have an operational relationship with him. Similarly, Lowman claims that, to his knowledge, the ambassador had met with the contras on no more than a handful of occasions: "He avoided it, and so did the embassy (excluding the CIA station)." For Casey or a congressional delegation, he "might arrange for a meeting" with the rebels. Neither Negroponte nor Lowman, however, admitted to "any significant amount of contact" in terms of daily operations. Nor was Alvarez running the show: "The fact is that it was a continuing problem for the CIA people concerned with the contras that the Honduran military wanted to have much more influence on the operations in Nicaragua." They "thought they knew better" than the guerrillas what had to be done. But actually the rebels were "pretty much running their own operations, planned perhaps with their CIA backers, but certainly not with the help of Negroponte."[37]

No doubt the reality lies somewhere in between. The ambassador was neither so innocent as he and his deputy claim, nor so deeply involved as the press had it. Negroponte himself was well-versed in the art of obfuscation. (So much so that some reporters dubbed him "the master of the pointless interview.") Nevertheless, our impression is that, on this issue at least, the truth is closer to the Negroponte-Lowman account than to the other. After a decade of conducting research on Honduras, we have been struck by the unreliability of the kind of testimony that went into some news reports. People lied a lot. Both the contras and the Hondurans loved to gossip, especially about their enemies and the gringos. Nor were U.S. sources overly wed to the truth. As two veteran observers of the Washington scene have remarked, "In a capital where deception is admired as an art, *lie* is perhaps the last dirty word."[38] The contra program was controversial; Negroponte had made enemies within the bureaucracy. Personalizing the issue was a way for dissenters to discredit a policy that they hoped to sink. (It is interesting, and probably significant, that in neither Bob Woodward's exposé on the CIA's secret wars nor Sam Dillon's book on the contras is Negroponte's name even mentioned. Nor is there much emphasis on his role in the works by Christopher Dickey and Roy Gutman, which describe U.S. relations with the rebels in considerable detail.)

What can be said with some confidence is that John Negroponte was a hands-on ambassador. Very little happened during his tenure of which he was unaware. He strongly believed in U.S. policy and aggressively promoted it. Though he could be abrasive, he was too competent to issue economic recommendations in the imperative.[39] Accounts of his daily contacts with Alvarez were clearly false. Nor is it likely that he had much of an operational role vis-à-vis the contras, though he had helped work out arrangements for their support with the Honduran military[40] and was kept well informed of their activities. Others handled operational matters. By the end of 1982, some 150 CIA agents were in Honduras, providing logistical support for raids into Nicaragua and helping the Argentines, the Hondurans, and a few Cuban-American contract employees train the guerrillas. Agency representatives and Alvarez held coordinating meetings on a weekly basis. There was no need for the ambassador to compromise himself by becoming too involved.

Negroponte's recommendations and demands were usually—though not always—accepted by the host government. (The Hondurans were particularly resistant to some of the embassy's economic advice.) On more than one occasion, he was accused of interfering in the country's internal affairs. But while his "imperial manner" offended some, he was popular with most Hondurans, who have an affinity for caudillos and were less concerned with a loss of sovereignty than with the need to assure the anticipated "rain of dollars." Negroponte symbolized the U.S. commitment. (He also, incidentally, had a genuine affection for Hondurans. He and his wife, Diana, would adopt three Honduran children. Even today, Mrs. Negroponte is still fondly remembered for her social work, some of which was done at no small risk to herself. When they left in 1985, even *El Tiempo*, the nationalist San Pedro daily, which is ordinarily highly critical of U.S. policy, ran a Doumont cartoon expressing thanks to the ambassador for all he had done: "¡Adios, amigo!" was the theme.)

Nevertheless, U.S. relations with Alvarez were destined to be rocky. In April 1982, Argentina attacked the British-held Falkland Islands, placing a severe strain on Washington's dealings with Latin America. As the Reagan administration began to tilt toward Britain, Negroponte sought to reassure the Hondurans. Alvarez, however, would have none of it: "Where is the Monroe Doctrine?" he ranted. "Who is the next one you betray? Honduras? El Salvador? Guatemala?

Costa Rica?" Later, he would remark that the situation reminded him of the old saying that the United States "has its mind in Washington, its heart in Britain, and its feet in Latin America."[41] For a while, it seemed that the Argentines would pull out of the contra operation, but in the end they stayed on through 1984.

In May another flare-up occurred when the CIA's Dewey Clarridge sent Edén Pastora, the legendary Comandante Cero, to meet with Alvarez. Pastora, disenchanted with the direction in which the revolution was moving and frustrated in his own considerable political ambitions, had left Nicaragua the previous year. In April, he had publicly denounced his old Sandinista comrades and formed his own organization to wage war against them. Clarridge wanted to bring him in as a leader of the anti-Sandinista resistance. To do this, however, he had to build bridges between Pastora, whose followers were gathering in Costa Rica, and Enrique Bermúdez, head of the contras in Honduras. This proved difficult. Pastora had not fought Somoza to turn Nicaragua back over to the national guard, and his meeting with Alvarez was little short of disastrous. Alvarez looked on the former Sandinista with suspicion, refused to address him by his guerrilla rank of *comandante,* and held him under virtual house arrest. Pastora was outraged. He wanted to be leader of the anti-Sandinista movement and claimed to be speaking for the Nicaraguan people. But Alvarez argued that only the FDN had earned that right. Later, Pastora complained that Alvarez had not been interested in unity and had declared that only the FDN could have access to Honduran territory.[42]

The consequence of Alvarez's veto of Pastora, as in the case of his continuing encouragement of the Argentine presence, was a weakening of the CIA's ability to manage the contra operation. How much difference this ultimately made is hard to say, because by now Dewey Clarridge was more or less in charge. Clarridge had his own agenda and seemed to be setting his own guidelines, and it was not always clear that he and his superiors in Washington were operating on the same wave length. His relations with Alvarez were increasingly strained, since he persisted in making promises he could not keep. Increasingly, U.S. policy was veering out of control.

As months passed and little progress was made in the war against the Sandinistas, Alvarez's frustration grew. In April, he had publicly supported the right of the United States to "intervene militarily" in Central America if that proved necessary to preserve the peace. But nothing had happened. Accordingly, he began to look for a way to force Washington's hand. When in August Honduran intelligence reported that the Nicaraguan army was making threatening gestures toward the border, Alvarez put his forces on red alert, moved six battalions into the El Paraíso region, and issued orders to destroy "every troop" and "piece of equipment" that entered Honduras. When the North Americans, whose intelligence did not support Alvarez's claims of a major Nicaraguan threat, inquired as to his intentions, they were told to prepare to "go to Managua. This is our chance."[43]

This was not quite what the Reagan administration had in mind. It was one thing to wage "low-intensity conflict" through regional proxies, quite another for one of those proxies to invade its neighbor. The latter might spark a full-scale war, requiring tens of thousands of U.S. combat troops. The U.S. Congress and public would not stand for such an intervention—especially in support of an aggressor. Accordingly, U.S. Embassy and military officials "reminded [the Hondurans] that they were not in the business of trying to foment a regional war." Nor was the United States "looking for an excuse to become involved" in such a conflict. The Southern Command (SOUTHCOM) showed Alvarez photographs of Nicaraguan troop movements and counseled him against taking any independent action. In the words of one high-level policymaker, "I think we were able to be sufficiently convincing on that score that we probably scared them half to death."[44] Alvarez came away from the experience disillusioned and bitter. The United States, he felt, "wasn't serious" about fighting the Sandinistas; it wanted "vassals, not allies."[45] "Only when El Salvador has fallen, and Honduras and Guatemala follow, only when all of Central America is communist, when it is already too late, will we realize the importance of this war to the death."[46]

Revolution and Counterrevolution in the "Oasis of Peace"

The United States was not alone in having been alarmed by this episode. From Mexico, Colonel Torres Arias issued a public denunciation of his old rival: Alvarez, he claimed, was an opportunist and megalomaniac planning an "adventure of madness." "His extremist, radical and repressive ideas" would "only lead the people of Honduras along the road of blood and fratricidal struggle as well as costly and irreparable international confrontations." Honduras had "neither the economic nor the military capability to impose a military decision on another state"; moreover, Alvarez's "psychotic" attempts to eliminate all opposition could only bring all the "horrors of terrorism, guerrillas, and civil war" to the country. Torres Arias called on the Honduran armed forces and Congress to remove him from power before it was too late.[47]

Now, Torres Arias was no gem. He had had close ties with the Somozas and was involved in gunrunning and narcotics. Between 1978 and 1981 he and Ramón Matta had set up a lucrative drug supply network with Manuel Noriega, then chief of army intelligence in Panama. These activities had aggravated Torres's relations with Alvarez, who was strongly opposed to such dealings, and were a factor in the former's diplomatic exile.[48] Apparently, too, the CIA had known about these operations but ignored them. Torres had been a strong asset. As the Honduran military's liaison with the contras, he had been one of the prime movers in bringing in the Argentines and supplying arms to the rebels.[49] Unfortunately, he was nondiscriminatory and nonsectarian: He would sell to anyone. In the 1970s, he had sold weapons to the Sandinistas. In the early 1980s, with a new market opening up in El Salvador, he began selling to the Farabundo Martí National Liberation Front (Frente Farabundo Martí para la Liberación Nacional—FMLN). When in 1981 he twice visited Fidel Castro in Cuba in meetings that had been arranged through General Noriega, the CIA became increasingly concerned. When Torres began to change his mind about the contras and oppose Honduras's support role, he was maneuvered out of power by Alvarez and his allies with the backing of the agency.[50]

Torres Arias' denunciation was widely distributed in Honduras, where it caused a sensation. He was stripped of rank and property and charged with treason. The truth was that he was saying things that many Hondurans were thinking but were afraid to express. The human rights situation, in particular, had seriously deteriorated in the preceding few years. Whereas between 1975 and 1979 there had been, on the average, ten to fifteen gross violations per year, late 1979 had seen a sharp increase. The following year, dozens of violations were recorded, and the targets were not only peasants and workers but members of opposition parties, students, journalists, priests, and Salvadoran refugees. In 1981, moreover, the number of violations increased once again. For the first time in Honduran history, there were numerous reports of political assassinations and "disappearances."

These years were also marked by an increase in terrorism and other forms of antigovernment activity. Bombings, kidnappings, bank robberies, building occupations, airplane hijackings, guerrilla attacks, mass demonstrations, strikes, and land seizures became the order of the day. Many of the payroll holdups and kidnappings were the work of the contras, and in one case at least General Alvarez called in their leaders and threatened them with expulsion.[51] Most of the activity, however, came from the left. Among the most notable actions were the March 1981 hijacking of a Honduran airliner by the Cinchonero Popular Liberation Movement, the September 1981 shooting of two U.S. military advisers and bombing of the Honduran Congress by the Lorenzo Zelaya Popular Revolutionary Forces, and the September 1982 Cinchonero occupation of the Honduran Chamber of Commerce in San Pedro Sula. In this last operation, 105 hostages were taken, including much of the country's business elite. (Among those held were the economic and treasury ministers and the president of the central bank.)

The culmination of this upsurge occurred in July 1983, when a ninety-six member guerrilla force led by José Maria Reyes Mata, a leader of the Revolutionary Party of Central American Workers (Partido Revolucionario de Trabajadores Centroamericanos—PRTC), entered Olancho from Nicaragua. The group was meant to be an advance party. But the plan was sabotaged almost from the beginning, when deserters informed the armed forces. A counterinsurgency campaign was mounted. The rebels were located and a cordon formed around them. Trapped and exhausted from their grueling march through the mountains, the guerrillas "pathetically waved their handkerchiefs," as officers in an air force plane used a megaphone to call on them to surrender. Later, the military would claim that most of the insurgents had died from combat, hunger, or fatigue. Subsequent reports from former military personnel and other sources, however, painted a more sobering picture: "In the first few days, six PRTC members turned themselves in. Once their statements had been taken, they were transferred to Tegucigalpa. But upon arriving, . . . Alvarez ordered that they be returned to Olancho. There a special intelligence squad . . . executed them." As for the others, one or two died from starvation and fatigue and about twenty—all apparently illiterate peasants—were turned over to their families. The vast majority (nearly seventy persons), being mostly students and professionals, were executed after capture. Among those so dispatched were Reyes Mata and a North American priest, James ("Padre Guadalupe") Carney.[52]

Almost from the beginning, there were rumors of North American involvement. The *Chicago Tribune* reported that the U.S. and Honduran militaries had coordinated intelligence and planning and that U.S. Army helicopters had flown Honduran troops into combat. Honduran radio and newspaper reports claimed that Reyes Mata had been captured by the Honduran army with the help of U.S. advisers.

U.S.-Honduran military exercises in the region coincided with reported battles. Subsequently, the State Department would admit that U.S. intelligence personnel had participated in the interrogation of two captured deserters. At the same time, it denied that the embassy had known that a U.S. citizen had been involved until the Honduran government had revealed that fact at a press conference.[53]

What can be said with certainty is that the episode would be used by the State Department and the Honduran military to "prove" their claim that Honduras was the target of communist subversion. And certainly the threat was real enough. Although the Sandinistas initially had paid little attention to the "solidarity" groups in Honduras—the radical left there had never been very effective and in 1979 was in no position to be of much use—this had gradually changed over time. In 1980 the Nicaraguans began to provide logistical support, training, arms, and advice for the proliferating factions seeking to overthrow the Honduran government. Gradually, too, the Salvadoran guerrillas had come into the game. By late 1981 the Revolutionary Army of the People had formed a joint Salvadoran-Honduran command in Tegucigalpa, directing a military organization of fifty, fifteen of whom were Salvadorans. The following summer, these elements sabotaged the main power station in the capital and bombed several U.S. businesses. The arms for these operations were brought from Nicaragua and processed through a "logistical center for war material transformation" located on the outskirts of Tegucigalpa. From there they were sent to various hiding places.[54]

None of these efforts had much effect. Revolutionary conditions did not yet exist in Honduras. The political culture remained strongly conservative; there was little popular support for the idea of turning the country into another Nicaragua. The radical left was not only small but hopelessly divided by the same "bureaucratized anarchy" that plagued the society as a whole. Although human rights violations existed and were on the rise, the situation was a far cry from the kind of indiscriminate and massive carnage that might have made radicals of large numbers of Hondurans. Indeed, the political system remained flexible enough to allow some reform, whether in land tenure or in the sharing of political power. Thus, hundreds of thousands of Hondurans could still sustain the hope that their lives might improve. Even in the face of rapidly growing socioeconomic difficulties, one could still be optimistic, for Hondurans had found a foreign patrón who would save them. The "rain of dollars" would cure all ills. Under the circumstances, it would have taken a massive effort on the part of the Sandinistas and the Salvadoran guerrillas to have created a subversive network capable of posing a serious threat to stability. The operations that were undertaken were exploratory, designed to test Honduran defenses and gauge the potential mass support for a revolutionary movement. In part, too, they were a response to Honduras's growing cooperation with the U.S. strategic plan. A message was being sent: If the Hondurans joined Reagan's wars, they could expect retaliation.

But General Alvarez and his security forces turned out to be more than a match for their enemies. Between 1980 and 1984 the Honduran military, with U.S. support, systematically uncovered and destroyed most of the nascent Honduran guerrilla movement, along with the Sandinista and Farabundo Martí support structures. "During these years, . . . there were no trials or lawyers to defend the accused. It was a period of rationally directed state terror against an identified enemy who was also willing to kill to change the system of government."[55] The name of the game was "decapitation." Repression was directed primarily against leaders or outspoken members of organizations considered subversive. The philosophy was simple: If you killed the head, the body would die. One could destroy the movement by destroying its leaders and potential leaders. While some would brand this strategy the "Argentine method," the numbers of dead would never approach those recorded in that country. Still, the Argentine influence on Alvarez was obvious and the techniques familiar: Critics were castigated as subversives and Sandinista sympathizers. Salvadoran refugees were harassed and abused. Scores of Honduran citizens, many innocent of any offense, were arrested, murdered, or "disappeared." Torture during interrogation became routine. Clandestine cemeteries began to appear.

As legal and social reinforcement for this campaign, in April 1982 an antiterrorist law, Decree 33, established draconian penalties for crimes against state security, including land invasions. In July 1983 Penal Code 24 reinforced its provisions. Meanwhile, the government had created a network of civil defense committees for the purpose of "heightening patriotic fervor," aiding the authorities in times of emergency, and "contributing to the vigilance and conservation of vital installations."[56] These were, in effect, neighborhood spy groups (*orejas*). They were soon supplemented by a national center for emergency information designed to "help the Honduran people inform the various agencies concerned with state security about any attitude that they consider suspicious and that concerns security."[57] A network of telephone hot lines was created. Since informers could remain anonymous, this provided a perfect opportunity for persons engaged in personal vendettas to denounce their enemies. These measures fostered an atmosphere of suspicion and distrust and led to the arrest of many innocent people.

Most of the dirty work was done by the FUSEP, its primary operational arm, the National Department of Investigations (Dirección Nacional de Investigaciones—DNI), and the death squad known as Battalion 3-16. This last, in particular, became the focus of much public attention. Founded by Alvarez in the late 1970s, Battalion 3-16 was originally known as the Department of Special Investigations. Until 1982 it was commanded by Captain Alexander Hernández, a graduate of the U.S. police training program under the now-defunct Office of Public Safety. In August of that year, however, he was implicated in death squad activities by Torres Arias and replaced.[58] (Hernández's subsequent career pattern suggested that even publicly recognized deeds of this sort were no obstacle to promotion: In December 1982, he was elevated to the rank of major by the Honduran Congress and sent as a military attaché to Buenos Aires. There he remained until the Argentine government, by then in civilian hands, declared him persona non grata in late 1984. Subsequently, he was named deputy director of the national police academy and, still later, head of the FUSEP advanced officer training school. By late 1992 he had attained the rank of colonel.)

While Battalion 3-16 operated—allegedly it has been abolished, though official pronouncements to this effect continue to be received with skepticism by many Hondurans—it was headquartered in Tegucigalpa, with a subordinate unit in San Pedro Sula. Small cells carried out surveillance and kidnapping throughout the country, bringing their prisoners to detention centers in the capital and San Pedro. Apparently, Alvarez himself often selected the persons to be questioned or "disappeared," channeling his orders through Colonel Juan López Grijalva, head of military intelligence. Other high-level officers said to be involved included the commander of the FUSEP, who provided arms transport and sometimes troops, the chief of the air force, who contributed air transport when necessary, and the director of the DNI, who provided both personnel and clandestine cells. The actual kidnappings were carried out by troops, mostly sergeants and below. There were separate squads for surveillance, kidnapping, and executions and separate personnel assigned as interrogators, torturers, and executioners. The last were primarily ex-soldiers recruited from the Central Penitentiary, where they were serving time for crimes of violence. To maintain secrecy, Alvarez ordered the assassination of many of his own executioners.[59]

In late 1981, moreover, the Argentines proposed that contra gunmen be used to supplement the work of Battalion 3-16. After Somoza's fall, the FDN intelligence chief, Ricardo Lau, had enlisted former national guardsmen to serve as contract killers. The Argentines now suggested to Alvarez that Lau's network be used to execute "subversives" kidnapped and interrogated by the Honduran military. Over the next several years, Lau's hit men played an important role in the Honduran military's extermination campaign, kidnapping and killing Honduran labor and student leaders as well as alleged Salvadoran gunrunners and Sandinista spies. Some of the FDN's most notorious assassins set up shop in Choluteca, where they worked closely with the intelligence section of the Honduran Army's 101st Brigade, a unit advised by U.S. military officers. Between 1982 and 1984, eighty-two Salvadorans disappeared in Honduras, many in Choluteca. Most were killed by Lau's death squad. Meanwhile, scores—and perhaps hundreds—of other killings were occurring in and around the contra base camps, where prisoners and suspected spies (including many contra recruits), personal enemies, and rivals were being eliminated in an orgy of paranoia, caprice, and sadism.[60]

Perhaps the most difficult and controversial aspect of these activities concerns the role of the United States. That the North Americans provided training and advice to some of the officers and troops involved in human rights abuses is incontrovertible. In addition, Lau's section was reportedly funded by the CIA.[61] There remain, however, serious questions as to the extent and kind of the involvement. General Walter López Reyes, former head of the Honduran armed forces (1984-1986), has claimed that the CIA chose some of the death squad victims—though he also sought to place blame for nearly all of the disappearances on the contras rather than on the Honduran military.[62] Moreover, José Valle López, who worked with one of the kidnapping squads, has charged that "a Mr. Mike from the U.S. Embassy sat in on many torture sessions and provided written questions. We handed over all documents to three U.S. women in charge of documentation. There were other gringos, too, with special equipment when we went on auto patrols."[63]

Other sources suggest a less direct U.S. role. Thus, a former FDN commander described to a North American journalist how he had helped organize a death squad with the approval and collaboration of the CIA and with cover provided by the Honduran government. According to this account, the contras were given Honduran army uniforms and official military identifications to conceal their identities. CIA advisers had been present at the meeting at FUSEP headquarters when the Honduran military had agreed to the arrangement. Subsequently "Colonel Raymond" (Ray Doty), the supervisor of all CIA agents working with the contras, had received weekly reports from Ricardo Lau. The CIA had "wanted comprehensive information about everything the unit had done and how much it had spent. The FDN was accustomed to filing written reports on all investigations, captures, and killings it had committed, but [Doty] specifically ordered Lau never to file written reports on the killings of people captured by the Hondurans and turned over to the contras." On one occasion, Doty was said to have been instrumental in preventing the release of a prisoner whom he feared might talk. (The man was killed instead.) On another, he allegedly congratulated the Nicaraguan commander for his skills as an assassin: "The jobs are very well done," he reportedly remarked. "Not even the CIA can do work like that."[64]

According to Florencio Caballero, a former Battalion 3-16 interrogator, CIA involvement with the unit was "extensive," but the Hondurans "constantly sought to deceive the U.S. officers about the true nature of their operations." Caballero and others had been trained in the United States in interrogation without physical torture. Although CIA officials knew when someone was detained and sometimes came to interrogate the prisoners themselves, he knew of no instance in which an agency officer "condoned or participated in torture or execution of a detainee. In fact, . . . the Hondurans had to invent stories to explain the deaths which occurred at their hands. The stock explanation . . . was . . . that the victim had been killed by fellow 'subversives' for giving information to the military."[65]

One must be wary of all such testimony. The left in particular had a strong interest in discrediting the United States. Yet Caballero's story has the ring of truth. The details he provides are impressive, and his evidence is unmarked by the "true believer's" uncritical support or uncritical condemnation. The obvious way to discredit the agency would have been to recite instances of physical torture or assassination, but Caballero did not do that. For that reason, his description of U.S. efforts to teach the Hondurans "modern" methods of interrogation is especially persuasive. In his words, the Americans "taught us psychological methods—to study the fears and weaknesses of a prisoner. Make him stand, don't let him sleep, keep him naked and isolated, put rats and cockroaches in his cell, give him bad food, serve him dead animals, throw cold water on him, change the temperature."[66]

Officially, of course, the United States denied everything: "At no time," declared a State Department spokesman, "has there been any

United States government involvement with alleged death squads in Honduras. United States officials in Honduras had no knowledge of nor did they condone abuses attributed to the Honduran armed forces and/or the FDN." Nor was there any truth to allegations that North American officials had sought to purge Honduran military officers who had pursued an honest investigation of the death squads. (Charges to that effect had been made by Major Ricardo Zúniga, the son of the former National Party leader.)[67]

These denials are not very convincing. From the very beginning, the State Department assumed the classic pose of the three monkeys: See no evil, hear no evil, speak no evil. At first, reports of torture and death squads were simply denied. Later, when they could no longer be ignored, their importance was minimized and the credibility of the critics questioned. The Honduran government, it was claimed, "neither condone[d] nor knowingly permit[ted] killings of a political or nonpolitical nature."[68] Similarly, the CIA had long been receiving reports on these abuses from its sources within the FDN and Honduran military intelligence. But it was not interested. There were more pressing priorities: Bermúdez and his officers were stealing U.S. aid on a grand scale. The Agency had to find some way of containing the corruption.[69] As for the embassy, it remained largely above the fray. On occasion, Negroponte privately protested "some of the worst abuses, and Embassy human-rights reports . . . note[d] a few of the most egregious cases. But in the main, the Americans appear to have helped organize an army intelligence machine they could not control, or perhaps did not want to control." In the words of one U.S. official, the CIA "knew what was going on, and the ambassador complained sometimes. But most of the time they'd look the other way."[70] The embassy too had other priorities, and human rights issues were only an obstacle to their achievement. In any case, there was little sympathy for the "disappeared." Some felt that they were no better than "pathological killers who deserved to be crushed like cockroaches."[71]

The Emasculation of an Incipient Democracy

It was a strange sort of democracy that was emerging—one in which human rights were increasingly abused and, with the notable exception of the president, civilians had virtually no power. In effect, the military functioned as a state within the state: "Military operations were carried out with foreign troops without asking the permission of the Congress or the president. At times, the foreign policy of the country went in one direction and the armed forces in another."[72] And this was accepted. "Eager to please Washington and fearful of their own military, many of Honduras' leading politicians" had become "spectators in their own . . . game."[73] If there were problems, the CIA would grease the way with bribery, as it was also doing with the media.[74] The result was that Congress rarely debated the great issues of the day. Suazo's rodista supporters regularly delivered a majority on key pieces of legislation. This docility led the lone Christian Democratic deputy, Efraín Díaz, to complain that "Congress legitimizes all the executive wants . . . it is not, practically speaking, an independent power."[75]

So too the judiciary. Though Congress appointed Supreme Court justices, Suazo's control over it enabled him to determine who would sit on that bench. In turn, the Supreme Court appointed all members of the lower courts, with predictable consequences: "The lack of life tenure and the political nature of the appointments process have had a profound and debilitating effect on the independence of the Honduran judiciary. The courts have been largely ineffectual as a check on the other branches of government, particularly in cases where the armed forces are accused of violating human rights."[76] In effect, Congress and the courts had become appendages of the ruling Liberal Party faction. Moreover, these political problems were aggravated by the lack of any established tradition of judicial activism. (Hondurans had watched the Watergate proceedings in disbelief, unable to comprehend how the courts could subject the executive branch to such close scrutiny.) Furthermore, members of Congress had no staffs; they therefore had to rely almost entirely on information supplied by the executive. This was true even on matters, such as the enactment of the budget, that were technically in the domain of the legislature. On one occasion, when Congress asked for more budget information, it was accused of trying to destabilize the government.

A major example of this legislative and judicial debility involved the decision to build a Regional Military Training Center (Centro Regional de Entrenamiento Militar—CREM) in Puerto Castilla. In 1981 Washington had embarked on an ambitious training program for midlevel Salvadoran officers as part of its effort to turn the tide in that country's civil war, but the program had run into difficulties. Most of the troops had been trained in the United States and El Salvador. There were, however, severe congressional restrictions on the number of U.S. military personnel allowed in the latter, as well as constant war-related interruptions and security problems, and the economic cost of bringing Salvadorans to the United States was prohibitive. When the head of SOUTHCOM, General Paul Gorman, came up with the idea of training these troops in a seemingly stable third country, Honduras, he found a receptive audience.[77]

This was an extraordinary notion, symbolic in a way of the Reagan administration's lack of understanding of and insensitivity to Honduran feelings. The Soccer War had only just been formally terminated. Salvadorans were still regarded with a great deal of bitterness, fear, and suspicion. An increasing number of Hondurans were becoming concerned lest their country become embroiled in their neighbor's civil war. Although the negotiations were secret, word leaked out and caused an uproar. The Honduran government refused to consult Congress and in general treated the whole affair as a fait accompli. Not until after the first contingent of U.S. trainers arrived in June 1983 was the issue finally debated by the deputies.[78]

The occasion required the participation of the president, the foreign minister, and the head of the armed forces. In separate closed-door sessions, General Alvarez and Foreign Minister Edgardo Paz Barnica explained the government's position. Suazo himself went on the air to reassure Hondurans that the CREM was just a "technical center for our armed forces." As usual, Alvarez was blunt, intimidating the deputies with their ultimate nightmare: "Honduras cannot be neutral in regard to the Salvadoran or Nicaraguan conflicts," he thundered. "Do you want the Salvadoran conflict to be resolved in El Salvador, or do you want to have it here?"[79] The legislators were duly impressed. When the issue of the agreement's constitutionality was raised, it was finessed with a simple change of words: Henceforth, the Salvadorans would be referred to as "students" and their North American instructors as "advisers." This done, Congress dutifully passed the legislation by seventy-eight to three.

Later Negroponte's deputy, Shepard Lowman, would concede that the initial agreement was probably unconstitutional but that the embassy had decided to go ahead with it anyway: "The constitution was ambiguous and the legal community divided. While the weight of opinion was that the CREM required prior legislative approval, there was a respectable minority view that it did not." In any case, the "Honduran body politic was very strongly in favor of it. Hondurans are quite conservative. And they were damned scared of the situation in El Salvador. They were afraid Salvador was going to go down the drain. So their basic inclination was to be helpful."[80]

There is truth in this. The commission appointed by the armed forces and government did conclude that the agreement was legal. Its reading of the constitution was, however, selective at best. The commission's judgment was based primarily on Article 21, which gives to the executive "in matters of its exclusive competence" the right to ratify and "adhere" to international conventions without the prior consent of Congress. Other legal sources, however, quickly pointed out that Article 16 required that all international treaties be approved by the legislature before being ratified by the executive and that Article 205 gave Congress the right to "authorize or deny the transit of foreign troops" and the "admission of foreign military missions" into the country. Notwithstanding the contradiction between an article requiring the prior approval of Congress for "all" international treaties and one that gives the executive the right to conclude some conventions (namely, those within its "exclusive" jurisdiction) without prior congressional consent, it is apparent from Article 205 that the issue at stake did not fall within the "exclusive competence" of the executive. One must therefore agree with the bulk of Honduran legal opinion that the constitution had been violated.[81] What is most striking is that the embassy was aware of the problem and chose to ignore it. It is one thing for Hondurans to violate their constitution, quite another for the United States to encourage them to do so. Ostensibly, the Reagan administration was trying to promote democracy in Honduras; yet in this instance it was also simultaneously undermining it. Hondurans could perhaps be forgiven for concluding that, for Washington, democracy was less an end than a means. When inconvenient, it could be ignored or manipulated.

This episode would come back to haunt the United States in more ways than one. Though the Honduran Congress had momentarily been pacified, the basic issue had not been resolved. Nationalists were offended by the way the agreement had been reached; many considered the affair an affront to soberanía and dignidad. For those Hondurans, the CREM became a symbol of North American penetration and Honduran submission. Moreover, there was still a fairly widespread feeling—nowhere more intense than in certain sectors of the military—that the Salvadorans were the main enemy. Whatever the outcome of the Sandinista experiment, a few years later Hondurans might well find themselves again fighting Salvadorans. The training now being lavished on their traditional enemy might one day be used against them. For a while, this sentiment was obscured by the near-unanimity of the congressional vote and contained by the tranquilizing effects of U.S. aid. Within a year, however, the illusion of Honduran complacency would be shattered.

One other issue must be mentioned, and this has to do with the regime's attempts to repress the peasant and labor movements. The provisions of the antiterrorist Decree 33 applied to such traditional forms of protest as land invasions, street demonstrations and factory occupations. To those familiar with the history of the agrarian movement, this was ominous: Much of the agrarian reform had been achieved only through the use of aggressive tactics. It was argued by peasant militants, with considerable reason, that one had to occupy the disputed lands and force the authorities to make the appropriate decisions. Now such tactics were being placed in jeopardy without any assurance that the authorities would behave fairly or responsibly once the land seizures stopped. As the occupations continued, human rights violations in the countryside sharply escalated.

Labor, too, suffered. This was a time of burgeoning unemployment and reduced social services. Protest brought the usual response: "decapitation." Militant leaders were "disappeared" or arrested and tortured. "Democratic fronts" were pursued with a vengeance. Progovernment groups were set up within unions where leftist influence was strong, leading to divisions that were then, in accordance with the law, resolved in the government's favor. During 1981 such fronts were able to win control of SITRATERCO and the students' union at the National University. At about the same time, the progressive cooperative Las Isletas, which had just been taken over by new management with broad campesino support, found itself besieged again. Subsequently, the Professional Teachers' Training Guild found its moneys confiscated and its headquarters "militarized" as the authorities granted a small group of dissidents legal recognition. The National Electrical Company Workers' Union (Sindicato de Trabajadores de la Empresa Nacional de Energía Eléctrica—STENEE) became infested at the grass roots with progovernment elements. When it launched a strike in September 1984, its legal status was suspended. Such abuses only intensified and spread the unrest. For a while, Alvarez would be able to keep the lid on this pressure cooker with repression. In March 1984, however, the cover would be lifted and a new political phase begun.

Notes

1. To use Philip Shepherd's image.

2. Richard Lapper and James Painter, *Honduras: State for Sale* (London: Latin America Bureau, 1985), p. 81.

3. Somoza was especially concerned that he be allowed to live in the United States, free from the fear of extradition, and retain his assets. In December 1978, he sent his cousin to feel out the State Department on these issues. The White House was never informed. Robert A. Pastor, *Condemned to Repetition: The United States and Nicaragua* (Princeton: Princeton University Press, 1987), p. 289.

4. *Washington Post,* 23 March 1980.

5. *New York Times,* 16 April 1980.

6. Thomas P. Anderson, *Politics in Central America* (New York: Praeger, 1982), p. 131.

7. *New York Times,* 9 and 18 August 1981. This episode had repercussions. Because U.S. law forbade military personnel to carry such weapons, the U.S. ambassador had the captain in question deported.

8. Interview, 11 April 1990; U.S. Department of State, *Country Reports on Human Rights Practices* (Washington, D.C.: U.S. Government Printing Office, 1981), p. 429.

9. This last from an official who investigated the incident in the field. See also *Washington Post,* 29 April 1981; *London Sunday Times,* 22 February 1981; Americas Watch/American Civil Liberties Union, *Report on Human Rights in El Salvador* (New York: Vintage Books, 1982), p. 169.

10. Viron Vaky, "Hemispheric Relations: Everything is a Part of Everything Else," *Foreign Affairs,* Vol. 59, No. 3, 1981, pp. 623-624.

11. Pastor, *Condemned to Repetition,* p. 231.

12. Interview with Gustavo Alvarez Martínez, 16 March 1986. Alvarez went to Paz six or seven times before the president gave his reluctant approval. "Don't get into trouble," Paz reportedly said. "If something goes wrong, I'll have your head." Roy Gutman, *Banana Diplomacy: The Making of American Policy in Nicaragua, 1981-1987* (New York: Simon and Schuster, 1988), p. 43.

13. Quoted in Christopher Dickey, *With the Contras* (New York: Simon and Schuster, 1985), p. 115.

14. Binns interview.

15. Gutman, *Banana Diplomacy,* pp. 46-47; confirmed in interview with Alvarez Martínez, 3 December 1988.

16. Peter Kornbluh, *Nicaragua: The Price of Intervention* (Washington, D.C.: Institute for Policy Studies, 1987), p. 20; Dickey, *With the Contras,* p. 108.

17. Unless otherwise noted, the following is based on Gutman's *Banana Diplomacy,* pp. 55-57, 65; and our two interviews with Alvarez Martínez.

18. Sam Dillon, *Comandos* (New York: Henry Holt, 1991), p. 65.

19. In the words of one U.S. official in Central America. *Newsweek*, 8 November 1982. The following month, one of the contras' U.S. advisers told one of us, "We are hoping the Sandinistas will make the same mistake Somoza did. If they can be provoked into retaliating against opposition leaders and fence-sitters, that will drive people to take up arms."

20. Honduran and Salvadoran leftists have conceded in a number of interviews that most of these victims were involved in gunrunning. *Washington Post* and *New York Times*, 14 February 1986.

21. Binns interview.

22. Stephen Volk, "Honduras: On the Border of War," *NACLA Report on the Americas*, No. 15, Vol. 6, November-December 1981, p. 32.

23. Interview with Mauricio Castañeda, of 19 January 1989.

24. In the words of Ambassador Binns.

25. Interview with Irma Acosta de Fortín, 3 February 1988.

26. Víctor Meza, as quoted in Gutman, *Banana Diplomacy*, p. 103.

27. We have heard this story many times. The Honduran historian Longino Becerra swears that it is true and claims to have personally received the information from Suazo's maid. Interview, 4 February 1989. Suazo, of course, denies the account, as do his former advisers. We are skeptical of the Becerra version (though Suazo's television antics did happen) but repeat it because (1) it fits the former president's character so well and (2) it says something about the Honduran political culture. Mainly, though, we just like the story.

28. Volk, "Honduras," p. 34; interview with Tita Zúniga, 8 February 1988; Binns interview.

29. Víctor Meza, "The Military: Willing to Deal," *NACLA Report on the Americas*, Vol. 22, No. 1, January-February 1988, p. 14.

30. Richard Alan White, *The Morass: United States Intervention in Central America* (New York: Harper and Row, 1984), p. 185.

31. Mark B. Rosenberg, "Honduras: Bastion of Stability or Quagmire?" in *Revolution and Counterrevolution in Central America and the Caribbean*, Donald E. Schulz and Douglas H. Graham, eds. (Boulder: Westview Press, 1984), p. 335.

32. We have heard this from three separate sources (two Americans and one Honduran) who were in positions to know but who do not wish to be identified.

33. Rosenberg, "Honduras," p. 335.

34. Interview with John Negroponte, 13 July 1988.

35. Gutman, *Banana Diplomacy*, p. 102.

36. Letter from *Newsweek's* editor, Maynard Parker, 18 January 1989. We have been assured by several of the reporters who worked on the story that the description of Negroponte and his role was based on "numerous" sources in "several" U.S. government agencies, as well as Honduran informants.

37. Interview with Shepard C. Lowman, 19 July 1988; Negroponte interview.

38. Jane Mayer and Doyle McManus, *Landslide: The Unmaking of the President, 1984-1988* (Boston: Houghton Mifflin, 1988), p. 194.

39. The letter in question was published in the Honduran press; *Newsweek* was simply wrong. See *Boletín Informativo,* No. 9, February 1982.

40. See Oliver North's electronic message to John Poindexter, 17 September 1986, in the Iran-Contra Committees' *Report* (Washington, D.C.: U.S. Government Printing Office, 1987), Appendix A, p. 775.

41. Gutman, *Banana Diplomacy,* pp. 105-107.

42. Ibid., pp. 107-110; also Dickey, *With the Contras,* pp. 147-151.

43. Gutman, *Banana Diplomacy,* p. 113.

44. Ibid.

45. Interview with Alvarez Martínez, 16 March 1986.

46. Quoted in *Inforpress Centroamericana,* 25 November 1982.

47. *Excélsior* (Mexico City), 31 August and 1 September 1982.

48. Alvarez interview of 16 March 1986. Confirmed by two other military sources.

49. Binns interview.

50. *New York Times,* 12 February and 5 April 1988. See also U.S. Senate Foreign Relations Committee, Subcommittee on Terrorism, Narcotics, and International Operations, *Drugs, Law Enforcement, and Foreign Policy* (Washington, D.C.: U.S. Government Printing Office, 1989), p. 74.

51. Alvarez interview, 16 March 1986; Binns interview.

52. Americas Watch, *Human Rights in Honduras: Central America's "Sideshow"* (New York, May 1987), pp. 139-140.

53. Michael Kelley, "Questions Surround Death of Padre Guadalupe," *Honduras Update,* Vol. 2, Nos. 2-3, November/December 1983, p. 8; Nancy Peckenham and Annie Street, eds., *Honduras: Portrait of a Captive Nation* (New York: Praeger, 1985), pp. 186-187.

54. U.S. Department of State, *"Revolution Beyond Our Borders": Sandinista Intervention in Central America* (Washington, D.C.: U.S. Government Printing Office, 1985), pp. 14-15; U.S. Departments of State and Defense, *Background Paper: Nicaragua's Military Buildup and Support for Central American Subversion* (Washington, D.C.: U.S. Government Printing Office, 1984), pp. 26-28.

55. James LeMoyne, "Testifying to Torture," *New York Times Magazine,* June 1988, p. 47.

56. *El Tiempo,* 11 August 1982.

57. Ibid., 23 September 1983.

58. Americas Watch, Human Rights, pp. 67-68, 127-128.

59. Ibid., pp. 128-129; Dillon, *Comandos,* p. 99.

60. Dillon, *Comandos,* pp. 63-64, 100, 117-125; see also Dickey, *With the Contras.*

61. Dillon, *Comandos,* p. 100.

62. Interview on *60 Minutes,* 29 March 1987.

63. Interview with Alison Acker, cited in Acker's *Honduras: The Making of a Banana Republic* (Boston: South End Press, 1988), p. 116.

64. Linda Drucker, "A Contra's Story," *The Progressive*, August 1986, pp. 25-28.

65. Americas Watch, *Human Rights*, p. 133; see also Dillon, *Comandos*, p. 101.

66. LeMoyne, "Testifying to Torture," p. 62; Americas Watch, *Human Rights*, pp. 133-134.

67. Americas Watch, *Human Rights*, pp. 118-119.

68. Ibid., pp. 119-121.

69. Dillon, *Comandos*, pp. 125-129.

70. LeMoyne, "Testifying to Torture," p. 47. We have been told essentially the same thing by several persons who were in the embassy during these years.

71. Quoted in Lapper and Painter, *Honduras: State for Sale*, p. 94.

72. Efraín González, then chief of staff of the armed forces, in *La Tribuna*, 13 October 1984.

73. Mark B. Rosenberg, "Honduran Scorecard: Military and Democrats in Central America," *Caribbean Review*, Vol. 12, No. 1, Winter 1983, p. 15.

74. See Walter López's charges in *Central America Report*, 1 May 1987. We have also been told this by several Honduran congressional sources. See also Dillon, *Comandos*, pp. 106-107.

75. Quoted in Lapper and Painter, *Honduras*, p. 98.

76. Americas Watch, Lawyers Committee for International Human Rights, and Washington Office on Latin America, *Honduras: On the Brink* (New York, February 1984), pp. 13-14.

77. Information from General Fred Woerner. That the CREM was a U.S. rather than a Honduran initiative has been confirmed by both sides. Negroponte interview; Lowman interview; interview with Ubodoro Arriaga, 9 November 1988.

78. As late as 4 June 1983, the president of Congress, Efraín Bú Giron, complained that the legislature had not yet received any convention having to do with military bases and that the only thing he knew about it was what he read in the press. Several days earlier, General Gorman had announced the CREM's creation. *La Tribuna*, 4 June 1983. The Suazo government was itself divided over the issue, with the minister of the presidency, Carlos Flores Facussé, strongly opposing the measure. Flores Facussé, personal communication.

79. *La Tribuna* and *El Heraldo*, 21 June 1983.

80. Lowman interview.

81. The arguments pro and con may be found in Edgardo Paz Barnica, *La Política Exterior de Honduras, 1982-1986* (Madrid: Editorial Iberoamericana, 1986), pp. 251-288.

4

The Backlash

The Honduran military is an unusual animal. In times of peace you have to feed it, and in times of war you have to defend it.

—Honduran saying

On Friday, 30 March 1984 Gustavo Alvarez accompanied by Oswaldo Ramos Soto, his close adviser and the rector of the National University, boarded a plane for San Pedro Sula to attend a meeting of the ultraconservative Association for the Progress of Honduras (Asociación para el Progreso de Honduras—APROH). Though this was a private political function, Alvarez expected to be met at the city's Armando Escalón Air Base by someone of appropriate rank. He was destined to be disappointed. Neither the base commander nor the head of the air force, General Walter López Reyes, was on hand, and Alvarez had to suffer the indignity of being met by the duty officer, a mere lieutenant. This was sufficient to send him into a rage. He phoned López, berating him and threatening him with dismissal. In turn, López was outraged. He wanted to take "personal revenge." He was talked out of this, however, by one of his fellow officers, who suggested that such actions be "institutionalized."[1]

Meanwhile, Alvarez and Ramos went on to the APROH meeting, where the former was to deliver a speech. The theme of the talk was simple and familiar: War was at the door; it was impossible to coexist peacefully with the Sandinistas. Dramatizing his argument, as was his custom, Alvarez persuaded the assembled audience of right-wing businessmen, bankers, and trade unionists to contribute some 127,000 lempiras to the organization's treasury. In addition, 140 of the attendees agreed to give another 1,000 lempiras a month each.

At seven the next morning Alvarez, Ramos Soto, and their bodyguards returned to the air base for their return flight to Tegucigalpa. Unknown to them, two hours earlier hostile forces had seized the main barracks in the capital and secured the communications between the country's various military units. Several thousand troops had surrounded Tegucigalpa. As Alvarez and Ramos made their way toward their aircraft, they were met by Colonel Roberto Martínez and the base commandant, Major Israel Navarro, who informed the general that he had a confidential phone call from President Suazo. Navarro and Alvarez went off to take the call, leaving the latter's bodyguards behind. When they arrived at the designated area, they found it surrounded by soldiers. Navarro abruptly informed Alvarez that he was under arrest and demanded that he surrender his pistol. In response, Alvarez shouted, "I don't take orders from my subordinates!" Navarro put a pistol to his head and presented him with a letter of resignation, assuring him that either his signature or his brains would be on the document momentarily. When Alvarez still refused to sign, he was handcuffed, thrown to the ground, and beaten. He was then put on a plane and flown to the capital. From there, he was sent to Costa Rica and exile.[2]

The embassy and the CIA station were taken completely by surprise by these developments.[3] Negroponte's only hint of trouble had been an ugly incident that had occurred in the COSUFFAA on 18 March, when Alvarez had berated several commanders in front of their colleagues. Among the recipients of this tongue-lashing had been Walter López.[4] At the time, Negroponte had not given the incident much thought. Alvarez had seemed invulnerable. He had just been promoted to major general and through a constitutional reform had acquired the title of commander in chief. In addition, he had created joint chiefs of staff to replace the old general staff, a move that promised to augment his growing power. The creation of three new brigades had further centralized the military command and given him even greater control over battalion commanders. Finally, the day after his ouster he had been scheduled to go to Washington for high-level meetings with the Reagan administration.

Not until midmorning did President Suazo learn of the coup. By that time, Walter López had four signed resignations in hand. In addition to that of Alvarez, who later denied having resigned, López had the signatures of the army chief of staff, the head of the FUSEP, and the commander of the navy. (Several days later, the army inspector general would become the fifth member of the COSUFFAA to resign.) He now phoned the president and invited him to a meeting with the high command. Upon his arrival, however, Suazo found only López, Colonel Erick Sánchez, and Colonel William Said Speer. (As commanders of tank units, Sánchez and Said Speer had been key participants in the rebellion.) The trio proceeded to explain the situation to the astonished president, who protested that the removal of Alvarez had been unconstitutional. At this point, Suazo was told that the plane was waiting; if he did not like the arrangement, he could accompany Alvarez to Costa Rica.[5]

Shortly thereafter, Negroponte met with Suazo and López. The latter assured the ambassador that Honduran foreign policy would remain essentially unchanged. At that, Negroponte decided to try to put the situation in the best possible light. He called together a half-dozen reporters and solemnly informed them that it had been President Suazo who had fired Alvarez; civilian rule, it seemed, was alive and well. Not until that evening did Suazo address the nation. When he did, he was remarkably circumspect, saying only that the armed forces had dismissed Alvarez and that he would assume the role of commander in chief until Congress approved a new military leader. In the days that followed, U.S. officials repeatedly characterized Alvarez's dismissal as a "strengthening of the democratic process," though constitutional procedures had clearly been violated. By now, Suazo Córdova was claiming full credit for what had happened, but nobody put much stock in this. In the words of Liberal Party deputy José Azcona, this had been "an internal military decision even if the Embassy says differently."[6] On 4 April, with the Congress building surrounded by troops and armored personnel carriers fitted with machine guns and air force planes buzzing overhead, the Honduran legislature voted to make Walter López the new armed forces commander. When one plane passed especially low just as a deputy cast his vote for the new chief, the assembly broke into spontaneous laughter. The Honduran sense of humor remained alive and well, even if Honduran democracy was not.

The Fall of Gustavo Alvarez: An Autopsy

What had happened? How was it possible for a commander so well entrenched to have fallen so easily? Again, one must stress the difference between appearance and reality. On the surface, things had seemed calm. Behind the facade, however, a plot had been brewing for months. In the beginning, the leaders of this movement had come from the intermediate ranks of the officer corps—from among the lieutenant colonels and majors of the sixth and seventh *promociones* (graduating classes) of the Francisco Morazán Academy. The idea had been to launch the coup in April, during Holy Week, or perhaps later, in June. According to the original plan, Suazo Córdova was to have been ousted along with Alvarez. Two circumstances, however, had forced the conspirators to strike early: The first was the COSUFFAA meeting of 18 March, when Alvarez had confronted some of these officers as well as some full colonels who had previously maintained their distance from the dissidents. (His outburst had been triggered by the demand that he account for the disappearance of US$1 million earmarked for the purchase of military equipment. The demand had been intended to provoke the temperamental Alvarez into an explosion, and it had succeeded. By the end of the meeting, key members of both younger and older generations had found common ground.) The second development was the beginning of congressional discussions, with approval almost certain to follow, of a new Constituent Law of the Armed Forces, which would have given the commander in chief almost absolute control over the institution and would have reduced considerably the influence of the young officers. (Specifically, Alvarez had wanted to cut the COSUFFAA from fifty-two to twenty-one members, limit its mandate, and virtually replace it with an eight-member Commanders' Junta loyal to him.)[7]

Perhaps, too, the coup was accelerated by an upsurge of human rights violations during these months. Some of the conspirators were worried that they might soon fall victim to a violent purge of the military. Others were concerned that some future government might try to bring human rights violators to justice. Be that as it may, the developments mentioned above were in themselves quite sufficient to force their hand. The young officers now found themselves obliged to make alliance with those colonels who had only recently been alienated by the *caudillo's* increasingly authoritarian and threatening dispositions.

With characteristic lack of diplomacy, Alvarez had succeeded in alienating a broad cross section of the officer corps, whose members felt an urgent need to act before it was too late. Their complaints were many. Some were offended by his increasingly blatant efforts to promote his own political ambitions. He had been building a personal power base outside the armed forces in the APROH, which had become an enormously influential policy center. (Alvarez was its president.) At the same time, he was meddling in party politics, apparently with the intention of securing the 1985 National Party presidential nomination. He had managed to get former president Melgar Castro, a close ally, elected head of the party's central committee. A few days after the 31 March coup, two National Party leaders who had opposed Melgar charged that Alvarez had tried to buy the nomination for 4 million lempiras (US$2 million at the official exchange rate).

Further, Alvarez's flirtation with Sun Myung Moon's Unification Church had caused no small discomfort to both his Catholic business allies and some high-ranking officers. The general had promoted the sect and its political arm, which aggressively espoused his own "simplistic and semi-mystical East-West view of the world." During 1983, the Honduran press had repeatedly drawn attention to Alvarez's connections with Moon and Bo Hi Pak. "The liaison was particularly ill-considered since it clashed with Suazo's own attempts to champion Catholic sentiment and undermined APROH's claims to be the principal barrier against the atheistic tendencies of the left."[8] The relationship also caused some embarrassment when Reverend Moon was arrested in the United States for tax evasion.

Then there were the charges of corruption. Alvarez had begun his climb to power with a reputation for honesty in an officer corps riddled with vice. Once there, however, he had rapidly amassed a fortune. His funding came from various sources: from public moneys as well as the APROH, from U.S. military and economic aid, and from CIA funds intended for the contras. He "enjoyed a wide range of business interests, including a principal shareholding in the U.S.-based Union Star company, which exported arms, liquor and other products to the Honduran Army." Reportedly, the officers who deposed him had written evidence that he and his cronies had embezzled some US$30 million of public funds.[9]

Beyond this, many officers were convinced that, one way or another, Alvarez would get them into a shooting war. In November, the APROH had suggested that the Nicaraguan problem could be solved by a U.S. invasion. About this time, Alvarez made an attempt to persuade his North American sponsors to establish a "liberated zone" in Nicaragua. A few weeks later, he boasted that he would celebrate his next birthday in Managua. In February, he declared himself ready to throw Honduran troops into the civil war in El Salvador. Many of Alvarez's colleagues had been critical of his willingness to train Salvadoran troops in the CREM. Now, moreover, there were over 12,000 contras camped within Honduras's southern border, and their chances of overthrowing the Sandinistas seemed remote at best. The thought of so many frustrated, angry, and armed counterrevolutionaries on national soil, beyond the control of Honduran authorities, straining the country's pitifully scarce socioeconomic resources and disrupting local life, was enough to cause many a military martinet to have second thoughts about the wisdom of the enterprise. In the words of one officer, "The army began to realize early in 1984 that it was being asked to do a lot for the United

States, but it was not getting much in return. They saw Alvarez as the culprit."[10]

Still, all this would probably not have been enough to provoke a coup had it not been for the general's increasingly threatening behavior *within* the armed forces. Alvarez's relations with his colleagues were always strained. On the one hand, he was respected for his competence; on the other, he was hated and feared for his ruthlessness and lack of tact. His machinations to attain the posts of armed forces commander and brigadier general without having fulfilled the requirements for those positions had been widely resented, as had his exile of Bodden and Torres Arias. His tendency to make decisions without consulting his colleagues was a major source of friction. The armed forces had changed substantially over the preceding decades; one-man rule was no longer fashionable. By increasingly bypassing the COSUFFAA, Alvarez was violating the tradition of collective decisionmaking. Now, with his rise to major general and commander in chief and the recent promotion of several of his closest allies to general, he seemed poised to establish his absolute power. The new Constituent Law of the Armed Forces would have excluded from influence most members of the sixth and seventh promotions, including the majority of the officers with direct command over troops. Those who were about to be victimized understood full well the implications of these changes. That these moves were being made by a man who had manipulated the rule book to secure his own advancement only added insult to injury. When at the 18 March COSUFFAA meeting Alvarez made the strategic blunder of lashing out at both senior and junior commanders, the die was cast.

López Reyes and the New Deal: The Constraints of Dependency

At first glance, it did not seem that the new regime would bring much change. The incorporation of the colonels into a conspiracy begun by less conservative junior officers had considerably diluted the movement's original purposes. Concessions had been necessary: Seniority and hierarchy would be respected; the possibility of punishment for those guilty of corruption and human rights abuses would be minimized. After the exile of those closest to Alvarez, changes were made in almost all military units. Power was decentralized and collegiality restored. The new chief, Walter López Reyes, did not even gain control over the key component of the military establishment, the army.

Indeed, he lost his position as air force commander, leaving him with only one post: commander in chief of the armed forces. But although the power of the intermediate ranks of the officer corps was in general enhanced, the placement of personnel at the highest level of the institution was determined by seniority. None of the original conspirators gained such exalted positions; the movement had been co-opted by the older generation.

Yet López Reyes (the nephew of Oswaldo López Arellano) turned out to be more independent that many observers had anticipated. In contrast to initial press reports, which stressed the unchanging nature of Honduran foreign policy, López began to treat Negroponte "as an appendage of a previous regime. He refused to confide in him and preferred to let him discover major decisions in the press." Similarly, for General Paul Gorman of the SOUTHCOM, it was suddenly much more difficult to get things done in Honduras. The contras, too, began running into problems, as López, with the support of his colleagues, "began to restrict their presence and activities. The contra project began to unravel, and the Hondurans began to reassess their role."[11]

The first issue to arise concerned the CREM. The new regime requested that the ratio of two Salvadorans to every Honduran trained at the facility be reversed. Fifteen years after the Soccer War, many Hondurans still regarded El Salvador as a greater threat than Nicaragua. The Hondurans had expected a favorable settlement of the border dispute in return for allowing Salvadoran troops at the CREM. They had been disappointed. Accordingly, López Reyes began to suggest that the Reagan administration bring its influence to bear.

Beyond this, the Hondurans were concerned about Salvador's "special relationship" with the United States. Honduras received far less U.S. economic and military aid than its neighbor. Under the auspices of the U.S. training program, the Salvadoran armed forces had already expanded to 41,650 soldiers, whereas Honduran forces numbered just 17,200. The balance of power between these two traditional enemies was being disrupted. Lacking the means to sustain a comparable buildup, Hondurans saw no sense in helping strengthen the Salvadoran military: Why sharpen the knife of one who can use it against you?

By this time, too, the Reagan administration was running into major congressional resistance to the contra program. The possibility that U.S. support might be cut off and/or that Washington might strike a deal with Nicaragua began to weigh heavily on Honduran minds. In the aftermath of Alvarez's ouster, there had been street demonstrations with anti-American overtones. That spring, moreover, U.S. Secretary of State George Shultz had visited Managua, raising fears that Honduras might soon find itself alone against the Sandinistas. If that happened, one observer remarked, Honduras would become "an orphan that has played a ridiculous role."[12] Already, national pride had been offended by the jokes that were circulating in Latin America: Honduras, it was being said, was a prostitute who did not even have the self-respect to ask a decent price for her services.

All this produced a considerable backlash. In May, the Hondurans tried to cancel the U.S.-sponsored Granadero 1 joint military exercises, but the Americans brought enough pressure to bear to change their plans. Shortly thereafter, General López surprised and angered the embassy by telling reporters—before he informed Negroponte—that Honduras wanted to renegotiate the CREM agreement. In a televised address, López spoke obliquely about "adjusting the expenses of developing the armed forces to the real capacity of the national economy" and the need to conduct military cooperation under "conditions of the most absolute respect for the vital interests and dignity of the republic." In addition, he pledged "full support for the negotiations the executive branch is conducting in the search for a peaceful solution to the Central American conflict, within the atmosphere of the Contadora initiative."[13] This last, in particular, raised some eyebrows in Washington. For eighteen months, the Contadora nations—Mexico, Venezuela, Colombia, and Panama—had been pursuing negotiated solutions to the region's conflicts. They had repeatedly been frustrated by the Reagan administration, with the Hondurans acting as cat's-paw. Now López Reyes seemed to be saying that Honduras could no longer be counted on to follow the U.S. lead.

The Hondurans now formed a high-level commission to reassess their relations with the United States, and they asked that the Reagan administration do the same. The CREM and the border dispute with El Salvador were the most obvious subjects of scrutiny, but they were not the only ones. The Hondurans let it be known that they wanted changes in the 1954 Bilateral Military Assistance Agreement. They demanded more control over U.S. army personnel and a clearer understanding of what would become of the facilities built during the military exercises that were now almost continuous. They asked that future joint maneuvers, said to be a strain on the country's financial resources, be reduced in scale. They also requested preferential trade status for such products as sugar and meat, a sharp increase in economic and military aid, and a bilateral defense pact.

The most troubling issue facing the two sides concerned the contras. "What am I going to do with 12,000 fighters here?" General López pointedly wondered aloud. By summer, the guerrillas' command center and a 120-bed hospital had been moved out of the capital to less conspicuous locations, and a training camp had been closed. The following January, Steadman Fagoth, leader of a Miskito counterrevolutionary group, was expelled from the country after holding a press conference in Tegucigalpa. In more congenial days, such behavior would have drawn no more than a gentle warning, but times were changing. During the last six months of 1984, the contras were repeatedly told to maintain a low profile even as the CIA continued to fly supplies into Nicaragua from bases in Jamastrán and Aguacate.

The fact is that the Hondurans had not yet made up their minds what to do with the guerrillas. Both the contras and their hosts were in limbo, dependent on forces beyond their control. The U.S. Congress had still not decided on a policy of its own. Lacking clear direction, Honduran authorities settled into a posture of watchful waiting. These were difficult months. Hondurans' indecision reflected their insecurity and the lack of obvious alternatives. It was not just a matter of 12,000 or so heavily armed contras; if the rebel campaign collapsed, as many as 100,000 sympathizers and family members might flee into Honduras. The country did not have the resources to absorb such an influx. The ultimate nightmare was that the insurgents might dissolve into uncontrollable marauding bands, sustaining themselves through gunrunning, drug smuggling, cattle rustling, and other illegal activities. Already Hondurans had been the victims of numerous human rights violations, and there was very little that the authorities could do about it. The contras had almost as many men under arms as the Honduran military. Any attempt to force them out might easily result in considerable bloodshed, a prospect that appealed to few Honduran officers.

In short, the Hondurans faced a serious "disposal problem." The situation was further complicated by the contradictions within government policy. Officially, there were no contras on Honduran soil. When told by an inquiring reporter that the rebel headquarters was in full view of his office, Foreign Minister Edgardo Paz Barnica professed ignorance. Only in February 1985 was the contra presence officially acknowledged, and even then the admission did not last for long. Deception had become a way of life.

Clearly, López Reyes and his colleagues had no fundamental complaint with U.S. policy. They wanted to be paid better, to have some of the most grating irritations to their nationalistic sensibilities removed, and to receive guarantees that they would not be left holding the bag. Most of all, they wanted a massive increase in economic and military assistance. Though aid from the United States and multilateral lending agencies had risen sharply since 1980, capital flight and debt service had largely nullified whatever benefits had been achieved. (After 1985, indeed, when the multilaterals abruptly halted their lending, the net transfer of aid would be almost nonexistent or negative.) As far back as July 1983 Suazo had sent Ronald Reagan a long letter, with an accompanying appeal for US$550 million over the next three years. The message was simple: Honduras had followed Washington's economic advice, but the austerity measures had led to growing unemployment:

> We greatly fear that if this situation continues it will become a politically destabilizing factor and weaken our people's belief in the capacity of the democratic system to resolve the problems that we are trying to remedy. . . . If we do not have the necessary outside support, these measures will have exactly the opposite political results from what we are aiming for. . . . Our people are beginning to ask themselves, openly and with increasing force, if our own best interests are being served by being so intimately aligned with the United States when we receive so little in return. We estimate that the requested budgetary assistance represents, in the long run, a relatively low cost when one takes into account the political and military risks that Honduras is assuming.[14]

López Reyes now raised the ante: US$1.7 billion (US$1.3 billion economic and US$400 million military) was demanded through the end of the decade.

In response to this new assertiveness, a few minor concessions were made: More Hondurans were admitted for training at the CREM. Military exercises were scaled down and the number of U.S. soldiers stationed in the country reduced. But this did not go very far toward satisfying Honduran demands. Indeed, by November the number of American military personnel would increase once again as it became evident that previous efforts to maintain a low profile were mainly a matter of the politics of Reagan's reelection. As months passed and little was accomplished, Honduran irritation grew. Some of this was taken out on Negroponte, who became the object of increasing public attack. In September, the government announced that it would no longer permit the training of Salvadoran troops at the CREM. The following month, Foreign Minister Paz Barnica declared that Honduras wanted to redefine its ties with the United States: "We want a more independent relationship on security issues and more assistance in helping build our economy and strengthening our democratic system. . . . My government has grown impatient with the lack of a concrete response."[15]

The State Department reacted with mock surprise: The United States had no objection to exploring possible changes! But in fact the department had not even formed a commission to consider such matters, something the Hondurans had requested months before. Existing levels of aid were viewed as entirely adequate. A modest increase might be possible but certainly nothing like the Hondurans had in mind. By the same token, talk of a special security pact was dismissed as unrealistic. Washington had never offered such a treaty to any Latin American country. An accord of this kind, it was argued, would vitiate the 1947 Inter-American Treaty of Reciprocal Assistance (the Rio Pact) and probably involve the United States in a commitment to Honduras should war again break out with El Salvador. In any case, it was the considered opinion of most Western observers that the Hondurans were bluffing. If the United States did not give them security guarantees, where could they turn?

Honduran nationalism had collided head-on with the constraints of dependency. The country had never had a strong nationalistic elite, and the López Reyes regime, though more so than most, was no exception. By November, the Hondurans were virtually begging for aid. In Washington, a high-ranking delegation even raised the possibility that the United States might be permitted to build a permanent military base. The State Department, however, refused to take the bait. Though it finally agreed to establish a commission to reassess relations, it sent the Hondurans home essentially empty-handed. Still, they seemed happy to have been accorded the time of day: "We met with the highest levels of the government of the United States," proudly declared Ubodoro Arriaga. "That hasn't happened before."[16]

Meanwhile, the contra program continued. The Hondurans proved unwilling to deprive the rebels of their sanctuaries. Indeed, as U.S. aid to the guerrillas diminished and (because of congressional prohibitions) eventually ended and the Argentines pulled out, the Hondurans, Salvadorans, and Israelis stepped up their support. Honduras became a major supplier of ammunition to the insurgents. El Salvador took over the job of maintaining the contra's small air force.

What were mere gringos to make of such behavior? Truly, Hondurans were a puzzle. In the words of one embassy cable, "At times, GOH [Government of Honduras] posturing and mixed signals can be the order of the day, and those of us involved in handling the day-to-day details of the relationship occasionally experience difficulty in discerning whether a particular Honduran complaint (of which there are invariably many) is merely a tactical ploy . . . or something more fundamental."[17] In the end, Honduran wavering and inconsistency led the Reagan administration to underestimate the depth of the discontent. In December, it asked Congress for a mere US$2.2 million extra over its original FY 1986 military aid request of US$86 million. U.S. officials knew that the Hondurans would not be pleased but reasoned that they would be unhappy with almost anything that the United States might do. The following month, Reagan's national security adviser, Robert McFarlane, was sent to Tegucigalpa to smooth things over. McFarlane assured his hosts that the administration would spare no effort to persuade Congress to renew aid to the contras. At the same time, however, he let it be known that a special security pact would not be forthcoming.

The Hondurans were furious, and they did not disguise it. In the words of one senior official: "We had a message and let me tell you, they got the message. There is a limit to the risk Honduras can take."[18] They especially resented McFarlane, whom they regarded as an arrogant, pompous, preening peacock. In the aftermath of the visit, the Sandinistas extended a series of peace feelers to the Hondurans. In turn, the latter made it a point of informing the Americans about these overtures and even about several indirect ones from Cuba via Panama. Some Honduran officers, it was hinted, felt that it was time to patch things up with the Nicaraguans.

The United States and Honduras: The Manipulative Alliance

The U.S.-Honduran symbiosis was changing. It had always been based on mutual interest. But now that the facade of mutual satisfaction had been stripped away, something far less attractive was revealed underneath: mutual exploitation. About this time the Sandinistas began to build up their military forces along the Honduran border. Anticipating an attack on the contra base camps, the Reagan administration belatedly began to formulate a "strategy for enticing the Hondurans to greater support for the Nicaraguan resistance." On 7 February, the Crisis Pre-Planning Group, composed of senior officials from the State Department, the CIA, the Pentagon, and the National Security Council (NSC) staff, recommended that the president send a letter to Suazo Córdova indicating continued U.S. support for the rebels and for the defense of Honduran sovereignty. It was also recommended that the United States expedite the delivery of military items already ordered; that up to US$75 million of the US$174 million in economic support funds embargoed to pressure Suazo into adopting monetary and tax reforms be released; and that CIA support be increased for several projects already under way in Honduras. Originally, it was suggested that the letter be delivered by Negroponte and that this communication be followed by the visit of a special envoy who would "verbally brief" the Hondurans on the "conditions" attached to the concessions. "For obvious reasons," noted one NSC memorandum, "we would not wish to include this detail in any written correspondence."[19]

Later, the question would arise whether there had been any quid pro quo—whether U.S. aid had been exchanged for continuing Honduran support for the contras. Robert McFarlane, in his testimony at the trial of Oliver North, claimed that there had. This drew angry protests from Suazo and López Reyes, who averred that the former national security advisor was "off his rocker."[20] George Bush, who by then (spring 1989) was president of the United States, also denied the charge. About the same time, moreover, the State Department's Michael Kozak testified before Congress that the plan had been scrapped after objections had been raised about the "conditionality." This issue was of no small import because the October 1984 Boland Amendment had barred the U.S. government from spending money, directly or indirectly, for military assistance to the contras. Although the testimony of the participants is often contradictory and the paper trail incomplete (much documentation having been shredded by North), we know that on 19 February President Reagan approved the plan to offer the Hondurans increased aid in return for their ongoing support for the rebels.[21] Subsequently, Reagan sent the proposed letter to Suazo through Negroponte, assuring the former of continued U.S. backing for the "freedom fighters." However, the idea of sending a special envoy was rejected.[22]

The matter apparently did not end there. The available documentation suggests that the bureaucratic struggle between the State Department and the NSC continued. McFarlane, North, and Raymond Burghardt still favored the sending of a special envoy to stress to the Hondurans the nature of the desired exchange.[23] Whether that envoy was ever sent remains uncertain, but two things should be kept in mind: First, after his April 1989 congressional testimony was called into question, Michael Kozak backed away from his claim that the plan had not been carried out. Second, in March 1985 Vice President George Bush visited Honduras to discuss with Suazo the "issues raised in President Reagan's letter."[24] According to a list of "admitted facts" submitted at the North trial, Bush told his host that Reagan had "directed expedited delivery of U.S. military items to Honduras." He also informed Suazo that the president had ordered that "currently withheld economic assistance . . . should be released; that the United States would provide from its own military stocks critical . . . items that had been ordered by Honduran Armed Forces; and that several . . . programs under way for the Honduran security forces would be enhanced." Although the document did not state that Bush himself had spelled out the trade-off, it did say that the president and other top officials had authorized "the entire plan" to send an "emissary who would very privately explain U.S. criteria for the expedited economic support."[25]

Had the decision not to send an envoy been reversed? If so, was Bush that envoy? One cannot be sure. The document quoted above is not explicit about such matters, and in any case its accuracy has been challenged.[26] Bush himself has denied any involvement in a quid pro quo. He is, however, hardly a disinterested spectator. He would deny a great deal in the years that followed his March 1985 visit, but his protestations would often smack of artfulness. At the time that the controversy over the special envoy arose, he was in the first months of his own presidency and had a strong interest in getting on with his term unencumbered by the kind of scandal that had made Reagan's last two years a nightmare. Similarly, the denials of Suazo and López Reyes must be seen within the context of their interest in protecting their own reputations as well as that of Honduras and the Honduran armed forces. (Actually, Suazo did not deny that there had been an exchange of favors—just that it had not involved the contras. Moreover, he asserted that it had been *he* who had set the "conditions": The Reagan administration had invited *him* to Washington. In return, he claimed to have demanded US$75 million and the security guarantees because—as he delicately put it—"I am not going to go to masturbate and sign joint communiqués that . . . I never understood and never will.")[27]

Perhaps more definitive information about the Bush connection will still come to light. Until then, however, we will have to settle for more tentative judgments. The available evidence indicates that the then-vice president was not the unwitting, occasional spectator he portrayed himself as being. Indeed, it would appear that he was an important link between the White House and the Honduran government, and not only with Suazo. In January 1986 he would meet with the incoming Honduran president, José Azcona. We know that prior to that meeting Oliver North would advise him to stress the importance of Honduran aid to the contras and to "raise the subject of better U.S. government support" for Honduras in return.[28] Whether he followed that advice is still uncertain.

But the real issue here is not the personal involvement of George Bush. The point is that the administration that he was representing repeatedly used aid as a bribe to secure continuing Honduran support for the contras. Whether the deal was explicit or implicit is not especially important. Tacit bargaining is just as real as a signed accord. This was a government obsessed with the notion of "plausible deniability." One had to have some cover, no matter how flimsy, that would permit the plausible denial of involvement in activities that might be politically dangerous and/or illegal. Obfuscation and deceit were integral parts of the administration's modus operandi. The evidence strongly suggests that most U.S. policymakers (the secretary of state being a notable exception) perceived the situation in terms of an exchange of U.S. aid for Honduran support of the guerrillas.[29] And it is impossible to believe that the Hondurans did not understand the relationship in those terms also. After all, "playing the gringos" was a time-honored tradition, and this was the opportunity of a lifetime—a golden chance to make them pay for what they wanted.

For months after the Bush visit, the two sides continued their uneasy courtship. In late April, the House of Representatives once again rejected Mr. Reagan's request for contra aid. Again, the Hondurans balked. For the preceding two months—ever since the 19 February presidential approval of the plan to offer them extra aid—they had been cooperating with the FDN's logistical efforts. Now senior military officers and other high functionaries resurrected the fear that the guerrillas might be disarmed and deprived of their sanctuaries. A senior Honduran officer told the rebel leader Alfonso Robelo that the House vote "finishe[d] the contras." A shipment of ammunition to the guerrilla base at Las Vegas was confiscated. In a memo to Ronald Reagan, McFarlane urged that the president telephone Suazo to make clear the U.S. commitment to maintain "pressure on the Sandinistas regardless of what action Congress takes."[30] This same day Reagan again authorized a secret plan to secure Honduran support for the contras by providing millions of dollars in aid.[31] These renewed assurances apparently had their intended effect. In their telephone conversation, Suazo pledged Reagan his full cooperation and promised to investigate reports that the Honduran military had been obstructing munitions shipments to the rebels.[32] Two days later, Walter López met with Negroponte and—according to the latter—informed him that the Honduran armed forces were "ready to continue helping the anti-Sandinistas if the U.S. government compensates them" with an increase in economic or military aid.[33] Shortly thereafter, the Honduran foreign minister, heading a high-level delegation to Washington, reaffirmed that his country did not plan to restrict the activities of the contras.

In the Byzantine world of Honduran politics, nothing is certain, and few things are stable for very long. In May, hostilities along the Nicaraguan border expanded dramatically. The Sandinistas attacked a Honduran border patrol, killing one soldier and wounding four others. The incident came on the heels of an incursion in which two Nicaraguan companies had crossed several kilometers into Honduras to assault FDN positions. Such attacks, along with cross-border artillery bombardments, forced some 1,000 Hondurans to flee their villages and brought unprecedented public attention to the danger posed by the contra presence.

The flare-up undermined the government's claim that there were no contras on Honduran soil. (In fact, during these months the embassy estimated that about half of the FDN forces—perhaps as many as 8,000 guerrillas—were in the country at any given time.) The assaults caused considerable economic damage and left the impression that the military was unable to defend national territory. In addition, there was widespread dismay over the effect of these incidents on Honduras's international image. In the words of one embassy cable, "Hondurans squirm over anything which contributes to a reputation of contributing to regional tensions or serving as a cat's-paw for the United States."[34] In an attempt to regain its credibility, the government ordered the removal of the main FDN base camp in Las Vegas to a more remote and less accessible site.

This was the situation in late May when Suazo, Arriaga, López Reyes, and Paz Barnica arrived in Washington to meet with Reagan and his advisers. Suazo had delayed acceptance of the invitation until 11 May pending acceptable negotiations on economic and security matters and an easing of domestic political turmoil. In a memo to the president, McFarlane noted that "Suazo's visit comes at a time of some stress in our relationship. Honduras has been key to our ability to project power in Central America and bring pressure on Nicaragua." The Hondurans

> maintain that their close association with us on regional issues—especially provision of a base for the FDN—costs Honduras international support and increases the likelihood of Sandinista aggression. The GOH [Government of Honduras] argues that these factors entitle it to increased economic assistance and more concrete security assurances. . . . The GOH has requested $1.37 billion between now and 1990, an amount which we have advised them is unrealistic. Suazo may also raise the GOH's unhappiness with the conditions we have attached to our aid. These conditions are designed to increase Honduras' export capability; and in practice we have been very flexible in applying them because of Honduras' national security importance.

McFarlane went on to suggest that "without making the linkage too explicit, it would be useful" for the president to "remind Suazo that in return for our help—in the form of security assurances as well as aid—we do expect cooperation in pursuit of our mutual objectives. In this regard, you could underline the seriousness of our security commitment, which the Hondurans seem to regard as the main *quid pro quo* [our emphasis] for cooperating with the FDN."[35]

The visit was a public-relations success even though it did not accomplish much of substance. At the end, a joint communiqué was issued by the two presidents approving minor changes in the 1954 Military Assistance Agreement. The United States agreed to "consult with and support" the Honduran government "in its efforts to defend its sovereignty and territorial integrity" in the event of "communist aggression." Elsewhere, the administration proposed that economic aid be increased from US$134.9 to US$142.9 million and military aid from US$62 to US$88 million. Obviously, these commitments fell far short of the "new deal" that the Hondurans wanted. Nevertheless, they accepted the terms as (in the words of one embassy source) the "best that they [could] get for the time being."[36]

No basic issues were resolved, and so the conflict continued. Honduran bitterness and cynicism increased. When toward the end of the year the military again cut off arms deliveries to the contras, North commented that "from previous meetings with López [Reyes], it is obvious that the Hondurans perceive the USG [United States government] is 'using' Honduras for its own political ends. They have learned that we withhold our assistance . . . in order to force concessions from them. They are now using this same tactic with us as a means of insuring that the U.S. government will come through for them. López and his colleagues recognize that the only leverage they have over us is their covert support for the Nicaraguan resistance."[37] The Honduran military was particularly disgruntled because it lacked some of the sophisticated equipment that the contras had. Consequently, in March 1986 an agreement was reached to give it ground-to-ground missiles. Nevertheless, in May the new Honduran president, José Azcona, "indicated to President Reagan that Honduras' continued support for the Resistance depended upon significant increases in . . . military aid."[38]

A few months later, on the eve of a congressional vote that allowed the CIA to resume aid to the contras, the chief of the agency's Central American Task Force, Alan Fiers, would travel to Honduras, Guatemala, and Costa Rica. In an October 1986 memorandum to Casey, he noted that "the Hondurans were, as always, nettlesome. Nevertheless, in the final analysis they agreed to fully support the program and to allow supplies to begin moving as scheduled. They were clear as to what they seek in return: support for the purchase of advanced aircraft."[39]

Manipulation was the name of the game, and quid pro quos—at times tacit and at times explicit—were the currency. Still, this type of bargaining did not always work. Witness the fate of the Regional Military Training Center: In June 1985 the Hondurans were informed that the United States would no longer participate in the CREM. Months of negotiation had been insufficient to reconcile differences over the Salvadoran issue. The United States had wanted to turn the base into a permanent facility to which troops from all over Latin America could come for small-unit training. Several formulas had been proposed to disguise the fact that Salvadorans would be allowed to participate. In the end, however, the Hondurans had balked. The situation in El Salvador was no longer as frightening as it had been a couple of years earlier; consequently, there was less need to strengthen the Salvadoran armed forces. The thought of entering into a long-term arrangement to provide military training to their traditional enemy remained profoundly disturbing to many. The project was therefore allowed to die; the U.S. pullout was simply the punctuation mark.[40]

López Reyes and the New Deal (Continued): The Easing of Repression and the Rise of Political Opposition

The overthrow of Alvarez Martínez changed more than just Honduran foreign policy. Prior to April 1984, political and social discontent had been effectively contained through repression. Now, under López Reyes, brute force was at least partially replaced by more sophisticated methods. The result was a rapid growth of domestic political opposition. The fall of Alvarez released the frustration and anger that had been building over the preceding two years. Even before it there had been popular unrest. To protest the kidnapping of Rolando Vindel, a leader of the electrical workers' union, there had been a work stoppage on 20 March. In response, the security forces had taken over the National Electrical Company, detaining three hundred workers and holding six union leaders on charges of subversion. More protests had followed. Between late March and the end of May, tens of thousands of Hondurans took to the streets. Some demonstrated against human rights violations, others against government economic and social policies, still others against war and the United States.

Shortly after assuming command, López Reyes had announced that there would be a full investigation of all human rights abuses and that the guilty would be punished. By early May, members of the high command were sitting down with human rights activists to discuss the problem of the "disappeared." Officials and politicians who had been silent now came forward. In August, Major Alexander Hernández and Captain Alonso Canales, who had been linked to rights violations, were sent into diplomatic exile. Several policemen who had engaged in torture were fired. The abuses did not cease, but they were on the decline,[41] and the high command was clearly trying to distance itself from them.

The hopes raised by this promising beginning proved vain. As in the case of Honduran foreign policy, the domestic changes that López Reyes and his colleagues brought about were limited. The institutional interests of and diffusion of power within the military precluded a full investigation. As the months wore on and none of the missing reappeared, López had to admit that the inquiry was stalled: "We are touching on matters and sectors of great delicacy," he confessed. "There are stumbling blocks, moments in which we don't have any way to move forward."[42] The problem, of course, was that the military could not really be expected to investigate itself. The exile of Hernández and Canales had been intended to placate human rights activists in the face of this lack of progress. Instead, it angered them. Critics protested that the two should have been arrested and punished. Demands were made that the investigation be opened to civilian participation.

At year's end, however, the military issued a communiqué revealing that only 8 of the 112 missing persons had been found. It was suggested that some of the "disappeared" might have fallen victim to a vendetta pursued by "non-Honduran irregular armed leftist and rightist groups." As for the possible involvement of government authorities, nothing definite could be proven. And even if such a connection were to be established, the commission could not identify those responsible, since some of the individuals interviewed had refused to cooperate. Human rights activists were especially angered by the military's failure to publish testimony from a number of small-town mayors regarding the existence of death squads and clandestine prisons. Commenting on the report, *El Tiempo* derided it as a cynical "whitewash" that "says nothing worthy of respect or credibility" but "leaves people with the disastrous impression that human life is worth nothing in Honduras and that there is not a single institution or power within the state to which the people can turn, in which they can trust, in the hour when the individual is a victim of abuse of power, arbitrariness, and institutional terrorism."[43]

By this time, the opposition was floundering. Though the removal of Alvarez had produced a spectacular flowering of grass-roots activity, there was no national party—or even coalition—to represent these forces. Within the Liberal and National Parties resistance to government policies was largely confined to minority factions, and outside those traditionally hegemonic structures there were only the small Christian Democratic Party and the PINU within the legal opposition. Suazo's rodista followers continued to control the state bureaucracy and used their patronage powers and ability to manipulate the election laws to exacerbate divisions among their opponents.

Government intervention in the internal affairs of opposition parties and interest groups was, of course, a long-standing tradition, firmly rooted in the Honduran political culture. (Philip Shepherd once remarked that the "first axiom of Honduran politics is to divide the opposition rather than present a coherent plan to govern.")[44] Moreover, it was a tactic that was aided by chronic institutional weaknesses. Internal divisions, both political and personal, had hopelessly fragmented the labor and peasant movements; egocentric individualism, political rigidity, and corruption were the order of the day. Suazo and his followers assiduously nurtured these divisions through such time-honored methods as bribery and the formation of "democratic fronts." Within organized labor, there were now three major federations with separate political allegiances. At the same time, the growth of peasant activism had led to the creation of dozens of organizations—many of them local—rather than to a coherent national movement. The small revolutionary movement was similarly splintered. As the 1985 election campaign approached, the traditional political parties themselves broke into deeply divided factions. No fewer than seventeen candidates would vie for the presidency (though only nine—including the Christian Democratic and PINU candidates—would be certified by the National Electoral Tribunal). The Honduran system of bureaucratized anarchy was reaching new heights.

After the Fall: The Bueso Rosa Affair

On 1 November 1984 the FBI arrested eight persons in Miami on charges of using U.S. territory to conspire against the life and government of Roberto Suazo. Five of the accused were also charged with smuggling cocaine worth US$10 million into Florida to finance the plot. Among those arrested were two Hondurans living in Miami: Gerard Latchinian, an international arms dealer; and Faiz Sikaffy, a businessman. Back in the 1970s, Sikaffy had bought what was then Honduras's only cement factory, illegally obtaining US$6 million from the National Investment Corporation to do so. Later, during the presidency of Policarpo Paz, he had persuaded the government to buy into the company but had used the funds to start separate businesses. Both the government and the company had ended up deeply in debt, and the former finally had taken over the enterprise. Now Sikaffy wanted it back.

Named as a coconspirator was the former military chief of staff General José Abnegado Bueso Rosa, then serving as an attaché in the Honduran embassy in Santiago, Chile. At one time, Bueso had been the second-most-powerful figure in the armed forces. He had been its liaison with the contras, the man with whom senior U.S. officials had made arrangements for the rebels' logistical, training, and other support activities. A close associate of Gustavo Alvarez, he had been sent into exile after the events of 31 March. When news of the conspiracy broke, Bueso sought asylum in the Paraguayan embassy. Denied it, he surrendered to Chilean authorities.

Bueso's ties with Alvarez inevitably raised questions. Sikaffy had revealed that the conspirators had planned to replace Suazo with an ex-general. Alvarez had been living in Latchinian's home in Coral Gables. Though Alvarez denied any knowledge of the plot, his disavowals were met with skepticism in Honduras, where the authorities announced that they would request his extradition on charges of corruption. Moreover, on 2 November, the government announced the termination of Alvarez's pet project, the ultraconservative APROH, for actions "contrary to existing public order and the democratic system."

This was quite a comedown. The APROH had been founded as a secret organization in the 1980 through 1981 time frame, before attaining legal recognition in 1983. By then it was rumored to have been operating as a kind of shadow cabinet for economic policy. In April 1981 the association's vice president, Miguel Facussé, and others had begun to draw up an economic action plan, most of which would eventually be adopted by the Suazo administration. Though the APROH was never quite the "invisible government" that critics considered it, it was a major center of paragovernmental influence. The overthrow of Alvarez, internal conflict, and a consequent deterioration of its links with the Liberal Party and the armed forces had left it little more than a shell.

It is still not clear whether or to what degree Alvarez and the APROH were involved in the coup attempt. Even the general's enemies concede that he strongly opposed drug trafficking, one of the central charges against the conspirators. Indeed, narcotics had been a source of considerable friction between Alvarez and the contras. On more than one occasion, meetings with guerrilla leaders in Alvarez's home in Colonia Florencia had degenerated into shouting matches as the general voiced his displeasure at rebel involvement in these activities. The response was always the same: "Our power comes from a power that is greater than yours."[45]

The full story of the contra involvement in the drug trade also remains to be told. As early as 1985, a secret CIA study reported that a "top commander" of the guerrillas operating out of Costa Rica had used cocaine money to buy arms. According to the CIA's Alan Fiers, "We knew that everybody around [Edén] Pastora was involved in cocaine. . . . His staff and friends were drug smugglers or involved in drug smuggling." Similarly, a U.S. federal drug investigator told two Associated Press reporters that virtually every contra faction in that country was implicated in such operations.[46] Even General Paul Gorman, certainly no enemy of the contras, has testified, "Everything

I know from human intelligence [deleted] would suggest that anybody that was in the game of subversion down there was in one way or another involved with drugs."[47] Traffickers had business relations with contra organizations; they provided them with cash, weapons, planes, and air supply services. Some of the people who were running guns to the insurgents were also flying narcotics back to the United States.

There is, moreover, public testimony that U.S. officials knew what was going on and did nothing. One senior CIA officer in the region, upon being told of these activities, instructed his contra informants not to get involved but indicated that it was all right to accept financial contributions from dealers. When the flights returned home with the "white stuff," they should just look the other way.[48] Knowledge of these activities went at least as high as the National Security Council staff. Oliver North's notebooks contain numerous references to narcotics, including one line ("Get Alfredo César on Drugs") that sounds as if he was thinking of using the issue to discredit certain contra leaders. On at least seven occasions, concern about protecting the secret supply network to the guerrillas prompted NSC involvement in criminal investigations. Four of those cases allegedly involved narcotics; in three of them North intervened. The most interesting of these involved Bueso Rosa.[49]

Bueso had spent eight months under arrest in Chile while U.S. authorities tried to extradite him. When he was finally brought to the United States, it was under a negotiated arrangement that left him free from indictment on narcotics charges. It soon became apparent, however, that Bueso expected to be exonerated completely. Indeed, the prosecution was soon informed that the State Department had an intelligence interest in the defendant. Bueso, it was said, might reveal earlier contra support operations; moreover, it was believed that he was destined for big things in Honduras. As it turned out, the individual who delivered this message (a military officer on loan to State) had no authority to speak for the department. Nevertheless, a few days before Bueso was to plead his case in the Federal District Court in Miami, officers in the Defense Intelligence Agency (DIA) scheduled a luncheon in his honor in the executive dining room of the Pentagon. Only a lengthy meeting including senior members from the State and Justice departments and the CIA persuaded the DIA officials to call off the affair.

But the matter did not stop there. After Bueso pled guilty to two counts of murder for hire, General Robert Schweitzer and Colonel Nestor Pino testified on his behalf at the sentencing. At the same time, the Reagan administration filed a sealed deposition to urge leniency. Bueso Rosa, it stated, had "always been a valuable ally to the United States." As chief of staff of the Honduran armed forces, he had been "primarily responsible for the initial success of the American military preserve in Honduras. For this service, he was awarded the Legion of Merit by the president, . . . the highest award that can be presented to a foreign military officer."[50] Duly impressed, the judge sentenced Bueso to a mere five years in prison, with immediate eligibility for parole.

Enter Ollie North. In a note to John Poindexter, his superior on the National Security Council, North warned that Bueso Rosa, if not further mollified, might "start singing songs nobody wants to hear." In September 1986 North met with the State Department's Elliott Abrams, the Justice Department's Steven Trott, and the FBI's Oliver Revell to press for pardon, clemency, deportation, or the reduction of an already reduced sentence in order to keep Bueso—in North's words—from "spilling the beans." In a subsequent meeting with Revell and Jim Michel of State, North argued that Bueso had been involved only tangentially in the plot (which was not the case). His arguments convinced at least one person; in early October Assistant Secretary of State Abrams reversed his department's previous position and agreed that the United States should do whatever it could for the Honduran. The idea at this point was to get the sentence reduced to time served and then deport Bueso to Honduras. Subsequently, there was also an attempt to have the government intervene in a parole hearing in order to obtain his immediate release.

There may also have been an effort to obtain Honduran involvement. The previous April, José Azcona, the newly inaugurated president, had written a letter to his North American counterpart requesting the latter's personal intervention in the case: Could not the charges be dropped or a pardon granted? Two months later, a second letter was sent through Attorney General Edwin Meese. (The first had been blocked by aides who did not want Reagan involved.) The message was essentially the same: Bueso Rosa deserved leniency. His record was otherwise unblemished, and it would be a pity to deprive both Honduras and the United States of his "valuable services." These activities provoked some nasty infighting within the bureaucracy as officials from the State and Justice Departments and the FBI protested such interference. In the end, the Justice Department—over the objections of the prosecution—asked that Bueso be transferred to a minimum security prison.

One of the mysteries surrounding this affair was why so many people were anxious to have Bueso Rosa freed. At one time or another, at least eight senior officials or former officials intervened in the case: North, Poindexter (who claimed that President Reagan was interested in helping Bueso), Abrams, the CIA's Dewey Clarridge, the Defense Department's Fred Iklé and Nestor Sánchez, and retired Generals Schweitzer and Gorman. No one ever made a detailed argument why Bueso Rosa deserved leniency. Perhaps, as Frank McNeil suggests, this was partly a case of "Rambo nostalgia"—a willingness to excuse almost anything for someone who was friendly to the United States and its "special projects."[51]

Some of the "songs" that Bueso Rosa might have sung almost certainly had to do with matters that, had they become public knowledge, could have seriously damaged the administration's Central American policy. The journalists Brian Barger and Robert Parry, coauthors of a groundbreaking piece on the contra drug connection, have reported that their sources were concerned that the publicity given to such activities might set back efforts to obtain more military funding for the rebels. By this time, too, Honduras was well along the road to becoming a "narco-state." The military had become deeply involved in trafficking. Drug lords were offering money to political parties while buying businesses and land to launder profits. Yet, in 1983 the Drug Enforcement Administration (DEA) office in Tegucigalpa had been closed. Subsequently, the embassy would repeatedly obstruct efforts by U.S. drug enforcement officials to investigate these matters. Although several law enforcement agencies continued to look into the contra drug involvement, investigators often came away with the feeling that their reports were "going into a vacuum."[52]

During his watch at the SOUTHCOM, General Gorman had repeatedly warned the joint chiefs and the Defense Department about the growing threat that drug cartels posed to U.S. and Latin American security. The administration, however, had other priorities. This was a period in which the State Department routinely channeled "humanitarian assistance" to the contras through companies owned and operated by narcotics traffickers, though information about the drug connection was readily available. During these years U.S. officials tolerated Manuel Noriega's involvement in the drug trade because the Panamanian dictator's support was considered important to the contra program.[53] The war came before everything else. Bueso Rosa was in a position to have named Honduran military officers and contras involved in the narcotics business. That had to be prevented.

Alvarez, who had made a fortune illegally while armed forces chief, was never extradited. Instead, he remained in Miami and was put on the Pentagon payroll as a consultant. In 1986 he was paid US$50,000 for work on a classified "sole-source" study of low-intensity conflict. The previous year he had received an undisclosed sum from the RAND Corporation for a paper on U.S. policy in Central America.[54] In addition, he underwent a religious conversion. He was still a true believer, motivated by "the fatherland, God, and liberty," but now he would replace communism with the devil as the symbol of everything he opposed.

Political Development or Political Decay? The Constitutional Crisis of 1985

The 1985 elections were a landmark of sorts. It had been decades since a duly elected Honduran president had served out his term in office. Successful elections would have provided evidence of a new political maturity and lent strong support to an important part of the rationale behind U.S. policy—namely, that the Reagan administration was helping the Hondurans to achieve democracy. Instead, the public was treated to a comic opera that effectively laid to rest any lingering notions that there was a constitutional process in Honduras or that Honduran politicians could be trusted to place the national interest above their own ambitions.

For months, rumors had been circulating that Suazo Córdova was planning to prolong his term in office. By autumn 1984 his "astute but lubricious manipulations" of the National Party's internal political struggles had "all but stripped" that organization of "any credible opposition platform." According to one North American scholar writing at the time, Suazo "has been able to maintain under his control several National Party deputies, who through the National Electoral Tribunal (Tribunal Nacional de Elecciones—TNE) have been legally recognized as the party's official leaders. Supposedly an autonomous agency with representatives from each of the country's four parties and a judge from the Supreme Court, the TNE itself is controlled by Suazo. Three of the five representatives respond to his wishes (the Liberal and National Party representative as well as the Supreme Court judge). While his methods of influence have varied, there seems to be consensus that the president provides monetary and employment pay-offs to his loyal followers."[55]

But the Nationals were not Suazo's only victims. Without the support of Alvarez, the president had found himself increasingly isolated as his party splintered beneath him. By now there were no fewer than five important factions, each with some measure of popular support. And in contrast to those in the National Party, the Liberal divisions partially reflected differences in program and ideology. Without a credible internal means of resolving these conflicts, they tended to fester and erupt in the kind of fratricidal strife that had plagued the party for years.[56]

Dissidents now accused the National Electoral Tribunal and the party's executive council of favoring Suazo's rodista faction in the selection of the Liberal candidate for the 1985 presidential elections. Many had been infuriated by the declaration of the rodistas' secretary general that the most formidable member of the Liberal opposition, José Azcona Hoyo, had no chance of becoming the party's nominee. The president's announcement that he would back the unpopular former minister of the presidency, Carlos Flores Facussé, only added fuel to the fire. The assumption was that Suazo wanted to be the power behind the throne. When in the aftermath of the assassination plot the government began to lash out at both the National and Liberal oppositions, the stage was set for a broad-based alliance designed to prevent the president from imposing his will on the electoral process.

By the end of 1984 there was a widespread feeling that Suazo had to be stopped. Economic crisis, human rights violations, corruption, incompetence, and now a thinly disguised effort to perpetuate himself in office had all but destroyed the government's legitimacy. Wags joked openly about the "buzzards" (actually grackles) that perched on the roof of the Presidential Palace, dubbing them the "presidential honor guard." Toward the end of December these various currents of discontent found expression in an unprecedented manifesto issued by an ad hoc group of distinguished Hondurans from all four political parties. The declaration called for (1) respect for the constitutional mandate prohibiting reelection, (2) an end to intervention in the internal affairs of political and social organizations, (3) punishment of those who had committed crimes against the national treasury, (4) party primary elections, (5) strengthening of agencies responsible for ensuring an honest electoral process, and (6) respect for the separaion of powers of the three branches of government.

These demands went far beyond "facade democracy" to insist on substance as well as form. As matters stood, there were no procedures for internal party democracy. Various factions simply called conventions in the name of the entire party, the legality of which would then be challenged by those who had been left out. In turn, court rulings tended to reflect the influence of the particular faction in power. By the same token, there was no real separation of powers: The autonomy of the Supreme Court had been effectively destroyed by Suazo's practice—contrary to his constitutional mandate—of directly appointing the justices. And since congressional candidates were usually selected by the dominant party leaders, Suazo had been able to maintain control over the Liberal majority and even, through his power to grant official recognition (by means of the National Electoral Tribunal) and other favors, to co-opt some of the National Party "opposition."[57]

Now, however, all this was changing. In January the Liberal Party's central executive committee vowed to expel any member who joined a proposed coalition against the president and threatened to expel the dissident M-LIDER (Movimiento Liberal Democrático Revolucionario) faction. By now Suazo was frantically manipulating the internal procedures of the rodistas to block his opponents from the nomination. In February he convened an "extraordinary assembly," attended mostly by his cronies, in his hometown of La Paz. In a move that stunned even veteran observers, the gathering nominated Oscar Mejía Arellano as the Liberal Party's candidate. Flores Facussé was out.[58]

At the time, M-LIDER's Carlos Roberto Reina remarked that "the ways of manipulating candidates have gone from the dramatic to the tragic, to the ridiculous, and finally will end in the comic."[59] He was right. Suazo's maneuvers brought howls of indignation from José Azcona and Efraín Bú Girón (the latter being president of Congress and also a presidential aspirant). Suazo now moved to preempt any appeal that they might make to the central executive committee by removing that body's president and secretary general. (Both had favored Bú Girón.) Two of Suazo's closest supporters were named to replace them. When the president of the committee objected, he was expelled from the rodistas. When the followers of Azcona and Bú Girón occupied the committee's offices in protest, Suazo sent troops to surround the building.

Thwarted by Suazo's maneuvers, the opposition rallied around the banner of electoral reform. Some Liberal and National Party dissidents joined the leaders of the Christian Democratic Party and the PINU in forming an umbrella group. Reforms were proposed that would have established party primaries, provided state subsidies for the various parties' election expenses, and facilitated the registration of new parties. Had they been adopted, the provisions would have permitted coalitions within the Liberal Party that might have broken Suazo's control. Moreover, factions could have split off and formed independent parties and received funds to do so. But the dissidents lacked the two-thirds vote in Congress to override a presidential veto. Consequently, a move was launched to restructure the Supreme Court with a view to readjusting the balance of power within the National Electoral Tribunal, where Suazo was still dominant. Bú Girón accused the court's president of having violated the law and abandoned his legal responsibilities by campaigning for Mejía Arellano. He then formed a congressional committee to investigate the "disastrous" administration of justice in the country and called upon the court's president and several other justices to explain themselves. Instead, the court ruled the congressional investigation unconstitutional, accused Bú Girón of treason, and launched an investigation of its own—into *congressional* corruption.

The country now descended into what can only be described as—politically speaking—a civil war. On 28 March Congress accused the chief justice and four of his colleagues of bending the electoral laws in Suazo's favor. By a vote of fifty to twenty-nine, the lawmakers dismissed the offending judges and appointed replacements. In turn, Suazo denounced the move as a "technical coup" and ordered the arrest of the new justices. The Supreme Court building was surrounded by troops. The new chief justice, Ramón Valladares Soto, was arrested; the others went into hiding. When the administration made tentative moves to charge the rebellious legislators with treason, Congress countered with an amnesty decree covering the deputies and the new judges. Needless to say, Suazo vetoed the measure. The legislators also approved the proposed electoral reforms, but these too were vetoed. Finally, in yet another display of indifference to the popular will, the dominant rodista clique called the party's national nominating convention two days earlier than scheduled and rubber-stamped Mejía Arellano as the Liberal nominee.

Little of this activity was in accord with the constitutional rules of the game. But then, in Honduras, constitutions are made to be broken. Constitutional procedures had not been followed in the establishment of the CREM or the removal of Alvarez, and they would be similarly ignored three years later when the Honduran drug czar, Ramón Matta Ballesteros, would be forcibly extradited to the United States. Although Congress had the right to appoint Supreme Court justices, it was by no means clear that it could remove them. Thus the Christian Democrats and the PINU, though quite willing to provoke a crisis over electoral reform, had opposed the dismissal of the justices. The constitution, they proclaimed, should not be sacrificed on the altar of partisan interests. Suazo and his followers were now hopelessly deadlocked with the Azcona and Bú Girón factions. Neither side was willing to compromise. Indeed, each was trying to intensify the confrontation by appealing to the armed forces to intervene on its behalf. Military intervention, however, was a touchy thing. The embassy made its position clear: The consolidation of democracy was its "number one priority," and this required elections. If the army interfered, it would be much more difficult to sell the American public and Congress on further aid. Negroponte and his deputy, Shep Lowman, repeatedly delivered this message, as would Negroponte's successor, John Ferch. In the weeks that followed, such arguments would help López Reyes control the commanders who favored "extraconstitutional action."

Still, the military could not remain uninvolved. As the situation continued to deteriorate, it assumed a posture of "active neutrality." In practice, this meant that it tried to balance one side against the other. Initially, López Reyes seemed to back Suazo. In a radio interview on 15 April, he had refused to support the dissidents and threatened to take "radical measures" should the stalemate continue. Yet, although the army complied with the president's order to surround the Supreme Court, only one of the new justices was arrested; the others were allowed to flee into hiding. More important, when Suazo threatened to declare a state of siege, the military refused to support him. López Reyes was walking a tightrope, leaning to one side and then the other in a calculated display of evenhandedness designed to preserve his institution's professional and "democratic" image and enable it to perform the crucial tasks of mediation that lay ahead.

It was a masterful performance. In April a new and potentially more explosive element had appeared. What had begun the previous month as a squabble among traditional politicians was transformed into a broad social movement encompassing the working class and the peasantry. A coalition of labor and campesino groups now demanded the restructuring of the Supreme Court, the release of Chief Justice Valladares, and electoral law reform, including party primaries. A general strike was threatened. On May Day thousands of demonstrators took to the streets. López Reyes now tilted to the left, seeking to co-opt these forces. In mid-April, he had opened discussions with selected labor and peasant groups in an attempt to find a solution to the "institutional breakdown" that had occurred.

Toward the end of the month, the chief of staff, Colonel Efraín González, declared that López's remarks of 15 April had been misinterpreted: The unions' demands were actually quite moderate, and the politicians should carefully consider them.

Slowly, a grand compromise was emerging. As the discussions dragged on, others—including the church and the political parties—were brought into the process. In the end, the army would reach agreements with the leading factions of both the Liberal and the National Party. On 20 May, following marathon negotiations at Toncontín Air Base, a settlement was signed by eleven members of the Liberal Party, eight members of the National Party, three Christian Democrats and three members of the PINU, fifteen worker and peasant leaders, and a representative of the armed forces. The plan, which came to be known as the Air Force Pact or Option B, was to allow all of the candidates' names to appear on the ballot. The candidate of each party who received the most votes would become the party's nominee and would be credited with all of the votes cast for the various candidates of that party. Option B effectively defused the crisis by eliminating the possibility that "official" candidates could be imposed on the rank and file. As part of the compromise, the imprisoned chief justice was released and the arrest warrants for the other judges were dropped. All five "congressional" justices withdrew from the court, as did all but one of the judges whom they had replaced. (The old chief justice remained in his post.) In turn, Congress appointed four new judges.

In the short run, at least, the settlement did not contribute much to the cause of electoral reform. With their own candidacies ensured, Azcona and Bú Girón abandoned their support for more substantive changes. The issue of primaries was postponed until after the elections. Instead, the deputies amended the electoral code so as to increase (from 82 to 134) the number of seats in the next Congress, thus enhancing their own chances of remaining in office. Again, there were questions as to the constitutionality of some of these measures, but, as usual, these were conveniently overlooked. The legislators seemed more interested in dividing up the 7.5 million lempiras appropriated to help finance the campaigns and in establishing an extraordinarily complicated formula for allocating congressional seats among the various lists of candidates.

The effect of these arrangements was to enlarge the field of candidates without significantly broadening the spectrum of political opinion. The National Party aspirants were all staunch conservatives, while the most important Liberals—Azcona, Bú Girón, and Mejía Arellano—were center-right.

While the M-LIDER candidate, Carlos Roberto Reina, was a social democrat, he had no chance of winning. Similarly, the Christian Democrats and the PINU remained marginal parties with little popular support. (Nor, given the new election-financing arrangements, which favored the large parties over the small, did this situation seem likely to change.) As in the past, the most influential factions and politicians were perfectly willing to sacrifice the country's fragile constitutional stability for the sake of their own aggrandizement. And, as in the past, it was the military and the gringos, rather than the civilian politicians, who remained the ultimate arbiters of Honduras's political destiny.

Elections Honduran-Style: The Politics of Surrealism

But there was more to come. The weeks following the May settlement witnessed a growing atomization of Honduran political institutions. By the time the National Electoral Tribunal met to decide which candidates were to be allowed on the ballot, there were eighteen presidential hopefuls, representing nineteen political movements. From this field, nine were selected. The campaign that followed was chaotic. The *suazocordovistas* challenged Azcona's nationality and tried to obtain his disqualification. In turn, the *azconistas* challenged Suazo's candidate, Mejía Arellano, on grounds that he had briefly served as interim president in 1983, when Suazo was receiving medical care in the United States. (The constitution prohibits anyone who has previously "exercised executive authority" from seeking the presidency.) Bú Girón's running mate, Ramón Valladares, was disqualified for having recently served as chief justice of the Supreme Court. (In fact, he had been arrested before he could take office.) The eligibility of the leading National Party candidate, Rafael Leonardo Callejas, was questioned because of alleged corruption when he was minister of natural resources in the 1970s. The candidacy of Juan Pablo Urrutia, oft-denounced as Suazo's man in the National Party, was blocked by the party's central committee until he accounted for US$87,000 that had disappeared while he was the committee's president a few years before. The Liberal Party's social democratic faction, M-LIDER, found that its official roster of candidates had mysteriously "disappeared" after being handed in to the party's central executive committee. About this time, its offices were burglarized.

In this increasingly surrealistic context, Suazo continued to weave his web of intrigue. On 22 August Walter López revealed that high-ranking military officers had been approached by officials from both major parties proposing that a coup be launched and Suazo's tenure extended for two more years. A month later, the president's supporters introduced a motion in Congress to restructure that body as a constituent assembly: The elections would be postponed for as long as two years while those clauses in the constitution that dealt with such matters were rewritten. Within minutes, fistfights had broken out on the floor, prompting General López to phone the president of Congress a warning that such behavior would not be tolerated.

Meanwhile, Suazo had begun to put pressure on Washington. On 10 October a privately owned plane loaded with nonlethal aid to the contras was seized at Toncontín Airport. The Hondurans had been issuing warnings about such activities ever since the U.S. Congress had authorized US$27 million in "humanitarian" assistance the previous summer; now they were taking action. The move was indicative of the schizophrenic nature of Honduran policy: At the same time that the government denied the guerrillas' presence, it had made private arrangements with their supply officers to keep the aid flowing. Unfortunately, Mario Calero, who was running the operation for his brother, Adolfo, had the bad judgment to allow an NBC television crew to come along for the ride. Although the contras needed the publicity, the presence of the crew placed the Hondurans in an untenable position. The government could no longer "plausibly deny" the guerrillas' presence; it had become trapped in its own web of deceit.

To make matters worse, at the end of the month *El Tiempo* made public what had long been an open secret in the capital—that the contras' "main center of military instruction and logistical support" was located a few miles west of Toncontín. The facility, known as the Fifth School Supply Center (La Quinta), had recently been expanded to accommodate the anticipated US$27 million in aid. In addition to training and storage facilities, the base had a helicopter launching pad (frequently used, according to witnesses) and a recording studio for the rebels' 15 September radio station on Mount Picacho.[60]

La Quinta was quickly closed down, but the damage had been done. Nor were the Hondurans the only ones caught in the lie. In early October, in his first press conference, the new U.S. ambassador, John Ferch, had assured everyone that there were no contras in Honduras. These revelations did nothing for his credibility. He now faced the task of getting the supply plane released and the aid moving again. This proved difficult, for Suazo viewed these issues as tools for extracting new concessions. Earlier, at a "very private dinner" at the home of Flores Facussé, the president had proposed to Ferch that the elections be postponed and that he, Suazo, continue in office for the next two years. More aid was demanded. The ambassador had, however, rejected the proposal. Subsequently, he and other embassy officials had repeatedly let it be known that the United States opposed these "unconstitutional" maneuvers. From this point on, relations between Ferch and Suazo were "virtually nil." Suazo sought to wrap himself in the flag of Honduran nationalism, accusing the embassy of interfering in the country's internal affairs.[61] After 10 October he blocked the flow of supplies to the contras altogether, hoping that the U.S. commitment to the rebels "would be stronger than some incomprehensible fastidiousness about the Honduran Constitution."[62]

But the United States held firm, and the election campaign continued. Aid in the amount of US$900,000 flowed into the country in an attempt to ensure that the balloting was successful. As the day of decision drew near, the Nationalists began to have second thoughts about the wisdom of the existing arrangements: Rafael Callejas was on a roll, and there appeared to be an excellent chance that he would obtain more votes than anyone else. Yet, the May compromise had expressly held that the new president would be the leading candidate from the *party* that obtained the most votes. Fearing that victory might be about to be snatched away from them by the more numerous Liberals, the Nationalists began to mutter darkly about the unconstitutionality of the agreement. The constitution, it was noted, stipulated that the presidency would go to the *candidate* with the most votes.

While the Nationalists mulled over their options, others too began to protest: Labor and peasant groups complained about a campaign that was devoid of serious debate. The National Registry charged that 15,000 foreigners had been given citizenship documents, that some voters were being registered twice, and that many on the rolls were deceased. Others claimed that state employees were being forced to contribute to the campaign of Suazo's favorite, Mejía Arellano. It was rumored that ballots existed with Mejía's name already checked.

Indeed, at this point Mejía's campaign was in such disarray that fraud seemed his only hope. An elderly Suazo look-alike, he attracted the public's anger with the president like a lightning rod. Detractors vandalized his posters in Tegucigalpa, splattering his picture with red paint. When he launched a series of advertisements using his initials, OMA, rumors spread that the letters stood for "Once Mil Arrugas" (Eleven Thousand Wrinkles), "Organización Mundial de Ancianos" (World Organization of Senior Citizens) or "Otro Muerto Andando" (Another Walking Corpse). Things got so bad that Suazo eventually arranged to have the photograph of the deceased Liberal hero Modesto Rodas put on the ballot in place of Mejía's, calculating no doubt that illiterate peasants might cast their ballots believing that they were voting for Rodas.

The president used every means at his disposal to promote his candidate. Mejía's propaganda could be seen prominently displayed in government buildings, including ministerial offices, the Central Penitentiary, and FUSEP headquarters. Once, Suazo used a borrowed U.S. military helicopter to drop leaflets on a Callejas rally accusing the Nationalist candidate of being a "sodomite with AIDS." When the *Miami Herald's* Shirley Christian asked the embassy's Cresencio Arcos to comment, Arcos replied that "the Marxists may have taken Nicaragua but the Marx brothers took Honduras."[63]

It had been that kind of a campaign. Huge amounts of money had been spent (reportedly, more than 6 million lempiras by the Callejas camp alone).[64] For weeks the public had been subjected to an unceasing barrage of propaganda. Fourteen persons had died in political brawls. The charges and personal invective continued right up to the final day of campaigning, prompting the church to issue a plea for sanity. In a rare display of class for a politician, Callejas announced that he would not contest an anticipated decision by the National Electoral Tribunal to uphold the terms of the May compromise. Subsequently, the board affirmed the validity of Option B, and the elections were held as scheduled.

On 24 November Hondurans flocked to the polls in an atmosphere that can only be described as carnival. Liberals wore red clothing and Nationalists blue in symbolic identification with their parties. Private cars and public transportation decorated with party banners honked their way to the polls. Some confusion arose when the U.S.-supplied invisible ink into which voters dipped their little fingers to prevent multiple voting did not darken immediately. As the process continued, however, fears of fraud gradually subsided.

In spite of all the charges there is little to indicate that the elections were anything but honest. The final results were as ambiguous and controversial as had been feared: Callejas won a clear plurality of the vote, 42.6 percent to Azcona's 27.5 percent, but the combined tally of Liberal votes came to 51.1 percent. Under Option B, Azcona had won. There was again some talk of challenging the constitutionality of the May compromise, but in the end the Nationalists decided not to do so. They would almost certainly have lost. Callejas had already pledged to respect the election results, and to have plunged the country into another crisis would have risked alienating the military and the embassy (whose overriding interest was political stability) and placed enormous strains on the already tattered fabric of Honduran democracy.

In any case, it was unnecessary. The *nacionalistas* had emerged united behind a single leader, Rafael Callejas, who had established himself as the most popular politician in the country and the early favorite to win the 1989 election. They controlled the largest single bloc (63) of congressional deputies. Because the legislative seats in each municipality went to the party of the winning presidential candidate in that municipality, Azcona could be confident of controlling only a minority of votes (46 out of 134). The implications were not lost on close observers: The president would be severely limited in his ability to set and realize a legislative agenda. To pass bills, he would have to be continually making pacts with other factions. His administration would be plagued by deadlock and inertia.

It was with this in mind that Azcona early on made an agreement (a *"pactito"*) with the Nationalists giving them control of the Supreme Court and half of the other judicial appointments, foreign service jobs, congressional vice presidents and secretaries, and directors of autonomous institutions in return for the right to choose his own cabinet (except for two Nationalists) and the president of Congress. Most important, a gentleman's agreement was reached that would enable him to submit legislation without constant fear of defeat.

This was a typically Honduran arrangement and had more or less predictable results. The last agreement of this kind that had been attempted—the national unity pact of the early 1970s—had been woefully unsuccessful, the two parties having taken advantage of the occasion to divide the spoils of office between them. Azcona's bargain seemed more of the same. The only thing it really ensured was that judges would continue to be selected on the basis of political loyalty rather than competence and that land reform would remain largely unimplemented, since the conservative National Party judges would be in an even better position to obstruct it. Nor did the Azcona cabinet offer much reason for optimism. The military selected the foreign and defense ministers. (Foreign Minister Carlos López

Contreras was a cousin of López Reyes.) Most other positions went to the president's longtime friends and supporters. In the uncharitable words of one scribe, "Most of the members of this 'new' cabinet, with few exceptions, bring with them a history of incompetence in past government positions."[65] Factionalism, corruption, incompetence, and stalemate appeared destined to continue.

As for his relations with the Honduran military and the embassy, Azcona appeared to be, if anything, even more dependent than his predecessor. Among the problems he inherited were a bankrupt economy, growing peasant and labor unrest, continuing human rights abuses, a politically powerful armed forces that had become dependent on U.S. aid, and a guerrilla war against Nicaragua that was creating serious socioeconomic disruption in southern Honduras. Though he had criticized the rebels' presence in the past, Azcona now seemed willing to allow them to continue their operations. Nor would there be any halt to the almost continuous U.S. military exercises in the country. Indeed, no sooner was the new president in office than it was announced that the United States would build yet another airfield, this one only 30 kilometers from the Nicaraguan border.

The Zúniga Affair and the Fall of Walter López

The civilian arena was not the only place in which the politics of surrealism was being enacted. Intrigues were also consuming the armed forces. The military remained deeply divided by service, rank, generation, personality, and politics, and by autumn 1985 subterranean rumblings could once again be detected. In September, the battered and decomposed body of the former army major Ricardo Zúniga Morazán was found in an unmarked grave in Danlí, near the Nicaraguan border, with a steel file driven into the heart.

This was no ordinary murder. Zúniga was the son of Ricardo Zúniga Agustinus, the long-time éminence grise of Honduran politics. Unlike his father, however, "Tito" had been an idealist. In 1982, he had been a liaison officer between the Honduran army and U.S. military attachés in the embassy. In this capacity he had come to resent the overbearing North American influence on Honduran political life. He believed that the Reagan administration's policies were turning the country into a "whorehouse." Although no friend of the Sandinistas, he regarded the contras as reactionaries and incompetents who could not hope to gain the popular support necessary to win their war. He was disgusted with the corruption he saw around him, the lack of professionalism in the Honduran armed forces, and the human rights abuses of Alvarez and his successors.

Zúniga had made his views known both in military circles and in public, in the process making powerful enemies. In interviews with U.S. reporters he had charged that the United States was turning a blind eye to these abuses and perhaps even encouraging them. As the representative of over twenty young reform officers (lieutenant colonels and majors from the sixth and seventh promotions) seeking to break the embassy's grip over Honduran politics, he had traveled to Washington in 1984 and 1985 to meet with members of the U.S. congress, their aides, and other contacts. The stories he recounted were hair-raising: Zúniga spoke of CIA bribes paid to key officers to maintain their support for the contras. He claimed that Battalion 3-16, the special security unit set up by Gustavo Alvarez with U.S. assistance, had gone far beyond its ostensible mission of rooting out Salvadoran and Nicaraguan gunrunners to become involved in the kidnapping and murder of dozens of Hondurans thought to be subversive. He argued that some low-level CIA personnel had known of these killings and that contras were being used as gunmen. He wanted to get the Nicaraguans out of Honduras and back into their own country so that they would not be "hanging around Tegucigalpa" trying to intimidate Honduran officers who did not support their cause. (Zúniga and several others had received death threats.) He also wanted to limit the presence and influence of the CIA.[66]

Not surprisingly, word of these activities got back to the high command. Zúniga was cashiered and for a brief time held under barracks detention. He refused to be intimidated, however, and continued to act as an informal adviser to the young officers until his disappearance in August.

There was, of course, an investigation. According to the official report on the incident, Zúniga had been murdered by an exiled Cuban businessman who had owed him money. But this satisfied few. For one thing, some 350,000 lempiras was still owed to the Zúniga family.[67] The Cuban had had nothing to gain financially by the killing. Moreover, the body had been found in an area where there were contra camps, and there were Nicaraguan accomplices involved. Then, too, Zúniga had been savagely tortured. Had his killers perhaps been trying to extract information? If so, about what? Answers were never provided. Indeed, as time passed and the accused was not brought to trial, new questions arose. It became clear that the Cuban had powerful protectors. Even the Zúniga family, with all its influence in the military, might prove incapable of bringing the accused to justice.

This was almost certainly a political killing: Zúniga knew too much, and he was talking. He had to be silenced. After he had been forced out of the military, some of his colleagues had been warned that they might be next. In an incident earlier that year, the high command had attempted to send one of the group's most influential members into diplomatic exile. The move had set off a fierce struggle in which the junior officers had prevailed. The transfer order was withdrawn. Now, however, these tensions reemerged as some in the Zúniga circle threatened to retaliate for the murder.

As the maneuvering grew more intense, the CIA became involved. The agency had been taken by surprise by the ouster of Alvarez. Determined that this would not happen again, it had penetrated Honduran military security, maintaining telephone taps and other surveillance.[68] In the process, it had been closely monitoring the activities of the young officers. On the assumption that they constituted a threat to U.S. policy, agency operatives sought to weaken and isolate them while strengthening the position of their seniors in the fifth promotion. In December, matters came to a head: The young nationalists were planning a barracks revolt but hesitated just long enough for the senior officers and the CIA to strike first. A preemptive purge was launched, with the most dangerous dissidents being removed from key army posts.[69]

By late January 1986, the purge had consumed even as powerful a figure as Walter López. On 30 January Hondurans were stunned by the announcement that General López would step down. The reasons given varied from "personal motives" to a dispute over the contra presence and fed a wave of speculation. The air was filled with calls from political and social leaders for the general to reconsider. Following a meeting with President Azcona, López declared his willingness to continue in his post "for the good of the country," but it was too late. López's enemies seized the moment. A COSUFFAA meeting was hastily convened. On 1 February it was announced that the general's resignation had been unanimously accepted and was "irrevocable." The matter having thus been decided, López headed for Houston, ostensibly to have a "medical checkup." There he stayed with his family for the next fifteen days—precisely the amount of time needed for a "constitutional" completion of the change of command. After that, he returned to the country, "without penalty or glory."[70]

As usual, neither the civilian president nor Congress had played much of a role in the decision. In effect, they had been presented with a fait accompli. As for the embassy, on the day of his removal López had sent an emissary to Ambassador Ferch asking for U.S. intervention on his behalf. The request had been rejected.[71]

But why had López fallen? The answer is complex. In part, he was the victim of the growing conflict between the fifth and sixth promotions. He owed his job largely to the young officers who had been so instrumental in overthrowing Alvarez. Those elements, however, had just suffered a serious setback, and his identification with them and the policies they represented had made him vulnerable. Moreover, López had taken a stand against Suazo's attempt to remain in office. He had antagonized the CIA and the embassy by obstructing the contra program and the CREM even as he had demanded more aid. Although such actions had enhanced his nationalistic and democratic image and brought him popular support, they had alienated some of the most senior officers in the armed forces. These elements, among the most reactionary and corrupt in the military, supported the contras and were subservient to North American policy. Over the years, Suazo had ensured their loyalty through hundreds of thousands of dollars in bribes. Their ascendancy, supported by elements in the CIA, boded ill for the future.

Yet, there was more behind López's ouster than a conflict between military generations or North American intervention. The armed forces were suffering from the same bureaucratized anarchy that was afflicting civilian institutions. López's critics included members of the sixth promotion as well as older officers. Some discontent was policy-based, some a matter of personality conflicts and service rivalries. There had long been bad blood between the army and the powerful air force. López, of course, came from the latter. He had been supported by many as a transitional replacement for Alvarez because no acceptable leader could be found in the army. After almost two years in office, however, he had not resolved what many reformers considered the most pressing issues of the day: The contras were still in Honduras; there had been no progress on the border dispute with El Salvador. Now, moreover, the government had apparently agreed to amendments to the 1954 Military Assistance Agreement with the United States that some felt would compromise national sovereignty.

For some time this discontent had been bubbling upward in the form of disrespectful and undisciplined talk and behavior. By late 1985, rumors of rebellion found their way into the local press: One of the most active and nationalistic of the young officers, Lieutenant

Colonel Mario Amaya, had refused transfer to the Fifth Battalion in the remote and primitive zone of La Mosquitia. The assignment was widely interpreted as an attempt by López Reyes to isolate Amaya from his allies in the fifth and sixth graduating classes. At the same time, the general was maneuvering to perpetuate himself in power by gaining greater control over military assignments and promotions. Already, indeed, he had announced his intention to remain in office a year beyond his designated term. Such actions reminded some of his former supporters of Gustavo Alvarez. Some of them now joined forces with the so-called "Group of Iron"—a hard-line conservative faction in the COSUFFAA—and withdrew their support. Thus, as in the case of Alvarez, López Reyes had succeeded in causing diametrically opposed elements to join forces against him.[72]

The precipitating event occurred on the eve of Azcona's inauguration. On that day, López made the fatal mistake of sending a confidential memo to the new president outlining the rampant corruption in the officer corps. Azcona, in a fit of self-righteousness, revealed the document to others who, in turn, "told the crooks." Shortly thereafter, López was ousted.[73]

Notes

1. Interviews with John Negroponte, 13 July 1988, and Gustavo Alvarez Martínez, 16 March 1986.

2. Alvarez interview; Longino Becerra, *Cuando las Tarántulas Atacan* (Tegucigalpa: Editorial Baktún, 1987), pp. 263-264; *La Prensa*, 6 April 1984.

3. Negroponte interview; interview with Shepard Lowman, 19 July 1988; conversations with CIA personnel in Tegucigalpa. Some reports claim that Walter López informed Negroponte of the impending coup, but we are skeptical. First, numerous sources, including Negroponte himself, deny it. Secondly, given the crucial importance of maintaining secrecy, it is unlikely that López would have jeopardized the success of the operation by notifying the U.S. ambassador, especially when he could not have been sure of Negroponte's reaction. Third, the subsequent development of their relationship strongly suggests that López did not regard Negroponte as a confidant. Indeed, quite the opposite. He seemed to relish keeping the ambassador in the dark.

4. Negroponte and Lowman interviews; interview with Cresencio Arcos, 14 July 1988.

5. *El País*, 6 April 1984; interview with Ubodoro Arriaga, 27 February 1989.

6. *New York Times*, 8 April 1984, confirmed by Ubodoro Arriaga.

7. Leticia Salomón, "La Doctrina de la Seguridad Nacional en Honduras," *Boletín Informativo Honduras,* Special No. 33, February 1988, pp. 12-15; Becerra, *Cuando las Tarántulas Atacan,* p. 263.

8. Richard Lapper and James Painter, *Honduras: State for Sale* (London: Latin America Bureau, 1985), p. 105.

9. Ibid., p. 104.

10. Roy Gutman, *Banana Diplomacy* (New York: Simon and Schuster, 1988), p. 190.

11. Ibid., pp. 191-192.

12. *New York Times,* 10 June 1984.

13. Ibid.

14. *El Tiempo,* 14 September 1983.

15. *New York Times,* 9 October 1984.

16. Arriaga interview; *La Prensa,* 6 December 1984.

17. "U.S.-Honduran Relations on the Eve of Dr. Suazo's Visit," May 1985.

18. *New York Times,* 23 January 1985.

19. NSC memorandum from Oliver North and Raymond Burghardt to Robert C. McFarlane, "Approach to the Hondurans Regarding the Nicaraguan Resistance," 11 February 1985; memorandum from McFarlane to George Shultz, Caspar Weinberger, William Casey, and John Vessey, "Approach to the Hondurans Regarding Nicaraguan Military Build-up," 12 February 1985.

20. Suazo's words. *La Tribuna* and *El Tiempo,* 17 March 1989.

21. Testimony of Robert C. McFarlane at the trial of Oliver North, in *New York Times,* 16 March 1989. See also the memo from McFarlane to Reagan, "Approach to the Hondurans Regarding the Nicaraguan Resistance," 19 February 1985. The document bears Reagan's initials, indicating his authorization to proceed.

22. Cable from the Secretary of State to the U.S. Embassy in Tegucigalpa, February 1985; memorandum from Robert McFarlane to President Reagan, "Approach to the Hondurans Regarding the Nicaraguan Resistance," no date; NSC memorandum from Oliver North and Raymond Burghardt to McFarlane, 20 February 1985.

23. North-Burghardt NSC memo to MacFarlane, 20 February 1985; McFarlane, "Approach to the Hondurans," n.d.

24. NSC memorandum from Robert Kimmitt to Nicholas Platt, n.d.

25. *Miami Herald,* 8 April 1989.

26. The document was drafted by attorneys for Oliver North and the Iran-contra prosecutor and was reviewed by the State Department before it was made public. Subsequently, however, State questioned its accuracy. Ibid., 1 May 1989.

27. *La Tribuna,* 17 March 1989.

28. *Miami Herald,* 8 April 1989.

29. Thus, for example, all of the participants at the 7 February meeting of the Crisis Pre-Planning Group agreed that "our expediting these items is conditional on continued Honduran support for the resistance." NSC memo for McFarlane from Oliver North and Raymond Burghardt, 15 February 1985.

30. McFarlane, "Recommended Telephone Call," 25 April 1985.

31. Testimony of McFarlane at the North trial. *New York Times,* 16 March 1989.

32. Cable from John Negroponte to Robert McFarlane, "President Suazo's Telephone Conversation with President Reagan," 26 April 1985.

33. Testimony of John D. Negroponte before the Senate Foreign Relations Committee, as reported in *La Tribuna,* 12 June 1989. Predictably, General López denied the charge. See his letter to Negroponte, in *Boletín Informativo Honduras,* No. 98, June 1989, p. 3.

34. Cable to the secretary of state, May 1985.

35. McFarlane, "Meeting with Honduran President Suazo," 21 May 1985. Again, that controversial phrase! In January, it had appeared in a North memo to McFarlane regarding attempts to get Guatemalan support for U.S. policy. It also showed up in the document of "admitted facts" in the North trial (in reference to the mysterious emissary who may or may not have been sent in early 1985). It was, apparently, a popular concept that everyone but George Bush understood.

36. Cable to the Secretary of State, "U.S.-Honduran Relations on the Eve of Dr. Suazo's Visit," May 1985.

37. *New York Times,* 18 May 1989.

38. Theodore Draper, *A Very Thin Line* (New York: Hill and Wang, 1991), p. 109.

39. *Miami Herald,* 19 May 1989.

40. Lowman interview.

41. This conclusion was disputed by the 1984 report of the Honduran Committee for the Defense of Human Rights. But the committee is highly politicized, and serious questions have been raised about the integrity of its reports. Both Americas Watch and Amnesty International accept that the situation did improve under López; see, for example, the former's *Human Rights in Honduras After General Alvarez* (February 1986).

42. *El Tiempo,* 1 August 1984.

43. Ibid., 31 December 1984.

44. Shepherd, "Six Keys to the Understanding of Current United States-Honduran Relations," Prepared Statement before the Subcommittee on Military Installations and Facilities, U.S. House of Representatives, 28 March 1984, p. 10.

45. This is sensitive information from someone who was present at some of these meetings. Although such testimony is by its very nature difficult to confirm through multiple sources, we have always found this individual to be reliable.

46. *Central America Report,* 10 January 1986; U.S. Senate Foreign Relations Committee, Subcommittee on Terrorism, Narcotics, and International Operations, *Drugs, Law Enforcement, and Foreign Policy* (Washington, D.C.: U.S. Government Printing Office, 1989), pp. 37-38.

47. Deposition of Paul Gorman, 22 July 1987, in Senate Select Committee on Secret Military Assistance to Iran and the Nicaraguan Opposition and House Select Committee to Investigate Covert Arms Transactions with Iran, *Report of the Congressional Committees Investigating the Iran-Contra Affair,* Appendix B (Washington, D.C.: U.S. Government Printing Office, December 1988), p. 10.

48. Frank McNeil, *War and Peace in Central America* (New York: Scribner, 1988), pp. 227-228; also U.S. Senate Foreign Relations Committee, *Drugs, Law Enforcement, and Foreign Policy,* p. 52 .

49. The following is based primarily on McNeil, *War and Peace,* pp. 227-232, 289-290.

50. Quoted in *Metro* (San José), 13 October 1988.

51. See McNeil, *War and Peace,* p. 231.

52. Joel Millman, "Narco-terrorism: A Tale of Two Stories," *Columbia Journalism Review,* September-October 1986, p. 50; *New York Times,* 12 February 1988.

53. U.S. Senate Foreign Relations Committee, *Drugs, Law Enforcement, and Foreign Policy,* pp. 42-49, 87-97.

54. George Black, "The Many Killers of Father Carney," *The Nation,* Vol. 246, No. 3, 23 January 1988, p. 85.

55. Mark B. Rosenberg, "The Current Situation in Honduras and U.S. Policy," Prepared Statement before the Subcommittee on Western Hemisphere Affairs, Committee on Foreign Relations, U.S. House of Representatives, 6 February 1985, p. 6.

56. A detailed account of this factional squabbling may be found in Mario Posas, *Modalidades del Proceso de Democratización en Honduras* (Tegucigalpa: Editorial Universitaria, 1989), pp. 99 ff.

57. Rosenberg, "The Current Situation," pp. 4, 5, 8.

58. According to Flores (personal communication), this was all part of a maneuver by Suazo to extend his term in office. "As I was not in agreement with this game and didn't want to be used, I withdrew."

59. *Central America Report,* 15 March 1985.

60. *El Tiempo,* 31 October 1985.

61. Interview with John Ferch, 23 June 1988; also Lowman interview.

62. Unpublished letter from Shepard Lowman to the *Washington Post,* 29 June 1988.

63. Arcos interview.

64. Aníbal Delgado Fiallos, *Honduras Elecciones 85* (Tegucigalpa: Editorial Guaymuras, 1986), p.69.

65. Susan Jessop, "Azcona Announces 'New' Cabinet," *Honduras Update,* Vol. 4, No. 5, February 1986, pp. 1-2 .

66. Interview with Ricardo Zúniga Morazán, 26 February 1985; see also Joel Millman, "Dead Men Tell No Tales," *Mother Jones*, Vol. 12, No. 3, April 1987, p. 48.

67. Interview with Tita Zúniga (Elizabeth Zúniga de Mazariegos), 8 February 1988.

68. *Central America Bulletin*, Vol. 5, No. 5, March 1986, p. 3. We have also been told this by a U.S. intelligence source.

69. These maneuvers were first reported in the *New York Times* by James LeMoyne (29 September 1985 and 31 January 1986). Several present and former U.S. government officials (including Shepard Lowman and John Ferch) have in conversations cast doubt on this account, but three sources, two Honduran and one North American, who were in positions to know have confirmed its essential accuracy. Though these informants have requested anonymity for reasons of career and "health" (as one of the Hondurans quaintly put it), we are inclined to believe them. Some of this testimony is detailed to the point of being self-incriminating. See also the *Washington Post*, 9 February 1986, and the *Christian Science Monitor*, 19 November 1985.

70. Víctor Meza, "La Caída de Walter López: Significado y Enseñanzas," *Boletín Informativo Honduras*, No. 58, February 1986; *Christian Science Monitor*, 19 November 1985.

71. Interview with John Ferch, 9 April 1990.

72. *El Día* (Mexico City), 5 through 7 February 1986; also conversations with two Honduran officers who were involved.

73. López Reyes to a high-ranking U.S. embassy official (not-for-attribution).

5

The United States and Honduras: From Crisis to Crisis

Fanaticism consists in redoubling your effort when you have forgotten your aim.

—George Santayana

By the mid-1980s the Reagan administration's Central American policy had taken on some of the most lamentable trademarks of the Honduran political culture: deception and self-deception, each reinforcing and perpetuating the other, mendacity as standard operating procedure, rampant factional conflict, incompetence, a penchant for Byzantine intrigue, and contempt for the law. At the root of the pathology was the president himself: Ronald Reagan—an actor turned politician who had stepped into the role of a lifetime. Without peer among U.S. presidents in terms of his skills of public communication, he was also perhaps the least knowledgeable on policy issues. ("Poor dear," smirked Margaret Thatcher, "there's nothing between his ears.")[1] A leading analyst of the administration's arms control policy once remarked that

> The best way to get . . . [his] attention [which tended to drift when confronted with matters of substance] was to suggest to him what he personally should say publicly about a foreign problem or a policy. Then the president would sit up, and his eyes would come back into focus. What he cared about was speeches—particularly his own speeches. He knew that his smooth delivery and easygoing, winning manner were huge assets. He would work at fine-tuning a speech with an enthusiasm that he rarely devoted to other duties.
>
> It was this aspect of Reagan's approach to the presidency that led him to see the announcement of the proposal as an end in itself. If

> the speech worked as a speech, then the policy must be a good one. If the speech came off, the policy could be sustained.[2]

Unfortunately, the obsession with effect led to an extraordinary neglect of truth. All presidents lie or at least distort the truth on occasion, but Ronald Reagan brought to the job an actor's conception of a world in which the line between fantasy and reality was blurred beyond recognition. Just as in the cinema artistic license is routinely used to enhance the impact of the film on the audience, so on the stage of politics Reagan did not hesitate to blend fact with fiction.[3] And neither did those whom he brought into his administration. The philosophy was simple: An ounce of publicity was worth a pound of performance. During these years, audience manipulation through the use of symbols and slogans was carried to unprecedented heights. The truth became a "problem to be solved," and the solution was an art form known as "spin control" (the "spin" being the interpretation that White House public relations experts gave to the news in order to make sure that it "bounced" the desired way).[4] In the process, disinformation became king, and language itself was increasingly drained of meaning. Thus, notwithstanding the *somocista* background of the vast majority of contra commanders and their record of human rights violations, they were routinely described by the administration and its supporters as "freedom fighters" (the "moral equivalent" of the Founding Fathers, in Reagan's unforgettable phrase). Conversely, the Sandinistas, who had virtues as well as vices, were portrayed in tones of monolithic black.

Under the circumstances, it was inevitable that U.S. diplomacy would be heavily laced with duplicity. Whereas the usual purpose of negotiations is to fashion agreements, under the Reagan administration precisely the opposite would be the case: The function of diplomacy would be to *prevent* accords. Time and again, the administration would seek to sabotage Latin American efforts to defuse the crises that were wracking the isthmus. Conflicts that might have been resolved by diplomatic means were perpetuated while the United States pursued the chimera of military victory.

The Sabotage of Contadora

The Reagan administration was, of course, far from monolithic. Within it were pragmatic professionals like George Shultz, Thomas Enders, and Philip Habib, who were genuinely committed to negotiating with the Sandinistas. Though accepting many of the premises of the hard-liners, they were willing to limit U.S. demands for internal change (i.e., the ouster of the Sandinistas) in return for guarantees on national security issues such as limiting the size of the Nicaraguan military and ending the supply of arms to guerrillas in neighboring countries. In contrast, right-wing ideologues like the CIA's William Casey, the State Department's Elliott Abrams, and the NSC's John Poindexter and Oliver North would accept nothing less than the overthrow of the Sandinista government. To them, loyalty to the contras was the litmus test of political correctness.

The president of the United States sets the tone for his administration. Through his appointments and pronouncements, he gives direction to policies even if he does not shape the details himself. In the case of Central America, Mr. Reagan's obsession with the anticommunist struggle gave a decided advantage to the hard-liners (the "war party," as Roy Gutman has called them). Time and again, the moderates found themselves outmaneuvered and neutralized. After mid-1982 they were increasingly marginalized—so much so that after the president's reelection in November 1984 there was a veritable revolution in the policymaking team. The next two years would mark the zenith of the zealots.

It was within this context that the U.S. diplomatic strategy evolved. In January 1983 the foreign ministers of Mexico, Colombia, Venezuela, and Panama had gathered on the small Panamanian island of Contadora to initiate a search for peaceful solutions to the region's mounting crises. Following the meeting, an appeal was issued to all Central American countries to reduce tensions and resolve their differences through dialogue and negotiation. These conflicts, it was stressed, had to be removed from Cold War politics, which only made them worse. Over the next year and a half, Contadora negotiators met periodically to work on a draft treaty. Their efforts presented the Reagan administration with a difficult problem. On the one hand, for political reasons, it could not publicly reject such negotiations. To have done so would have placed on itself the onus of having obstructed the peace process. On the other hand, it was profoundly suspicious of these efforts. The fear was that a settlement might be reached that would leave the Sandinista regime intact and undermine U.S. policy. The participation of Mexico, in particular, was a matter of concern. Under the López Portillo government, that country had embraced the Sandinistas and even (with Venezuela) provided them with petroleum at special prices. Mexico had recognized the Farabundo Martí guerrillas as a "representative political force" that should be allowed to participate in a negotiated solution to the Salvadoran civil war. It had criticized the United States for trying to force-fit the Central American crisis into an East-West frame of reference that distorted the indigenous roots of these conflicts. In turn the Reagan administration had reacted, in the words of one NSC summary paper, by trying to "turn around" the Mexicans and European social democrats, "in the meantime keep[ing] them isolated" while the United States co-opted the negotiations issue by "demonstrating a reasonable but firm approach to negotiations and compromise on our terms."[5]

On 7 September 1984 the Contadora foreign ministers presented a draft treaty for the signatures of the five Central American governments. The initial reaction of the administration was positive. Secretary of State George Shultz praised Contadora's efforts as "an important step forward." He added, however, that Nicaragua had already rejected "key elements" of the plan. Other State Department officials also praised the effort. The draft was not everything the United States wanted, they said, but it was basically sound; naturally, the Sandinistas would never accept it.

Two weeks later the Nicaraguan government announced its readiness to embrace the treaty "without modifications." The State Department was stunned. Almost immediately, it began criticizing the treaty as "unsatisfactory" and "one-sided." Intense consultations with Honduras, El Salvador, and Costa Rica were launched. None of those countries had given any indication that they would refuse to sign, but now, under U.S. pressure, they backed away. In mid-October, Honduran Foreign Minister Edgardo Paz Barnica hosted a meeting in Tegucigalpa to discuss alterations in the treaty. The gathering was not part of the regular Contadora process, and Nicaragua—charging that the United States was manipulating the negotiations—did not attend. The amendments drafted represented a wholesale revision of the accord. Issues that had been discussed and agreed on were raised all over again. The "counterdraft" did not prohibit U.S. military exercises in Honduras; the restrictions on foreign military advisers were modified; the protocol binding the United States to uphold the agreement was eliminated. This time it was the turn of the Nicaraguans to say no.

Administration hard-liners were exultant. In the words of a secret NSC memorandum: "We have effectively blocked Contadora group efforts to impose the second draft to the Revised Contadora Act. Following intensive U.S. consultations ... the Central Americans submitted a counterdraft ... [that] shifts concern within Contadora to a document broadly consistent with U.S.

interests. . . . We have trumped the latest Nicaraguan/Mexican efforts to rush signature of an unsatisfactory Contadora agreement. . . . Contadora spokesmen have become notably subdued recently on prospects for an early signing . . . although the situation remains fluid and requires careful management."[6]

Later, the chief Honduran negotiator at Contadora, Jorge Hernández-Alcerro, would conclude that the Reagan administration had made a serious mistake. Not only had it left the impression that it was dictating policy, but a more flexible position might have resulted in an acceptable agreement. At minimum, the Sandinistas' bluff would have been called. For their part, the Hondurans had taken the talks seriously. First-rate personnel had been assigned to them and detailed preparations made. In truth, their negotiators were far better equipped to deal with the adversary than were their U.S. counterparts.[7]

Any agreement that would have required the United States to accept the continued existence of the Sandinista regime was anathema to the White House. On 23 November the deputy national security adviser, John Poindexter, passed a message to his superior, Robert McFarlane: "Continue active negotiations but agree on no treaty and agree to work out some way to support the contras either directly or indirectly. Withhold true objectives from staffs."[8] This said much about the administration's hidden agenda. The hard-liners viewed negotiations with communists as a snare and a delusion and diplomacy as a way of losing what could be attained by military means. During these years, the United States was engaged in an elaborate exercise in gamesmanship. Time and again, the State Department would resort to the classic technique of obstructionist diplomacy known as the "joker ploy": Demands would be made that the Sandinistas could not possibly accept, ensuring that the negotiations would fail and placing the blame squarely on Managua. When Nicaraguan responses seemed to meet its publicly stated concerns, the United States would simply ignore them or increase its demands.

The fate of the Manzanillo talks was a prime example: Between June and November 1984, at the request of the Contadora countries, the United States and Nicaragua held a series of bilateral meetings, all but one in Manzanillo, Mexico. The U.S. negotiating position was so extreme that it could not be taken seriously. While demanding major concessions from the Sandinistas with regard to the size of their armed forces, the reorganization of their domestic politics, and their relations with the Soviet bloc (all Soviet and Cuban military personnel had to be withdrawn), the Reagan administration offered nothing in return beyond a vague promise to take Nicaraguan actions "into account." Indeed, U.S. envoy Harry Shlaudeman was given strict instructions *not* to explore ways in which differences between the two sides might be narrowed. In the words of one State Department source, "The administration really doesn't want a settlement. . . . No one knows whether the United States should invade Nicaragua, but people don't want to foreclose that option by signing some kind of agreement." Indeed, the hard-liners had opposed even sitting down with the Sandinistas.[9] Washington soon broke off the meetings on a pretext.

Then there was the Reagan "peace plan" of April 1985. Under the guise of promoting negotiations, the president embraced a contra demand for a dialogue with the Sandinistas. Colombian President Belisario Betancur, who had been at the proposal's unveiling and who had initially treated it as a positive development, quickly backed off when it became clear that the plan was nothing more than preparation for war in disguise: If the Sandinistas refused to talk with the contras—as seemed certain—military aid to the rebels would be resumed.

During these months, the White House was locked in a war with Congress over the contra aid program. In late April 1985, Reagan informed the Senate that he planned to resume talks with Nicaragua. Yet, when the legislators acquiesced and granted him the aid he wanted, the promise was abruptly forgotten. In July, the Contadora foreign ministers called on the two sides to resume bilateral talks. The Sandinistas immediately agreed; the United States just as quickly refused.

Meanwhile, though the Contadora talks would continue to drag on, they were losing steam. Within the Reagan administration the hawks were now ascendant, and their priorities were neither negotiations nor containment. In the words of newly appointed Assistant Secretary of State Elliott Abrams, a settlement with Nicaragua was impossible: "It is preposterous to think we can sign a deal with the Sandinistas . . . and expect it to be kept."[10] Washington was repeatedly able to block an accord through a combination of its own efforts and those of its allies in the "Tegucigalpa group" (Honduras, El Salvador, and Costa Rica). Thus, just before the September 1985 gathering of the Contadora foreign ministers, Abrams met with the U.S. ambassadors to Central America to alert them to the need for developing "an active diplomacy in order to hinder the attempts at Latin American solidarity that could be directed against the U.S. and its allies, whether these efforts are initiated by the Support Group [Brazil, Argentina, Uruguay, and Peru], Cuba, or Nicaragua."

Although it was preferred that the Contadora process continue, "a failure would be more desirable than a bad agreement."[11]

In the days preceding the 12-13 September Contadora meeting, Shlaudeman visited the countries of the support group. At the same time, Honduras and Costa Rica echoed U.S. demands that the Sandinistas negotiate with the contras as a prerequisite for an accord. Just prior to the opening of a forty-five-day "permanent session" of Contadora in early October, Secretary of State Shultz met with representatives of the Tegucigalpa group and Guatemala to lay out U.S. positions and concerns. Among other things, he emphasized an "internal reconciliation" in Nicaragua. The United States, he said, would not be bound by any peace agreement that might be signed. In a move that was widely interpreted as an attempt to weaken Contadora and make it more amenable to U.S. pressure, he proposed that the Dominican Republic and Ecuador, both strong U.S. allies, be added to the support group. Two days later, Washington again announced that it would provide military support to Honduras should a conflict with Nicaragua break out. The day before the opening of the "permanent session," Honduras put its armed forces on red alert.

It was within this context that the Panamanian high command on 9 October charged that the United States was involved in a "seditious" plan to include Panama within a "regional operation designed to neutralize and destroy the Contadora Group." About this time, the National Security Council reportedly sent a delegation to the region on a secret mission to persuade friendly governments not to sign an accord.[12] Meanwhile, various North American functionaries let it be known that, come what may, the Reagan administration intended to continue its policy of "pressuring" Nicaragua. Within Contadora, Honduras and El Salvador led the charge. The Sandinistas' position that foreign military maneuvers in the region be prohibited was rejected, and so were their demands for security guarantees against U.S. aggression and for a "reasonable balance" of Central American military forces based on each country's security needs. These were not outrageous conditions. Washington had been using "joint" military exercises in Honduras to intimidate the Nicaraguans, supply the contras, and strengthen the Honduran military in ways that went far beyond the intentions of Congress. Prospects for peace were dependent on *mutual* restraint. One could not expect much from the Sandinistas unless the United States was willing to make concessions—above all, to concede the continued existence of the revolution. But that the White House was unwilling to do. In Reagan's words, the goal was to "remove [the Nicaraguan government] in the sense of its present structure," to make the Sandinistas "say 'uncle' . . . to the rebels."[13] Capitulation, not compromise, was the name of the game. Not surprisingly, the Sandinistas declined to play.

North American Instrumentalism, Honduran Interests, and the Functionality of Conflict

By now the Hondurans had been largely reduced to the status of a U.S. pawn. Though their interests frequently differed from those of Washington and they could often be troublesome, their lack of an alternative to the U.S. economic lifeline severely limited their ability to develop an independent policy. They were too susceptible to bribery and pressure. Moreover, notwithstanding the risks involved, a continuation of the war against Nicaragua was in the interest of Honduran elites and of many ordinary people as well. It ensured a continuing, large-scale influx of North American money that, if it did little to solve the country's socioeconomic problems, at least kept the economy from collapsing.

Meanwhile, fortunes were being made. Much of this assistance was siphoned off by corruption. Later, Vice President Jaime Rosenthal would charge that AID funds were being wasted on a massive scale through mismanagement and graft. By 1986, moreover, the Honduran armed forces were being financed to the tune of US$88.2 million. No one had any illusions about U.S. willingness to continue this largesse under conditions of peace. As with economic aid, much of this assistance was also misappropriated—how much no one will ever know, but the trail led to the very top of the hierarchy. Nor were the funds sent to the contras through Honduras immune from this pilfering. In June 1986, the General Accounting Office (GAO) disclosed that US$1.4 million in "humanitarian" aid had been diverted to the bank accounts of the Honduran high command; additional payments had gone to other officers, leading politicians, and their relatives.[14]

Now, this was nothing new. Before Congress barred the CIA from direct involvement with the contras in 1984, it had been common practice to pay key Honduran officers for their cooperation. But when in August 1986 the legislators approved US$100 million in aid to the rebels, they created a gold-rush atmosphere. The Hondurans scrambled to get into the action. For some time, the Supermercado Hermano Pedro in Comayagüela had been operating as a front for the participation of several officers in contra-supply operations. The supermarket had been the largest Honduran recipient of payments from the US$27 million in "humanitarian" aid that Congress had voted for the rebels in 1985. In May 1986, however, it had been disclosed that the store had been billing the U.S. government for thousands of uniforms that had never been delivered. At the same time, questions were raised about other transactions. One U.S. official with knowledge of the operations conceded that the embassy had tolerated Hermano Pedro's irregular practices as a way of rewarding the Honduran officers involved.[15]

Publicity was the last thing the colonels wanted. In late July 1986 they offered the contra-supply racket to another businessman who, it was expected, would maintain a lower profile than the Hermano Pedro's owner, Rodolfo Zelaya. On 8 August Honduran troops raided and ransacked Zelaya's home, arresting his family and the vigilantes guarding the premises. Outraged, Zelaya accused Colonels Roberto Núñez Montes and Wilfredo Sánchez, the heads of military intelligence and the FUSEP, of mounting the raid to intimidate him into surrendering his business. As a result of denunciations by his allies in the National Party, the armed forces briefly suspended the two officers. Behind the scenes, however, senior officers were already preparing to share future profits, legal and illegal, from the increasingly lucrative sales to the guerrillas. Accepting the inevitable, Zelaya sold out and sought refuge in Miami.

Also during this period there was a struggle for control of the contra arms market. Prior to the 1984 aid cutoff forced by the Boland Amendment, the CIA had handled all weapons purchases directly. After the cutoff, however, a fierce competition had broken out between rival arms dealers. In this struggle, in which millions of dollars were at stake, the main competitors were retired General Richard Secord and two other enterprising former military men, Ronald Martin and James McCoy. In conjunction with the head of Honduran military intelligence, Colonel Héctor Aplícano, and other high-ranking officers, Martin and McCoy set up an "arms supermarket" to service the rebels. Oliver North was able to bypass the Martin-McCoy network by forcing the FDN's Adolfo Calero to receive weapons only from Secord. That, in turn, rankled the Hondurans. In spring 1986, Secord was called in for a chat with the high command. The message was blunt: "From now on you will buy from us." Already Martin, McCoy, and the Hondurans were anticipating the bonanza to come from Reagan's US$100 million aid request. Hundreds of tons of weapons and munitions were pouring into the

Honduran military installation at Aguacate. Unfortunately, these activities offended the sensibilities of the CIA base chief, James Adkins, who smelled drugs. In October 1986, when Adkins and his aides began to purchase weapons with the US$100 million, they refused to buy from the "supermarket." This led to a flare-up between the CIA official and the new Honduran military commander, Humberto Regalado, who almost expelled the American from the country.[16]

Given these temptations, it should not be surprising that Honduran foreign policy was geared to the obstruction rather than the promotion of peace. The interests of Honduran elites, both civilian and military, were clear: War was functional so long as it did not involve *them* and the contras did not become a destabilizing force within Honduras.

During these years, Honduras was turned into an instrument of U.S. policy. Between 1979 and 1986, U.S. military aid increased more than twentyfold. The society became highly militarized. Everywhere uniformed and armed teenagers could be seen guarding office buildings and private residences. Simultaneously, the U.S. presence grew by leaps and bounds. Joint military exercises, often involving massive numbers of U.S. troops, became an almost constant feature of Honduran life. Between October 1981 and August 1987, no fewer than fifty-eight of these operations were conducted. Although the numbers fluctuated, by 1986 there were about 1,200 U.S. military personnel in the country at any given moment. Civilians too participated in the influx. The number of AID projects mushroomed; the Peace Corps contingent became the largest in the world. Increasingly, Honduras began to assume the appearance of an occupied country.

It is difficult to gauge the full effect of this buildup, for official figures usually obscured as much as they revealed. The Honduran military budget was reported to be grossly understated in an effort to hide the drain of these activities on national resources. As late as fall 1983, the U.S. embassy was still trying to maintain the fiction that military expenditures were a mere 6 percent of the budget. Other observers, however, estimated that 15 to 20 percent was more realistic, with much of this being hidden in the education, communications, and presidential budgets.[17]

One of the functions of the "joint" military maneuvers was to provide the Honduran armed forces—and the contras—with much larger amounts of military assistance than U.S. legislators were willing to authorize. In effect, the Reagan administration was making an end run around Congress. Permanent and semipermanent improvements of Honduran military facilities were made. Hardware, supplies, and other necessities were flown in, then left behind after the exercises were over. Most important, the maneuvers provided a pretext for building a U.S. military infrastructure that would have been difficult to finance by other means. By 1986, the United States had spent millions of dollars on military construction projects; a dozen C-130-capable airfields had been built, improved, or proposed, most along the Nicaraguan and Salvadoran borders. (Prior to the exercises, there had been only three C-130-capable airfields in the entire country, and two of those had been civilian. The Honduran air force, of course, had no C-130s.) Two radar stations, one on Cerro La Mole south of the capital and the other on Tiger Island in the Gulf of Fonseca, had been constructed. There were tank traps, fuel storage areas, air intelligence installations, and semipermanent facilities for North American servicemen. Palmerola Air Base, near Comayagua, had become the most important center of U.S. espionage operations in the region. OV-1 Mohawk reconnaissance planes would regularly fly out of it and other bases en route to El Salvador, where they provided government forces with intelligence on guerrilla concentrations and movements. Similar services were provided the contras to help them avoid Sandinista army sweeps. Meanwhile, roads were being constructed to link new bases and airfields with existing highways, towns, and ports or to supply rebels in remote areas of southern Honduras. The airfields at Aguacate, Jamastrán, Puerto Lempira, Rus Rus, and Mocorón became major contra-supply depots.

Not surprisingly, questions of legality arose. In September 1984, the House/Senate Arms Control and Foreign Policy Caucus issued a report entitled *U.S. Policy in Central America: Against the Law?* Among other things, it listed nineteen U.S. and eleven international laws that might have been violated. Most had to do with aid to the contras (the Boland Amendment, in particular, had explicitly prohibited the use of U.S. funds to overthrow the Nicaraguan government); a few, however, involved U.S. construction activities. Nor was this the first time that such issues had been raised. Democratic critics such as Senator James Sasser and Representative Bill Alexander had repeatedly voiced concern about the building of "permanent" military facilities. Suspicions were reinforced by a 1984 GAO report charging the Defense Department with improper use of funds for much of the military construction and training that had been conducted in the preceding two years.[18] Clearly, contingency plans were being made, and Congress was not being adequately informed.

Yet, if Congress was being deceived, it was also a willing dupe. Most members of Congress understood (or at least suspected) where the Reagan administration was heading. All too many chose either to support that policy or to avoid the debate. For such legislators, calculated self-deception had become the order of the day. As in the early years of the Vietnam War, they did not *want* to know too much. The Gulf of Tonkin mentality and the doctrine of "plausible deniability" were alive and well. Congressional "oversight" had taken on a double meaning.

The Zenith of the Zealots

By the mid-1980s the United States had established a formidable, semipermanent military capability in the heart of Central America. U.S. officials were openly discussing an invasion. Indeed, the administration was now using that prospect as a psychological weapon against Congress as well as the Sandinistas. In a classified report to the legislators in May 1985, the president proclaimed that the eventual use of military force "must realistically be recognized" if other alternatives failed. About the same time, Secretary of State Shultz warned the members that if they did not renew aid to the contras they would hasten "the day when the threat will grow, and we will be faced with an agonizing choice about the use of American combat troops." Within some circles, optimism about such an operation was becoming euphoria. An invasion of Nicaragua would be easy. The majority of Nicaraguans would welcome it, as would other Central Americans. The Sandinistas had become so unpopular that the biggest problem would be preventing "severe retribution" against them. In the words of one military officer, "They've lost the support of the people. . . . They'll get their heads chopped off."[19] Such predictions were made of the same stuff as earlier forecasts of a contra victory, but in any case the theory would not be put to the test. To his credit, Ronald Reagan was always much more cautious about committing troops to the region than were the fire-breathers in the "war party." The White House remained wary of congressional and public reaction, and the Sandinistas were not disposed to provide it with a pretext for such an operation.

Unknown to Congress and the public, however, the administration had for months been engaged in an unprecedented effort to evade restrictions on its Central American policy. Evasion of the law, of course, was nothing new. In July 1983 Congress had placed a limit of US$24 million on the amount that the CIA could spend on its

Nicaraguan project. Director Casey's response had been to ask the Defense Department to give the contras US$28 million in weapons and aircraft free of charge. The Pentagon had delivered three small planes and some night-vision equipment before it decided that the arrangement was probably illegal and refused further requests, but by then the agency had decided to step up military action. "Managua by Christmas!" was the rallying cry. When the offensive began, the Sandinistas had been shocked to find that the rebels had acquired a well-equipped navy and air force. CIA "Q-boats" dashed into Nicaraguan harbors and set fuel tanks afire. At least one battle drew a U.S.-crewed helicopter into direct combat with Sandinista gunners. Other agency helicopters strafed Sandinista positions. A rebel-piloted Cessna attempted to bomb the military airfield at Managua International Airport but crashed into the passenger terminal, causing embarrassing civilian casualties. Nicaraguan ports were mined in an effort to disrupt the supply of arms and fuel.

These were, of course, acts of war, and they were not an aberration. During these years proponents of what the media liked to call the "Reagan Doctrine" advocated aiding anticommunist groups throughout the world as a means of combatting Soviet expansionism without having to resort to nuclear weapons or large-scale conventional combat. By mid-decade the CIA would be working on a half-dozen secret wars. Some of these were massive and only formally covert (Nicaragua, Afghanistan, Cambodia, and Angola); others were smaller and hardly noticed at all (Chad, Ethiopia). Behind the rhetoric of the "Reagan Doctrine" and the tactics of low-intensity conflict was the notion of supporting insurgencies against communist governments and counterinsurgencies against communist guerrillas. Since Central America contained both (Nicaragua and El Salvador), it became the main laboratory for experimentation. CIA Director Casey, for one, believed that the stakes were huge and historic. The opportunity had to be seized; the war was too important to be left to politicians. Casey virtually "oozed contempt" for the House and Senate: "He saw no useful role for the intelligence committees and as much as told them so. The congressmen, with little real power to find out what was going on inside the agency, put Casey through long secret hearings, testy sessions that ended in a few minutes of studied camaraderie, after which the legislators shook their heads in wonder and Casey stalked away muttering, 'Assholes.'"[20]

But Congress could not be ignored. Even prior to the uproar over the mining of Nicaraguan harbors, it had become apparent that the legislators would not supply the funding needed for the successful prosecution of the contra war. Alternative sources were needed. One solution was to solicit money from friendly countries. Between 1984 and 1986 Saudi Arabia would provide US$32 million to the rebels' cause. Brunei would contribute US$10 million (which through a clerical error wound up in the wrong Swiss bank account). Taiwan and South Africa would supply smaller amounts. When Congress became aware of these operations, Casey would deny any U.S. involvement. Meanwhile, a young lieutenant colonel on the National Security Council staff was given the task of holding the resistance together, "body and soul." During these years, Oliver North embarked on a wide range of activities on behalf of the rebels. He wooed conservative fund-raisers and put the contras in touch with private citizens willing to make large donations. He advised the guerrillas on strategy, helped them compile shopping lists for weapons, and provided them with highly classified CIA reports and maps. In October 1984, however, with the Boland Amendment, Congress had prohibited the CIA "or any other agency or entity involved in intelligence activities" from spending money in support of the contras "directly or indirectly." The intention was straightforward enough. In the words of its author, Representative Edward Boland, the measure "clearly ends United States support for the war in Nicaragua." There were "no exceptions."[21]

Casey and North found an exception—or, perhaps more accurate, were able to convince themselves that they had found one: The Boland Amendment, they argued, did not apply to the National Security Council, since that agency was not "involved in intelligence" in the same way the CIA was. This was a thin rationale for the continuation of contra-supply activities. (President Reagan's Executive Order 12333, issued in December 1981, had explicitly directed that the NSC "act as the highest Executive Branch entity that provides review of, guidance for, and direction of the conduct of all national foreign intelligence, counterintelligence, and special [covert] activities, and attendant policies and programs.") Nevertheless, it provided at least a semblance of legitimacy. From this point on, the NSC staff—especially North—moved into the gray area left by the congressional restrictions, assuming activities that the CIA was no longer able to undertake itself.

Nevertheless, the Boland Amendment took a heavy toll. Nineteen eighty-five was a difficult year for the contras; after two years of relative success, they were nearly routed. By Christmas they had been driven out of north-central Nicaragua and reduced once again to a cross-border raiding force. The main fighting units were sitting in their Honduran camps "without boots, ponchos, hammocks, and—for many—hope." Arriving columns "looked like prisoners returning from Buchenwald."[22]

It was at this point that a fateful decision was made to channel funds earned from the covert sale of arms to Iran to the contras. For some months the administration had been engaged in a campaign to free U.S. hostages being held in the Middle East. In August 1985 U.S. antitank missiles had been sent to the Khomeini regime through Israel. In January 1986 Amiram Nir, a senior adviser to the Israeli prime minister and the man in charge of Israel's counterterrorism program, met with Ollie North and the newly appointed special assistant for national security affairs, Admiral John Poindexter. At that meeting, Nir suggested that the Iranians be overcharged for the weapons they were receiving and that the profits be funneled to the "freedom fighters" in Nicaragua.

The proposal was enthusiastically received. Both North and Poindexter thought it "a neat idea." Bill Casey was ecstatic, calling the plan "the ultimate irony, the ultimate covert operation."[23] Whether anyone bothered to tell the president remains unclear. Mr. Reagan would later deny it, and North and Poindexter would back him up, but then, these are not very reliable witnesses. Reagan, of course, had a strong personal interest in denial: He could have been impeached, his place in history sullied forever, had a link been established. Later, during Poindexter's trial, the defense would argue that Reagan had authorized the admiral's actions, calling into serious question the veracity of the latter's 1987 congressional testimony.

As for Oliver North, stories of his deceptions are legendary: He had lied to colleagues about having had one-on-one meetings with the president; lied to Poindexter about a telephone conversation with Costa Rican President Oscar Arias in which he had allegedly threatened Arias with a loss of U.S. aid; misled anyone who would listen about his wartime exploits. Parts of his official NSC biography were fabricated. In the words of one colleague, "With Colonel North you could never be certain that what he was telling you was true or was fantasy or was being told you deliberately to mislead you, so my normal modus operandi when receiving information from Colonel North, as I'm sure it was for most other people who knew him for some time, was to take everything with about four grains of salt and try to sort it out from there."[24] Others went farther, suggesting that North was not entirely operating in the world of reality. (He had a history of psychological problems, having been briefly hospitalized in 1974 for "emotional stress.") Perhaps it is best simply to say, with

Theodore Draper, that he "had a touch of fantasy in his makeup that made him overdo, overestimate, and overstate. [He] was a strange combination of the naive, the driven, the fanatical, and the self-deceived. . . . a soldier in a civilian setting, refighting an old war [Vietnam] in new and different circumstances."[25]

As for Reagan's knowledge of the diversion, there are reasons to believe that he knew much more than he let on. The president, after all, had actively participated in fund-raising activities with Colonel North. In February 1985 he had authorized "enticements" for Honduras to aid the contras. Subsequently, he had phoned Suazo Córdova to secure the release of military supplies that were being held up by the Honduran army, and when his request had been granted he had personally approved an increase in aid. Mr. Reagan had been briefed on a clandestine Costa Rican airstrip built by the North network to aid the contras at a time when such assistance was prohibited. He had approved a paramilitary operation to airdrop cannons to the rebels so they could attack a ship bearing arms for the Sandinistas. By his own admission, he had been "involved in the decisions about support to the freedom fighters. It was my idea to begin with." The available evidence, in short, suggests that not only was he kept informed of the contra-supply operation but he occasionally stepped in, when needed, to help.[26]

Still, one cannot entirely dismiss the possibility that Reagan may have been ignorant of the diversion. As the Tower Commission diplomatically noted, the president's "management style" was not one that ordinarily involved him in the details of policy. (This is putting it mildly. On one occasion, when he was governor of California, he had astounded not only critics, but even some of his own advisors, by his inability to tell reporters a single item in his own legislative program.) His own testimony in the 1990 Poindexter trial presented the sad portrait of an old man, hopelessly forgetful and confused: Mr. Reagan could not remember the senior military officer in his own administration; he could not recognize one of the main contra leaders; nor could he recall that Robert McFarlane, one of his closest advisers, a man whom he had seen every day for months at a time, had pleaded guilty to charges of withholding information from Congress. As for the primary conclusion of the Tower report, he could only say wonderingly, "This is the first time I have ever seen that."[27] Perhaps this was a performance—he was after all an actor—but there is enough evidence on the public record to make a plausible case that this president was, in policy matters, simply incompetent.

[Note: At this writing, the special prosecutor's Iran-contra report has not yet been released. It is expected, however, to strongly support the interpretation that Reagan knew about and was deeply involved in these activities.]

But there was another important issue here. For some time, Bill Casey had apparently been toying with the idea that private covert operations could be set up, secretly funded by foreign contributions and arms sales, and run, also in secret, out of the Old Executive Office Building next to the White House. North would testify that it had always been the "intention to make this a self-sustaining operation. There [would] always be something there which you could reach out and grab when you needed it. Director Casey said he wanted something you could pull off the shelf and use at a moment's notice."[28] Since the organization would be "independent of appropriated monies," it would not be accountable to Congress. Nor need its activities have been restricted to Central America. Potentially, it could have been used anywhere in the world.

Of all the ill-advised schemes conceived during the Reagan years, this was perhaps the most dangerous—an invisible government, accountable to no elected official (including, apparently, the president of the United States). Though the plan was never put into effect, by early 1986 the forces that had conceived it had come to dominate Central American policy. That would spell trouble for those who took a more pragmatic approach.

An Envoy's Story: A Cautionary Tale for Doves Living in a Nest of Hawks

John Ferch had come to Honduras as ambassador believing in the Reagan administration's professed interest in negotiated settlements. He had viewed Contadora as more of an opportunity than a threat: The Sandinistas were "panicking," he felt, and under continuing pressure might make major concessions. Moreover, when all the fighting was over, Central Americans would still have to come to terms with their military establishments. Contadora might provide a way to reduce the size and power of those traditionally parasitic organizations so that democracy could have a chance. With this in mind, he had decided early on to adopt a more detached approach to the Honduran military than Negroponte's. He would try to strengthen the civilian government by dealing with Azcona first and only then with the COSUFFAA.[29]

Beyond this, Ferch wanted to change the proconsular image of the U.S. ambassador. Though he had interceded in the Honduran political process to thwart Suazo's machinations and ensure that the 1985 elections were held, his normal style was noninterventionist. Early on, he had instructed one of his aides to "cool it. This is not the John Negroponte show anymore. We don't run this country."[30] He had refused to intervene on López Reyes's behalf in January 1986. He even declined to advise Azcona on cabinet nominations when asked. The problem with U.S.-Honduran relations, he felt, was that there had been too much interference in Honduran affairs. He was determined to treat Azcona with the respect that a head of state deserved. Partly because of this, the two men enjoyed excellent relations, and they quickly came to an agreement on the release of US$67.5 million in aid that had been withheld because of Honduran unwillingness to take certain economic measures advocated by the AID.

The contras were not one of Ferch's priorities. He had known little about the program prior to his arrival. Before leaving Washington, he had tried to pry information out of North with scant success. He was unaware of the supply network being set up by Secord. His own relations with the rebels were minimal. Initially, his doubts about the program led him to adopt a hands-off attitude. In late 1985, however, the CIA station chief informed him that there were rumors in Washington that Ferch opposed the contras, and thereafter he felt obliged to take a more active interest. Around the turn of the year he met Enrique Bermúdez and other rebel leaders for the first time. Subsequently he had breakfast with them on several occasions, always trying to maintain a balance between keeping them at arm's length and keeping current.

This was not quite what Assistant Secretary of State Elliott Abrams had in mind. In contrast to his predecessors for more than a decade, Abrams had "no experience in a diplomatic post abroad, no regional expertise, and no background as a foreign policy professional." However, he did have a "quick mind, a combative manner, and boundless ambition."[31] He reminded some of a roving shark. Over the next several years, he would earn a reputation for ruthlessness and deceit that was extraordinary, even by the predatory norms of Washington. In the process, he would alienate Congress, politicize and divide his own department, and become almost universally despised by Latin Americans.

Abrams wanted to reverse the revolution in Nicaragua. He believed that Ronald Reagan would never leave office with the Sandinistas still in power. He felt that John Ferch was too weak an ambassador to do what had to be done. He was "not proconsular enough"; he did not support the contras. In turn Ferch believed, naively, that he could ignore the rebels; he never quite understood that they were central to U.S. policy. And so like two ships passing in the night, he and Abrams kept talking past one another.[32] Trouble was inevitable.

By October 1985 day-to-day policy toward Nicaragua was being run by a triumvirate. The Restricted Interagency Group (RIG), officially composed of twelve to fifteen members, had in terms of real work been boiled down to three: Abrams, North, and the CIA's Alan Fiers. On 9 December Ferch was called to Washington for a meeting with Abrams. He was told that there was a perception that he did not support U.S. policy. Ferch denied the charge, but the following day he attended a meeting with Abrams, North, and Fiers. The gist of the message was that the RIG wanted someone in control of the contras. By this time Secord's supply operation in Honduras was in motion. Ferch was being tested to see whether he could be trusted, and at the time he dodged the issue. When he returned to Tegucigalpa, he sent Abrams a secret cable indicating his readiness to carry out his instructions—so long as they were put in writing. He never received a response. Later Ferch would conclude that this request was the straw that broke the camel's back. He had no problem with implementing the RIG's instructions—he thought of himself as a "good soldier"—but he did want some assurance that the orders were legal. Abrams's refusal to put them in writing convinced him that they were not. His days as ambassador were now numbered.

An Envoy's Story (Continued): The Holy Week "Invasion"

On 20 March 1986 the House of Representatives rejected Reagan's request for US$100 million for the contras, and the administration panicked. The next day, a Friday, Abrams descended on Toncontín Airport with a "flying circus" to try to reassure the Hondurans. In fact, the latter were not greatly concerned about the vote. The embassy had already assured them that this was only a temporary setback; the contras would not be abandoned. But Abrams wanted to reinforce the message. As a goodwill gesture, he promised the Honduran military an unspecified amount of aid and left a Pentagon colonel behind to work out the details. Over the weekend, a wish list of weapons, totaling US$70 million, was compiled.[33]

This was the beginning of Holy Week. On Saturday, Sandinista troops poured over the Honduran border in a raid on contra base camps. The attack presented an opportunity for the United States and a dilemma for the Hondurans. It played into the hands of the Reagan administration, strengthening its bargaining position vis-à-vis Congress and giving Abrams the ammunition he needed to make good on his promise to the Honduran military. At the same time, it threatened to drag the Hondurans into a shooting war and expose once again the mendacity of their official position that there were no contras on Honduran soil.

There was here a basic conflict of interests, and it led to very different reactions. For its part, the Reagan administration sought to magnify the seriousness of the incursion. A media blitz was launched. Fifteen hundred troops, it was claimed, had "invaded" Honduras. When, on 24 March, the Hondurans asked for U.S. helicopters to ferry troops to the border area, they were told to put their request in writing. When they hesitated, Ferch's deputy, Shepard Lowman, met with Azcona and urged him to send a letter acknowledging the raid and requesting emergency military assistance. President Reagan, he said, was ready to approve up to US$20 million. Lowman also asked Azcona to do something about his press secretary, who had publicly denied Washington's claims of a major incursion and asserted that this was all just part of the White House's "political and propaganda tactics" to obtain contra aid.[34] "We are trying to help you," he complained," and you leave us with our mouths open."[35] By evening, Azcona still had not declared a state of alert. Washington was getting nervous, and so John Ferch paid an early morning visit to the president. "You don't have a choice on this one," he told Azcona. "You've got to get a letter up there right now. They're going bonkers up there. This is absurd, but you've got to do it."[36] At this point the Honduran bowed to the pressure and wrote a letter to his North American counterpart asking for air transport and other material assistance. In response, the Reagan administration sent the US$20 million in aid. U.S. pilots were rushed in to fly Honduran troops to the border. General John Galvin, the head of the SOUTHCOM, was dispatched to "coordinate" with the Honduran military.

Even after their formal request, the Hondurans continued to deny the U.S. version. That very day a government spokesman declared that the aid was the "initiative" of President Reagan. On 1 April reporters were told that Honduras was being pressured into provoking a war with Nicaragua and this was why the government was moving with such caution. Two days later, officials informed the press that fewer than eight hundred Sandinista troops had crossed the border and that the incursion was similar to three hundred previous crossings that Washington had chosen not to publicize. At the same time, a senior Honduran official bemoaned his country's dependency. The United States, he noted, "has a great capacity to influence us." It had been the Reagan administration that had decided to publicize the attacks; it was in the U.S. interest "that this situation have the connotation of an international incident." Sandinista forces were already withdrawing. Honduras had fallen into a U.S. "trap" in the aid debate. Subsequently, Foreign Minister López Contreras reiterated that the incursion did "not represent a major threat." On 7 April the government issued a communiqué denying that Azcona had asked the United States for US$20 million in aid.[37]

These statements irked the Reagan administration, but, more than that, they once again raised questions as to its veracity. Seeking to contain the damage, the White House and the State Department issued a denial of the Honduran charges. And on 8 April Elliott Abrams, testifying before Congress, rejected the notion that the Sandinista attack had been exaggerated. Indeed, he claimed that it had been "played down." That was too much for Representative Peter Kostmayer, who retorted, "Frankly Mr. Secretary, I am not surprised at anything you say to this committee anymore. . . . I am not surprised at the level of your audaciousness. An increasingly large number of people are beginning to regard administration statements as simply untruthful."[38]

In reality, neither the Hondurans nor the Americans had a monopoly on mendacity. U.S. attempts to portray the aid request as a Honduran initiative ignored the fact that Abrams had promised military assistance *before* the crisis. At the same time, it is clear that once the fighting began the Hondurans did not have to be pressured into asking for help. The Sandinista incursion was real enough; though aimed at the contras rather than Honduras, it was a violation of territorial integrity. It struck at the self-image of the armed forces even while providing them with a golden opportunity to secure the aid that Abrams had pledged but might otherwise have been unable to deliver. Azcona had therefore telephoned William Walker, the deputy assistant secretary of state for inter-American affairs, and asked for help. About the same time the Honduran armed forces commander, Humberto Regalado, had called the embassy and asked for sixty helicopter sorties. These were Honduran initiatives, and they were not coerced. The problem arose when Walker and subsequently Lowman asked Azcona to put the request in writing. To have done that would have drawn international attention to the contra presence, belying the Hondurans' official position that there were no guerrillas on Honduran soil and exposing them to charges of being the real aggressors. It was at this point that U.S. pressure was brought to bear.[39]

Later, Abrams commented that "U.S. choppers and crews couldn't be [provided] on the basis of an informal telephone call."[40] U.S. law required a formal request. Still, there is the larger question of whether the threat was exaggerated. The CIA's analysts had treated the Nicaraguan attack as a routine incursion, little more than a move against an obvious "target of opportunity."[41] Was all the hullabaloo really necessary?

It seems clear that U.S. motives went far beyond a simple desire to support an ally under attack. This was one factor, but it was not the only one and not necessarily the most important. The US$100 million aid request that Congress had denied was almost four times the amount approved in 1985. The campaign for its passage had begun with a burst of hyperbole and intimidation. The president had denounced the Sandinista regime as a cancerous growth that could become a "mortal threat to the entire New World." Images had been conjured up of Soviet missiles "on our doorstep," of hundreds of thousands of Central American refugees pouring into the United States, of the collapse of the region's fledgling democracies, of a threatened Panama Canal: "Those who would invite this strategic disaster by abandoning yet another fighting ally of this country will be held fully responsible." Reagan's director of communications, Pat Buchanan, had gone even farther, calling the vote on contra aid a test of the Democratic Party's loyalty: Henceforth, everyone would know whether the Democrats stood with Ronald Reagan and the resistance or with Daniel Ortega and the communists.[42]

In the short run, the tactic had backfired. Democrats and Republicans had been offended. Rather than attempting to build a bipartisan consensus, the administration had appealed over the head of Congress to the American people through a crude television advertising campaign. On 20 March, however, the House rejected the proposal, leading North and Abrams to panic. There followed the latter's trip to Honduras and his promise of military aid.

It was within the context of this bruising domestic political struggle that U.S. pressure on Honduras must be understood. The Senate was scheduled to take up the contra issue the following week.

The battle in both houses would continue for months. The temptation to exaggerate the seriousness of the incursion was enormous. Rejecting the analysis of his own intelligence experts, Casey insisted that the issue be portrayed as a Sandinista attempt to "knock out" the contras "while we debated." The president himself called the offensive a "slap in the face of everyone who voted against aid to the freedom fighters thinking it to be a vote for reconciliation." In the weeks ahead, U.S. officials would repeatedly cite the incursion as evidence of the need to approve the aid, and eventually the legislators would acquiesce.

On 15 April President Azcona finally abandoned the fiction of the contras' nonpresence, admitting that the rebels freely crossed back and forth along the border. Honduras, he said, did not have the resources to patrol the eleven-hundred-kilometer demarcation line with Nicaragua. When asked why the Honduran military did not at least close down the rebel camps, he responded irritably, "What do you want? That I spend millions . . . here to guard their [the Sandinistas'] backs?" Toward the end of May, he went to Washington and repeated this theme. He also urged Congress to restore aid to the rebels so that they could leave Honduras to "fight within Nicaragua."[43]

An Envoy's Story (Concluded): End of the Line

The "crisis" being over, there remained the little matter of the fate of the U.S. ambassador. Secretary Abrams wanted a "field commander" to carry out policy in Honduras, someone who would keep the Hondurans in line and actively support the contra program, and John Ferch was clearly not the man for the job. Fairly or not, Ferch had been blamed for the embarrassing lack of coordination between U.S. and Honduran policies during the Holy Week "invasion." Some of his superiors had been angered by what they perceived to be his sympathy with Honduran resistance to the economic conditions attached to U.S. aid. Reports had begun to circulate that his relations with the Honduran military were deteriorating: General Regalado was said to be displeased. He and his colleagues felt that the ambassador, in his efforts to strengthen the civilian government, was cutting the armed forces out of national security policy. (He had even gone to Washington to complain.) Then there were the rumors of a morale problem in the embassy. An undersecretary of management had been sent down to Tegucigalpa and come back with reports of disarray.[44]

The bottom line, of course, was that Abrams and his hard-line colleagues did not trust John Ferch. Sensitive operations were being conducted in Honduras, some of which were illegal, and an ambassador was needed who would cooperate or at least turn a blind eye to them. In April, Secord's contra-supply operation, "Project Democracy," made its long-awaited first flight, hopping from Honduras over the border into northern Nicaragua to drop 3,440 pounds of grenades and ammunition to the guerrillas. Many more such drops would be made in the months ahead. By now Ferch's CIA "subordinates" were working closely with North and Secord under an arrangement that involved, in effect, two chiefs of station: the embassy station, which coordinated all U.S. intelligence activities in the country, and a CIA "base," which took primary operational responsibility for the war. The division was standard practice in nations where the agency was developing a major paramilitary capability; it was designed to distance and shield the ambassador and the embassy from charges of espionage and other unseemly practices by giving them "deniability." In this case, it protected them too well: Neither John Mallett at the embassy station nor James Adkins at the base told Ferch about the Secord operation. Nor was this the only activity hidden from the ambassador. Ferch and his deputy, Shep Lowman, seem to have been unaware of the CIA's intervention in Honduran military politics, in particular its efforts to isolate the dissidents in the sixth promotion.[45] In the highly compartmentalized and secretive world of covert operations, some parts of the foreign policy apparatus were hiding from others.

The upshot of all this was a prolonged and nasty campaign to discredit Ferch. And ultimately it succeeded. In June, just two days after the House finally approved the US$100 million contra-aid package, Ferch was fired. As his successor the administration appointed Everett Ellis Briggs, an "enthusiastic supporter" of the guerrillas, with responsibility for all of the embassy's activities "including oversight of the contra program."[46] Finally, Abrams would get the "strong man" he wanted.

Military Politics and Human Rights: The First Year of the Regalado-Azcona Administration

The embassy was not the only power center in Tegucigalpa with new leadership. The Hondurans had a new president and a new armed forces commander. The question was whether it would make any difference. To be sure, in some respects José Azcona was a vast improvement over the power-hungry, corrupt, and erratic Suazo. Tall, silver-haired, and dignified, he looked like a president, and he was honest. Unfortunately, he was also of questionable competence. In part, this was a matter of personality. In the words of one high-level U.S. embassy observer, "Azcona didn't govern; he reigned." He was a lazy, indecisive, passive president who "didn't like to kick ass." When confronted with a problem that he didn't want to deal with, he would pretend it didn't exist. During the 1988 riot, when the U.S. embassy annex was being torched and looted by an enraged mob, Azcona would remain incommunicado as a frantic Ted Briggs repeatedly telephoned the presidential residence for help. His refusal to take the difficult steps necessary to deal with the country's economic crisis while it was still manageable meant that problems would grow worse and that the pain of adjustment would be much greater when the situation could no longer be ignored.

To be fair, the problems he faced were formidable: The economy was in a shambles; human rights abuses continued to fester; there was growing labor and peasant unrest; thousands of contras remained camped on Honduran soil. Moreover, the basic equation of national politics had not changed. In the balance between the presidency, the military, and the embassy, the civilian president was still a distant third. And to make matters worse, Azcona did not have the solid congressional majority that would have enabled him to take strong measures. From the moment he stepped into office, he was a lame duck.

Azcona's military counterpart, Humberto Regalado Hernández, had been promoted to general on 19 February, only two days before he became armed forces chief. He was a member of the "Group of Iron," the sector of the military that supported General Alvarez during the years in which the "National Security Doctrine" had been imposed without quarter. He had been a member of the armed forces commission that absolved the military of responsibility for the "disappeared." His brother, Marco Tulio, belonged to Battalion 3-16.[47] Given Regalado's background and the continuing weakness of civilian political and judicial institutions, it is not surprising that respect for human rights was one of the first casualties of the new regime.

Under López Reyes, there had been notable improvement. Although illegal detentions, torture, and other "lesser" abuses continued, they represented more of a "constant, low-grade fever that [had] never been fully cured" than a "violent, racking disease." Most important, the number of people killed and "permanently disappeared" had dropped sharply. There had been no documented political killings of Hondurans in 1985. The most serious incident had involved Salvadorans: On 29 August troops had fired on unarmed refugees in the camps at Colomoncagua, killing three and wounding fifty others.[48] During 1986, however, the situation sharply deteriorated. Several dozen people died under mysterious circumstances during the first half of the year, most notably Cristóbal Pérez, a well-known leader of the radical Unitary Federation of Honduran Workers (Federación Unitaria de Trabajadores de Honduras—FUTH). By summer, a self-proclaimed anticrime organization calling itself the "Commandos of Death" was killing off habitual criminals and delinquents in the capital. The situation was serious enough to prompt President Azcona to issue a public expression of alarm. Although he attributed the killings to personal acts of vengeance, he also suggested that there was police involvement. As usual, not much was done about it.

As the weeks passed, the climate of violence became increasingly politicized as the military indicated its determination to silence dissent. This period witnessed the reactivation of the civil defense committees, community spy networks that encouraged the anonymous denunciation of suspected subversives. At the same time, General Regalado announced measures to combat a "communist plot against Honduras" designed to discredit the contras, force the withdrawal of the United States, and denounce the "disappearances." There would be investigations of all those thought to be plotting against the nation, with every Honduran a possible suspect. The army publication *Proyecciones Militares* launched a vitriolic attack on journalists and students for being part of "the focus of subversive infection." A government communiqué warned that those who supported another government in an action against their own would be subject to criminal penalties.

In August, moreover, an unsigned, mimeographed "death list" was circulated, accusing more than a dozen prominent civilians of being "the Honduran revolutionary leadership." Among those mentioned were Carlos Roberto and Jorge Arturo Reina, the leaders of the M-LIDER (social democratic) faction of the Liberal Party; Carlos Montoya, president of Congress; Manuel Acosta Bonilla, a former government minister and a leading nacionalista; and Víctor Meza, one of the country's most respected journalists. In an interview Meza, the "Lone Ranger" of the Honduran left (a sobriquet reflecting the suspicion with which he was held by those who disliked his penchant for criticizing the Sandinistas as well as the contras, the United States, and the Honduran military), averred that the purpose of the list was to "create a war climate, a climate of terror and repression, to quiet the voices of those who criticize the developing war with Nicaragua."[49] A spokesman for the U.S. embassy minimized the importance of the list, hinting that it might even have been manufactured by the left to discredit the Honduran government.

But the terror could not be so easily dismissed. In early August, the car of Rodrigo Wong Arévalo, the news editor of Radio América and an outspoken critic of military corruption, was destroyed by a bomb. A month later, the office of the Committee for the Defense of Human Rights in Honduras (Comité para la Defensa de los Derechos Humanos—CODEH) was bombed twice within a single week. The organization's director, Ramón Custodio, received a bouquet of flowers with a death notice attached. In November, a youth burst into Custodio's medical clinic and left a package tied with a ribbon on his desk. The "gift" was smoking. Custodio defused the device, and no one was hurt. In January, the union activist Leonor Meza's truck was bombed. This was the eighth terrorist bombing in six months and the third since the beginning of the new year. Shortly thereafter, in the wake of repeated threats against her life, Meza fled into exile.

Meanwhile, General Regalado had consolidated his position. In September a coup had been launched by Colonels William Said Speer (commander of the armored cavalry), Guillermo Thuman Cordón (chief of infantry), and Lufty Azzad Matute (headmaster of the Francisco Morazán Academy). The three were part of a group of about twenty officers who were "hard-liners but nationalists." In contrast to Regalado and the "Group of Iron," they were critical of the contra presence (but thought that if nothing could be done about it then at least Honduras should receive more benefits) and tended to view El Salvador rather than Nicaragua as the primary threat to national security. Their names were said to have appeared on a CIA list of "dangerous persons" in 1984, along with "Tito" Zúniga's; reportedly, the agency considered their group "impenetrable."[50]

The plan had been to replace Regalado with Thuman Cordón, but it had backfired. The general was able to muster the support of Colonel Leonel Riera Lunatti, the head of the Public Security Force, who in turn rallied the sixth promotion behind Regalado. Riera Lunatti was an ambitious opportunist and thoroughly corrupt, but he understood the frustrations of junior officers whose upward mobility had long been blocked by their seniors. He knew also that they were as susceptible to corruption as the older generation. In the purge that followed, members of the sixth promotion found their positions in the command structure strengthened and their opportunities for personal enrichment expanded. They would now be swept up in the "gold-rush fever" engendered by the US$100 million in contra aid as Regalado and Riera Lunatti gave new meaning to the Honduran maxim that a good commander is one who lets his colonels thieve freely.

In December 1986 the Honduran Congress met in special session to consider the military's nominees for a three-year term as armed forces commander. Until then Regalado had been only the interim commander, serving out the term begun by Walter López. The balloting itself was a mere formality, the general winning with only one vote in dissent. This did not mean, however, that he had become the new Alvarez. On the contrary, he had been granted formal command by his colleagues on condition that he not rule. This would be a collective leadership in which Regalado—in spite of his own hard-line instincts—would have to play the role of mediator between contending factions. Moreover, because of the shift in the balance between military generations, it would be a leadership in certain respects even less inclined to follow U.S. policy unquestioningly. Many in the sixth promotion were critical of the contra presence. Almost immediately, that issue would be revived.

Contragate: The Reagan Administration and the Resistance in Crisis

By late 1986, the contras were occupying more than twenty villages in a 450-kilometer area of the Honduran departments of El Paraíso and Olancho. They had rechristened the area "Nueva Nicaragua" and its unofficial capital, the town of Capire, "Managuita." There was also a large rebel presence in Choluteca and Gracias a Dios. Altogether, it was estimated that there were at least 56,000 rebels and their dependents in the country. Their impact had been devastating: Many communities had become uninhabitable because of fighting between the contras and the Sandinistas. Villages had been repeatedly occupied or shelled. Scores of people had been killed in the ongoing clandestine counterintelligence war between the rebels, who assassinated suspected Sandinista spies, and Nicaraguan soldiers, who attacked rebel collaborators. Many others had fallen victim to contra violence. Assassinations, murders, armed robberies, kidnappings, torture, intimidation, property seizures, and cattle rustling had become a part of everyday life. Land mines were a constant danger. Since July, the

Sandinistas had kept up to 1,000 regular troops on patrol in the Las Vegas salient. Most of the area's population had been forced to flee. Damage to the local economy was in the tens of millions of dollars.

There had been protests, of course. The coffee growers' guild, which represented some 33,000 producers, denounced the rebels for damaging crops and frightening away workers and petitioned the government for indemnification. Motions were introduced in Congress to expel the "illegal armed groups." Opposition cut across the political and social spectrum, embracing right-wing nationalists as well as leftists, coffee growers as well as workers and peasants. Public opinion polls consistently showed that an overwhelming majority of Hondurans opposed the guerrilla presence. National sovereignty was being violated; control over the border areas had become a fiction. Increasingly, the specter of "Lebanonization" began to creep into the debate. What would happen if the United States abandoned the rebels? Visions of 15,000 frustrated, angry, and heavily armed guerrillas, along with tens of thousands of their dependents, permanently camped on Honduran territory—a renegade army engaged in large-scale gunrunning, drug dealing, extortion, robbery, and murder—were enough to sober all but the most fanatical anticommunists in the military.

The army was developing strategies for annihilating the rebels in the event of a confrontation, but as things turned out, this was unnecessary. In late October the contra-aid bill was finally signed into law, and the guerrillas gained a new lease on life. The US$100 million package included US$70 million in military aid. (The remainder was euphemistically labeled "humanitarian" assistance.) The rebels were ecstatic. Over the course of the next year, they announced, they would double the size of their fighting force and expand its operations to three-fourths of Nicaragua.

Yet, even in this moment of triumph, events were unfolding that would thrust the Reagan administration into its most serious crisis and undermine the contras' quest for a military victory. On 5 October a Sandinista ground-to-air missile downed a decrepit cargo plane over Nicaragua. The following day the flight's loadmaster and sole survivor, Eugene Hasenfus, was captured, and he immediately began to talk. Hasenfus claimed to have been hired by the CIA to supply arms to the rebels. Television crews were brought in and a media event staged. The Reagan administration responded with an orchestrated attempt at "spin control." The RIG met and decided to ask the contras to publicly accept responsibility for this and other flights. Reagan, Shultz, and Abrams all categorically denied that the U.S. government was involved. In fact, the operation had been directed by Ollie North from its inception, and its discovery had immediate and far-reaching repercussions: The Secord supply operation was halted. A multitude of investigations were set in motion. Journalists swarmed around the issue like flies around carrion. Two weeks later, the House Judiciary Committee asked Attorney General Meese to appoint an independent prosecutor to investigate possible violations of the law. North's entire support program began to unravel.

Two days after Hasenfus was shot down, Casey was informed that disgruntled investors and middlemen were threatening to reveal the administration's arms sales to Iran. On 3 November, a Beirut magazine reported that Reagan's former national security adviser, Robert McFarlane, had visited Iran the previous May, bearing gifts. The article led to a flood of press revelations about efforts to "exchange arms for hostages." And to make matters worse, on 4 November the Democrats regained control of the Senate and strengthened their majority in the House. Reagan had now lost his working majority in Congress.

On 25 November, in a nationally televised press briefing, Attorney General Meese announced that profits from the arms sales to Iran had been diverted to the contras. Heads now began to roll: North was fired. Poindexter resigned. Suddenly the president himself seemed terribly vulnerable: Either Mr. Reagan had known and approved of these operations (a potentially impeachable offense) or he had been ignorant of what his underlings had been doing (in which case serious questions had to be raised about his competence). Finally, on 15 December, as he was preparing to testify before Congress, Bill Casey collapsed in his office. He was rushed to Georgetown University Hospital where he underwent surgery for a lymphoma, a cancerous tumor on the brain. Five months later, he would be dead.

By late November both the Reagan presidency and the contras were in shock. It was increasingly doubtful whether a crippled administration could persuade an outraged Congress to provide the kind of ongoing, massive funding that might give the guerrillas a fighting chance. "We may now be seen as nothing more than the pet project of a lame-duck president," lamented one rebel leader. "If that's the way it is, we're finished."[51]

In late October, moreover, heavy fighting had again broken out inside the Honduran border as Sandinista troops pursued hundreds of fleeing contras. Fighting continued sporadically throughout November and early December, eventually dragging the Honduran military into the fray. In the process, President Azcona ordered fighter-bombers to attack Nicaraguan positions and requested another U. S. airlift of Honduran troops to the airfield at Jamastrán.

In the face of this concatenation of developments, coinciding as it did with the growing influence of the sixth promotion, embarrassing press revelations of the Honduran military's role as intermediary between Israeli arms suppliers and the contras, and a sharp upsurge of antirebel sentiment among the general public, Regalado and his colleagues decided that something had to be done. Accordingly, the Reagan administration was informed that the guerrillas would have to leave the country. In response, the newly arrived U.S. ambassador, Ted Briggs, presented his hosts with a timetable under which the contras would be sent into Nicaragua over the next four months. Reluctantly, the Hondurans accepted. In doing so, however, they made it clear that they were unwilling to have the four months stretch into eight.[52]

The Slow, Painful Death of the Contra Policy: The Beginning of the End

Nineteen eighty-seven was a pivotal year for the contras. For the first time, they had been given the support they needed to inflict major damage on the Sandinista regime. A hundred million dollars was an extraordinary amount of money for an army this size—around US$7,000 per guerrilla—and it enabled the CIA to overhaul what had been a very ragged fighting force. Rebel commanders now received direct training from Green Berets. The contra air force was rebuilt. Aguacate Air Base was transformed into a vast intelligence center and air-supply hub. The rebels were armed with Redeye surface-to-air missiles; their intelligence system was improved; they were given a new name—the "Nicaraguan Resistance"—and a coherent political message.[53]

The results were not unimpressive. By midyear, some 10,000 insurgents were in Nicaragua, and they were taking it to the enemy. The Sandinista helicopter force, a key element in the government's ability to maintain the upper hand during the previous two years, was reeling under the assault of the Redeyes. Within a matter of months, almost half of the helicopters had been destroyed. In two CIA-directed battles, the guerrillas overwhelmed a half-dozen rural towns, seizing missile stocks and destroying Soviet radar installations. Meanwhile, thousands of peasants, impressed by the surge, were flocking to the contras as recruits and collaborators.

All this wore the Sandinistas down. The effects could be seen most dramatically in the economy, which "moved during the year from decline to disorder to downright chaos. Government military spending was already gobbling more than 50 percent of the national budget, and through the year the country's streets, markets, and other infrastructure—already eroded by years of wartime austerity—crumbled into ruin. The government was financing its operations by printing worthless currency, and inflation surged from 700 percent early in the year to 15,000 percent at its close. With prices spiraling out of control, industry collapsed, farms stood idle, living standards plummeted. . . . Begging children clogged Managua's streets. Hospitals had no anesthesia, pharmacies no aspirin, groceries no food." The offensive never came close to defeating the Sandinistas militarily, but it did demonstrate to them the costs of continuing the war. Eventually, they sued for peace.

But as significant as these gains were, the contras remained dependent on forces beyond their control—in particular, on the U.S. Congress. Moreover, money, training, and weapons were not enough to stem the rot eating away at the movement's insides. By early 1987, the rebels were the focus of no fewer than seven U.S. criminal investigations, ranging from the theft of aid to arms smuggling and drug trafficking. An Americas Watch report accused them of increasing human rights violations. Factional infighting was tearing the resistance apart. Ex-guardsmen distrusted ex-Sandinistas; those in the field resented those in the base camps; footsoldiers despised officers; contra leaders in Honduras regarded the directors in Miami as overpaid bureaucrats.

As always, Bermúdez and the high command were the cause of much resentment. Dissidents accused them of incompetence and corruption. The charges were indisputable, but they produced only superficial changes. State Department efforts to dilute the power of the somocistas and their allies and strengthen the hand of more reputable elements had run into heavy opposition from the CIA. Whatever their liabilities, Bermúdez and his cronies were obedient. This was a quality much valued by the agency, which wanted to run the war unencumbered by resistance from any misguided Nicaraguans who might have thought that *they* should be in charge. In March, frustrated that the promised changes were being blocked, the leading contra moderate, Arturo Cruz, resigned. The facade of democracy and civilian control so crucial to the administration's strategy for prying aid out of Congress had all but ceased to exist.

All this fed the growing doubts about the desirability and sustainability of the contra policy. Though some political unity was restored after a major gathering of the rebel leadership in May, both this and the guerrillas' military gains went virtually unnoticed in Washington. There the continuing debate over aid would be almost entirely divorced from what was happening on the battlefield. For much of the year, the Iran-contra scandal dominated the discourse. Gradually, however, it was joined by another, even more potent, force: the Central American peace process. There was a new president in Costa Rica, Oscar Arias Sánchez, and he was calling for a new political strategy to force the Sandinistas to loosen their grip on power. In the U.S. Congress, where the prospects for future military appropriations were highly uncertain, his appeals would strike a responsive chord.

The history of contra aid had been one of ongoing struggle between supporters and opponents, marked by periodic cutoffs, resumptions, and restrictions that had prevented the fashioning of any kind of concerted and coherent policy and that had enabled the Sandinistas and their Soviet-Cuban allies to counter U.S.-contra efforts through their own massive military buildup. Barring a congressional decision to cut off aid once and for all, that pattern seemed likely to continue: The rebels would be given enough to enable them to survive and fight on but would not be able to win. Democrats would be able to protect themselves against Republican charges that they had "sold out the freedom fighters." And Nicaragua would continue to bleed indefinitely.

Thousands of contras were now returning home. Yet, in spite of claims that there was no longer a counterrevolutionary presence in Honduras, some of the rebels had simply moved deeper into the countryside, where they were less noticeable. Peasants in the remote Patuca River area of Olancho were reported to be selling their lands to the newcomers, who were setting up their bases anew. In May approximately 3,000 Sandinista troops dislodged a large concentration of contras in the San Andrés de Bocay area of Jinotega. As the rebels fled back across the border, Honduran border guards tried to block their way, and fighting erupted. A few days later, Honduran authorities canceled a contra meeting scheduled in Tegucigalpa.

The Hondurans were still torn between the desire to get rid of the rebels and the economic realities of their situation. They were still dependent on U.S. aid. To have taken too firm a stand would have left them vulnerable to retaliation and cut them off from lucrative contra-aid profits. A forcible expulsion of the guerrillas would have meant fighting and bloodshed—the last thing the military wanted. Once more the Hondurans equivocated, publicly pretending that the rebels were gone while privately sanctioning a continuing (though much reduced) presence. It was a facade that could not be maintained indefinitely. Early the following year, *El Tiempo* revealed that hundreds of contras were still in El Paraíso, having recently set up camp at the headquarters of the Sixth Infantry Battalion, about fifty kilometers from the capital.[54]

The Slow, Painful Death of the Contra Policy (Continued): The Road to Esquipulas and Beyond

Nineteen eighty-seven witnessed the resurrection of an old administration nightmare—namely, that the Central Americans themselves might negotiate an end to the hostilities, leaving the Sandinistas in power. Throughout the previous year, the United States had continued to undermine the Contadora process. When Nicaragua accepted the third Revised Contadora Act in June, Secretary of State Shultz had announced that the four Central American "democracies" would repudiate it. Nor, he claimed, would they any longer accept the "tutelage" of the Contadora countries. Sure enough, not long thereafter the Tegucigalpa group and Guatemala rejected the act. At times, U.S. tactics bordered on the petty. Toward the end of the year, when the UN and Organization of American States (OAS) secretaries general offered the services of their institutions to Contadora, Washington tried to prevent the OAS chief, João Baena Soares, from traveling to Central America. On this issue, the administration generated only resentment. Nevertheless, by year's end it was clear that Contadora was going nowhere.

In December Costa Rican President Oscar Arias, frustrated at this lack of progress, journeyed to Washington with a peace plan of his own. Originally, the Arias proposal was embraced by the Reagan administration as a means of further undermining Contadora. It included a call for "democratization," with elections in Nicaragua to be monitored by the OAS and negotiations between the Sandinistas and the contras. The proposal was so close to Washington's position, however, that it raised suspicions about Arias's role. Subsequently, the measure was modified. Demands for talks between the Sandinistas and the rebels were shelved, as was the call for immediate elections. Even so, the plan presented at the February meeting of the Central American presidents in San José was much weaker than Contadora on the crucial issue of foreign military intervention. No mention was made of military advisers, maneuvers, or bases; moreover, the proposal's concentration on internal democratization was a point that the United States had been insisting on for some time.

Nevertheless, as the plan continued to be modified, Washington began to distance itself. Elliott Abrams suggested that the proposal did not make sufficient demands on the Nicaraguan government. As it became clear that the contras were being frozen out of the negotiating process (unless they sought amnesty and became part of the unarmed opposition), the administration's reservations turned into barely disguised hostility. By June 1987 officials were openly expressing concern that the forthcoming meeting of Central American presidents in Esquipulas, Guatemala, could benefit the Sandinistas at a time when the United States was trying to isolate them. On 17 June President Arias met with Ronald Reagan at the latter's request. The Costa Rican was told in no uncertain terms that his plan was inadequate and that the United States would not be bound by it. Economic pressure was applied, bureaucratic excuses being found for delaying US$140 million in aid approved for Costa Rica in FY 1987.

In July the Central American foreign ministers met in Tegucigalpa, along with representatives of the Contadora group, to discuss a draft of the Arias plan. Unexpectedly, they were confronted with something else: The Hondurans presented a plan of their own—or, at least, so they said. Oddly, their proposal was in both Spanish *and* English (when all of the participants spoke Spanish) and was bound in a professional-looking booklet. It had all of the earmarks of having been prepared by a certain North American agency, and Arias himself said that it reflected U.S. objections to his proposal.

In August matters came to a head. Once again, a decision on contra aid was approaching. After months of gloom a growing number of U.S. officials had come to view the prospects of success with renewed optimism. The previous month's testimony by Ollie North before the select congressional committee investigating the Iran-contra scandal had generated an enormous groundswell of sympathy. Almost overnight, public opinion polls showed a 36 percent shift in favor of aid to the resistance. The congressional investigators were noticeably intimidated. Even so, key Republican legislators warned that, in the absence of evidence that Reagan was willing to pursue a new diplomatic approach to the region, a simple request for more military aid would probably be defeated.

The opportunity was immediately seized. On 4 August—just two days before the Central American presidents were to meet in Esquipulas to consider the Arias plan—the administration came up with a "peace proposal" of its own. For all its deviousness, this was a brilliant maneuver—a classic example of gamesmanship that held out the promise of at once undermining Arias and securing the desired aid. This was a bipartisan proposal of sorts; indeed, it had been drawn up by the speaker of the House, Jim Wright, who had voted against contra aid in the past but was eager to put Central American policy back on the track toward negotiations.

It almost immediately became apparent that this was another joker ploy. Once again, the administration had set forth terms that it fully expected the Sandinistas to decline. Among other things, the plan called for an end of military aid to Nicaragua from the communist countries. U.S. officials expressed doubt that Managua would accept the plan's broad proposals for "democratization" or the idea that negotiations would begin before the contras had been disarmed and disbanded. In the words of one senior official, "If the White House had thought the plan was acceptable, they would have changed it."[55] The beauty of it was that the Democrats seemed to have been co-opted. Once Managua had rejected the proposal, Congress would have little choice but to renew aid. After all, the Democrats had been calling for negotiations for years. Now the White House had responded with a plan cosponsored by the Democratic speaker of the House (a fact that administration officials eagerly pointed out) that called for negotiations to begin immediately and be completed by 30 September. If the Sandinistas refused to cooperate, the onus for failure would be on them. In that event, the other parties, including the United States and the contras, would be free to pursue such actions as they deemed necessary—a scarcely veiled reference to the resumption of guerrilla warfare.

But the administration had been too clever. The Sandinistas rejected the proposal out of hand. Many Democrats reacted with irritation toward Speaker Wright, who they felt was being used and whose commitment now threatened to box them into a corner. Moreover, the White House had miscalculated the impact that the proposal would have on the Central American presidents meeting in Esquipulas. The latter had not even been informed that a new initiative was under way. Indeed, it had been assumed that the shock of the announcement would throw the conference into disarray and probably scuttle their efforts to work out a peace agreement. But the maneuver backfired. Even the Hondurans were offended by U.S. insensitivity. In the end, the ploy had precisely the opposite effect from what was intended: It acted as a catalyst to the deliberations. The presidents felt that, if they did not reach an agreement, the Reagan-Wright proposal would be the only alternative, and negotiations would break down completely. On 7 August they signed a preliminary accord that was significantly different from that proposal.

The administration was now caught in a trap of its own making. In Washington, Speaker Wright immediately embraced the Esquipulas agreement, warning the White House that it would be unwise to seek further military aid for the contras while peace talks were under way. Suddenly, it was Washington, not Managua, that was isolated and on the defensive. "Can Ronald Reagan say no?" mused one U.S. official. "After . . . years of saying we would support whatever the Central American nations want, what else can we say?"[56]

The Esquipulas agreement called on the Central American governments to open dialogues with unarmed opposition groups, declare political amnesties, and seek cease-fires in the region's guerrilla wars. Outside aid to insurgents was prohibited; the territory of one country could not be used to attack another. Internal "democratization" was required: There was to be a lifting of censorship and states of siege, a guarantee of "total political party pluralism," including freedom of the press and political organization, and periodic, internationally supervised, elections. Monitoring groups were to be established to press the plan's provisions. National reconciliation commissions were to be organized in each country. The United Nations, the OAS, the Central American foreign ministers, and the Contadora group would be asked to play a part in the verification process. A 7 November deadline was established for the simultaneous implementation of the requirements.

The accord was far from perfect. The language was sometimes too general. There were no sanctions or other mechanisms for bringing about cease-fires. There was not even a call for direct talks between the Nicaraguan government and the contras or the Salvadoran government and the FMLN. The plan also left unresolved such key security issues as how to reduce growing armies, weaponry, and foreign military influence. Still, it was a good beginning. Some of these issues could be negotiated in time, and there would be plenty of that. The 7 November deadline would come and go. The fighting would continue.

The Guatemalan agreement struck a crippling blow to the administration's Nicaraguan policy, but slowly the White House pulled itself together and tried to regain the initiative. One of the first signs that the struggle would not be abandoned came in mid-August with the resignation of Philip Habib, the president's special envoy to Central America. Habib had come to his post fresh from a diplomatic triumph in the Philippines, where he had played a pivotal role in the U.S. decision to support Cory Aquino and democracy. He had taken his new assignment seriously. As had John Ferch, he had assumed in the beginning that the White House was interested in negotiated solutions, but experience had taught him otherwise. Habib had lent his reputation to the Reagan policy and in so doing had provided legitimacy to the contra aid effort. Once in office, however, he was never allowed to do any serious negotiating and became a "man without a mission." He had not been involved in the formulation of the Reagan-Wright plan—indeed, he had been highly critical of it—and when the Central American presidents signed the Guatemalan accord he had urged that their efforts be supported. Habib considered the pact a golden opportunity: He wanted to build on it, "filling the gaps, strengthening the security aspects . . . and making sure the Central American democracies got it together." He felt that he could "end the war on terms acceptable to us."[57]

But that was not the message that Elliott Abrams wanted to send. Abrams was no longer the administration's spokesman on Capitol Hill, having been declared, in effect, persona non grata for repeatedly misleading Congress. Within policymaking circles, however, his influence continued to grow. Abrams thought that Habib was out of line—that he considered himself a "negotiator" when in fact he was only a "symbol." Habib's recommendations were a "weak" alternative to the "strong," prorebel policy that was needed. The secretary wanted to push hard for another battle on contra aid and favored telling the Central American allies, "Either you work closely with us to protect your national security or your national security isn't going to be protected."[58]

In the short run, Abrams won. Habib's plan was vetoed, and he resigned. A few days later, U.S. envoys to Central America were instructed to convey the White House's "concern" about the Esquipulas accord to their host governments. The following day, a senior official announced that the plan could not work unless the United States provided long-term support to the contras after a cease-fire. Only continuing pressure could force the Sandinistas to live up to their agreements.

There followed a concerted campaign to undermine the accord. On 25 August President Reagan pledged unwavering support for the contras over their 15 September radio station. Subsequently, Secretary of State Shultz announced that the administration would seek US$270 million in new aid. The president declared the peace plan fatally flawed even as other officials dismissed Sandinista compliance as "cosmetic" and "sham." In early October the United States issued a list of demands that, it claimed, were necessary to ensure "real" democratization in Nicaragua. The conditions were so excessive as to be nonnegotiable, prompting Jim Wright to complain that the "extreme right wing" had taken over Central American policy: "It is becoming increasingly difficult to avoid the conclusion that the president is trying to torpedo the peace process."[59]

In October, also, Oscar Arias was awarded the Nobel Peace Prize. The announcement increased his prestige enormously and gave renewed impetus to the Esquipulas plan. The Costa Rican president had become an international celebrity. Everyone was impressed but the Reagan administration, whose officials increasingly referred to the Nobel laureate with barely disguised contempt. Toward midmonth, U.S. tactics began to shift again. Rather than trying to add more conditions to the Guatemalan accord, officials began to argue that it should be applied in the strictest possible fashion: If the Sandinistas had not negotiated a cease-fire with the contras by the 7 November deadline, they should be accused of noncompliance. That could then be used to support the US$270 million aid request. Meanwhile, the number of armed encounters from June on increased three- to fourfold compared with the beginning of the year. In October the CIA doubled the amount of arms delivered to the rebels. As the contras stepped up their attacks, so did the Sandinistas, leading to some of the fiercest fighting yet.

Esquipulas: Two Approaches to Compliance

The Arias plan contained both opportunities and risks, and it soon became apparent that some governments were more willing to incur the latter than others. Though the accord required all of the signatories to comply with its terms, there was an unspoken consensus that only Nicaragua would be held strictly accountable. Both regionally and in the United States, attention was focused primarily on the issue of *Sandinista* compliance. Still, the agreement was about as favorable as Managua could have hoped. If fully implemented, it would almost certainly have meant the end of the contras. Deprived of their foreign sanctuaries and arms supplies, they would have withered away. They were not recognized as a negotiating force; the internal "dialogue" was to be limited to the *unarmed* opposition and those who accepted amnesty. With the guerrillas thus weakened, there seemed an excellent chance that order could be restored and Sandinista hegemony maintained. Beyond that, Nicaragua desperately needed peace. Tens of thousands of people had been killed; damage to the economy exceeded US$2 billion. The populace was exhausted. Without peace, the government had no hope of attaining its socioeconomic goals. The society would continue to disintegrate. The revolution would be destroyed.

The plan was not without risk. As Alexis de Tocqueville recognized long ago, the most perilous moment for a bad government is when it seeks to mend its ways. During the Sandinistas' years in power, the economy had been largely destroyed, and living conditions had plunged to Depression-era levels. Although government policies were only part of the reason for this decline, increasing numbers of Nicaraguans held the Sandinistas responsible. Beneath the system of controls imposed by the regime, discontent seethed. There was no way of gauging the breadth or depth of this alienation or predicting the public response once those controls were lifted.

On balance, however, the agreement was clearly in the Sandinistas' interests, and they embraced it enthusiastically. The government indicated that it would meet its obligations even if the other signatories did not. It set up a national reconciliation commission that was reasonably representative of both pro- and antigovernment views and chaired by the regime's most influential critic, Archbishop Miguel Obando y Bravo. Censorship was suspended and an existing amnesty law broadened. Several Catholic priests who had been expelled from the country for their procontra activities were allowed to return. Nicaragua's most influential newspaper, *La Prensa,* closed for sixteen months for its opposition to the regime, was allowed to reopen. The ban on Radio Católica was lifted. The so-called Law of the Absent, which allowed the seizure of property of those who had gone into exile, was repealed. A dialogue was opened with opposition parties. In early November, under increasing international pressure, the government agreed to initiate indirect cease-fire talks with the contras. The following month, the two sides met in the Dominican Republic and began to negotiate their differences. The road ahead would be long and difficult, but at least progress was finally being made.

In contrast, in Honduras the armed forces and government viewed the agreement with profound suspicion. Before leaving for Esquipulas, President Azcona had assured the military and the United States that he would agree to nothing more than a loosely worded joint communiqué. When in the wake of the Reagan-Wright proposal the other presidents had agreed to sign, he had felt obliged to go along; he did not want to shoulder the blame for sabotaging the conference. Subsequently, the Hondurans tried to limit the accord's impact by questioning its validity, selectively interpreting its provisions, and claiming exemption from its requirements.

The Honduran position was that the Guatemala document was not a peace treaty, merely a "procedure for eventually arriving at a treaty."[60] As such, it was not binding, and they were not obliged to comply with the requirement of free and timely elections. Nor, initially, was Azcona willing to set up a national reconciliation commission: Such commissions were only "for those countries that have an armed conflict." It was "absolutely inconceivable to introduce a commission of reconciliation where there is nothing to reconcile."[61] At the Central American foreign ministers meeting in San Salvador on 19-20 August, Foreign Minister López Contreras arrived a day late. The conference accomplished nothing; the Hondurans obstructed the formation of the special commissions that were to study how the plan's objectives could be achieved. Subsequently, the government seized every opportunity for delay, with the result that two months after the accord had been signed the Hondurans had still not taken a single step toward compliance.

The fact of the matter is that the plan *was* binding on the signatories, entailing "the obligation . . . to comply simultaneously" with what had been agreed upon "in the time frame established."[62] But it raised serious problems for the Hondurans. Compliance with the election provisions would have exacerbated an already intense controversy. By law, municipal elections were scheduled for November. But since these would have threatened the Liberal Party's political hegemony, Azcona had opposed them, and the National Electoral Tribunal had postponed them. Beyond this, there was a fear that a national reconciliation commission would provide a platform for the left to denounce the military and embarrass the government. In the aftermath of the signing of the agreement, the Catholic church and a coalition of small leftist groups put intense pressure on the president to form the required commission and open a national debate on human rights. A shouting match ensued, with the bishops and the left accusing the military of numerous abuses and the latter responding with a highly publicized campaign against the "enemies of democracy" who were said to be infiltrating "all structures of society."

The most difficult issue, however, was still the contras. Although officially they had left the country, in reality their airstrips were still in operation. At night, planes continued to fly over Nicaragua, dropping supplies to guerrillas in the field. For the Hondurans, this was a no-win situation: If they allowed the International Verification Commission to inspect the border areas, the rebels would be discovered, and the military would be obliged to remove them.

Bloodshed was likely. If the authorities refused to permit such an inspection, they would be blamed for obstructing the peace process. Their response was to stall.

As weeks passed, this became increasingly difficult. Pressure was brought on the Honduran government to comply. In September the Costa Ricans agreed to form their own national reconciliation commission, undermining Azcona's claim that the requirement applied only to those countries beset by civil war. Grudgingly, the Hondurans followed suit. In November a reconciliation commission was set up and an amnesty law passed. But neither of these actions had much effect. The commission's powers were sharply circumscribed. It was not allowed to investigate the repression of the Alvarez years or the presence of the contras. It would operate for sixty-nine days before disbanding, leaving its job largely uncompleted. Similarly, the amnesty affected only a handful of political prisoners, and although it did lead to the release of many peasants arrested for land seizures, it did not repeal the notorious antiterrorist law.

Meanwhile, as the time approached for the International Verification Commission to visit Honduras, efforts were made to conceal the contras' presence. Rebel spokesmen closed their offices near Toncontín Airport and moved to Miami. Guerrilla bases were reduced to a minimum level of operation that could be shut down during the commission's visit. Only at the last minute, when there was no longer time for the visitors to make preparations, did the government consent to on-site inspection. And even then it denied access to Aguacate and Swan Island, where the supply program was still in operation. In the end, the commission never went beyond Tegucigalpa.

Notes

1. Peter Jenkins, *Mrs. Thatcher's Revolution: The Ending of the Socialist Era* (Cambridge: Harvard University Press, 1989), p. 210.

2. Strobe Talbott, *Deadly Gambits* (New York: Alfred A. Knopf, 1984), p. 78.

3. Whether he was aware of this was the subject of some debate within the White House. Lou Cannon concluded that "at some level" he probably did know the difference but didn't care. The stories were simply a means of creating an effect. And certainly his aides didn't object. In the words of White House spokesman Larry Speakes, "If you tell the same story five times, it's true." Lou Cannon, *President Reagan: The Role of a Lifetime* (New York: Simon and Schuster, 1991), pp. 37-42, 54-64. Quoted materials on pp. 56, 60.

4. Jane Mayer and Doyle McManus, *Landslide: The Unmaking of the President, 1984-1988* (Boston: Houghton Mifflin, 1988), p. 35. The expression "The truth was a problem to be solved" is attributed to the political essayist Leon Wieseltier.

5. *New York Times,* 7 April 1983.

6. *Washington Post,* 6 November 1984.

7. Interview with John Ferch, 9 April 1990.

8. *New York Times,* 20 August 1987.

9. Ibid., 2 November 1984.

10. Ibid., 18 August 1985.

11. This from a classified briefing paper to the ambassadors. *Excélsior,* 8 September 1985.

12. *La Jornada,* 10 October 1985; *Uno Más Uno,* 11 and 13 October 1985; *Central America Report,* 1 November 1985.

13. Press conference, 21 February 1985.

14. U.S. General Accounting Office, *Central America: Problems in Controlling Funds for the Nicaraguan Democratic Resistance,* Report to the Chairman, Subcommittee on Western Hemisphere Affairs, Committee on Foreign Affairs, U.S. House of Representatives, GAO/NSIAD-87-35, December 1986. Between 1984 and 1986 as much as US$97 million may have been raised for the contras. This was considerably more than the FDN's own estimates of its needs. More than US$20 million could not be traced. *New York Times,* 8 April 1987.

15. *Miami Herald,* 9 May 1986.

16. Sam Dillon, *Comandos* (New York: Henry Holt, 1991), pp. 175-176.

17. See Philip L. Shepherd, "The Tragic Course and Consequences of U.S. Policy in Honduras," *World Policy Journal,* Vol. 2, No. 1, Fall 1984, p. 118.

18. The report called these practices a "significant departure from the past." The United States "does not generally leave facilities, materials, or equipment behind." Moreover, the exercises had been improperly used to conceal aid to the contras. *Miami Herald,* 1 July 1984.

19. *New York Times,* 4 and 5 June 1985.

20. Mayer and McManus, *Landslide,* p. 77.

21. See Theodore Draper, "The Rise of the American Junta," *New York Review of Books,* Vol. 34, No. 15, 8 October 1987, pp. 47-48.

22. Roy Gutman, *Banana Diplomacy* (New York: Simon and Schuster, 1988), pp. 282-283.

23. Testimony of Oliver North and John Poindexter before the Select Committee on Secret Military Assistance to Iran and the Nicaraguan Opposition, 8 and 15 July 1987.

24. Theodore Draper, *A Very Thin Line* (New York: Hill and Wang, 1991), pp. 114-116, 348-349, 531-534; Cannon, *President Reagan,* pp. 626-627; Mayer and McManus, *Landslide,* p. 68.

25. Draper, "An Autopsy," *New York Review of Books,* Vol. 34, No. 20, 17 December 1987, pp. 69-70.

26. See Draper, *A Very Thin Line,* pp. 108-109; Cannon, *President Reagan,* pp. 714-718; *New York Times,* 5 May 1989.

27. *New York Times,* 23 March 1990.

28. Mayer and McManus, *Landslide,* p. 82.

29. Except where otherwise noted, this section is based on interviews with John Ferch, 23 June 1988 and 9 April 1990.

30. Ferch's comment to one of his aides, as reported by the latter (not-for-attribution).

31. Gutman, *Banana Diplomacy,* pp. 315.

32. This from a high-level embassy source (not-for-attribution).

33. Interview with Ferch's deputy, Shepard Lowman, 19 July 1988; *Philadelphia Inquirer,* 7 January 1987.

34. *Philadelphia Inquirer,* 7 January 1987; Lowman interview; *El Tiempo,* 25 March 1986.

35. From a Honduran government official quoted by the Associated Press in *El Nuevo Diario* (Managua), 4 April 1986.

36. *Philadelphia Inquirer,* 7 January 1987; Ferch and Lowman interviews.

37. *La Tribuna,* 26 March 1986; *ACAN* (Panama City), 2 April 1986, in Foreign Broadcast Information Service, *Daily Report: Latin America,* 3 April 1986; *Cadena Audio-Video,* 7 April 1986, in ibid., 8 April 1986; *New York Times,* 3 and 4 April 1986; *Los Angeles Times,* 3 April 1986.

38. *Miami Herald,* 9 April 1986.

39. Ferch and Lowman interviews; Ferch testimony in the *Philadelphia Inquirer,* 7 January 1987; *New York Times,* 4 April 1986.

40. *Washington Post,* 8 January 1987.

41. Gutman, *Banana Diplomacy,* p. 324.

42. This discussion is based primarily on ibid., pp. 321-325. Quoted materials are on page 322.

43. *El Tiempo,* 15 April 1986; *New York Times,* 29 May 1986.

44. This paragraph is based on information in the Ferch interviews and from conversations with several State Department and embassy officials.

45. Or at least they deny knowledge of these activities. Ferch believes that the embassy station chief was also kept in the dark about the Secord operation, but I have been told otherwise by another high-level embassy official (not-for-attribution).

46. Interview with Ted Briggs, 9 April 1990.

47. Americas Watch, *Human Rights in Honduras: Central America's "Sideshow"* (New York, May 1987), p. 130.

48. The purported reason for the attack was that the military had been trying to capture Salvadoran guerrillas who had been using the camps as a safe haven and source of resupply. This may well be true. Nevertheless, critics pointed out that since May the camps had been surrounded by a

Honduran military cordon and that all refugees had been required to report at checkpoints and carry Honduran identification. Americas Watch, *Human Rights in Honduras After General Alvarez* (New York, February 1986), pp. 5, 35.

49. *Miami Herald*, 19 August 1986.

50. Interview with Ricardo Zúniga Morazán, 26 February 1985; *Central America Report*, 10 October 1986.

51. *New York Times*, 1 December 1986.

52. *St. Petersburg Times*, 6 December 1986; *Central America Report*, 19 December 1986.

53. These paragraphs are based primarily on Dillon's *Comandos*, pp. 168ff. The long quote is on p. 184.

54. *El Tiempo*, 12 January 1988.

55. *New York Times*, 6 August 1987.

56. Ibid., 8 August 1987.

57. Gutman, *Banana Diplomacy*, pp. 349-351.

58. Ibid., pp. 349-353.

59. *Central America Bulletin*, November 1987.

60. *La Prensa*, 10 August 1987.

61. *Inforpress Centroamericana*, 20 August and 17 September 1987.

62. Ibid., 13 August 1987.

6

A Journey into the Depths: Economic Crisis and Social Decay

Everything that God put here is beautiful. It is only the things that man put here that are ugly.

—Doris Morazán

Flying into Tegucigalpa can be a hair-raising experience. The city is nestled at the foot of tall mountains. Typically, planes come in over the ridges, then dive quickly to the airport far below. It is one of the most dangerous descents anywhere. It is not quite so bad on TAN-SAHSA flights because the Honduran pilots navigate close to the mountains. ("Our pilots are trained to fly between the trees" was the way one TAN official put it.) On the other hand, the less experienced U.S. pilots, fearing downcurrents, try to stay clear of the hills. They come in higher, and their drop is steeper. Landings are like going down a roller coaster, veering sharply to avoid foothills and then coming in low and fast over Bulevar Toncontín. If a pilot comes in too low, he risks hitting one of the trucks or buses passing the airport (and every now and then there is an accident, and someone is killed). If he comes in too high he may not be able to stop on the eighteen-hundred-meter runway; the plane could easily go through the neighboring barrio and across the Bulevar de las Fuerzas Armadas to plunge into the gorge of the San José River. Toncontín is one of the few airports in the world where passengers often break into spontaneous applause upon landing.

Between 1958 and 1983 no fewer than ten international studies concluded that Toncontín did not meet the minimum conditions for safe air navigation. The maximum angle for a safe descent was 2.5 percent; the trajectory at Toncontín was 7.6 percent. By the same token, takeoffs required aircraft to rise as rapidly as possible in order to clear Mount Picacho on the other side of the city. Some of the oldest commercial planes still in operation flew in and out of Toncontín. This kind of daredevil navigation placed enormous strains on pilots, aircraft, and motors. Yet in spite of the obvious dangers and repeated warnings from professional associations, Honduran authorities continued to react with negligence, apathy, and bureaucratic obstruction.[1]

Ordinary people approached this situation with the same wry humor they accorded their other national idiosyncrasies. On Sunday evenings, just before sunset, a crowd would gather in the parking lot of the Infinito discotheque across the street to watch the planes come in. Families would bring sodas and beer. Bets would be made as to which planes would land safely and which would not. It was great entertainment.

In another sense, however, the descent into Toncontín was symbolic of the state of Honduran society. In socioeconomic terms, the country was going down fast, and the passengers seemed to be stuck in a state of suspended animation, holding their breath, waiting for the crash, amazed that they had thus far been able to escape the chaos that was engulfing Nicaragua, El Salvador, and Guatemala. How long, many wondered, could peace be maintained?

The Economic Crisis: Onset and Causes

In the early 1980s the central bank conducted a revealing study on the development of the nation's economy. It found that between 1960 and 1982 the economy had grown by an average of 4.4 percent a year but that this growth had done almost nothing to improve the abysmal conditions in which the vast majority of Hondurans lived. In 1960, 81 percent of the population had been classified as extremely poor; in 1982, 81 percent were still extremely poor.[2]

About this time, the economy took a sharp plunge downward. Between 1979 and 1982 the growth of the GDP fell from 6.8 percent to -1.7 percent. Per capita growth dropped from 2.9 percent to -5.2 percent. Thereafter, the situation gradually stabilized, with the economy growing 2.8 percent in 1984 and a little over 3 percent in 1985-1986. This was not enough, however, to overcome the rapid population increase, and so per capita GDP continued to decline. By 1986 the country had experienced seven consecutive years of negative per capita growth. Meanwhile, real wages and salaries plunged 7.7

percent in 1983 and continued to fall (though less dramatically) in the years that followed. Unemployment increased from between 7 and 15 percent in the 1972-1980 period to perhaps as much as 26.5 percent in 1986. At the same time, a dramatic change occurred in the pattern of government spending. Whereas in 1980 nearly two-thirds of that expenditure went for civilian socioeconomic programs and only one-third for defense and debt, by 1984 precisely the opposite was the case: Defense spending and debt service absorbed close to two-thirds of the government's budget and only 35 percent went to other activities.[3] Not surprisingly, those hit first and hardest were the poor.

The causes of the crisis were complex. A major factor was a sharp decline in the terms of trade. Between the late 1970s and early 1980s, international recession took a heavy toll on the prices Honduras received for its exports. Coffee fell from over US$3 a pound to less than US$1.40 on the world market. The country's other agricultural products also generally experienced low prices. At the same time, the volume of exports declined substantially. As a result of the second oil "shock" of 1979, the price of imported petroleum increased. From an index of 100 in 1978, the terms of trade fell to 92 in 1980 and 73 in 1982. Meanwhile, the foreign debt began to soar, and so did interest payments. Between 1980 and 1985 the debt doubled, exceeding the US$3 million mark in 1986. From this point on, debt service surpassed new aid disbursements. Between 1986 and 1988 service charges consumed about half of all export earnings. Furthermore, as the country became increasingly militarized and joined the United States in virtually continuous military maneuvers, oil became an increasingly important part of the Honduran import basket. From 1982 to 1984 it accounted for about 21 percent of the cost of all imports, up from 16 percent in 1980-1981. In combination, these factors led to a growing trade gap and balance of payments problems.[4]

Beyond this, regional warfare and economic disintegration took a heavy toll. Intraregional trade collapsed. Foreign interests proved unwilling to invest in an area torn by civil strife and economic crisis. During these years, capital flight and disinvestment reached alarming levels. Although such things are impossible to calculate with confidence, the leading U.S. scholar on the Honduran economy has estimated that during the first five years of the crisis (through 1985) capital flight was probably around US$1.5 billion. Other sources are more conservative. Credible estimates for the decade as a whole range from about US$800 million to well over US$2 billion. In comparison, U.S. economic aid between 1980 and 1989 was only US$1.15 billion.[5]

As the crisis deepened, the government found itself having to choose between unpalatable and risky alternatives: On the one hand, it could attempt to finance needed imports and growing militarization by imposing severe austerity measures that would cut even further into personal income and consumption. On the other, it could try to cover the rising balance of payments and fiscal deficits by securing more foreign and domestic credit. Since the former was politically difficult and risked triggering massive social unrest and political instability, the government opted for the latter. Initially, it borrowed anywhere it could, including from the International Monetary Fund (IMF). In 1983, however, the IMF deal collapsed and the Hondurans turned increasingly to internal credit to keep the economy afloat. In the process, government involvement in the economic arena grew considerably. Public investment became the primary demand factor stimulating the economy as the state borrowed huge sums of money from the central bank. By 1986 the economy was drowning in freshly printed lempiras, paving the way for a surge of inflation toward the end of the decade. After 1985, moreover, multilateral lending virtually ceased. Honduras increasingly came to rely on U.S. aid—especially economic support funds—to finance its balance of payments deficits. Gradually, the country was being transformed into an "economic garrison state" and an "international welfare case."[6]

Economic Crisis and Social Decomposition

With economic decline came an acceleration of social disintegration. Although Honduran statistics leave much to be desired (there are no complete and reliable figures on employment, for instance—just estimates and projections), there is universal agreement that an already grim situation became much worse after 1980. Even by the most conservative calculations, there were over half a million people unemployed or underemployed by 1986, and a more realistic figure, based on the assumption that the rate of underemployment was much greater in the countryside than the cities, would probably be around 800,000 (though the previous year the College of Economists had put the total at over 900,000). How many of these were unemployed as opposed to being employed part-time is impossible to say. The UN Economic Commission for Latin America estimated open unemployment at around a quarter of the workforce. Other sources were more conservative, one placing the figure as low as 8.2 percent. (The latter, however, did not include hidden unemployment, for which no information is available. Moreover, the estimate of rural unemployment—4.4 percent—seems extremely optimistic.) Perhaps the best guess at the overall unemployment rate would be between 15 and 21 percent. Estimates of rural underemployment were similarly varied, ranging from 30 to 89.1 percent, with another 30 to 44 percent underemployed in the cities.[7]

Under the circumstances, those who survived often did so by joining the ranks of the "self-employed." During these years, the informal sector of the economy swelled to record proportions as the number of itinerant vendors increased dramatically. On the average, one could earn 13 to 14 lempiras a day (US$6.50-$7.00 at the official exchange rate) by selling lottery tickets, clothing, chewing gum, fruit, newspapers, prepared foods, cold drinks, auto accessories, toiletries, and other items in downtown Tegucigalpa or at the San Isidro market in Comayagüela. The vast majority of these vendors, having lost their previous jobs, had set up shop after the early 1980s. Most were dissatisfied with their lot, though many had learned to accept it with the same fatalism that the poor had always used as a defense mechanism in the face of circumstances that they were powerless to change. Most could survive but not much more, since their growing numbers meant more competition, which in turn drove down the prices that they could charge for their goods and services.[8]

These activities, though essential for survival, contributed in no small part to the growth of crime and squalor in the capital. Petty thieves flourished in the stalls of San Isidro. The streets were increasingly littered with garbage. Children ran wild while mothers attended their *chiclera* stands. Those who could not afford to set up a business of their own often became professional beggars, haunting the sidewalks and doorways, sometimes entering restaurants to hover around the tables of gringos who might give them a few scraps out of pity or embarrassment. Mothers and grandmothers trained children to beg or steal. Crippled mendicants set up shop around the National Cathedral. Everywhere small boys offered to "guard" parked automobiles. For a small fee they would guarantee that your car would not be vandalized; if you declined to pay, it would.

Meanwhile, lower-class families disintegrated. Cultural values had, of course, always fostered irresponsibility in Honduran family life. Male self-esteem was closely tied to machismo. One of the ways of proving oneself a man was through sexual conquest and impregnation. (As one Honduran feminist put it, "The male ego is located in the penis.") Consequently, there was little sense of obligation to wives and children. Men did not have to be faithful. Many simply left their women (most relationships were never established legally in any case) and started new families elsewhere. Rarely was birth control practiced. The church forbade it. Men felt that it robbed them of their masculinity; children, after all, were proof of one's virility. And so Honduran males spread seeds of joy (and anguish) throughout the land.

Female attitudes tended to complement those of the men. Women often defined their identity and social role in terms of the production of babies, and this self-perception was reinforced by a considerable amount of social and economic pressure. In the words of one close observer of Honduran society: "If a woman hasn't had children by the time she is twenty, people begin to ask what is wrong with her." At the same time, women had traditionally been dependent on and subservient to males. Many were willing to accept the role of mistress in the hope that their men would provide for them and their children.

Thus, even before the current crisis, family life—especially in the lower classes—was marked by great instability. Hard times, however, considerably aggravated the problem. Women became even more anxious to attach themselves to men, and men found it harder than ever to provide. When the pressures of daily life became too great, the easiest way out was to leave. In most cases, the women would try to care for their offspring as best they could. One could not but be struck by the strength and courage of many of these mothers, who succeeded in holding together the remnants of their family in the face of overwhelming obstacles. But the task was often impossible, and the number of abandoned children grew. Youngsters were forced to survive on their own in the streets of Tegucigalpa and other urban centers. Juvenile delinquency thrived; child prostitution and involuntary servitude became significant social problems; criminal violence and official and semiofficial counterviolence assumed alarming proportions. It became commonplace to find the homeless under bridges or along the banks of the Choluteca and Chiquito Rivers in conditions of indescribable squalor: Since there were no sewage treatment plants in Honduras, filth was simply dumped into the rivers where people bathed, washed their clothes, and got water to cook with and drink. Small wonder that one often encountered children on the riverbanks poaching their brains with *resistol,* a cheap glue. Sniffing numbed the pain of hunger and deprivation and for a time allowed them to escape into a more pleasant world of illusion. Unfortunately, it also had devastating side effects. In time glue sniffers came to resemble walking zombies. Every year some 150 of an estimated 5,000 habitual users died.[9]

This was a poor foundation for the construction of a stable and prosperous society. Nor did the situation in the countryside help matters. Most country people lived on a per capita income of US$70 a year, a sum that covered only about 28 percent of their basic consumer needs. Between 1980 and 1988 real rural salaries had declined by around 23 percent. Underemployment was rampant. (Some sources estimated that a mere 11 percent of the workforce was employed full-time.) Only 65 percent of rural residents had access to health services and only 55 percent to potable water. Perhaps as many as 75 percent were in some stage of malnutrition (though much of this was the result of improper diet rather than the absence of food). In spite of the agrarian reform, some 150,000 families—fully a third of the rural population—remained landless. The number was increasing by at least 8,000 a year as "competitive exclusion" and rapid population growth more than offset the modest gains made under the Liberal administrations of the 1980s. There were now more landless families than before the 1972 reform. Moreover, the quality of the land that had been distributed was often so poor (and technical assistance and credit so scarce) that many of these properties were no longer being cultivated. About a quarter of the peasants who had received lands from the National Agrarian Institute had since abandoned them.[10]

As if this were not enough, campesinos also had to deal with the double scourge of the Nicaraguan presence and severe drought. Thousands of peasants along the southern border were being driven off their lands by the contras. Fighting between the Sandinistas and the rebels had turned the area into a war zone, plagued by frequent bombardments, firefights, and human rights violations. Workers were afraid to harvest crops because of land mines. In El Paraíso, at least thirty-four *aldeas* (small villages) had been abandoned. Although damage estimates varied, a moderate assessment would probably be around US$20 million, with some 12,000 Hondurans affected.[11] Worse yet, in 1986 a combination of floods and drought led to a disastrous loss of basic grains, producing widespread famine in Choluteca, Valle, and other southern departments. Several hundred thousand people were severely affected, and some died of starvation. In desperation, peasants left their homes in search of food, pouring into Choluteca and other cities. To its discredit, the Azcona government was slow to respond to the emergency. Local Liberal and

National Party bosses restricted the distribution of emergency food to members of their own party or faction. It was not a pretty scene.

The troubles in the countryside accelerated a long-standing pattern of rural-to-urban migration. In Tegucigalpa, which had grown tenfold since 1950, the hillsides became increasingly congested with makeshift *tugurios* (shanties). Between 1973 and 1983 the population had grown from 305,000 to 600,000, overwhelming existing housing facilities and leading to a rapid proliferation of land invasions by *paracaidistas* (parachutists) seeking to establish new settlements. On the other side of the Choluteca River, downtown Comayagüela was surrounded on three sides by one- and two-room shacks made of crude lumber and scrap materials, with wooden or corrugated metal roofs often held in place by rocks. The heat and dust were suffocating. Of the 115 barrios served by the social work facilities of the Central District's Metropolitan Council in 1982, 48 had no water and another 45 had it only in limited areas. Thirty-eight were without electricity; 80 had no sewage system.[12] Many shacks had dirt floors. Some of these communities were extremely vulnerable to mudslides and floods during the rainy season. During the dry season, water became exceedingly scarce.

This was more than just a temporary problem. Massive deforestation was changing the traditional patterns of rainfall at precisely the moment when rapid population growth was placing unprecedented demands on the capital's water supply. Increasingly, water had to be rationed or trucked into even middle- and upper-class neighborhoods. The natural sources were running out. Indeed, the entire southern part of the country from Tegucigalpa to the Nicaraguan border was in danger of becoming a desert.[13]

One culprit was slash-and-burn agriculture, another bureaucratic indifference. The Honduran Forestry Development Corporation, disabled by clientelism, had never been able to acquire the motivation and competence to do what was necessary to defend the environment. Thus, for all the timber that was cut down, little reforestation occurred. The prevailing attitude was exploitation: The wealth was there, so take it and the future be damned. Meanwhile, people still widely used wood for fuel. Campesinos cleared the land in the manner of the ancients, by burning, which resulted in widespread forest fires and soil damage. Cultural values (Catholicism, machismo) encouraged big families. Peasants still regarded large numbers of offspring as an asset. Children could help work the farm and provide a form of social security in one's old age. The upshot was that too many people were occupying too little good land. The soil was becoming overworked and was losing its fertility; forests were being destroyed; erosion and mudslides had become major problems; usable water was disappearing; arable land was turning to dust.

Water and housing, of course, were not the only items in short supply. The number of jobs, schools, and medical facilities could not begin to keep up with the exploding urban population. Even in the cities, most of the people were affected by malnutrition, internal parasites, or infectious diseases. Alcoholism and mental illness were spreading rapidly as socioeconomic conditions worsened, but as late as 1986 there were only thirty-seven psychiatrists in the entire country. In spite of what can only be described as an ongoing medical state of emergency, some four hundred recent medical graduates were unemployed.[14] In any case, most people could not afford decent health care, so they either suffered in silence, resorted to home cures or *brujas* (witch doctors), or placed themselves at the tender mercy of the medieval *médicos* in San Felipe hospital (where one North American missionary reported seeing diarrheic babies left to lie in their own excrement).[15]

This was the "country of *nada*," where demoralization and despair reigned and hope for the future was but a fleeting illusion. In the words of Edward R.F. Sheehan, "An air of hopelessness, a sense of the futility of ever truly changing anything, pervades the entire country. The favorite Honduran word is *nada*—nothing. *'El gobierno no hace nada . . . la iglesia no tiene nada . . . no tenemos nada . . . yo soy nada'* ('the government does nothing, the church has nothing, we have nothing, I am nothing')—phrases we heard everywhere. The people are passive and fatalistic, low in self-esteem. (In Spanish, Honduras means 'the depths.')"[16] "In 15 Years Honduras Will Be a Country of Retards," blared one newspaper headline in response to the latest report on the stunting effects of malnutrition on childrens' physical and mental development.

The starvation was emotional as well as physical. People desperately needed to believe in something. Almost anything. In their search for spiritual sustenance, many turned to evangelical religions. The 1980s witnessed a massive Protestant penetration of Honduras. If people could not believe in themselves, they could at least find hope and comfort in a higher authority. Unfortunately, the ultraconservative nature of many of these sects had the effect of reinforcing the passivity and fatalism of the mass political culture. As in the days of Karl Marx, religion was still the opiate of the people.

The U.S. Response

Philip Shepherd once observed that statistics on the current crisis are more like symptoms of a disease than its causes; moreover, that it would be myopic to suppose that the economy was just passing through a difficult but temporary phase after which everything would be well again. On the contrary, "the current crisis is less important than the profound chronic crisis Honduras has suffered for a very long time. When the current crisis passes, as it probably will eventually, Honduras may 'only' have 250,000 unemployed instead of 300,000 at present. . . . We are not simply talking about the problems of short-term economic reversal but also the extraordinary poverty, misery and inequality in which more than three-quarters of Hondurans have long found themselves. The need is for profound changes at all levels and policies which will enable Honduras to get out of the chronic crisis as well as the current one."[17] This is very true. Yet, when all is said and done, there remains a basic problem: How does one induce foreign elites with a vested interest in the status quo to promote change? In particular, "how can we hope to reform systems of power which seem responsive only to the threat of their destruction when we begin by guaranteeing their survival"?[18]

Under the Reagan administration, ideological and security concerns were paramount. Social justice was a secondary issue, if that. Washington could encourage the militarization of Honduras even though this meant diverting scarce resources away from sorely needed socioeconomic programs. Militarization led to a huge increase in foreign and domestic debt; it siphoned off funds that would have been better used to spur on economic development and raise living standards. It also led to a "boom" of sorts in the urban service sector as numerous hotels, bars, discotheques, restaurants, and houses of prostitution sprang up to cater to the growing U.S. presence. In turn, these highly liquid operations served as conduits for capital flight and currency speculation. Such activities had little to do with self-sustaining development that could generate economic recovery and employment on an ongoing basis. They were, however, a source of considerable short-term wealth (not to mention increased dependency), and they did help secure the cooperation of Honduran military, political, and business elites in the holy war against the Sandinistas.

U.S. priorities were reflected in the kind of economic aid provided. After 1981, a major shift occurred. Whereas previously economic support funds had constituted less than one-half of 1 percent of all U.S. economic aid (1946-1981), between 1982 and 1986 they amounted to around 55 percent. Defined by law as "security aid," these funds, taking the form of large-scale cash transfers, served to "close the balance of payments gap and fiscal deficit, thus 'bailing out' the economy, subsidizing military spending, and propping up elite consumption." Most of this aid went to the purchase of U.S. goods and services. Transferred directly to North American firms, contractors, and consultants, much of the money never got to Honduras. And that which did helped maintain middle-and-upper-class lifestyles by enabling the recipients to continue importing luxury items.[19] In contrast, development assistance, which had accounted for some 69 percent of U.S. economic and military support from 1946 to 1981, fell to 21 percent between 1982 and 1989.[20]

Beyond this, the administration's economic program—dubbed "Reaganomics for Honduras" by the local press—paid inadequate attention to the basic needs of the vast majority of the populace. On the contrary, its short-term stabilization policies were discriminatory and regressive, threatening to shift most of the burden of economic recovery onto the poor. At the same time, its export-led, direct-foreign-investment private-sector strategy offered established businessmen, agro-export elites, and U.S. investors new opportunities for self-enrichment. The administration pushed hard to get the Hondurans to adopt an IMF-style austerity program, but some of its recommendations were too much even for the Suazo government. Devaluation of the lempira, in particular, raised the specter of massive popular unrest, since it would have seriously depressed the purchasing power of the poor. Even the middle class would have been hurt because of the increased cost of imported goods. Consequently, in spite of repeated U.S. pressure to devalue, cut social spending, privatize unprofitable state enterprises, and otherwise reduce the fiscal and balance of payments deficits, the Hondurans resisted. Caught between the demands of its economic ideology and the need to maintain Honduran stability and cooperation, the Reagan administration usually subordinated its economic concerns to the contra program.

After 1985, however, the situation began to change as the Honduran bargaining position declined and José Azcona proved less resistant to North American pressure than his predecessor. By early 1986 the U.S. military presence and the contras were firmly established. The country continued to be in dire straits economically, and there seemed little likelihood of recovery without continuing, massive foreign aid. Shortly after Azcona's election, the Reagan administration "broke through the dike of Honduran resistance." Honduras increasingly began to comply with the "conditions" attached to U.S.

aid. From this point on, Honduran economic policy would be heavily influenced by the Agency for International Development, which would act as a virtual "shadow government," with parallel bureaus corresponding to Honduran ministries and agencies. The AID would constantly monitor Honduran "progress," cutting off funds when "U.S.-imposed targets [were] not met, threatening, prodding, and generally harassing," dictating the "broadest national fiscal and monetary policies down to the smallest grassroots development projects."[21] Even so, the Azcona government continued to resist the bête noire of devaluation.

By 1987 the economy was showing some signs of recovery. The GDP grew by 4.2 percent, exceeding population growth for the first time in years. Inflation was almost negligible; the lempira had stabilized. At the same time, however, the government was plagued by massive fiscal deficits, an overvalued exchange rate, shortage of foreign exchange, and declining private-sector confidence. About a fifth of the workforce was still unemployed, with many more employed only part-time. Real wages and salaries continued to decline. For the first time in years, corn and beans had to be imported. Moreover, things did not seem likely to get much better. In spite of considerable effort to "sell Honduras" to foreign investors, there were few takers. Indeed, the banana transnationals were threatening to pull out unless they were granted lower taxes and special concessions. Attempts to promote the privatization of state-owned enterprises were having little success. The Central American wars dragged on, frightening away investors and spurring capital flight. Prices for most of the country's raw-material exports remained depressed, with little relief in sight. Meanwhile U.S. efforts to promote nontraditional exports (melons, cucumbers, seafood, clothing, softballs, etc.) were generally not going very well. Hondurans had little experience in the marketing of such goods. In the words of the U.S. embassy, the program's potentials remained "underdeveloped."[22]

Part of the problem, too, was that Honduran institutions had only a limited capacity to absorb technical assistance and administer projects. Beyond the pervasive problem of corruption, the state lacked the expertise/competence to run large, complex aid programs effectively. It also lacked the capital to finance its share of project costs. Nor did there seem much likelihood that it could fund the recurring costs (e.g., maintenance) of completed projects in the future. Moreover, the bureaucratic obstacles remained formidable. The government's centralized procurement process averaged over one hundred steps and required about seven months to complete. (In some cases, the process took over two years.)[23] State agencies were overstaffed and inefficient. One could walk into almost any of the myriad bureaucracies in the capital and find three or four persons sitting around doing nothing for every one who was working. In a very real sense, they had "taken possession" of their jobs.[24]

Even when there was a genuine desire to respond to a particular problem, the capability was often limited or nonexistent. Thus, one study of the National Agrarian Institute found that the management had "inherited a motor vehicle pool which theoretically contained about 400 vehicles," most of which were "junk." In all of the INA, including the seven regional offices, there were only twenty-four vehicles in operation. There were problems in every area of administrative support. There was "no personnel system other than a small office which handle[d] the paperwork." Office space was "poorly assigned, poorly furnished, overcrowded, and clearly demoralizing." Supplies and equipment were in short supply.[25] In such circumstances, noted one North American observer, the old saying "Obedezco, pero no cumplo" ("I obey, but I do not comply") took on new meaning: Administrators *could* not comply because the resources were not available.[26]

In spite of all this, the AID stressed the positive: The vast majority of children under five had been immunized against childhood diseases; infant mortality had declined; thousands of new housing units and classrooms had been constructed; 330 kilometers of new rural farm-to-market roads had been paved; hundreds of thousands of person-years of employment had been generated.

There were, of course, real accomplishments here. Some individual projects *had* done well. But such portraits also tended to obscure the forest from the trees. More detached observers were almost unrelievedly pessimistic. In the words of one high-ranking embassy official, the country was "going to hell in a handbasket."[27] A resident Department of Agriculture consultant found the economic problems "intractable," with "no light ahead."[28] Some thought that the AID had a vested institutional interest in a rosy portrait. A U.S. government auditor of AID projects complained that agency personnel tended to be self-congratulatory, arbitrary, and insensitive to Honduran feelings and needs. A Peace Corps volunteer who worked closely with the AID lamented that the people she interacted with cared little for development work. Rather, their commitment fell more along the lines of "paycheck, housing allowances, per diem, and the next post."[29] It was an assessment that was shared by many others.

The Growth of the Corruption System

Beyond the inadequate resources, the incompetence, the unfavorable terms of trade, and so on, there was the pervasive problem of corruption. This was something that the embassy—and the AID in particular—could never really come to terms with. The tendency was to pretend that the problem did not exist or, at least, was marginal and controllable. In part, this was the product of a certain culture-boundness. North Americans have a tendency to project their own values onto others. It was easy for them to assume that their Honduran allies saw the world as they did and would behave accordingly. When evidence to the contrary began to appear, the instinctive response was selective perception—minimization, if not denial, of the obvious.

Then, too, there were the limitations imposed by political reality: Elite selection in Honduras was still largely an internal affair. The Reagan administration could not always choose whom it would deal with. If it tried too blatantly to interfere in such matters, it risked a nationalistic backlash that might seriously undermine its Nicaraguan strategy and draw unwanted attention to one of the country's most unsavory features. U.S. policy was based on cultivating an image of virtue for its Central American allies: These were the "good guys" as opposed to the villains in Managua. It was not at all clear that Congress would be willing to continue pouring hundreds of millions of dollars into a country governed by scoundrels, especially when a scandalous proportion of that aid—30 to 50 percent, according to Vice President Jaime Rosenthal[30]—was either wasted or siphoned off by the corruption system. In short, a closer accounting was politically inconvenient. As one frustrated U.S. auditor remarked, "You have to *look* for corruption, and we hardly try."[31]

This was much more than a matter of a few high-ranking officials helping themselves to cash that was not theirs. There were over a hundred publicly identified cases of corruption in the Suazo administration alone. The president himself had been deeply involved in payoffs and the misappropriation of funds, reportedly distributing more than US$4 million to his friends during his last two months in office.[32] "Like the mythical Hydra, graft [had] slowly invaded every available space in public administration. Bribery, buying and selling influence, fraud, and simple robbery of public funds [had] become an indispensable lubricant without which state machinery [would] not turn."[33] To gain approval to set up a small business, one had to go through a long list of procedures, each of which was a "toll booth manned by a bureaucrat" who would "exact his share of the economic rewards."[34] The military too got its cut. Knowledgeable sources in the capital claimed that a full colonel could be bought for US$40,000 and an influential civilian for US$5,000. This, of course, was not counting payments to the subordinates who controlled access.[35]

The private sector also partook of the spoils. The business community had come to think of the government as a piñata. Private enterprise was largely an illusion because Honduran firms depended on all kinds of subsidies, special treatment and tax breaks.[36] In the process, fortunes were made. The most notorious case was that of the National Corporation of Industrial Development (Corporación Nacional de Desarrollo Industrial—CONADI). Set up under the López Arellano government in 1974 for the purpose of fostering a national industrial sector, the CONADI provided low-cost loans to private investors. Between 1975 and 1980, it authorized 102 million lempiras (US$51 million) in direct loans and 208 million (US$104 million) in loan guarantees to industrialists at a ratio of 8.08 lempiras for every lempira of private capital invested. To finance its operations, it borrowed heavily on international capital markets, where its dealings were underwritten by the Honduran government. Unfortunately, many of the recipients found it more profitable to convert their lempiras into dollars and deposit the money in foreign banks. There was also an abundance of poor investments and incompetent or corrupt administration. The CONADI's policies were often governed by political criteria. Lending rules were widely violated. Technical advice was ignored. Loans were made without adequate collateral or documentation, sometimes in amounts disproportionate to the capital available. By 1981, the CONADI was bankrupt. As of May 1986, it owed 631 million lempiras to its lenders, and almost 630 million of that had been already lent. Of the companies that had received loans, only five percent were financially sound. Of the thirty-four companies that had absorbed 94 percent of the loans, sixteen were bankrupt, and the remainder would have been unable to meet all their financial obligations had they been required to do so in the short run. In some cases, the companies involved were nonexistent.[37]

One of the most striking symbols of the CONADI scam was the unfinished Sheraton Hotel, which sat on Tegucigalpa's Bulevar Miraflores like some great bombed-out hulk from a World War II air raid. Such unfinished shells of buildings dotted the Honduran landscape, courtesy of the government-private enterprise gravy train. The money trickled through the fingers of numerous bureaucrats, politicians, bankers, businessmen, contractors, and military officers until there was nothing left. Then the construction stopped, leaving the state with a debt of over US$300 million and virtually nothing to show for it.

Some of Honduras's wealthiest and most influential entrepreneurs drank from the CONADI trough. The Facussé family, in particular, was deeply involved. As vice president of the APROH and primary author of the famous "Facussé memorandum" (which argued that the only way out of the national crisis was to "sell" Honduras to the foreign investor), Miguel Facussé would become one of the leading architects of the Suazo administration's economic program. His nephew, Carlos Flores, would become Suazo's political adviser and, subsequently, a candidate for president. Back in the 1970s, however, the family's agribusiness and chemical companies had borrowed heavily from the CONADI. Mejores Alimentos alone had acquired a debt of over US$31 million—22.8 percent of the CONADI's loans. Another US$20 million was owned by Azucarera Central and involved such luminaries of private enterprise as Gilberto Goldstein, Paul Vinelli, Edwin Rosenthal, and Miguel Bendeck. The list of loan recipients included so many members of the Honduran establishment that it was in no one's interest to shed too much light on these transactions. Though President Azcona formed an investigating commission, he acknowledged that for all practical purposes the money was lost forever. Needless to say, indictments were not forthcoming.

Subsequently the Honduran government, under AID pressure, moved to "privatize" its CONADI holdings. In the short run, however, there were few takers. The low profitability of the enterprises, the lack of foreign and domestic capital, and the highly politicized nature of the project kept away most potential investors.

The CONADI scandal illustrated one of the most glaring weaknesses of the U.S. aid program. How could one promote economic growth when so many of the people on the receiving end were dishonest or incompetent or both? U.S. policy was dependent on the very people who were responsible for the mess the country was in. Nor did it help that, to facilitate the disbursement of assistance, more than half of U.S. aid was by 1984-1985 in the form of cash transfers, which required little management or oversight. Not surprisingly, they led to enormous waste.

One can hardly exaggerate the scope and depth of the problem. Corruption was not restricted to political, military, and business elites; it pervaded every segment of society. As Doris Morazán observed, there was a widespread feeling that if you could not protect your possessions you deserved to lose them. In such an atmosphere, petty theft thrived alongside grand larceny. La mordida flourished. Journalists took bribes intended to influence their reporting; postal employees robbed the mail; bureaucrats "facilitated" the obtaining of drivers' licenses and export permits; prison officials sold privileged treatment to criminals wealthy enough to afford it; policemen took "protection money"; "vigilantes" conspired with housebreakers; at Toncontín Airport black marketeers plied their trade under the very noses of the authorities. These hallmarks of social decay were everywhere. Hondurans had always been vulnerable to such temptations. Now, however, economic hard times had combined with the massive influx of North American money to break down whatever restraints remained.

The Narcotics Trampoline

By the mid-1980s, the corruption had taken a new turn. Honduras had become a major bridge for international drug trafficking. During his watch as head of the U.S. Southern Command in Panama (1983-1985), General Paul Gorman had warned his superiors in the Pentagon and the joint chiefs of staff about the danger that these activities posed for hemispheric security. But no one had been interested.[38] The administration viewed national security in more traditional terms; its obsession with the communist menace blinded it to the new threats that were emerging. Indeed, in 1983 the Drug Enforcement Administration office in Honduras had been shut down in spite of extensive reports from its head that senior Honduran military officers had become involved in the cocaine trade.[39] Efforts by U.S. officials to investigate were resisted by the embassy and higher authorities. On more than one occasion, the administration intervened in court proceedings involving Honduran drug traffickers with CIA links.[40] Not much, it seemed, had changed since the early 1980s when the agency had winked at the illicit activities of Colonel Torres Arias.

Yet, things *were* different. By 1986-1987 the trafficking was completely out of control. Senior officers, primarily associated with the navy and military intelligence, had formed an alliance with Juan Ramón Matta Ballesteros to turn the country into the main drug transshipment point between Colombia and the United States. In the process civil society, as well as the military, was being rapidly corrupted as the traffickers offered drug money to politicians and political parties and bought up businesses and land to launder their profits. In the estimate of one senior Honduran leader, the country was so poor and the army so corrupt that the dealers "could probably buy the officers and most of the National Assembly over the next five years."[41]

At the center of the scourge was Matta Ballesteros. Raised in the mean streets of Tegucigalpa, a barefoot, hardscrabble youth who would never learn to read or write, he had made his way to the United States for the first time at the age of sixteen. Over the next two decades he would be deported five times, but he would always return, armed with a false name and a forged passport. He had been, among other things, a field hand in Texas and a grocery clerk in New York City, and along the way he had become involved in organized crime—initially as a "chemist" in a small drug smuggling ring and eventually as "director" of an enormous, vertically integrated conglomerate. In the 1970s, he became the partner of a Guadalajara-based Mexican drug baron named Félix Gallardo, and over the next decade the two men transformed the regional drug trade from a backwoods bootleg operation into a sophisticated multinational enterprise. Between 1978 and 1981 Matta, with the help of Torres Arias, penetrated the Honduran armed forces. Subsequently, military involvement grew rapidly as the Medellín cartel channeled massive amounts of narcotics northward to the United States. In the process, Matta became one of the richest men in Honduras, with an estimated fortune of US$2 billion.

Matta's exploits were not limited to drug trafficking. In the late 1970s, he had been arrested in connection with the Ferrari killings. He stood accused in Mexico of having murdered thirteen Colombians and was involved in the 1985 torture-killing of the U.S. drug enforcement agent Enrique Camarena. He was an accomplished escape artist, having walked out of one jail in the United States and another in Colombia. Arrested in Cartagena in April 1985, he had been consigned to Bogotá's La Picota penitentiary while the government processed U.S. extradition requests. In September, the warden of that institution was assassinated after having personally frustrated a Matta escape attempt. Transferred to El Modelo, reputedly the most secure facility in the country, in March 1986 Matta made a spectacular escape greased by a US$1 million bribe. Almost immediately, he resurfaced in Honduras, where the constitution forbade the extradition of Honduran nationals. After a few months in the Central Penitentiary, living in specially designed quarters with a private kitchen, dining room, bedroom, and bath and furnished with a new color television set, Matta was absolved of the Honduran charges against him. Significantly, the presiding judge felt obliged to issue a public declaration that he had neither been bribed nor pressured to reach a favorable conclusion.

In November 1986 Matta left the Central Penitentiary for the more luxurious surroundings of the Colonia Los Angeles. There he lived until the dramatic events of April 1988. In the interim, he bought military officers and government officials, ensuring his continued security and influence. He even became something of a local legend—a modern-day Robin Hood who defied the gringos and stole from the rich to feed the poor. He built schools, was the employer of hundreds of Hondurans in a time of massive unemployment, and regularly received the legions of the impoverished at his mansion, where he handed out 20-lempira bills in the fashion of a true patrón. An aura of mystery and glamour surrounded him. Those passing his house would fall silent, attributing to him supernatural powers or, at least, a monitoring system capable of hearing even whispered conversations.

Meanwhile, the narcotics business flourished. There were in Honduras numerous unattended airstrips and unpatrolled islands from which drugs could be transshipped to the United States. Of the 215 registered airstrips, only 3 had effective security systems. Between late 1986 and early 1988, perhaps as much as fifty tons of cocaine moved through the country—about half the estimated consumption in the United States. In October 1986 a Colombian plane carrying a ton of the drug was seized in La Ceiba. In July 1987 DEA agents in Chicago seized US$1 billion in cocaine hidden in a shipment of Honduran bananas. Including earlier deliveries, the smugglers had brought more than five and a half tons into the country over the preceding year. In November, authorities in Florida discovered more than four tons of cocaine concealed in two shipments of Honduran wood. Other caches were found in frozen fish and shrimp. (The Reagan administration's efforts to promote nontraditional exports were bearing unanticipated fruit.) At year's end, the drug lord Jorge Ochoa Vásquez was captured by Colombian authorities while driving a Porsche Turbo belonging to the Honduran military attaché to Bogotá, Colonel William Said Speer. The estimated value of the car was US$260,000. Some observers wondered how Said Speer could have afforded such an automobile on a mere colonel's salary; others thought they knew.

Only slowly and reluctantly did U.S. authorities recognize the full dimensions of the crisis. When charges were made that Honduran officials were involved, Ambassador Briggs expressed his government's regret about this "false and baseless speculation."[42] In interviews and congressional testimony, Elliott Abrams absolved the Honduran leadership: General Regalado had warned of the danger that drugs posed to his country; he had asked for aid to help combat the problem. At his request, the DEA office in Honduras was being reestablished. As in any army, of course, there were a few bad eggs, but that did not mean that the institution itself was corrupt. Those who accused the armed forces of drug trafficking and human rights violations were playing politics, using these issues to undermine U.S. Central American policy.[43]

In fact, the accusations were coming from a wide variety of sources, with diverse motives—not only from the Honduran left but from Honduran conservatives, U.S. journalists, and State Department officials, supporters as well as opponents of U.S. policy. In February 1988 James LeMoyne blew the whistle in a *New York Times* exposé that chronicled CIA-embassy tolerance of these activities. The following day the *Los Angeles Times* reported that Reagan administration officials suspected Regalado himself of protecting Colombian traffickers. An unnamed State Department official was quoted as saying, "We don't know the extent of the Honduran military's involvement in drugs, but our educated guess is that all of the senior officers have knowledge, many are involved . . . and they are all reaping the profits."[44]

Bureaucratized Anarchy and Social Protest: The Labor Movement

If demoralization, passivity, and fatalism were major components in the Honduran social equation in the 1980s, one should not make the mistake of assuming that all Hondurans were submissive. Some raised the banner of protest. In fact, the number of urban social conflicts increased sharply between 1982 and 1988. In 1982-1983 there had been 52 such incidents; in 1987 alone there were 178, and the number was continuing to grow. The vast majority of these actions centered upon narrow economic demands (most were initiated by unions), but some were political or at least combined economic with political themes.[45] Continuing socioeconomic crisis and the easing of repression after the Alvarez years encouraged protest on the part of a multitude of disaffected interest groups. By 1987, the clamor was becoming deafening.

Organized labor had, of course, long been an important sociopolitical actor in Honduras. Though it was not at the center of power, it was strong enough for those who were to have to take it into account. Workers were a constituency that not only had to be "listened to, consulted with and accommodated, but also . . . curbed, co-opted and divided."[46] And the latter was made all the easier by the chronic inability of union leaders to cooperate with one another.

Honduran society is an alphabet soup of acronyms, and the labor movement is no exception. At mid-decade, there were four different umbrella groups or *centrales*, representing various political tendencies and strategies, composed of a vast array of federations, associations, unions, and enterprises. The oldest and largest of these, the Confederation of Honduran Workers (Confederación de Trabajadores de Honduras—CTH), was ostensibly social democratic in orientation, but its leaders generally gave the impression of being opportunists. Historically, the CTH had been the most conservative of the centrales; receiving much of its funding from the American Institute for Free Labor Development, it was often charged with being a pro-United States, pro-government, "business union." The organization's longtime general secretary, Víctor Artiles, had been a member of Gustavo Alvarez's ultraright-wing business group, the APROH. This did not, however, prevent him from running for Congress on the social democratic ticket. Nor did the confederation's social democratic orientation prevent its president from actively participating in the conservative National Party.[47] This kind of opportunism did not sit well with some workers. At one May Day celebration, Artiles was booed off the platform amidst flying oranges, bananas, and other debris.

The CTH, in short, was a heterogeneous amalgam with no real ideological integrity, vulnerable to external penetration and manipulation and plagued by ideological and personality conflicts, internal power struggles, and corruption. Part of the problem was generational conflict, with the old guard fighting to hold onto its leadership in the face of the challenges posed by younger cadres. There was considerable discontent, particularly among the rank and file, with the leadership's lack of militancy. Many felt that the organization was stagnating and were trying (with some success after mid-decade) to push it leftward. Accusations of graft abounded. Rarely were such claims seriously investigated, however, with the result that charges and countercharges tended to cancel one another out, obscuring the very real abuses that existed and fostering an atmosphere of cynicism and corruption. Under these conditions, the left often proved just as vulnerable to the temptation of easy riches as the right.

Then there was the problem of "outside" intervention. Conservatives in the labor movement had powerful allies. "Reliable" elements received funding from the Honduran government, the AIFLD, and other sources. The result was the further division of the rank and file. At times, unions would be split into parallel organizations, with only the progovernment faction granted legal recognition. "Democratic fronts," a time-honored stratagem, had been used with great effect against Las Isletas and the CTH affiliate SITRATERCO in the 1970s and continued to be employed in the 1980s.

From mid-decade on, moreover, a new threat arose in the form of *solidarismo,* a promanagement ideology imported from Costa Rica that was designed to weaken and/or destroy the union movement.[48] In essence, the proponents of solidarismo maintained that the workers did not need unions to defend their interests—that the interests of business and labor were basically the same. The fundamental objective was to increase production so that the wealth created could be distributed equitably in accordance with the principles of efficiency and justice. To achieve this, it was argued, class struggle had to be replaced by the spirit of human solidarity. Existing unemployment and pension funds were to be converted into savings accounts to be managed by the new solidarity associations. The first such organization appeared in 1985 in Polymer Industrial, a subsidiary of United Brands. By the decade's end, some two dozen other groups had been established in such major enterprises as Cervecería Hondureña, a subsidiary of Castle and Cook (Standard Fruit); the American Pacific Mining Company of El Mochito; the National Electrical Energy Company; the national telecommunications company (HONDUTEL); and the Banco de El Ahorro and the Banco Futuro. The intent, clearly, was to divide the labor movement and destroy the bases of its leadership.

Beyond this, however, the unions were their own worst enemies. Not only were the centrales divided internally but they were continually interfering in each other's affairs. The worst offenders were the CTH and the FUTH. The latter had been born in 1981 out of an ideological and personalistic dispute within the CTH and had originally been dominated by the Honduran communist parties (pro-Soviet and Maoist). Ever since, CTH leaders had been convinced—not without reason—that the FUTH was trying to destabilize their organization by encouraging leftists to assume control of it and luring others to join the FUTH. The CTH elite retaliated in kind, joining the government in efforts to divide the FUTH and co-opt its member groups. Partly as a result of this external interference and partly as a consequence of an internal power struggle in which more moderate elements gained control of the organization, from mid-decade onward the FUTH was subjected to factional conflicts that threatened to tear it apart.

None of the major centrales was immune to intervention and conflict. The promise of legal recognition was used to co-opt the most professional of them, the reform-minded, Christian-Democratic-oriented General Central of Workers (Central General de Trabajadores—CGT). With the attainment of legal recognition in 1983, some of the CGT's most prominent leaders moved to embrace the National Party, their combativeness decreasing accordingly. By the end of the decade, the organization would actually be more conservative than the CTH (though in part this would also be due to the latter's shift to the left). The CTH too was sometimes subjected to government interference. The most blatant cases, however, involved the FUTH: In 1982 the military seized the offices of the national teachers' union, ejecting its leadership. The organization's moneys and office equipment were confiscated. Legal recognition was granted to a small group of progovernment teachers who proceeded to take their "union" out of the FUTH and realign it with the CTH. Two years later, moreover, the authorities struck again. When the members of the national electrical workers' union, STENEE, walked off the job, its legal recognition was suspended. A labor commission was formed to negotiate with the government. But since FUTH had never had legal recognition and STENEE's status was now in limbo, their representatives were denied admission. Instead, the commission was composed of leaders from the more conservative CTH and CGT. Not surprisingly, few gains were made.[49]

The first law of Honduran politics is divide and conquer, but there are always harsher measures that may be taken: The "disappearance" of STENEE's Rolando Vindel, the assassination of the FUTH's Cristóbal Pérez, the threats against Leonor Meza were object lessons. Militancy carried with it grave risks and costs that not everyone was willing to bear. The consequence of outside manipulation and repression, combined with the severe internal weaknesses of the workers' movement, was the growing atomization of organized labor.

Bureaucratized Anarchy and Social Protest: The Peasants

The campesino movement was, if anything, in even worse condition. Some 20 percent of the peasants were organized—an impressive accomplishment in a predominantly agrarian society—but the forces of ideology, personality, clientelism, corruption, external manipulation, and repression that had played havoc with labor had fragmented campesinos as well. By the mid-1980s, there were three major organizations: the CTH-affiliated Association of Honduran Peasants formed in 1962 with the help of the AIFLD as a counterweight to the more militant (now defunct) National Federation of Honduran Peasants; the CGT-linked National Peasant Union which had emerged in the late 1960s out of peasant leagues formed by the Catholic church; and the Federation of Honduran Agrarian Reform Cooperatives (Federación de Cooperativas de la Reforma Agraria—FECORAH), which had arisen in the early 1970s out of the agrarian reform process with the support of the National Agrarian Institute. In early 1985, however, breakaway groups from these organizations created the National Central of Rural Workers (Central Nacional de Trabajadores del Campo—CNTC) as a radical alternative to the three majors. And later that year, the Federation of Honduran Peasants (Federación de Campesinos de Honduras—FCH) was formed through a union of three other groups. Nor was this all. Over the years six different organizations had emerged from the ANACH and five from the UNC. These divisions had spawned subdivisions, and so on down the line, until there were no fewer than fifteen campesino groups in operation. As one AID official quipped: "While Honduran soil may not be the best for most crops, it sure is fertile ground when it comes to peasant organizations. You just plant one, and a half-dozen new ones crop up."[50]

Meanwhile, agrarian unrest was mounting. Between 1982 and 1986 some 260 conflicts occurred in the countryside, often resulting in imprisonment, torture, or loss of life.[51] Much of this activity took place at planting time (around May) and involved land invasions or *recuperaciones*. Under General Alvarez, these seizures were treated as terrorist acts, with the perpetrators subject to five-to-twenty-year prison sentences. At the same time, Alvarez's APROH openly maneuvered to take over the direction of the ANACH. After the strongman's ouster, a more flexible approach was adopted. Efforts were made to co-opt moderate peasant leaders by accepting them as legitimate negotiating partners. When the UNC staged a coordinated series of land invasions in April 1985, leading to the arrest of some 140 campesinos, Walter López met with its leaders and agreed to a prisoner release. In the meantime, the UNC and the INA had formed a joint commission to study the suitability of the occupied lands for inclusion in the agrarian reform. During the massive land recoveries of May 1987, López's successor, Humberto Regalado, even struck a populist pose, wooing peasant leaders with protestations of sympathy and promising to use his influence with Azcona to bring about a negotiated settlement. (Reportedly, he complained that the government was not interested in agrarian reform—that the only way for it to move forward would be for the military to take over, but the United States would not stand for that.)[52]

As in the case of labor, legal recognition was a major instrument of co-optation. As one scholar lamented, "Peasant organizations struggle to win government recognition, which entitles them to a series of benefits (such as funds to pay organizers and the right to sit on the National Agrarian Council—a government-landowner-peasant body which settles land disputes). But once groups achieve this status they are beholden to the state, as the government begins to pay staff salaries, provide cars, lawyers, etc. So achieving legal status has often tempered militancy. Organizations only gain government recognition . . . once they have moved toward a more conciliatory position."[53]

Because of the extreme poverty of the sector and the more personalistic nature of its leadership-base relations, campesino organizations were even more vulnerable to this kind of manipulation than labor. Perhaps the most blatant instance involved the UNC. Long the most militant of the campesino organizations and the spearhead for the massive land invasions that became the trademark of the peasant movement, the UNC in 1984 was finally accorded legal recognition. In return, it moved sharply to the right, embracing the National Party and the military. In 1986 the progressive faction of the UNC was expelled at the organization's Seventh Congress (though a core of cadres remained committed to reviving its combative tradition). About the same time, it was reported that the UNC general secretary, Marcial Caballero, was working for military intelligence.[54]

Corruption and bribery have many faces. The UNC presented one, the INA another. When civilian government was restored in 1982, many people assumed that agrarian reform would be a priority. Idealists flocked to the INA in the belief that their presence could make a difference. In the beginning, regional administrators sometimes even organized land invasions themselves.[55] But the illusion did not last long. Neither the AID nor the Honduran government was interested in a real agrarian reform. (Land titling and agricultural reform, yes, but not much more.) When this became obvious, disillusionment set in. Corruption, always a problem, became rampant. In the process, the INA became increasingly bureaucratized and conservative, a major obstacle to reform. Administrators were hired for political reasons rather than because of their professional capabilities.

Lacking skills, experience, and interest, they dragged their heels as the situation in the countryside deteriorated.

During these years, the INA became an instrument of division. With the aid of conservative, anticommunist leaders in the UNC, the ANACH, and the FECORAH, INA Director Mario Espinal set out in 1986 to destroy the institute's militant trade union (Sindicato de los Trabajadores del Instituto Nacional Agrario—SITRAINA), blaming it for the failure of the agrarian reform. (By the early 1990s almost 97 percent of the INA budget would be devoted to salaries).[56] Campesinos were incited to occupy the INA's central and regional offices. The SITRAINA's dissolution was demanded, and eventually it was decapitated. Peasants were set against workers and against each other. (The most radical of the peasant groups, the CNTC, sided with the SITRAINA.) The cause of unity was dealt yet another telling blow.

Still, the movement would not go away. In May 1987, in response to Azcona's failure to live up to a promise to deliver 30,000 manzanas of land before the rainy season, tens of thousands of campesinos launched over two hundred simultaneous land seizures. All of the major peasant organizations were involved. By this time, even most of the conservative campesino leaders had become convinced that as long as Mario Espinal remained director of the INA there would be no agrarian reform. In the negotiations that ensued, all of the organizations except the UNC (which opened its own separate talks with the government) demanded his ouster. On this point, the administration balked. ("I would prefer to leave the Presidential Palace," said Azcona.) On others, however, it was more forthcoming. Among other things, it promised to set up an agrarian commission to adjudicate the specific cases in dispute. The government pledged to implement a program of land and titles, to provide credit, technical assistance, and training, to draft a national agrarian reform plan, and to release those who had been arrested during the incursions. In early June the commission announced that some 20,000 manzanas would be handed over. In just fifteen days more land had been adjudicated than in the previous eighteen months.

Once the commission's work was done, however, the initiative reverted to Espinal and the INA. By mid-June charges were again being raised that the reform was being sabotaged. At the beginning of July the major peasant groups (minus the UNC) met to consider their progress. The commission was proclaimed a failure. The legalization of the occupied lands was being thwarted by bureaucratic obstruction. In the process, the government had gained valuable breathing space. In the words of one observer, "Thus closes, at least for the moment, a chapter in the sad history of the agrarian struggle. . . . A chapter in which the campesinos, in some cases through good faith, in others through calculated opportunism, were manipulated by the government and the military. And the time bomb lit by the massive recoveries of May was deactivated."[57] (In March 1988 President Azcona finally gave in to peasant demands and removed Espinal from office.)

Bureaucratized Anarchy and the Revolutionary Opposition

In October 1986 guerrilla warfare once again came to Honduras, when several dozen members of the Cinchonero Popular Liberation Movement were discovered operating in the Nombre de Dios Mountains, some hundred and ninety kilometers northeast of Tegucigalpa. Over five hundred soldiers, reportedly accompanied by U.S. advisers,[58] were dispatched to track them down. Roads leading to the zone were militarized. The civil defense committees were reactivated. Dozens of suspected guerrilla sympathizers were detained. Eight rebel camps were discovered, along with an arms cache and a small amount of marijuana. Honduran military sources immediately accused the insurgents of having received aid from Nicaragua and Cuba and claimed that they had a well-organized logistical support system in the departments of Yoro, Cortés, Atlántida, and Francisco Morazán. For their part, the guerrillas professed to have ninety members in their column, but most sources put the number substantially lower.

The Cinchoneros were not alone. By 1987 five other groups had also declared themselves in favor of armed struggle. The U.S. Southern Command estimated the total number of militants to be as high as 1,000, though the number of armed and active combatants probably did not exceed a fifth of that.[59] Indeed, some of these groups were little more than paper organizations. The Cinchoneros themselves, after several years of revolutionary activity in the early 1980s (the high point of which had been the seizure of the San Pedro Sula Chamber of Commerce in August 1982), had been decimated by General Alvarez's counterinsurgency operations. Except for a brief spate of bombings in Tegucigalpa in late 1984, little had been heard from them in recent years.

The other revolutionary groups were similarly ineffective. The most notable of these organizations were the Popular Revolutionary Forces—Lorenzo Zelaya, the Morazanista Front for the Liberation of

Honduras, and the Revolutionary Party of Central American Workers. (This last was best-known for its July 1983 "invasion" from Nicaragua, during which the North American priest James Carney was killed.) None of these groups had ever shown any signs of having mass support, much less the ability to coordinate their activities. As with so many other Honduran social and political movements, bureaucratized anarchy had ravaged the revolutionary left. Partially as a consequence, its attempts to promote guerrilla struggle were never much more than sound and fury, signifying nothing.

The Frustrations of Nationalism and Dependency

One recalls the comments of a retired North American music teacher who had come to Honduras to help put together a national symphony. After many months of effort he left, disgusted with his hosts' inability to cooperate with one another. Everything, he complained, was "ego and power." Turf rivalries and personality conflicts had brought the project to the point of collapse. And now foreign funding had run out.

Honduras was an extraordinarily splintered society. It was not just the workers and peasants who were divided but virtually all organized movements: the political parties, the Catholic church, the armed forces, the business community, the revolutionary opposition. Division and strife—a generalized inability to cooperate on behalf of the common good or the national interest—were deeply ingrained in the culture.

Beyond this, Honduran nationalism was still weak and poorly defined. Although politicians were quick to pay lip service to nationalist slogans and symbols, their actions often belied their words. Beneath all the rhetoric and the other surface manifestations, Hondurans harbored serious doubts about their own nationalist credentials.

At the same time, they seemed enamored with almost everything North American. They listened to U.S. music, wore U.S. T-shirts, drank Coca-Cola, and increasingly longed to escape their own desperate circumstances by emigrating to the "land of opportunity." Public opinion polls consistently revealed that a large majority looked favorably on the United States (93 percent, according to one U.S. Information Agency [USIA] survey) and felt that it would come to their aid if they were attacked by a foreign power (88 percent).[60] Smaller but nevertheless substantial majorities continued to favor U.S.

military activities in their country (including the joint exercises) and supported aid to the contras. As one embassy report commented, "Increased American activity in Honduras has not encountered the kind of public controversy locally that it has in the U.S. Public opinion surveys conducted since 1985 . . . have consistently highlighted a healthy consensus in favor of a continued U.S. presence here."[61] Even critics of U.S. policy were sometimes forced to face these realities. As one of them lamented, "Nowhere else in Central America do U.S. officials and visitors get told so much of what they desperately want to hear—that the Sandinistas are a mortal threat, that the Salvadoran guerrillas are even worse than the government there. . . Americans 'feel at home' in Honduras . . . in a way they do not anywhere else . . . because Hondurans are so obliging in a way that is not true even in Costa Rica, a nation with which we probably share much closer values."[62]

The embassy's complacency was, however, ill-founded. Public opinion was not one-dimensional; moreover, it was changing, sometimes in ways that were not reflected in the polls. If in the beginning Hondurans had reacted with optimism or indifference to the growing U.S. involvement, by the mid-1980s many had begun to have second thoughts. At first, this usually took the form of grumbling that Honduras was not receiving enough aid for its services. As the war in Nicaragua dragged on, however, and the contra presence became increasingly disruptive and semipermanent, discontent assumed other manifestations and spread beyond the relatively narrow confines of leftist university and labor circles to embrace moderates and conservatives who were traditionally friendly to the United States.

The peace process itself accelerated this malaise. As the Arias plan inspired hope for an end to the Nicaraguan conflict, the fear that the United States might abandon Honduras grew. The feeling spread that Honduras was being used—or, at least, that its relationship with the United States was more beneficial to the Reagan administration than to Hondurans.[63] Resentment mounted: The rain of dollars had not materialized "as promised"; the socioeconomic crisis continued unabated. Increasingly, Hondurans began to feel that their dignidad was being violated. By early 1988, 30 percent of the USIA's annual survey respondents said that the United States lacked respect for Honduras (up from 18 percent the previous year). Twenty-four percent felt that U.S. treatment of Honduras was unfair (up from 13 percent). These were warning signs. Not unexpectedly, they were ignored.

Part of the problem lay in the instrumental nature of U.S. policy. Honduras had been relegated largely to the status of a tool or weapon in the Reagan administration's ongoing wars against Central American communism. Nationalists felt this intensely. They believed that the United States showed little interest in Honduran needs and "aspirations as an independent nation." Even General Alvarez could feel the indifference. Once, after his removal, he remarked that, in all his years as a high ranking official in frequent contact with U.S. personnel, rarely had the Americans expressed any interest in Honduran concerns or hopes for the future. Rather, the focus was almost entirely on "strategic information."[64]

Beyond this, North Americans could be extraordinarily insensitive to Honduran feelings. In 1983, for example, the Honduran and U.S. armies had seized a large cattle ranch in Puerto Castilla and converted it into the site for the Regional Military Training Center (CREM). The property was owned by a U.S. citizen, Temístocles Ramírez, who protested the seizure and filed a claim against the U.S. government demanding compensation. But questions as to the validity of the title soon arose. The Honduran Constitution forbade foreign ownership of property (such as Ramírez's) located within forty kilometers of the coast. In addition, Honduran law stipulated that state lands (which these properties had been prior to their acquisition) could be sold only for public benefit. The case was further complicated by the competing claims of Garífuna tribes dating to the turn of the century, by Ramírez's failure to petition Honduran courts, and by the fact that the company in question, Ganadera de Trujillo, was not actually his but belonged to a Honduran corporation, Inversiones Centroamericanas, that held 90 percent of the shares. Finally, the Honduran government, although conceding that some compensation should be paid, put the figure far lower than Ramírez's demands. Among other things, it seemed, he owed several million dollars in back taxes.

Notwithstanding these very real issues, the Reagan administration had threatened to exclude Honduras from its share of the initial distribution of funds from the Caribbean Basin Initiative. Under pressure, Suazo Córdova had agreed to compensate Ramírez. However, no action was taken. The dispute dragged on until finally, in 1987, the U.S. House of Representatives resolved to withhold US$20 million in foreign aid until the matter was settled. The move touched off a storm of protest in Honduras, where almost all political groups opposed indemnification. Nationalists cited the case as yet another North American violation of Honduran sovereignty. Once again, national laws were being subordinated to the interests of foreigners:

Ramírez had acquired these lands illegally (presumably through bribery). The confiscations had been made at the behest of the Reagan administration for the benefit of its pet project, the CREM. Ramírez had recognized U.S. responsibility by bringing suit against the United States. And now the United States expected Honduras to pay! (Twenty million dollars, though Arthur D. Little had assessed the value of the property at only $5.2 million.) The dispute provided a natural channel for displacing pent-up frustrations and resentments.[65]

Even more damaging, potentially, was the "Saigonization" of areas near U.S. military facilities. Here the old colonial town of Comayagua was the most striking case. Until the early 1980s, Comayagua was a sleepy little city about halfway between Tegucigalpa and Lake Yojoa on the northern highway. In 1982, however, the United States moved into Palmerola Air Force Base about 3 kilometers from the town. In the years that followed, this initially small installation spread over surrounding lands, eventually becoming home for some 1,200 U.S. troops rotating in and out of the facility. At first, the locals benefited. The base brought employment, customers for local businesses, and money. But gradually the undesirable side effects of the U.S. presence became evident: Prostitution flourished. By mid-decade, Comayagua housed twenty bordellos and ninety registered prostitutes. Hundreds of others were unregistered. On weekends, dozens were trucked in from the capital. Boys loitered in the central park and its environs soliciting dollars on the black market and offering to lead GIs to drugs and women. Not surprisingly under such circumstances, venereal disease spread rapidly. La Flor de Vietnam, a penicillin-resistant strain of gonococcus that had emerged in Southeast Asia during the 1960s, became common.

In early 1986 several prostitutes tested positive for the AIDS-related virus HTLV-III. A panic followed. Fear of contracting the disease caused people to stay at home as much as possible. Merchants and ranchers from surrounding areas avoided coming to Comayagua. Boom turned into bust. The assumption, of course, was that the plague had been brought by the gringos. About this same time, moreover, it was reported in the local press that North American troops had been involved in several child prostitution cases. Though the charges were never proven, these issues provided a convenient vehicle for radicals to whip up anti-American sentiment. Shock and outrage rippled through Honduran society. Congress ordered an investigation. In an editorial entitled "The National Shame and the Boys of Reagan," *El Tiempo* called for a thorough review of U.S.-

Honduran relations, declaring that "now we enter a foreseeable phase of development of a profoundly anti-North American sentiment in Honduran society that . . . did not previously exist. Nor was it desired."[66]

The concepts of dignidad and soberanía have much stronger and more compelling connotations than their English equivalents. No matter that these ideas were often ignored or violated by Hondurans themselves, they could still provoke intense reactions in that minority of citizens whose personal identity and self-esteem were closely linked to nationalistic values. This was one of the most crucial of the many contradictions in the Honduran political culture. If the psychology of dependence (the patrón-peón mentality) had led Hondurans to seek a foreign benefactor in a time of trouble, there were always those who understood that the embrace of the foreigners carried with it an inherent diminution of sovereignty and a potential loss of dignity. Moreover, as these realities became increasingly apparent, others could no longer ignore them. Honduras had been seduced; now it might well be abandoned. Desperately, Honduran leaders began to look elsewhere for sources of economic sustenance. The opening of commercial negotiations with the USSR and Czechoslovakia in 1987 produced a flurry of optimism that the "Soviet option" might lessen the country's dependence on the United States. But the illusion was short-lived. The communist states had problems of their own.

In Comayagua that August, a Chinese restaurant frequented by U.S. soldiers was bombed. Six Americans and as many Hondurans were injured. Though U.S. authorities quickly declared the town off-limits, the attack was an omen. Increasingly, U.S. soldiers would become the targets of violence. Beneath the surface of continuing U.S.-Honduran amity, a nationalistic reaction was building. All that was necessary was the right incident to spark an explosion.

Notes

1. *El Heraldo,* 4 October 1988.

2. *El Tiempo,* 14 October 1983.

3. United Nations Economic Commission for Latin America (ECLA), "Notas para el Estudio Económico de América Latina y el Caribe, 1985, Honduras," 13 June 1986; ibid., "Notas, 1988," 6 July 1989; *"Diagnóstico del Desempleo y Subempleo en Honduras,"* Boletín Informativo Honduras, Special No. 8, January 1984, p. 3; Philip L. Shepherd, "The Case of the Invisible Aid," *NACLA Report on the Americas,* Vol. 22, No. 1, January-February 1988, p. 36.

4. Ian Walker, *"Deuda y Ajuste Estructural: El Caso de Honduras, 1980-1988,"* Boletín Informativo Honduras, Special No. 50, September 1990, pp. 3-4, 16-17, 20-21; J. Mark Ruhl, "The Economy," in *Honduras: A Country Study*, James D. Rudolph, ed. (Washington, D.C.: American University Press, 1984), p. 109. Oil imports did drop sharply after 1984.

5. This includes Economic Support Funds. Based on the AID figures listed in *Boletín Informativo Honduras*, No. 115, November 1990, p. 5. The US$1.5 billion capital flight estimate comes from a conversation with Philip L. Shepherd.

6. Philip L. Shepherd, "The Honduran Economic Crisis and U.S. Economic Assistance: A Critique of Reaganomics for Honduras" (Unpublished manuscript, 1987), pp. 22-23, 29.

7. Roberto Flores Machado, "La Situación del Empleo en Honduras," *Cuadernos de Realidad Nacional*, No. 3, January 1988, pp. 1-4; ECLA, "Notas, 1988," 6 July 1989; Julio Antonio Bueso, *El Subdesarrollo Hondureño* (Tegucigalpa: Editorial Universitaria, 1987), pp. 192-193. Complicating the problem of estimating rural unemployment is the fact that it varies widely with the season and the crop.

8. David and Bobbie Andrews, "Los Vendedores Ambulantes en Tegucigalpa" (Paper presented at the Conferencia VII Semana Científica, Universidad Nacional Autónoma de Honduras, 18 October 1989).

9. *El Tiempo*, 11 June 1988.

10. *Análisis y Propuestas Sobre las Seis Recomendaciones en Materia Agraria Formuladas por la Misión Presidencial Agrícola de los Estados Unidos de América a Honduras* (Tegucigalpa: Instituto Nacional Agrario, n.d.); Raúl Ruben, *Notas Sobre la Cuestión Agraria en Honduras* (San José: Universidad Libre de Amsterdam, 20 July 1989), pp. 37-38; Mario Ponce, "Honduras: Agricultural Policy and Perspectives," in *Honduras Confronts Its Future*, Mark B. Rosenberg and Philip L. Shepherd, eds. (Boulder: Lynne Rienner, 1986), p. 133; Charles D. Brockett, "Public Policy, Peasants, and Rural Development in Honduras," *Journal of Latin American Studies*, Vol. 19, Part 1, May 1987, p. 82; Bueso, *El Subdesarrollo*, p. 192.

11. Centro de Documentación de Honduras (CEDOH), *Desplazados de Guerra Hondureños*, Chronology No. 10, October 1988, p. 1.

12. Leticia Salomón and Bethenia Galo, *"El Proceso de Urbanización en la Capital de Honduras,"* Boletín Informativo Honduras, Special No. 19, September 1985, pp. 2-5; Hilda Caldera, *"Las Invasiones Urbanas en Tegucigalpa,"* ibid., Special No. 26, July 1986, pp. 10-12.

13. Interview with Becky Myton, one of Honduras's foremost environmentalists, 28 May 1989.

14. Bueso, *El Subdesarrollo*, pp. 19-27.

15. Marion Howland, personal communication, 5 October 1988.

16. Edward R. F. Sheehan, "The Country of *Nada*," *New York Review of Books*, Vol. 33, No. 5, 27 March 1986, p. 11. Actually, the country was named by Christopher Columbus, who was struck by the depth of its natural ports, but Sheehan's point is well taken. Hondurans do tend to have poor self-concepts. They

often describe themselves as a lazy people. Even their jokes and stories have a self-deprecating quality about them.

17. Shepherd, "The Honduran Economic Crisis," pp. 32-33.

18. Tom J. Farer, "Political Development in Central America: Democracy and Humanitarian Diplomacy," Testimony before the National Bipartisan Commission on Central America, 29 September 1983.

19. Shepherd, "The Case of the Invisible Aid," pp. 33-35.

20. Based on AID figures as reported in ibid., p. 33, and *Boletín Informativo Honduras,* No. 115, November 1990, p. 5.

21. Shepherd, "The Case of the Invisible Aid," pp. 35, 37.

22. U.S. Embassy, *Handbook on Honduras: Defense, Development, Diplomacy, and Drug Control,* spring 1989. An exception was the lobster and shrimp industry, which took off after 1986, producing more than 11 percent of the value of the country's agricultural exports in 1988-1989.

23. U.S. General Accounting Office, *Providing Effective Economic Assistance to El Salvador and Honduras: A Formidable Task,* Report by the Comptroller General of the United States (Washington, D.C., GAO/NSIAD-85-82, 3 July 1985), pp. ii-iii, 18-19.

24. The *"tomar posesión"* syndrome. When a Honduran begins a new job, he says *"Yo tomo posesión"* ("I am taking possession"), the implication being that he owns it or has a right to it (whether he does any work or not). This is one of the idiosyncrasies of the Spanish language, which both reflects and helps shape thought, values, and action in subtle yet often important ways.

25. Jack Vaughn et al., *Final Report: An Administrative Analysis of the National Agrarian Institute of Honduras* (Arlington: Development Associates, Inc., 1983), pp. 7-8.

26. Mark B. Rosenberg, *Democracy in Central America?,* Occasional Paper Series No. 44, Latin American and Caribbean Center, Florida International University, March 1985, p. 26.

27. Interview with Don Johnson, 9 August 1989. Johnson was Ambassador Briggs's political counselor.

28. Conversation with Clarence Dunkerley, 20 July 1989.

29. Letter from Jan Brockman, 12 June 1990.

30. *Boletín Informativo Honduras,* No. 71, March 1987, p. 1.

31. Private conversation. (Not-for-attribution.)

32. *Boletín Informativo Honduras,* No. 78, October 1987, p. 1; CEDOH, *La Corrupción en Honduras, 1982-1985,* Chronology No. 3, September 1985.

33. Víctor Meza, "The Military: Willing to Deal," *NACLA Report on the Americas,* Vol. 22, No. 1, January-February 1988, p. 20.

34. Interview with former U.S. ambassador to Honduras Everett Briggs, 9 April 1990.

35. This from two friends who claimed to have paid such sums.

36. Jaime Rosenthal, in *El Tiempo,* 11 March 1987.

37. The information from this and the following paragraphs is largely from "CONADI: Destapando una Caja de Pandora," *Inforpress Centroamericana*, No. 703, 21 August 1986, pp. 6-8.

38. U.S. Senate Committee on Foreign Relations, Subcommittee on Terrorism, Narcotics, and International Communications, *Drugs, Law Enforcement, and Foreign Policy: Panama*, 100th Congress, 2nd Session, 8, 9, 10, and 11 February 1988, Part 2 (Washington, D.C.: U.S. Government Printing Office, 1988), pp. 46-49.

39. U.S. Senate Committee on Foreign Relations, Subcommittee on Terrorism, Narcotics, and International Operations, *Drugs, Law Enforcement, and Foreign Policy*, (Washington, D.C.: U.S. Government Printing Office, 1989), p. 76.

40. The Bueso Rosa affair is the most notorious example, but see also Mort Rosenblum's account of the Molina case in "Hidden Agendas," *Vanity Fair*, March 1990.

41. *New York Times*, 12 February 1988.

42. Quoted in Rosenblum, "Hidden Agendas," p. 116.

43. *El Heraldo*, 23 February 1988; *Boletín Informativo Honduras*, No. 83, March 1988, pp. 8-9.

44. *Los Angeles Times*, 13 February 1988. A similar report appeared in the *Miami Herald*.

45. Bohanerges Mejía and María Elena Méndez, "Honduras: Crisis y Demandas Populares," in *Honduras: Panorama y Perspectivas*, Leticia Salomón, ed. (Tegucigalpa: CEDOH, 1989), pp. 179-195.

46. Damián Fernández, "The Honduran Labor Movement" (undated draft manuscript, circa 1985), p. 2.

47. Mario Posas, *"El Movimiento Sindical Hondureño Durante la Decada del Ochenta,"* in Boletín Informativo Honduras, Special No. 44, October 1989, p. 5; *"APROH: Origen, Desarrollo y Perspectivas,"* ibid., Special No. 9, March 1984, p. 4.

48. The rest of this section is based mainly on an interview with Mario Posas, 16 March 1991, and Héctor Hernández F., *Solidarismo y Sindicalismo en Honduras* (Tegucigalpa: FUTH, 1991), pp. 38-82, 100-126.

49. I have mentioned only three of the centrales. The fourth, the Independent Federation of Honduran Workers (Federación Independiente de Trabajadores Hondureños—FITH), was founded only in 1985 and was still in the process of consolidation. Since this was written, the FUTH has joined the FITH and several other organizations to form a new central, the Unitary Confederation of Honduran Workers (Confederación Unitaria de Trabajadores Hondureño—CUTH).

50. Medea Benjamin, "Campesinos: Between Carrot and Stick," *NACLA Report on the Americas*, Vol. 22, No. 1, January-February 1988, pp. 24, 26; Bueso, *El Subdesarrollo*, pp. 126-128; Margarita Oseguera de Ochoa, *Honduras Hoy: Sociedad y Crisis Política* (Tegucigalpa: CEDOH, 1987), pp. 123-125. Since this was written, other groups have emerged, most notably the progovernment National Campesino Congress (Congreso Nacional Campesino—CNC) and the Coordinating Council of Honduran Campesino Organizations (Consejo

Coordinador de Organizaciones Campesinas de Honduras—COCOCH), an umbrella group bringing together organizations critical of Callejas's agrarian policy.

51. Bueso, *El Subdesarrollo*, p. 105.

52. Interview with Medea Benjamin, *Honduras Update*, Vol. 5, Nos. 9-10, June-July 1987, p. 3.

53. Benjamin, "Campesinos," p. 26.

54. Caballero had previously been a sergeant in the army. Nor was he the only UNC leader to carry a military identity card. Posas interview; CEDOH, "25 *Años de Reforma Agraria*," Boletín Informativo Honduras, Special No. 30, September 1987, pp. 8, 12.

55. Information from Augusto Suarez Lozano, one of the INA regional directors during this period.

56. *Boletín Informativo Honduras*, No. 122, June 1991, p. 2.

57. "La Situación Campesina: Las Recuperaciones de Mayo y sus Resultados," *Boletín Informativo Honduras*, No. 76, August 1987, pp. 3-8; "Los Resultados de la Comisión," ibid., p. 9.

58. According to townspeople in the area. *El Tiempo*, 30 October 1986.

59. The communist historian Longino Becerra put the number of armed combatants at a few dozen, but this seems low. Interview with Becerra, 4 February 1989. The SOUTHCOM estimate is from *Latin American Weekly Report*, 5 November 1987.

60. U.S. Information Agency, "Marginal Figures for January 1987 Survey of Public Opinion in Central America."

61. U.S. Embassy, *Handbook on Honduras*, Fall 1987, p. 14.

62. Philip L. Shepherd, "Six Keys to the Understanding of Current United States-Honduran Relations," Prepared Statement before the Subcommittee on Military Installations and Facilities, U.S. House of Representatives, 28 March 1984, p. 10.

63. By early 1988 over half (53 percent) of the USIA's Honduran respondents felt that the United States benefited more from the relationship than Honduras. That represented a 15 percent increase over the previous year. USIA, "Marginal Figures," January 1987 and 1988.

64. David Ronfeldt, *U.S. Involvement in Central America: Three Views from Honduras* (Santa Monica: RAND Corporation, July 1989), pp. 2, 5.

65. Information on the Ramírez case is from our interview with Ubodoro Arriaga, 27 February 1989; *El Día* (Mexico), 9 July 1987; *Boletín Informativo Honduras*, No. 75, July 1987, pp. 1, 16; and *New York Times*, 30 April 1987.

66. *El Tiempo*, 13 March 1986.

7

The United States, Honduras, and the End of the Contra War

Once we were a dictatorial cesspool; now we are a democratic cesspool.

—Honduran legislator

In September 1987 an unusual trial began before the OAS Inter-American Court of Human Rights in San José, Costa Rica. The case involved two Hondurans, Saúl Godínez and Angel Velásquez, and two Costa Ricans, Francisco Fairén and Yolanda Solís, who had "disappeared" in Honduras in the early 1980s. The proceedings were the culmination of a six-year process in which relatives of the deceased, with the aid of the Committee for the Defense of Human Rights in Honduras and the Committee of Relatives of the Disappeared/Detained, had brought the case to the attention of the Inter-American Commission on Human Rights, which had agreed to prosecute it. The defendant was the government of Honduras.

In the course of this landmark trial—the first ever in which a government had been brought before the court on charges of death squad activity—it was revealed that between 1981 and 1984 Honduras had implemented a carefully planned program to eliminate persons suspected of subversive activity. Among those who testified was Florencio Caballero, a former interrogator and defector from Battalion 3-16, who said that he and two dozen other army men had received training in the United States, as well as courses in Honduras led by U.S., Honduran, Chilean, and Argentine instructors. During the testimony, names were named—most notably, those of Lieutenant Colonel Alexander Hernández, the former commandant of Battalion 3-16 and a cousin of armed forces chief Humberto Regalado Hernández; Lieutenant Marco Tulio Regalado Hernández, the younger brother of the latter; and former army sergeant José Isaias Vilorio, who had been an agent in the National Department of Investigations and had reportedly maintained the files of the death squad. All three men were summoned to give testimony before the court when it reconvened early the following year.

On the morning of 5 January 1988, José Vilorio was shot to death in Tegucigalpa as he was waiting to board a bus. The assassin draped a red and black flag with the insignia of the Cinchonero guerrillas over the body. Subsequently, someone purporting to represent the Cinchoneros published a statement claiming responsibility for the killing. Doubts remained, however. Skeptics pointed out that, potentially, the military had a great deal to lose and the Cinchoneros much to gain from Vilorio's testimony. Only the previous day, Attorney General Rubén Zepeda had announced that the DNI aide would appear before the court. It made no sense, at this juncture, for the left to assassinate him. Even military and police officials conceded that the flag and the statement could have been intended to confuse investigators. As usual in such cases, no further leads were produced.

Other witnesses were being subjected to intimidation. In late December Ramón Custodio, the controversial president of the CODEH, had charged that the First Infantry Brigade was planning to kill him. His announcement had led the secretary of the Inter-American Court, before which Custodio had been a witness, to send a letter of concern to the Honduran foreign minister, Carlos López Contreras. López had dismissed the threat as a "smokescreen" and accused the left of trying to create martyrs. The next day Vilorio was assassinated.

Moreover, on the evening of 14 January Miguel Angel Pavón and Moises Landaverde were gunned down in San Pedro Sula. The killings traumatized Honduras. Pavón was a regional director of the CODEH and a PINU alternate deputy to Congress. A constant thorn in the side of the military, he had been the first witness in the proceedings. The previous year posters had appeared in several cities bearing his photograph, along with those of Custodio and three labor leaders. Captions had depicted the five as "terrorist delinquents" and "promoters of subversion."

The CODEH immediately blamed the armed forces, the government, and the U.S. embassy for the killings. And in fact the official handling of the case bore all the marks of a cover-up: Evidence mysteriously disappeared; witnesses changed their testimony; the police failed to cooperate. Though Judge Fátima de Pineda repeatedly subpoenaed the DNI to produce the agents who had been on duty at the time of the crime, her requests were ignored. Nor would the police release to the court the names of the officers who had initially investigated the killings. Bullet cases seen near the car disappeared. The victims' briefcases and address books were confiscated. Rather than conducting a serious investigation, the government sought to use the crime as a means of discrediting Ramón Custodio and the CODEH. Foreign Minister López Contreras even implied that Custodio was the leader of a terrorist plot and that Pavón and Landaverde had been the first victims. The murder was never solved.

The Azcona administration's response to the Inter-American Court was not much more forthcoming. True, it participated in the proceedings. Honduran representatives cross-examined witnesses and argued points of law and fact. But few documents were provided to support their protestations. The authorities repeatedly ignored requests for vital material evidence, leading the court to complain about their "obstructionism." Though the government did eventually produce Alexander Hernández, Marco Tulio Regalado, and the chief of military intelligence, Roberto Núñez Montes, their testimony was singularly unenlightening. All three claimed ignorance or refused to answer on national security grounds.

In early February, Humberto Regalado, in his capacity as commander in chief, announced the discovery of a "subversive plan," purportedly sponsored by the Sandinistas, to launch guerrilla war throughout Honduras. There had been a modest resurgence of revolutionary activity during the latter half of 1987, but the notion that the left could mount a nationwide offensive struck knowledgeable observers as fantasy. Many assumed that Regalado's pronouncement was intended to legitimate a stepped-up campaign of intimidation. These months witnessed an increasing number of assassinations and disappearances. Between February and July, there were at least nine bombing incidents. Some of this activity came from the left. Most, however, seemed to be the product of either the armed forces or right-wing death squads.[1] This fed speculation that the military might once again be embracing the doctrine of national security.

The Slow, Painful Death of the Contra Policy (Continued): The End of Military Aid

In early January General Colin Powell, President Reagan's special assistant for national security affairs, joined Elliott Abrams on a tour of Central America. They bore a blunt message: Honduras, El Salvador, Guatemala, and Costa Rica would face serious consequences should the U.S. Congress fail to continue the contra-aid program. The Central American presidents were about to meet in San José to evaluate the progress of the Esquipulas peace accord. The administration wanted them to denounce the Sandinistas. Such a proclamation would presumably carry great weight in Congress, where votes on aid were scheduled for the next month. Powell told his hosts that they should not expect to rely on the United States for additional economic assistance if the Sandinistas were relieved of the necessity to fight a guerrilla war. If the contras were abandoned, he warned, there would "not be a sudden surge of interest in things Central American or other kinds of aid."[2]

But Washington no longer had the bargaining power to enforce such demands. Furthermore, the Sandinistas, by taking an increasingly conciliatory negotiating position, were making it difficult to charge them with obstructionism. Even prior to the summit, they had begun indirect talks with the contras. Following the San José meeting, Daniel Ortega announced that his government would lift the state of emergency and accept direct talks. He expressed willingness to broaden the amnesty to include the armed rebels and political prisoners arrested since 1982. Although this was to be done following the arrangement of a cease-fire and the reintegration of the contras into civilian life, he added that even in the absence of a cease-fire Nicaragua would be willing to release the prisoners—provided that another country would receive them.

On 3 February, by a margin of just eight votes, the House of Representatives rejected an administration-backed resolution that would have provided at least US$43 million in economic and military aid to the contras over the next four months. The following day, a federal grand jury in Miami indicted Panamanian strongman Manuel Noriega on drug and racketeering charges. The indictment triggered an immediate crisis with Panama that was further inflamed by congressional testimony from former Noriega adviser José Blandón. Suddenly, the administration's Central American policy seemed extremely vulnerable. Officially, the White House was optimistic: "U.S. policy is not in disarray," insisted one spokesman. "Rejection of contra aid means we lost, but it is a temporary setback. The situation in Panama is unrelated, and ultimately we believe our goal of democracy in Panama will prevail."[3]

Others were not so sure. "What are we supposed to do now with the contras?" a senior Honduran official wondered aloud. The mood in the embassy was grim. The day after the House vote Ambassador Briggs met with Azcona to reassure him of the administration's continuing commitment. U.S. diplomats urged their Honduran counterparts not to panic: The situation remained fluid; they should wait and see what developed. Nevertheless, on 5 February General Regalado announced that the military had drawn up a plan to prevent the rebels from returning to Honduras en masse. Democratic senators, he added, must consider how refugees already in the country could be assisted in leaving. About this same time, Foreign Minister López raised anew an earlier plan to disarm the rebels. Toward the end of the month the COSUFFAA, led by members of the sixth promotion, overwhelmingly rejected a "hard-sell" U.S. proposal (which included offers of compensatory aid) that Honduras take greater responsibility for the guerrillas' logistical support.

The contras themselves reacted to these developments with understandable bitterness. Aristides Sánchez no doubt spoke for many when he denounced the United States as a "country in decline."[4] Some defiantly vowed to fight on. Others were more resigned, though many, like Mr. Macawber, were still hopeful that something would turn up. Though aid was scheduled to run out at the end of February, the rebels still had enough supplies to last several months. Meanwhile, presumably, Congress could be persuaded to pass some kind of compromise that would enable them to survive.

On 3 March, however, in a stunning blow to Speaker Wright's efforts to pass a US$30.8 million "humanitarian aid" package, rebellious liberal Democrats joined conservative Republicans in rejecting a compromise. The defeat came after a frantic attempt by the Democratic leadership to put together a winning coalition and left the speaker reflecting on Will Rogers's remark that, as a Democrat, he didn't belong to any organized political party. For their part, the Republicans were ecstatic. President Reagan expressed his delight with what had transpired and urged the legislators to develop an aid package "of sufficient quantity to sustain the freedom fighters." If they did not, he warned, "the prospects for peace and democracy inside Nicaragua [would] diminish quickly."[5]

The administration had seriously miscalculated. The defeat left the contras without any assistance for the first time since Reagan had authorized the CIA to begin financing them. In spite of White House efforts to put together a new package, it soon became apparent that a renewal, if possible at all, might take months to achieve. Within the administration, fatigue and demoralization now spread rapidly. There was a growing sense that the vote had been a watershed. Reports began to circulate that ways of disengaging from the rebels were being considered. White House Chief of Staff Howard Baker was said to be hoping that the whole issue would simply fade away. The special public diplomacy office that had been created to lobby Congress was closed.

Contra leaders could read these signs as well as anyone, and they drew the obvious conclusion: This was a slow-motion Bay of Pigs. Relations between the administration and the rebels now became increasingly tense as the latter's accusations of betrayal became more frequent and shrill. For the guerrillas, the most immediate impact of the cutoff involved their dwindling supply of food and ammunition. In accordance with U.S. law, CIA shipments had ceased as of 29 February. The best estimates suggested that provisions would begin to run out by May. Accordingly, rebel leaders began to consider ways of stretching supplies to last until the end of the year. The most obvious option was to pull back into Honduras all but about 1,000 of the combatants inside Nicaragua and sharply curtail the operations of those who remained.

But another massive influx of contras was the last thing the Hondurans wanted. Suddenly, the Reagan administration had another potentially explosive problem on its hands. Open war between its two allies had now become a very real possibility. One way or another, the means had to be found of keeping that peace while continuing the larger war. Backbones had to be stiffened. Honduran loyalty had to be maintained. The contras had to be preserved as a unified movement and provided with incentives that would keep them fighting. Part of the solution, obviously, was to persuade Congress to restore aid. The question was how.

In mid-March the White House received a boost from an unexpected source—the Sandinistas. Earlier that month 6,000 Nicaraguan troops had launched an offensive to dislodge rebel camps in Boaco, Chontales, Río San Juan, southern Zelaya, and the Bocay region of northeastern Jinotega, near the Honduran border. When a contra column in densely jungled Bocay stumbled into an ambush, its members turned and fled toward their Honduran sanctuaries with their assailants in pursuit. The latter did not stop at the border. Once in Honduras the force of some 1,500 Nicaraguan soldiers found itself within striking distance of a lightly defended supply depot that held almost half of the guerrillas' rapidly diminishing cache of weapons and ammunition. At this point the Reagan administration was close to panic. In the words of one senior presidential adviser, "Our private feeling is that . . . this is it. This is going to be the equivalent of taking people off the rooftop of the Saigon embassy. We're about to see an end of the war."[6]

Other observers, however, had a sense of déjà vu. The similarities to the 1986 Holy Week "invasion" were striking. Once again, the Americans seemed much more alarmed by the incursion than the

Hondurans. Foreign Minister López and military spokesman Colonel Suárez Benavides initially denied having any information about the Sandinista presence.[7] President Azcona, who was in bed with the flu, was unavailable for comment. An official silence was maintained while the government and military resisted Washington's efforts to get them to act. Once again, several thousand U.S. troops were dispatched. For their part, the Hondurans were careful not to get too deeply involved. As in 1986, they were happy to receive more "emergency" military aid (a request was quickly granted) but reluctant to get into a border war. And so again they went through the motions: U.S. helicopters flew Honduran troops to within 50 kilometers of Nicaragua—but at a place one hundred sixty kilometers from the fighting. The Sixteenth Infantry Battalion was ordered to march toward the battle zone, but by the time it had crossed the rugged jungle the Sandinistas had withdrawn. This was war Honduran-style, in which charade masked a very different underlying reality. Once again, the client had employed passive resistance to thwart pressures from its patron. "Obedezco, pero no cumplo" was still as relevant to understanding Honduran behavior as it had been in colonial times.

On 18 March Ambassador Briggs and President Azcona sought to allay speculation that the United States had secretly asked the Honduran government to make a public request in order to justify the U.S. show of force. In separate news conferences, the two men solemnly described the process whereby the Hondurans had requested aid and the United States had responded. Skeptics, however, noted that President Reagan had approved the sending of troops and the Pentagon had begun to prepare for deployment before Azcona's request had been received and, moreover, that the Honduran's letter had not specified the kind of aid desired. Furthermore, the question of Sandinista intentions remained open to debate. During the incursion, White House and State Department spokesmen had on more than one occasion claimed that Nicaraguan soldiers had seized, destroyed, or overrun rebel supply depots. When it became apparent that this was not true, many observers concluded that the administration had exaggerated the threat. (This was, incidentally, a conclusion that was reached even by some U.S. troops on the ground. In the words of one officer who was in the area, "I don't know what Washington was doing. The Sandinistas were nowhere near the headquarters.")[8]

Most suspicious of all was the way in which the White House sought to use the incident to pressure Congress on the contra aid issue. In the midst of the uproar, Elliott Abrams revealed that the legislature would soon receive another aid request. Sources in the administration noted that this was part of a strategy to "shame or scare" Congress into reversing itself. The genesis of the current "crisis," they claimed, had been the February and March votes. As a result of the cutoff, the Nicaraguan army had become more aggressive. The theme was immediately embraced by the president, who launched a campaign for renewed aid over the radio: The cutoff had given "the communist dictators a chance to smash their opponents." The "freedom fighters were in desperate need." There wasn't a moment to lose.[9] By 23 March no fewer than three proposals had been advanced in Congress. Ultimately, a compromise was reached, and on 1 April the president was able to sign a US$47.9 million "humanitarian" assistance package. The contras, it seemed, were not yet entirely dead.

Was the March invasion a concocted crisis, or was it real? In retrospect, the administration's concern seems understandable enough. One could not be sure of Nicaraguan intentions. The "invasion" appeared to be a major threat to the guerrillas at a moment when they were especially vulnerable. That the Sandinistas did not take advantage of the opportunity to deal the rebels a more telling blow may say less about their supposedly benign intentions than about their concern for the North American reaction. U.S. moves to dispatch troops and bolster Honduran defenses may well have helped prevent a more serious assault. Not only was this "prudent deterrence" but it was also an opportunity to show the Hondurans that the United States would stand by them.[10] At the same time, it is clear that the "crisis" was not unwelcome. The White House made every effort to use the episode as a weapon in the ongoing battle over aid. It did not hesitate to overdramatize the threat and distort the facts, and in the end it was largely successful. Reagan did not get everything he wanted, but what he did get was substantial.

In other respects, however, the tactic had negligible or damaging consequences. Although it may have stiffened Honduran backbones, it never alleviated their suspicion that the aid being restored would be just enough to keep the contras alive (and in Honduras) but not nearly what was needed to give the rebels a fighting chance in Nicaragua. Any benefits achieved in military and government circles were more than offset by the angry public reaction. "Does the state of Honduras really exist?" thundered the liberal daily *El Tiempo*. "Why is it that those of us here are the last to find out what is going on?" lamented the conservative *La Tribuna*. "The official [Honduran] sources . . . never know anything about anything. We have to wait for the State Department to give a briefing to Congress or the press in order to find out belatedly what is happening in our own country."[11] The sense that the United States was once again treating Hondurans with disdain—manipulating them and violating their national sovereignty—cut across traditional political lines: Congress had not been consulted; the constitution had been violated. A Doumont cartoon showed Azcona bending to kiss the boots of the North American troops. No doubt *Tiempo* spoke for many when it denounced the president's acquiescence as "illegal" and "humiliating": "There is indeed an invasion of our territory, but it is one designed to promote the interests of the Reagan administration."[12]

Before this reaction could have its effect, however, the contras themselves made a decision. On 21 March Sandinista and rebel delegations met in Sapoá, Nicaragua. Two days later, a cease-fire was signed. The agreement called for a sixty-day truce and talks on a definitive cease-fire. Contra soldiers would enter protected enclaves in Nicaragua, where they would receive only humanitarian aid from neutral organizations. In turn, the government agreed to guarantee freedom of expression. Exiles would be allowed to return and become part of political, economic, and social life, including municipal and national elections. An amnesty would be granted to all political prisoners, to be implemented gradually as further progress was made and a final cease-fire attained.

The agreement came as a shock to the Reagan administration, which expressed skepticism that the Sandinistas would keep their part of the bargain. But there was not much that could be done. Washington had failed to reassure the contras, who, sensing that they were being abandoned, had decided to make other arrangements.

Cocaine Politics: The Matta Affair and the Attack on the Embassy

Shortly before dawn on 5 April, more than one hundred "cobras" (members of the elite Honduran security unit), accompanied by Interpol and DNI agents and two unidentified North Americans, broke into the Colonia "Los Angeles" mansion of Juan Ramón Matta Ballesteros. Matta was located and, once in hand, whisked away to the airport and put on a plane bound for the Dominican Republic. There local authorities, informed that he was sought by the United States, placed him on a flight to New York. The next thing Hondurans knew he was on his way to a maximum security prison in Marion, Illinois, to await trial on various charges related to cocaine smuggling and the kidnap-killing of U.S. DEA agent Enrique Camarena.

The public reaction was explosive. "They Are Kidnapping Matta," blared the headlines in *El Tiempo*. "The Executive Power Is Responsible," proclaimed *El Heraldo*. The opposition cut across ideological lines, with Hondurans ranging from the ultraright-wing rector of the National University to the radical left rushing to denounce this "violation" of national sovereignty. The president of Congress declared the action illegal. (The constitution forbade such extraditions.) A majority of deputies urged that the government demand Matta's return. The chief justice of the Supreme Court denied that the seizure had been given judicial sanction. Out in the streets, people smoldered. The consensus was that Matta had been kidnapped: "The constitution was trampled, and with it our rights as citizens," complained one observer. At the university, students protested by burning the U.S. flag and a copy of the Honduran Constitution.

The latter, of course, had been violated many times before: Congress had not been consulted when U.S. reinforcements had been brought into the country during the Holy Week crisis. Nor had it been properly informed with regard to the construction of the CREM or the removal of Generals Alvarez and López Reyes. Honduran coastlands had been given to a U.S. citizen even though such transactions were illegal. This time, however, the violation had come on the heels of another, particularly offensive "abuse": the March U.S. "invasion." Pent-up feelings of national impotence and humiliation now combined with the peculiar symbolism of a man who embodied the frustrated aspirations of hundreds of thousands of poor Hondurans. "Narco" or not, Matta was one of their own. Brought up in bitter poverty, he had never forgotten his origins. Indeed, he had become a kind of patron saint to the poor, dispensing charity, building schools, and employing hundreds of people in a time of massive unemployment. Living openly in Comayagüela, he had defied the gringos and bought some of the most powerful figures in the Honduran military and government. And now he had been seized "like a dog picked up on the streets and taken away to the pound."[13]

On 7 April, moreover, the Honduran journalist David Romero broke a sensational story over Radio América. According to Romero, an embassy source had told him that during a recent visit former Ambassador John Negroponte had presented President Azcona with a memorandum bearing the signature of Elliott Abrams. Allegedly, the memo had threatened to release the names of high-ranking Honduran military officers involved in drug trafficking unless Matta were turned over. It also promised that if the government cooperated it would be rewarded by the release of an AID disbursement that was being withheld. Among the officers on the State Department's list were said to be the chief of military intelligence, Roberto Núñez Montes; the minister of defense, Wilfredo Sánchez; the chairman of the joint chiefs of staff, Roberto Martínez Avila; the Honduran representative on the Inter-American Defense Board, Carlos Reyes Barahona; and the commander of the navy, Leonel Gutiérrez Minera.

The U.S. reaction was immediate and unequivocal: "A complete fantasy," declared an embassy spokesman. There was "never a list of five colonels"—or, at least, the list that Romero had "did not come from us."[14] Although Negroponte (at the time an adviser on the National Security Council) had indeed visited the country, it had been a purely private trip. He and his wife were in the process of adopting their third Honduran child, and he had come down to go through the required screening exam. He had brought no letter from Abrams. He had seen Azcona and a few other present and former officials, but these had been strictly courtesy calls. No "operational matters" had been raised.[15] As for the Honduran government, on 10 April it released its official response, branding the Radio América report a "tendentious lie."

The origin of the document has never been verified. It may well have been a forgery; this would not have been unusual in the Honduran political milieu, where rumor and mendacity are commonly viewed as legitimate means of discrediting one's enemies. At the same time, U.S. diplomats are not noted for their candor and veracity and might be expected to deny such allegations. Only the previous month, Elliott Abrams had publicly urged the Hondurans to expel Matta.[16] Perhaps it is best just to say, with Víctor Meza, that whatever the truth about this mysterious list, they did turn him over. And while Ambassador Briggs was technically correct in asserting that this was a Honduran operation ("We did not snatch him"),[17] it is equally clear that the authorities were responding to U.S. pressures.

By late 1987 the tide had turned within the Reagan administration with regard to the issue of narcotics trafficking. For years it had turned a blind eye to the drug activities of some of its allies in the war against the Sandinistas, even entering into financial arrangements with traffickers willing to help supply the contras. There was no small irony here. Matta's SETCO had been one of four companies owned and operated by drug dealers that had been contracted by the State Department to transport "humanitarian" assistance to the rebels. (In 1984-1985 SETCO had been the primary company used by the Honduras-based FDN to carry food and military supplies.) In each of these cases information about the drug connections had been available to federal law enforcement agencies. Yet, apparently, that intelligence was never tapped; there had been no serious attempt to screen the suppliers.[18] At minimum this was willful negligence, one more in a long series of instances in which administration policymakers and operators chose to "see no evil."

After mid-1987, however, this posture was increasingly difficult to maintain. Mass protests in Panama, impending indictments of General Noriega in Florida, embarrassing news stories in the *New York Times* and elsewhere, and growing congressional outrage (manifested, in particular, in the hearings being conducted by Senator John Kerry) made it increasingly difficult to play the ostrich. Though the administration continued to be deeply divided on the Noriega issue until well into 1988, arrangements to obtain Matta were set in motion as early as the previous autumn. A blueprint for the arrest was drawn up. The chief of operations of the U.S. federal marshals was sent to Honduras to negotiate the details. When the subject was finally seized, North American agents would be present, both on the ground and in helicopters, to make sure everything went as planned.[19]

This was a touchy business for more reasons than one. High-ranking Honduran military and police officials were still on Matta's payroll, and care had to be taken that they not find out about the operation and alert him. To make matters worse, some of the "antinarcos" within the armed forces—especially in the sixth promoción—were nationalists who could not be trusted to go along with the plan. Consequently, only Regalado and a small group of officers were involved in the planning. Among those conspicuously absent was the powerful head of the FUSEP, Colonel Leonel Riera Lunatti, reportedly a friend and business associate of Matta.[20] There is some doubt, too, whether Azcona knew what was in the offing. A month before he had publicly declared that his government would not permit Matta's extradition. Some reports claim that he had not learned of the plan until the operation was under way. Faced with a fait accompli, he had quickly acquiesced, having "fallen into someone else's game."[21]

The Matta affair had strong repercussions within the armed forces. Officers who had not been informed were infuriated by the seizure. Factional rivalries spilled over into the streets. On 7 April the rector of the National University, Oswaldo Ramos Soto, met with senior military officers, who encouraged him to organize a *manifestación* (demonstration).[22] Pudgy, pompous, and given to shrill, long-winded speeches ("a man totally enamored with the sound of his own voice" was the assessment of one diplomat),[23] Ramos was enormously ambitious and completely without scruple. In the words of Ambassador Briggs, he was, quite simply, "a crook." Later Briggs would place much of the blame for what was about to happen on him.[24]

At dusk, members of the United University Democratic Front, a powerful rightwing student organization, set out for the embassy. In the course of their march they picked up an odd assortment of protesters: leftists from the Escuela Superior, residents of the barrios along the way, Matta employees. By seven-thirty, about 1,000 people had gathered in front of the embassy. A few dozen began to stone the building. When nothing happened they grew bolder: The compound's windows, security stations, and grass were set on fire; automobiles were overturned, smashed, and torched; the American flag was burned. Watching from the roof of the building, Briggs's political counselor, Don Johnson, had a sinking feeling as his own car went up in flames. Repeated calls for help to Azcona and other Honduran officials produced no response. For two hours riot police remained parked in back streets awaiting orders. Less than a kilometer away, firemen sat on a bridge. Implored by a U.S. official to act, they did nothing. Meanwhile, in Casamata barracks overlooking the scene from Mount Picacho, the FUSEP's Riera Lunatti bided his time. Only after the rioters had broken into and torched the embassy's annex were the police finally ordered to disperse them. By the time peace was restored, two persons would be dead four dozen wounded, and some US$6 million in damage done.

That the demonstration was encouraged by elements in the military is clear. Similarly, it is apparent that Azcona played almost no part in it. He had been kept largely in the dark about the worsening situation. He had avoided responding to Briggs's repeated telephone calls, since to have done so would have forced him to acknowledge his inability to get the high command to do his bidding.[25] Typically, he chose to pretend that the problem did not exist.

Beyond this, the details are murky. The most probable explanation for the incident is that a message was being sent. Corrupt elements in the military were hoping to frighten the Americans into limiting their antidrug activities, so as to avoid endangering those officers involved in narcotics. One Honduran journalist with excellent army contacts claims that Riera Lunatti had received a direct order from the Estado Mayor, with Colonel Núñez Montes on the other end of the phone, to hold back his troops.[26]

Other sources envisioned a more complex scenario.[27] According to this version, the march had been ordered by Riera Lunatti's enemies with a view to discrediting him. Though he had been kept in the dark on the Matta deportation, the troops involved in the seizure had been under his command. He had therefore had to accept the blame for the affair. (There had even been public demands that he be put on trial.) Now, moreover, he had been placed in a situation of having to use force to quell the resulting disturbance. The intent had been to make him look repressive and incompetent and thus further weaken his position. But Riera had turned the tables on his foes. He had refused to order his police to break up the rioters until authorization was granted by the high command. By forcing others to assume collective responsibility, Riera had prevented his enemies from making him a scapegoat. When the COSUFFAA finally went public, its official statements emphasized the "granite unity" of the armed forces: The FUSEP had captured Matta and sent police to the embassy on orders from the high command. Riera Lunatti had not held back his troops because of the Matta seizure. Charges that military officers were involved in the narcotics trade were part of a vast disinformation campaign intended to defame and discredit the armed forces and deter them from the war against drug trafficking.

There were also less sinister interpretations. Some observers argued that the delay in sending the police was due to incompetence and timidity: There had been a breakdown in communications. Azcona had not been available; Riera had not been able to reach Regalado and, failing to secure higher authority, had stalled to avoid being blamed for a nasty scene.

Whatever the truth, the Matta affair and the embassy riots seriously undermined the legitimacy of civil and military institutions. Many Hondurans came away from these developments convinced that senior officers had delivered Matta in exchange for impunity for themselves. At the same time the Reagan administration, by dealing with military rather than civilian authorities in the Matta capture, had effectively recognized the "true center of power," further weakening an already fragile democracy. Beyond this, anti-U.S. sentiment had now become more widespread than ever. This was the first violent demonstration against the United States in memory. And even if the vast majority of Hondurans deplored the actions of the protesters, some (about 6 percent, according to one poll) supported them. No doubt many others agreed with the Honduran lawyers quoted by *El Tiempo* that "here, gringos do whatever they want."[28] It would be weeks before things returned to normal. For months afterward North Americans would occasionally be subjected to harassment: orange peels and other trash thrown from buses, hisses, and shouts of "¡Puta gringa basura, fuera de mi país!"

The Passing Parade

These were exciting weeks. Two days after the riots, Gustavo Alvarez returned to Honduras, declaring that God had sent him back to stay. While in exile in Miami the former strongman had taken a heavy dose of Pentecostalism, and he now wanted to share his faith with his countrymen. In addition, he wanted to clarify his status with the armed forces. Ever since his ouster, his name had been under a cloud; he wanted the cloud removed. He had not returned to make trouble or meddle in politics, he emphasized, but he would be willing to lend his services to the military if the high command so desired. This was enough to send shivers through the body politic. To the suspicious, the former general's religious conversion seemed camouflage for more sinister motives. Those who had lost friends and relatives during the heyday of the national security state demanded his arrest and punishment, but nothing came of this. Following a brief judicial investigation, Alvarez was allowed to return to his home and family.

On 12 April, moreover, Vice President Jaime Rosenthal announced that he was resigning from his post as Azcona's economic adviser because of "profound differences" with the administration. Relations between the two men had been deteriorating for some time. Rosenthal had masterminded the 1986 economic plan but had been excluded from the preparation of the 1987 plan because of his criticisms of the AID's development programs. Furthermore, he had presidential ambitions of his own, and his newspaper, *El Tiempo*, had been unrelentingly critical of the government and the military. In the course of all this, disagreements had become personalized. Rosenthal had found himself increasingly isolated, opposed to much of what was being done and despairing of ever being able to have a positive impact. The seizure of Matta had been the last straw.

Rosenthal's withdrawal further weakened the Azcona administration by narrowing its base of legitimacy. By now, however, the moral rot that pervaded Honduran society had undermined all of its political institutions. In mid-May yet another scandal hit the military when General Regalado's half-brother, Rigoberto Regalado Lara, was arrested in Miami trying to smuggle twenty-six pounds of cocaine through customs. Regalado Lara was the Honduran ambassador to

Panama. He was also a "courier" in the Medellín drug network in which Honduras was a "bridge."[29] The government immediately suspended him from his duties, declaring that the United States was free to prosecute. Regalado Lara was not entitled to immunity, since the United States was not his country of assignment, and to have fought the issue would have brought his brother under suspicion. Already there had been reports, emanating from within the U.S. government, that Regalado Hernández had been protecting narcotics traffickers.[30] To make matters worse, the general had allowed his old friend Torres Arias to return to Honduras. In the late 1970s Torres had been an associate and sometime-rival of Ramón Matta in the burgeoning Honduran drug trade. Now he became an unofficial adviser to Regalado.[31] Visitors to the Hotel Maya casino soon grew used to the sight of him dropping thousands of dollars nightly at the gambling tables.

Regalado Hernández and his allies needed to stay on the good side of the gringos. One way of doing that was to selectively cooperate with their antinarcotics efforts. Appearances were crucial. Thus, in late 1987 Regalado had announced that the military was seeking the help of the DEA. About the same time, he began to encourage the crusading activities of Miguel Izaguirre, a flamboyant judge from the north coast city of Tela. Izaguirre had arrived in Tela in June 1987 to find that a series of cases had been dismissed because his predecessors had been afraid to pursue them. Within two months he had handed down the first conviction and prison term for cocaine trafficking in Honduran history, and others had soon followed. By early 1988 ten more Hondurans had been convicted on drug charges; nearly three dozen suspected dealers were in jail awaiting judgment; two major Honduras-based foreign traffickers had been arraigned. In the process, several attempts had been made on Izaguirre's life. Increasingly, he began to surround himself with an arsenal, carrying an AK-47 with him wherever he went, even into court.

Izaguirre could not have done all this without the support of the armed forces, and he said as much. That in turn led to charges that he was being "manipulated by the military" and was running a "narcoshow." Certainly it was no accident that his investigations always seemed to be confined to civilians: He received special protection from the armed forces and even drew a salary as an unofficial adviser to the 105th Infantry Brigade. Nevertheless, in early June it was announced that the Supreme Court had fired him, ostensibly for accepting cases outside his jurisdiction. This was like setting off a powder keg. Izaguirre had previously charged that there existed a "drug state parallel to the traditional state of law." Now he declared that narcotics traffickers had corrupted Congress, the Supreme Court, and the office of the attorney general. He began naming names.

The reaction was immediate: The president of Congress, Carlos Montoya, denounced Izaguirre as mentally deranged. He threatened to sue and to implicate the military. Others raised similar cries. A congressional commission was formed to determine whether the armed forces were protecting Izaguirre. At this point, the high command backed off. Regalado and his colleagues had no desire to get into a war with Congress and the courts; they were too vulnerable. Accordingly, the legislators were informed that the military did not support Izaguirre in his accusations. The judge from Tela would be allowed to fade into obscurity.

The Contras in Honduras: Peace and Disintegration

Meanwhile, contra unity and morale were rapidly crumbling. Unable to supply their forces inside Nicaragua, rebel commanders began ordering their troops to pull back into Honduras, where the U.S.-supplied "humanitarian aid" was being distributed. Border camps that had been abandoned the previous year began to swell once more with insurgents and their families. Morale plummeted. Peace, it seemed, would be more corrosive than war. The contras began to fight among themselves.[32] For about a year they had been able to maintain a surprising degree of unity as the "US$100 million offensive" raised their prospects and induced their leaders to set aside their personal and political differences for the good of the cause. Now, however, the vacuum in Washington spread to the resistance. Things fell apart.

In April dissidents circulated a petition signed by fifty-one field commanders and their aides demanding the replacement of Enrique Bermúdez as supreme commander. Most of the complaints were longstanding: The rebels accused Bermúdez of being an autocratic, corrupt, and incompetent leader whose lack of strategic vision and ties to the old national guard had severely hampered the movement. They said that he was an armchair colonel who did not know what was happening in Nicaragua because he had never fought there; that he and his subordinates had plundered supplies and stolen the salaries of those who were doing the fighting; that he had tolerated human rights abuses and was subservient to the CIA. Field officers fumed as the army fell into chaos while its supreme commander retreated incommunicado to Tegucigalpa. They were outraged as he frustrated their efforts to reorganize the military leadership and promoted his own cronies. Bermúdez had criticized the Sapoá accord and demoted several commanders who had been participants in or supporters of the negotiations. Now the dissidents began to receive encouragement from Adolfo Calero, the most powerful of the civilian directors and the chief contra architect of the cease-fire.

Matters came to a head the following month. For weeks Washington had been trying to "micromanage" the conflict. The rebellion was threatening to tear the movement apart. The perception was that the dissident commanders had been "spoiled" by their participation in the Sapoá talks. A rebel ascendancy meant chaos and capitulation, whereas what was needed was stability and continuity. When CIA attempts to bribe and intimidate the dissidents were unsuccessful, Honduran military help was recruited: A series of pro-Bermúdez meetings attended by several hundred contra officers and fighters, with CIA agents conspicuously present, was arranged. Food supplies were cut off to some dissident units. At the same time, Bermúdez stripped the rebellious officers of their U.S.-supplied vehicles and the stipends that had gone for family support.

When all else failed, it was decided to have the Hondurans seize and deport the dissidents. The necessary requests were made by both the Reagan administration and Bermúdez. In early May military authorities in Tegucigalpa detained seven contra officials, subsequently shipping them to Miami. The main dissident commander, Diógenes Hernández ("Fernando"), was lured into a trap and deported. About this time Bermúdez arrived in Honduras to find 2,000 defiant rebels bivouacked in base camps, refusing to obey his orders. Several commanders from the Southern Front now declared their support for the dissidents. Fighting broke out between pro- and anti-Bermúdez factions.

In the face of these developments, the civilian directors of the resistance sent two of their members to Honduras to make a firsthand evaluation. There one of the directors, Pedro Joaquín Chamorro, told a CIA official that the directorate had the authority to replace Bermúdez. The response mocked his pretensions: "I admire your idealism, but let's be realistic." This was, of course, symptomatic of the basic problem. The CIA had chosen Bermúdez to organize and lead the contra army. Over the years it had thwarted at least two attempts by rival commanders to oust him. The agency had also appointed the original members of the civilian directorate and paid their salaries. When the civilians' image as U.S. puppets proved an obstacle to congressional funding, U.S. officials began to stress the directorate's political independence and its control over the military wing. In fact, the CIA had never wanted the civilians to be an autonomous force; their function was to serve as window dressing.

But the directors had come to take themselves seriously. Back in Miami Chamorro, who had concluded that the rebellion was indeed a threat to the movement's cohesion, expressed outrage at the CIA's heavy-handedness: The dissident commanders, who had risked their lives and endured years of hardship for the cause, were now being treated as traitors. The agency even tried to pressure the directors to deny them access to resistance headquarters. In the words of one CIA official, "These people don't know the kinds of pressures we can bring. We haven't even begun the pressure."[33]

During the weekend of 14 May, Chamorro proposed to the directorate that it remove Bermúdez and install one of the dissidents as supreme commander. In the midst of the session, Bermúdez's ally Aristides Sánchez left the room, ostensibly to make a copy of the document. Instead, he telephoned the CIA's John Mallett. A speaker phone was set up in the meeting room, and with the directors listening the proposal was read to the American. Mallett exploded in a tirade, calling Chamorro an "imbecile" and accusing him of trying to turn the movement over to the Sandinistas. The Nicaraguans were speechless. When, some twenty minutes later, Mallett paused for breath, he was rebuked by Adolfo Calero, who protested that he and his colleagues would not "respond to insults and gross language." In the end, however, the CIA got its way. By this time, the "rebellion within the rebellion" had peaked and was rapidly losing steam. With Fernando and the other deported commanders separated from their troops and the latter dependent on the Honduran military for supplies, Bermúdez soon regained control.

At the end of May Bermúdez joined the contra negotiating team and immediately began putting roadblocks in the way of a peace settlement. The Nicaraguan government had advanced a proposal that went far beyond any of its previous offers to institute political change. At the time, there had been widespread optimism in both delegations that an agreement could be reached. In early June, however, the supreme commander told a Miami radio audience, "You cannot negotiate with the Sandinistas; nor can you expect them to respect freedom of expression or human rights." Rebel negotiators now began to make demands well outside the framework accepted at Sapoá. The proposals were apparently part of a joker ploy. As one

Sandinista negotiator commented, "Bermúdez wants the talks to fail so he can blame us and try to get more military aid from Congress."[34]

But Bermúdez was not the only obstacle to peace. The CIA had long been trying to undermine the negotiations by encouraging the domestic opposition in Nicaragua to engage in antigovernment protests and other disruptive activities aimed at provoking a Sandinista overreaction. Repression could provide the contras with a pretext for stalling or even withdrawing from the peace process. Moreover, elements within the Sandinista leadership were themselves undermining the negotiations. At times, there almost seemed to be a tacit alliance between the hard-liners on the two sides. Somehow, Tomás Borge's security forces always seemed most active when peace talks were in session, lending credibility to claims that the Sandinistas could not be trusted. In early June, the police detained fifteen opposition leaders as they sought to march to the National Assembly to present a letter of protest. The following month, an anti-Sandinista rally led to massive violence in which dozens of demonstrators and ten policemen were injured. Several dozen protesters, including several prominent figures, were arrested. Predictably, the peace negotiations led nowhere.

Meanwhile thousands of contras, some of them near starvation, were streaming back into southern Honduras. U.S. helicopter pilots dropping medicine and food to desperate refugees along the Coco River witnessed people ripping open bags to get at the raw meat, then vomiting when their stomachs rejected it. By late August some 11,000 guerrillas and several tens of thousands of their dependents were occupying a 190-square-kilometer area north and east of Yamales, the site of the main rebel bases. By now Bermúdez was threatening to abandon the peace talks altogether unless the United States sent more military aid, but Congress declined to do so. Within the Reagan administration, Elliott Abrams was increasingly besieged and isolated. More pragmatic elements had gained control of Central American policy. The U.S. elections were fast approaching, and no one wanted to resurrect so unpopular and divisive an issue. The contras had become unmentionable.

At this point the Hondurans tried to take matters into their own hands. In October, Foreign Minister López Contreras addressed the United Nations, where he told the assembled delegates that Honduras had had enough. He proposed that an international peacekeeping force be set up to "guarantee the nonuse" of national territory by foreign insurgents and to relocate the combatants first to sites in Costa Rica and Guatemala and then to Nicaraguan and Salvadoran territories far from Honduran borders. This was the last thing that the Costa Rican and Guatemalan governments (not to mention the White House) wanted, and the proposal was stillborn. The Hondurans showed their displeasure by suspending negotiations over a new military protocol that would have granted the United States greater access to Honduran bases and permission to build new permanent military installations. They let it be known that when the talks were resumed the issue would be linked to the future of the contras. At the same time, the Honduran military scored a nationalistic point by announcing that henceforth Palmerola would be known as the Enrique Soto Cano Air Force Base; it was, after all, a *Honduran* installation.

The rebels remained where they were. Congress would continue to provide "humanitarian aid," but military assistance was another matter. These months witnessed the continued slow disintegration of the contras as hundreds of guerrillas abandoned their camps and sought to slip through Mexico into the United States. Before leaving, many sold their arms, contributing to an upsurge of violent crime in Tegucigalpa and other Honduran cities. By the year's end the insurgency was effectively paralyzed, peace negotiations had dissolved in a flurry of mutual recriminations, and even sympathetic observers were dismissing the rebels as a thing of the past.

Politics and Human Rights: The CODEH and Its Enemies

On 29 July the Inter-American Court of Human Rights issued a landmark decision, finding that the government of Honduras had violated the American Convention on Human Rights by causing the disappearance of Angel Manfredo Velásquez. This was the first time that the court had found a government guilty of such activities. Six months later it declared Honduras responsible for the disappearance of Saúl Godínez. Finally, on 15 March it ruled in favor of Honduras in the Fairén-Solís case. The decisions were lauded by human rights activists as important precedents in international law, but the reception at the State Department and the embassy was less enthusiastic. For some time the Reagan administration had been trying to minimize the significance of these proceedings. The State Department had ignored them for as long as it could, even to the point of remaining silent in the face of the campaign of violence and intimidation that had been launched against the witnesses. When it did refer to the cases, it sought to misrepresent and discredit them by suggesting that they were unfair, politically motivated, and vindictive.[35]

Most of the rancor, however, was directed against the Committee for the Defense of Human Rights in Honduras and its president, Ramón Custodio. Custodio had long been a thorn in the side of North American and Honduran authorities, who accused him of "willful exaggerations," outright falsifications, and "partisan political attacks" designed to discredit and destabilize Honduras and undermine U.S. policy. Ambassador Briggs considered Custodio an "old-fashioned, hard-line communist with terrorist proclivities" who "cared nothing about human rights."[36] State Department and embassy publications typically dismissed the CODEH as an "antidemocratic leftist organization" and Custodio as a "Marxist ideologue." Even John Ferch had been suspicious. He had seen intelligence reports that Custodio was "on the Cuban payroll," and though he knew that such reports were often less than definitive ("as much guesswork and rumor as anything else"), he had decided to maintain a discrete distance.[37]

Part of the State Department's dislike for Custodio was a product of ideology and policy; part was personal. During the Alvarez years, Custodio had publicized human rights violations at a time when U.S. authorities were vehemently denying their existence. He had exposed the administration's lies for what they were; and he was hated for it. Beyond this, Custodio's reports *were* highly politicized. He openly embraced the radical left, adopting its propaganda as his own. His human rights reports always maximized the negative, sometimes to the point of straining credulity. In the aftermath of Alvarez's overthrow, when the country was breathing a sigh of relief at the easing of the repression, Custodio had continued to insist that little had changed. He had, moreover, personalized his charges, accusing John Negroponte of directing a "terrorist ring" set up by the Pentagon and the CIA for the purpose of eliminating Honduran leftists and later charging Ted Briggs with being the "intellectual author" of the Pavón-Landaverde assassinations.[38]

Such excesses raised serious questions about Custodio's judgment even in leftist circles. He ran the CODEH as if it were his own personal fiefdom, making it vulnerable to charges that it was a "phantom committee" and that international aid was being misappropriated. He had an enormous ego. His arrogance made him difficult to work with and led even some of his supporters to suspect that he was as interested in power and publicity as anything else. Yet, there was no doubt about his courage. Over the years, Custodio had been the target of numerous threats and assassination attempts. One recalls seeing posters slapped on the walls of downtown Comayagüela, featuring a bull's-eye superimposed over his face and the inscription "THE ONLY GOOD COMMUNIST IS A DEAD COMMUNIST." Whether a covert communist, as the embassy claimed, or merely a left-wing activist, as seems more probable, he was always larger than life.

But the Reagan administration was not interested in human rights. In the words of Americas Watch: "Despite its special relationship with the Honduran military, there is no indication that the United States has used its influence to press seriously for an end to human rights abuses. . . . Instead, the U.S. has acted as apologist for the. . . military, consistently denying, often in the face of overwhelming evidence, its involvement in gross abuses of human rights." Even in 1988, administration spokesmen continued to maintain that they had seen "no evidence" of "systematic human rights abuses" during the Alvarez years. (In contrast, the Inter-American Court, which included both a Honduran and a U.S. judge, found abundant evidence.)[39] In Tegucigalpa, the embassy continued to refer to the "more than 100 *alleged* disappearances which *supposedly* occurred" [emphases added], maintaining that there had been "only one possible case of politically motivated disappearance since 1984."[40] Washington had other priorities, and human rights scandals were perceived, accurately enough, as obstacles to their attainment.

Nor did the administration stop with an obfuscation of the human rights situation; it wanted to discredit Custodio and the CODEH. In this regard, the embassy was especially zealous. This was one of the largest State Department outposts in the world. U.S. diplomats exercised more influence over domestic politics than in any other Latin American country. And under the leadership of Everett Briggs, the institution had taken on many of the characteristics of a fortress under siege. Briggs had come to Honduras expecting to be the administration's "white knight" in the region. He had obtained the appointment by courting Jesse Helms and the "hard right," and his abrasiveness and insecurity combined with his zealous promotion of the contra cause to set the tone for the entire embassy. "You couldn't tell whether Briggs was smelling you or looking at you," recalled one of his State Department colleagues.[41] And so it was with many of his staff. During the tumultuous spring of 1988, spokesmen practiced throwing questions at one another to ensure that public information would have the proper "spin." Reporters were treated with distrust and contempt; critics were considered enemies and had their access restricted. When the CODEH published a report claiming that there had been 107 "extrajudicial executions" during the previous year, the embassy leaped at the opportunity to debunk it.

There followed a detailed counter-report. Of the one hundred incidents for which evidence was available, the embassy found that sixty-three were "undoubtedly" not what they were purported to be; in another thirteen cases the abuses committed, although reprehensible, did not fit the generally accepted definition of "extrajudicial execution." Among the other incidents listed were acts of passion (personal vendettas, drunken brawls, family squabbles), killings attributable to individuals or groups apparently unaffiliated with the military, deaths as the result of shoot-outs between the police and criminals, acts of self-defense, and even traffic accidents involving U.S. servicemen. The embassy concluded that only eleven of the cases at issue involved "possible" extrajudicial executions.[42]

Custodio had thrown in everything but the kitchen sink, and he had been caught in the act. No amount of explanation could erase the devastating impression that he was manufacturing his data. The gringos could not have been more pleased. In a public letter to the hapless doctor, the embassy's first secretary, Norma Harms, could not resist twisting the knife. After thanking Custodio for responding to the embassy study, she went on to say, "We received with satisfaction your admission that CODEH's work is not perfect, with which we agree completely. . . . We would like to ask you for the favor of sending us more information concerning your latest accusations with regard to 'extrajudicial executions' and 'political assassinations' supposedly carried out in 1988. Specifically, we are thinking of doing another study of these cases using the same format we used in our most recent studies."[43]

Neither Custodio nor the embassy was free from sin in these matters. The embassy, by shifting the focus of blame from human rights violators to human rights monitors, was attempting to obscure the continuing serious abuses by violence-prone elements in the military. Moreover, its attacks coincided with and lent encouragement to the much broader campaign by Honduran authorities to intimidate, discredit, expel, or otherwise eliminate anyone who drew attention to military corruption and human rights violations. In February the *New York Times's* James LeMoyne had been barred from the country after publishing articles on the armed forces' involvement in death squads. During the spring disturbances, *El Tiempo* had come under heavy government pressure for its critical editorials and reporting. In the aftermath of the first Inter-American Court ruling, the campaign intensified. In August, the bodies of common criminals once again began to be found along roadsides. When a U.S. human rights monitor investigated the incidents, he was informed by one of the judges handling the cases that the police themselves were responsible.[44]

In October Héctor Orlando Vásquez, a former CODEH activist who had briefly headed the group's San Pedro office, accused Custodio of misappropriating the organization's funds. The CODEH accused Vásquez of being a police informant, claiming that he had purloined its files and turned them over to the authorities. Vásquez in turn suggested that Custodio had been involved in the Pavón-Landaverde assassination and accused him of recruiting guerrillas and orchestrating incidents to discredit the armed forces. Although the State Department let it be known that it considered Vásquez a "reliable source,"[45] others were not so sure. Vásquez himself soon backed away from the most serious of his charges, admitting that he had no evidence that Custodio was involved in the Pavón case. Some of the lesser accusations were also disproved. The full truth, however, was never established.

But then, truth was not the point. Vásquez's charges were immediately picked up by Custodio's enemies, who proceeded to orchestrate an extensive campaign, replete with press conferences and television spots in which violence was linked to human rights activists. Nor was the CODEH the only target. In November, an arrest warrant was issued against the local Americas Watch consultant, Joseph Eldridge. Eldridge, whose reporting had been "driving the embassy up the wall,"[46] had made the mistake of publishing in the *Los Angeles Times* an op-ed piece critical of the Honduran military. In a decision that came from the very top of the armed forces hierarchy,[47] Eldridge was barred from the country. Toward the end of the month, moreover, the *Washington Post* correspondent Julia Preston was expelled for having published an article that quoted a military defector as saying that Battalion 3-16 had been responsible for the Pavón-Landaverde murders. Throughout this period, the authorities repeatedly raised the specter of legal sanctions against those who spoke out.

Violence and Social Decomposition: The Assassination of Alvarez Martínez and Other Acts of Terrorism

Nineteen eighty-nine began like the previous year—with a flurry of violence. On 7 January Manuel Adán Rugama, a top aide to contra commander Enrique Bermúdez, was assassinated in Tegucigalpa. On

23 January, Ramón Matta's lawyer was gunned down. Two days later, Gustavo Alvarez was killed. This last was for Hondurans particularly disturbing. Since returning from exile, the former military chief had immersed himself in fundamentalist religious activities, baring his soul to anyone who would listen, trying to convert the unconverted. Always, he had been haunted by the fear of assassination. He had made too many enemies. He did not know who would kill him, but he suspected his former colleagues the most. He knew too much about drugs and corruption, disappearances and assassinations. The military had tapped his phone and placed him under surveillance; it knew his habits and agendas, and while it had offered him protection his family remained suspicious. Alvarez refused to have a bodyguard or even carry a gun: "Only God," he liked to proclaim, "watches over me now."[48]

God did not watch closely enough. On 25 January a hit squad ambushed Alvarez's Toyota pickup three blocks from his home in the capital's Colonia Florencia. The vehicle's driver was killed instantly. The truck careened across the road. As Alvarez scrambled to get out, the killers opened fire once more, riddling his body with nineteen bullets. Subsequently an anonymous caller, purportedly a Cinchonero, phoned Radio América to claim credit for the deed. But responsibility was never definitively established. Although the embassy was convinced that the left had committed the act, the Alvarez family continued to harbor suspicions of the military.[49]

What disturbed many Hondurans the most about these killings was the aura of professionalism surrounding them. All three crimes had involved teams of assassins who had stalked their victims with machine guns. After firing an initial burst of bullets, they had moved in and fired again to make sure that the job was done. Nothing was left behind but corpses, 9-mm shell casings, and, in one instance, an empty Uzi magazine. Two of the hit squads had their own getaway trucks, and the other commandeered a van. None of the killers were recognized by witnesses, and the crimes were never solved.

Others viewed these events as evidence of profound social disintegration. Political violence had now acquired a dynamic of its own. In the words of one commentator, "The organized groups that traditionally have exercised their monopoly have begun to lose it. . . Violence has become a weapon within the reach of everyone . . . or almost everyone. It is becoming the preferred method for resolving social struggles, group confrontations, and, at times, even personal grudges."[50] Indeed, no sooner was Alvarez cold than a death squad calling itself the Anticommunist Action Alliance published a list of leftists whom it threatened to kill in retaliation. There followed a series of bombings in Tegucigalpa, San Pedro Sula, Comayagua, and La Ceiba. Anonymous threats were received by governmental and nongovernmental agencies. On 24 February an armed forces communiqué announced the discovery of 170,000 pounds of explosives in a safe house in La Ceiba.

It seems clear that the violence was coming from both ends of the political spectrum and from nonpolitical sources as well. The disintegration of the contras had released hundreds of unemployed guerrillas into Honduran society. Many were frustrated, bitter, and prone to violence. They were not necessarily political; many were only too happy to sell their guns to anyone with money. Those who had been in command positions, in particular, had access to weapons caches. Honduran officers were deeply involved in this traffic, often finding buyers and taking a share of the profits. The largest customer was the Salvadoran FMLN, but there were others also.[51] This was all part of the hidden legacy of the contra war.

Another part of that heritage was a marked increase in attacks on North Americans, especially military personnel. Anti-American sentiment was never widespread, and it never produced another disturbance on the order of the April riot. But there continued to be a few violence-prone leftists and nationalists who resented the U.S. presence. To these Hondurans the huge, recently implanted Coca-Cola sign on the hill overlooking downtown Tegucigalpa was an insulting reminder of the North American penetration of their country and the proprietary attitudes that came with it. From June 1988 onward, a series of public disclosures and rumors concerning the negotiation of "secret" agreements covering "permanent" military base rights and drug traffic control measures (including a treaty that would have given U.S. authorities access to information about Honduran financial accounts) heightened their fear that national sovereignty and law were being violated.

Thus it was that in the aftermath of the spring 1988 riot the radical left began targeting gringos in a more systematic fashion. In July four U.S. servicemen were wounded in an attack by Cinchoneros. In October a series of anti-U.S. demonstrations was launched in protest of the draft protocol on military bases. In December the roof was blown off Peace Corps headquarters by a bomb planted by the Morazanista Front for the Liberation of Honduras. (After the 1984 Kissinger commission report on Central America, the Peace Corps contingent in Honduras had been doubled to almost four hundred, the largest such delegation in the world. Its functions, as much political as socioeconomic, were designed to make the U.S. presence and policies more palatable to Hondurans. Needless to say, it quickly became a target of nationalist critics.)

The new year brought more of the same. None of these activities did much damage, but they did cause alarm at the embassy, which in these final months of Briggs's tenure appeared as isolated and paranoid as ever. By now construction was under way on an addition to the building that would give it all the appearance of a vast fortress. It seemed almost symbolic.

From Costa del Sol to the Baker Plan: The Road to Peace

Meanwhile, a new administration had taken office in Washington. In November 1988 George Bush had soundly defeated the Democratic presidential candidate, Michael Dukakis. Like Ronald Reagan, Bush was a staunch conservative. Unlike the former president, however, he was a pragmatist with a long history of experience in foreign affairs. What this would mean for Central America could only be speculated.

The Hondurans, of course, were anxious to press their own concerns with the new administration. For weeks Azcona had been emphasizing the need for an early resolution of the contra problem. In mid-January 1989 he had met with the president-elect to impress upon him the U.S. responsibility in these matters and to urge him to find a solution "as quickly as possible." Bush, however, had remained noncommittal. He was not yet in office and had not even selected his nominee for assistant secretary of state for Latin American affairs. He needed more time to formulate a policy for the region.

But Azcona was impatient. He was under heavy pressure domestically to do something about the contras, and so when Daniel Ortega proposed in early February that those rebels who wanted to leave their camps be disarmed and resettled, he gave the proposal his qualified support. The next week, the Central American presidents met in the Salvadoran beach resort of Costa del Sol. There the Hondurans formally proposed that the guerrilla bases be dismantled. An agreement was reached to draw up a plan within ninety days to close the camps and relocate the rebels and their dependents in third countries. In turn, the Sandinistas agreed to release most of the 3,300 contras and former national guardsmen who were still in prison and to prepare the way for national elections. As part of these arrangements, the five governments promised to halt all aid, other than humanitarian assistance, to insurgents in neighboring countries. The Nicaraguans further agreed to permit all political parties full access to the mass media and make whatever legislative and electoral reforms were necessary to "allow political actions and organization in the broadest sense." There would be a four-month period for the opposition parties to organize, followed by a six-month campaign culminating in presidential, legislative, and municipal elections on 25 February 1990.

The agreement shocked the Bush administration, which found itself overtaken by events before it could organize initiatives of its own. Accordingly, the State Department's reaction was cautious. The contras, for their part, were skeptical: The accord seemed to them unworkable because it did not call for direct negotiations with the Nicaraguan government and placed too much faith in Sandinista promises. Nevertheless, it was clearly a step in the right direction. In agreeing to elections and an elaborate scheme of verification (including international human rights observers and periodic progress reports) the Sandinistas had gone a long way toward meeting the demands of the domestic opposition. At the same time, the agreement received support from an unusual source: The Honduran military had long had a vested interest in perpetuating the war. It had benefited enormously from the dramatic increase in U.S. military and economic assistance during the 1980s. Now, however, the high command had come to the conclusion that the Bush administration had no choice but to continue high levels of aid, at least for the near future. Thus, little time was lost in announcing support for the plan.

The Costa del Sol summit meeting galvanized the Bush administration into action. In its aftermath, both the president and his secretary of state, James Baker, publicly pledged not to abandon the contras. The United States, they asserted, had a "moral obligation" to continue providing "humanitarian assistance" until such time as the Sandinistas complied with their promises. In private meetings with congressional leaders, however, Baker quietly indicated that a major shift in policy was under way. Reaffirming the administration's intention to ask Congress for more nonmilitary aid for the rebels, he also revealed that it would offer to lift economic sanctions against Nicaragua if the Sandinistas moved toward democracy. Whereas Reagan had relied almost entirely on coercion, a balance would now be sought between force and diplomacy.

Underlying this shift were the personality and perceptions of James Baker. Under the Reagan presidency, the United States had been pursuing a "policy of insufficiency." It had been trying to achieve a military objective with means wholly inadequate to the task. Baker had come to accept the failure of the Reagan policy, believing it to be the product of a lack of unity and purpose: The executive branch had been going in one direction and Congress in the other. He no longer considered the contras to be a significant military threat to the Sandinistas, and he was not disposed to try to force the issue. He did not fear the prospect of peace. He was no zealot.

During these weeks Baker spent days in closed-door sessions with Jim Wright and other congressional leaders, trying to hammer out a bipartisan consensus. At the same time, efforts were made to get the Hondurans back on board. On 13 March the undersecretary of state for political affairs, Robert Kimmitt, was sent to Tegucigalpa to persuade Azcona to allow the contras to remain in Honduras until after the scheduled Nicaraguan elections. Honduran officials began to speak of the principle of "simultaneity": The guerrillas, it seemed, would be around for another year. Azcona and López Contreras now began to call for more "humanitarian aid" for the rebels to keep them from becoming a security threat to Honduras. Once again, Hondurans had had to adjust their course to the prevailing northern winds.

Nor were they the only ones. For weeks the contras had been in a state of suspended animation. A month into the Bush presidency, they had still had no high-level communication with the new administration. They were frustrated and apprehensive. As the new U.S. policy developed in the weeks that followed, their initial uncertainty turned to alarm. In mid-March six of the rebel leaders were summoned to the State Department, where they were informed that the United States would no longer support their military operations. Henceforth, the administration would emphasize peaceful civilian activities in Nicaragua in the hope of challenging—and perhaps ending—Sandinista control in the elections scheduled for the following year. In the meantime, an aid package was being negotiated with Congress. Contra forces were to be maintained intact so that pressure could be kept on the Nicaraguan government. Those forces, however, were to refrain from military action. The struggle would be conducted by political means.

This came as a rude shock to many of the rebels. Much had changed in the few short weeks since the Reagan administration had left office. U.S. policymakers had long paid lip service to an electoral solution as a means of obscuring their real intentions; now the cover story had become policy.

One thing that had not changed, however, was the reality of U.S. dominance: Washington was still calling the shots, and not only with respect to strategy. Pressure was now being put on the rebels to clean house. For some time reports had been circulating that some of the guerrillas had tortured prisoners and committed other human rights violations in their Honduran camps. This was a potentially explosive issue, one that could easily sabotage the administration's delicate negotiations with Congress. Two years earlier, in an effort to placate the legislators and ensure continued funding, the State Department had created a contra human rights office. The system had acquired a life of its own, with some department and rebel monitors aggressively pursuing their investigations. In the process, they had repeatedly come into conflict with the U.S. embassy, whose officials obstructed their work, suppressed or minimized the importance of reports on human rights violations, and tried to protect Bermúdez and his cronies from what Ambassador Briggs viewed as a vendetta by Washington liberals.[52] Embassy officials tended to resent any criticism of the guerrillas, often complaining that the latter were the "only armed resistance in history that went into the field with human rights monitors looking over their shoulders."[53]

By early 1989, however, the embassy had lost much of its credibility. In February Representative David Obey publicly complained that he found the mission "most uncooperative" on these matters. Subsequently, an unidentified State Department official characterized Ambassador Briggs as "less than helpful"; at minimum, the embassy "could have put more pressure" on contra commanders to investigate and correct the abuses.[54] Others went farther, suggesting that the ambassador and his aides were walking a "fine line between willful ignorance and intentional obstruction." Some hinted that the embassy and the CIA had become accessories to the crimes—that they had known about them and done nothing.[55]

The issue could no longer be ignored. In late 1988 GAO auditors had toured the contra stockades and found evidence of pervasive torture; congressional Democrats were informed. Since existing legislation barred aid to any group that systematically violated human rights, the administration felt that it had little choice but to pressure the contras to prosecute the worst offenders. Accordingly, a military tribunal was convened. Eleven commanders, including two top leaders, were convicted of murder, torture, rape, or other crimes. As punishment, they were expelled from the movement.[56]

On 24 March a bipartisan accord was reached with Congress to continue funding the rebels through February 1990. Under a gentleman's agreement, this nonmilitary aid would be subject to legislative review in November. Any one of four congressional committees could halt the flow if it determined that the administration was not acting in good faith. By the same token, it was generally understood that if the contras resumed military operations Congress would shut off aid altogether. These were extraordinary concessions, but without them the administration did not have the votes to continue aid. In any case, Secretary Baker wanted to avoid the debilitating battles with Congress that had for so long afflicted the Reagan government. The agreement provided a graceful way for the United States to extricate itself without seeming to abandon its allies. President Bush could now take the high road. In his own words, "We do not claim the right to order the politics of Nicaragua. That is for the Nicaraguan people to decide. The Esquipulas accord requires a free, open political process in which all groups can participate."[57] It was a message that could not have been more welcome to congressional ears.

Tela and Beyond

The Baker Plan did not end the war. Even as the United States was encouraging the contra leaders to return to Nicaragua and continue the struggle by other means, it sought to preserve the guerrilla army in Honduras. The assumption was that the contras had to be maintained as a fighting force; otherwise the Sandinistas would renege on their promises.

But there was a conflict here that could not be ignored: The Central American presidents had pledged to agree within ninety days on a plan for the "voluntary demobilization, repatriation, or relocation" of the rebels. The process had not been spelled out, but the Nicaraguan government, at least, assumed that the dismantling would begin on the ninety-first day. In this it was destined to be disappointed. The ninety days passed without an agreement. Worse from the Sandinista perspective, contra forces began to violate the cease-fire with increasing regularity, and the U.S. Congress seemed unwilling to do anything about it.

By summer the peace process had once again stalled, and the situation on the battlefield was deteriorating. Thus it was that on 5 August the Central American presidents met once again, this time in Tela, Honduras. By now everyone except the Bush administration, the far right in the Republican Party, and the contras wanted to see the latter disband. When, shortly before the meeting, the Sandinista government agreed to a series of concessions to the domestic opposition, the latter consented to participate in the coming election and joined in the call for the rebels' dissolution. Even the Hondurans were now ready to be counted. When Azcona and López Contreras arrived in Tela, they were armed with a demobilization plan of their own.

The tone for the summit had been set, and not even an intensive lobbying campaign by the United States could change things. Telephone appeals from George Bush and visits from high-ranking State Department officials fell on deaf ears. When the other presidents agreed to "internationalize" responsibility for disbanding the guerrillas, Azcona jumped at the opportunity. The resulting agreement provided a specific timetable for the contras' departure. The key clauses called on the United Nations and the Organization of American States to form an International Commission of Support and Verification (Comisión Internacional de Apoyo y Verificación—CIAV) to distribute food, medical supplies, clothing, and other necessities while overseeing the dismantling of the camps and the relocation of the rebels. The guerrillas were to surrender their arms, equipment and military supplies to the commission, which would help repatriate the ex-fighters in Nicaragua and negotiate the relocation in third countries of those who refused repatriation. The CIAV would also monitor the treatment of the returning contras in Nicaragua and report any violations of their rights. A UN peacekeeping force would be formed to patrol the Honduran-Nicaraguan border and prevent any infiltration by the guerrillas. Demobilization was to be completed within ninety days of the establishment of the CIAV or by 5 December at the latest.

The problem was that the rebels, who had not participated in the conference, did not feel bound by its results, and the CIAV had no means of forcing them to disband. The December deadline therefore came and went with the contras still very much alive. By then, however, the focus of the anti-Sandinista struggle was rapidly shifting from the battlefield to the political arena. The February elections were approaching. At last, the Nicaraguan people would have the opportunity to decide their own fate at the polls.

The End and the Beginning: The Nicaraguan Elections

It was a bad season to be an incumbent in Central America. Governing parties had recently lost elections in Costa Rica, El

Salvador, and Honduras. Now it would be Nicaragua's turn. The socioeconomic indicators were ominous: The country had been devastated by back-to-back wars. Tens of thousands of people had been killed. The survivors were exhausted, the economy out of control. Over the past three years, the gross domestic product had fallen 11.7 percent, a drop of 21.5 percent per capita. Unemployment and underemployment were rampant. Inflation was 1,700 percent. Real wages had fallen from an index of 100 in 1980 to 29.2 in February 1988 and to 1 in December 1989. Milk consumption had plunged by 50 percent in 1988 alone. Tuberculosis and malaria were spreading widely. Infant mortality and illiteracy were rapidly increasing. Hospitals lacked basic supplies; the educational system was collapsing; consumers had to wait in endless lines for food and fuel.[58] Through a combination of war and economic sanctions, the Reagan administration, aided enormously by the Sandinistas's own mistakes, had succeeded in discrediting the revolution. For years more than half of the government's budget had been devoted to the military as resources that should have gone into socioeconomic development were siphoned off by the war effort. Inevitably, most of the regime's promises of a better life had gone unfulfilled.

It is a truism of electoral politics that economic hard times redound to the benefit of the out-of-power party. No incumbent could have been expected to win an honest election after having presided over the decline that the Sandinistas had overseen. In addition, the government's woes were compounded by the nature of the opposition: Daniel Ortega's rival in the presidential race was none other than Violeta Barrios de Chamorro, the widow of Pedro Joaquín Chamorro, the martyred publisher of *La Prensa*. Doña Violeta, as almost everyone called her, was widely revered as a symbol of national reconciliation. Her campaign was a masterpiece of public relations, skillfully manipulating the deeply rooted religious instincts of the Nicaraguan people even as it played to their desperate longing for peace. In contrast, the Ortega campaign could hardly have been more inappropriate. In the midst of so much suffering, Sandinista strategists organized a rollicking, modernistic extravaganza that seemed to support the opposition's contention that this was a cynical, corrupt government.

The Sandinistas had lost touch with reality. Most Nicaraguans wanted peace and reconciliation. They understood that only under those conditions could the socioeconomic crisis be overcome and a better life constructed. In perspective, the victory of Chamorro and her National Opposition Union (Unión Nacional Opositora—UNO) coalition would be based as much on a rational calculation of the alternatives as on any visceral hatred of the Sandinistas: A Chamorro victory offered hope—the *possibility* of a better future. An Ortega triumph, in contrast, seemed to promise only more of the same—more conflict with the United States, more war with the contras, and more interminable socioeconomic deterioration. For most Nicaraguans, the choice was obvious. The final vote was not even close: On 25 February 1990 Chamorro was swept into office with 54.7 percent of the vote to Daniel Ortega's 40.8 percent. The UNO captured fifty-one of the ninety-two seats in the National Assembly. A new era had begun.

War's End

The UNO had won the election, but could it govern? The victorious opposition was composed of no fewer than fourteen political parties, some of which had nothing in common beyond their dislike for the Sandinistas and their desire for a share of the political pie. There were conflicts between conservatives and communists, old-line politicos and newly arrived technocrats, Chamorro family insiders and those outside the new president's personal entourage. Conflicts of personality abounded. Could Doña Violeta hold this ungainly coalition together?

Of even more immediate importance was whether Mrs. Chamorro and her advisers could negotiate the transition of power and bring the civil war to an end. These issues were inextricably intertwined. Though the Sandinistas had lost the election, they remained by far the best organized and most popular political party in Nicaragua. They controlled the armed forces, the police, the bureaucracy, and the most powerful unions. Without their consent, no transfer of power would occur.

The Sandinistas' primary concern, of course, was their own future. It was one thing to give up control of the government, quite another to surrender the institutions of armed force. Without some kind of power-sharing arrangement, de facto if not formal, it seemed unlikely that they would surrender political office. Most of all they were worried that their bitter enemies, the contras, would take advantage of the transition to assume power or, at least, become the nucleus of a new right-wing army. The Sandinistas needed assurances that they would not now become the targets of a vendetta. The contras, they insisted, would have to be disarmed.

This was easier said than done. The Bush administration had recognized the need to purge the rebel ranks of the corrupt elements that had dominated it since the beginning. In August 1988 Enrique Bermúdez had moved to Miami to join the political directorate and avail himself of the US$180,000-a-year salary that the CIA provided directors. There he had increasingly lost touch with developments in Honduras and Nicaragua. Even some of his closest allies had turned against him. In July 1989 the State Department had quietly orchestrated a shift in power from Bermúdez to the general staff and its new chief, Israel Galeano (Commander "Franklin"). In early 1990 he was deposed altogether. This did not mean that there would be any softening of the rebels' position, however. From their camps in Honduras and Nicaragua, they remained defiant. Even after 25 February they continued to resist disarming, maintaining that their continued existence as a military force was necessary to ensure Sandinista compliance with the election results. Anticipating international pressures to disband, thousands of rebels began to return to Nicaragua, taking their arms with them.

By now everyone wanted the contras to dissolve except the contras. The guerrillas had become the single most formidable obstacle to peace. No longer dependent on U.S. military aid, they were in danger of becoming a Frankenstein's monster. Many were embittered by Washington's "betrayal" and adamant that they would not lay down their guns until the Sandinistas relinquished control of the armed forces. To make matters worse, the latter now began to back away from the conciliatory gestures they had made in the immediate aftermath of the elections. By early March they were issuing defiant warnings against government interference with their control of the military and the police. Daniel Ortega even went so far as to declare that he could not guarantee a peaceful transition unless the contras were immediately disbanded. By this time, a new U.S. ambassador, Cresencio Arcos, had arrived in Tegucigalpa. Arcos had been in the embassy when the contra war was just beginning in the early 1980s. He had served five years under a series of ambassadors. He knew the country. Even after returning to Washington in 1985, he had continued to have Honduran responsibilities, dealing with contra issues (humanitarian assistance, human rights) at the State Department and the White House before becoming Elliott Abrams's deputy for Central America. When the bottom had fallen out of the aid program in 1988, Abrams had instructed him to "hold this thing together with bailing wire" until the next administration could take over. He was the head "contra-handler" at State, the logical person to finish what he had been working on for so long. Informed that he would be returning to Honduras, he was told, "You were present at the creation of this f—— mess. Now you can go back and shut it down."[59]

Arcos understood that his superiors did not care what he accomplished in Honduras so long as he solved their political problem. His task was to deliver the contras. During these weeks heavy pressure was brought to bear on the rebels, who were told in no uncertain terms that they would have to lay down their arms before the United States would provide money for their reintegration into Nicaragua. With the help of the Hondurans, a meeting was arranged between Chamorro's representatives and the contras at Toncontín Air Base. On 23 March an accord was signed calling for an immediate cease-fire inside Nicaragua and the beginning of a general demobilization. Those troops still in Honduras were to be disarmed no later than 20 April (five days prior to the new government's inauguration). Those already in Nicaragua would gather in designated "security zones" under UN and OAS supervision until they could be disarmed and reintegrated into civilian life.

But the Toncontín accord did not end the matter. Only on 19 April were the final details of the demobilization agreed upon. And even then, the process dragged on. On 22 April Mrs. Chamorro informed the other leaders of her UNO coalition that Humberto Ortega would be retained as head of the Nicaraguan armed forces. This was an extraordinary move. By satisfying the Sandinistas' demands concerning the military, Chamorro and her advisers were hoping to co-opt them, securing their support not only for the political transition but for other changes, including the dismantling of the powerful Interior Ministry, which controlled the security police, and sharp reductions in military manpower. The retention of Ortega, it was felt, would help calm tensions and avoid confrontations with the Sandinistas' followers, who were already demonstrating their ability to disrupt vital services through strikes and demonstrations. Above all, Chamorro and her advisers recognized the danger of replacing the Sandinistas with an extreme anti-Sandinista government. They wanted to demonstrate that they were not seeking revenge and that there was a place for their opponents in the new political order. The aim was national reconciliation.

It was a brilliant tactical move, but it was also an explosive one. The revelation threw the UNO into immediate crisis. The appointment was denounced as a betrayal. Relations between Chamorro and the fourteen veteran party leaders in the coalition had never been close; now they were dangerously close to rupture.

Nor was the Bush administration pleased. A few days earlier, Assistant Secretary of State Bernard Aronson had been dispatched to Managua with a message that Ortega's continued presence could jeopardize the more than US$300 million in aid being considered by Congress. The administration was concerned that, with Ortega still at the helm, the military would continue sending arms to the guerrillas in El Salvador. Aronson also warned that the contras might now refuse to abide by the demobilization agreement. His fear was well founded. From a security zone in northern Nicaragua, Commanders "Franklin" and "Rubén" denounced Chamorro for having "sold out" to the Sandinistas. The guerrillas now stopped disarming and began to make new demands. By the end of May fewer than 2,000 had turned over their weapons.

The deadlock was finally broken on 30 May, when the government agreed to establish twenty-three "development zones" in rural areas where the rebels could settle, provide their own security, and participate in local government. The former combatants were also promised that they would be given priority in recovering farmlands confiscated by the Sandinistas. A substantial portion of the U.S. aid package (which had been passed by Congress in spite of the Ortega reappointment) would go to facilitating their return to civilian life. Accordingly, the demobilization was resumed. On 15 June President Chamorro announced that she had ordered a one-third reduction in the size of the Nicaraguan military and the creation of an all-volunteer force. By her side, endorsing the proposals, was Humberto Ortega. Amazingly, the president had broken the deadlock between the Sandinistas and the contras. The war was over.

Postscript: The Wages of Sin

In May 1989 Hondurans learned that they were not yet rid of Elliott Abrams. The former assistant secretary of state had decided to go into the lumber business with, among others, retired General Paul Gorman. Honduras, with its vast (though increasingly endangered) forests, provided an obvious opportunity for profit. Asked about his new job, Abrams responded, "I am making a lot of money. It is marvelous."[60]

He was not the only former Reagan administration official to profit from his past activities and contacts. Both before and after conviction for illegal Iran-contra activities, Oliver North was able to fashion a lucrative new career for himself, touring the United States, speaking to adulatory audiences. Right-wing political groups organized US$100-a-plate dinners to pay his court costs. The former lieutenant colonel received as much as US$25,000 a lecture. In speech after speech he would bring the crowds to their feet with ringing denunciations of the "imperial Congress" and the "sad swamp on the Potomac." To many conservatives he seemed the "most marketable political commodity in the United States," just the man to rejuvenate the Republican Party in the 1990s.[61]

Ronald Reagan too was enjoying being a private citizen. In October, he collected a US$2 million "honorarium" for a nine-day visit to Japan, where he gave speeches defending Japanese investments in the United States—in particular, Sony's proposed US$3.4 billion takeover of Columbia Pictures. Reagan also used the occasion to raise millions of dollars for his presidential library through donations from the Japanese government and private enterprise. The episode touched off a storm of criticism back home. Some Americans, it seemed, found distasteful the spectacle of a former president making a fortune by promoting the penetration of his country by its major economic rival.

Notes

1. On the Pavón-Landaverde and Inter-American Court cases, see especially Americas Watch (AW), *Honduras: Without the Will* (New York, July 1989), pp. 9-15, 69-77. A description of the bombings may be found in *Boletín Informativo Honduras,* No. 87, July 1988, pp. 1-2.

2. *Miami Herald,* 14 January 1988.

3. Ibid., 16 February 1988.

4. Ibid., 5 March 1988.

5. Ibid.

6. *Newsweek,* 28 March 1988.

7. *El Heraldo* and *El Tiempo,* 18 March 1988.

8. This from one of General Woerner's aides at the SOUTHCOM (not-for-attribution). In the words of one pro-contra journalist, the administration's reaction was "hysterical overkill." Glenn Garvin, *Everybody Had His Own Gringo* (Washington, D.C.: Brassey's Inc., 1992), p. 227.

9. *Miami Herald,* 20 March 1988.

10. The request for troops was initiated by the commander in chief of the SOUTHCOM, General Fred Woerner, who considered Honduran morale even more important than the need to deter the Sandinistas. He also thought that it was a "great opportunity" to practice a deployment under "neat" conditions to "see what we were capable of doing" (personal communication).

11. *La Tribuna,* 17 March 1988; *El Tiempo,* 18 March 1988.

12. *El Tiempo,* 18 March 1988.

13. In the words of one Honduran. *Miami Herald,* 11 April 1988.

14. Interview with the embassy press officer, Chip Barkley, 21 February 1989. Romero told one of us that he had been shown the letter (he did not have a copy) by someone in the embassy. He said that he was convinced that it was genuine. Interview, 7 March 1991.

15. Interview with John D. Negroponte, 13 July 1988.

16. *El Tiempo,* 7 March 1988.

17. Interviews with Ted Briggs, 9 April 1990, and Víctor Meza, 15 April 1989.

18. U.S. Senate Foreign Relations Committee, Subcommittee on Terrorism, Narcotics, and International Operations, *Drugs, Law Enforcement, and Foreign Policy* (Washington, D.C.: U.S. Government Printing Office, 1989), pp. 42-49.

19. *El Heraldo,* 7 and 8 April 1988; *Miami Herald,* 10 and 14 April 1988.

20. Information from two Honduran military informants; interview with Ambassador Briggs, 9 April 1990; interview with Briggs's political counselor, Don Johnson, 9 August 1989. The allegations of Riera's friendship with Matta were first reported in *El Tiempo* and *El Heraldo,* 13 April 1988.

21. *Miami Herald,* 14 April 1988; *El Heraldo,* 7 March 1988.

22. This from a military source who was in position to know; see also *New York Times,* 15 April 1988.

23. Johnson interview.

24. Briggs interview.

25. This from a high-level Honduran government source; see also *New York Times,* 13 April 1988.

26. This source, whom we have found to be reliable in the past, claims (not-for-attribution) to have been told this by Núñez Montes. We have also been told this story, minus the reference to Núñez Montes, by a Honduran colonel and a U.S. embassy official. See also *El Heraldo,* 20 April 1988.

27. This scenario is based primarily on *New York Times,* 15 April 1988.

28. *El Tiempo,* 7 April 1988.

29. David Romero, personal communication; confirmed by two other sources.

30. *Los Angeles Times,* 13 February 1988; *El Heraldo,* 15 February 1988.

31. Interview with Longino Becerra, 4 February 1989; interview with Víctor Meza, 18 March 1991; conversations with four other well-informed sources.

32. Unless otherwise noted, this section is based on Sam Dillon, *Comandos* (New York: Henry Holt, 1991), pp. 218-230; R. Pardo-Maurer, *The Contras, 1980-1989: A Special Kind of Politics* (New York: Praeger, 1990), pp. 106-124; and Garvin, *Everybody Had His Own Gringo,* pp. 235-239.

33. *Miami Herald,* 19 May 1988.

34. *New York Times,* 11 June 1988.

35. See, especially, AW, *Honduras: Without the Will,* pp. 85-87.

36. Briggs interview.

37. Interview with John Ferch, 23 June 1988.

38. Briggs interview.

39. AW, *Honduras: Without the Will,* pp. 79, 88, 90.

40. U.S. Embassy, *Handbook on Honduras: Democracy, Defense, Development, Diplomacy,* spring 1989. Emphases added. In contrast, Americas Watch found seven such cases from mid-1987 to mid-1989 alone.

41. Dillon, *Comandos,* p. 198.

42. "Press Summaries of CODEH's List of Alleged Extrajudicial Executions by Honduran Authorities in 1987," p. 17.

43. Letter from Norma Harms to Ramón Custodio, 1 August 1988.

44. Interview with Joe Eldridge, 10 April 1990.

45. U.S. Department of State, "Rebuttal of Americas Watch Critique of Department's 1988 Report on Human Rights in Honduras" (mimeo, 1989).

46. Thomas Dodd, personal communication.

47. So Eldridge's wife was informed by a high-ranking Honduran immigration official.

48. Interview with Gustavo Alvarez Martínez, 4 December 1988.

49. Interviews with the embassy's Don Johnson and a member of the Alvarez family who requested anonymity.

50. *Boletín Informativo Honduras,* No. 93, January 1989, p. 1.

51. See, especially, the detailed testimony of former contra commander Horacio Arce ("Mercenario") in *El Día* (Mexico City), 6-7 November 1988. See also *El Tiempo,* 28 September 1988, and *New York Times,* 17 March 1989.

52. On this subject, see especially Dillon, *Comandos,* pp. 230-233, 252-298.

53. Johnson interview.

54. *New York Times,* 23 March 1989.

55. Dillon, *Comandos,* pp. 255, 279.

56. This was the high point of the contra human rights effort. Subsequently the conviction of Commander "Mack," the powerful chief of intelligence, was reversed, and he was reinstated. In August another tribunal absolved a dozen other commanders. By then, however, Congress had voted to continue aid, and the administration was no longer much interested in contra human rights abuses.

57. *New York Times,* 25 March 1989.

58. Carlos Vilas, "What Went Wrong," *NACLA Report on the Americas,* Vol. 24, No. 1, June 1990, p. 12.

59. Interview with Cresencio Arcos, 4 March 1991.

60. *El Heraldo,* 31 May 1989.

61. *New York Times,* 7 May 1989 and 21 April 1990.

8

The Invisible Country

Gracias a Dios que hemos salido de estas Honduras.

—attributed to Cristóbal Colón

Scotty Reston once said that North Americans are willing to do anything for Latin Americans except read about them. Honduras is living proof of this. The Nicaraguan revolution had marked the beginning of an era of unprecedented U.S. attention to Central America. Indeed, under the Reagan administration, Washington's concern with the region had amounted to an obsession. The White House had defined the situation in strategic Cold War terms and set the policy agenda accordingly. The press and, to a lesser extent, the public had followed—if not in agreement, then at least in terms of attention paid. In contrast, the Bush administration had had very different perceptions and priorities. Well before the 1990 election defeat of the Sandinista government, it had moved to demote the region from its high place among U.S. foreign policy priorities. And, again, public attention had followed suit. In 1988 the *New York Times Index* listed twenty-nine articles dealing primarily with Honduras; in 1989 the number was seven, and in 1990 it was two. Honduras—and to a lesser extent the region as a whole—had reverted to its historical status as an obscure backwater far removed from the attention of both U.S. policymakers and the public—an invisible country.

It is surprising that a change in administrations could make so much difference. Granted, the revolutions in the communist world and the end of the Cold War made it much easier to reevaluate the Central American crisis. Congress's refusal to continue funding the contra war made it virtually impossible for the Bush administration to pursue the policies of its predecessor and politically costly even to try. The stalemate in the Salvadoran civil war had largely eliminated the fear of a communist victory in that country; there, as elsewhere, the prospects for peace seemed to be improving. All these developments helped President Bush and his secretary of state redefine the Central American problem in noncrisis and nonmilitary terms.

Yet, North American perceptions notwithstanding, the crisis was not over—at least not for Central Americans. The fighting in El Salvador dragged on. In Nicaragua, the peace remained fragile. In country after country, the socioeconomic conditions that had helped create conflict were worse than they had been a decade earlier. Nicaragua, in fact, appeared mired in permanent crisis: The economy was a basket case. And just as the former opposition had been determined to make Sandinista Nicaragua ungovernable, now the Sandinistas were doing the same to the Chamorro government. By 1991 hundreds of ex-contras, angered at the Sandinistas' continued control and repressive use of the coercive apparatus of the state and disillusioned with the promises and performance of the government, were again taking up arms. Now, moreover, they were being joined by demobilized former members of the Sandinista army, whose return to civilian life was marred by widespread unemployment and poverty.

In socioeconomic terms, for Honduras the crisis had in fact grown considerably worse. A new president was in office with a bold neoconservative plan to restructure and revivify the economy. Unfortunately, for many, the cure seemed worse than the disease. Meanwhile, the military was going through its own agonies. Riven with continual struggles over power and spoils, various factions began to tear each other apart in an orgy of cannibalism. The only good thing about the situation was that the institution's increasing debility offered an opportunity for civilian structures to flourish. As had occurred so often in the past, development and decay continued to go hand in hand.

Political Modernization and Democratization: The 1989 Elections

In November 1989, Rafael Leonardo Callejas and the National Party were swept into office in the party's most impressive electoral triumph of this century. The final results had Callejas winning the presidency over his Liberal opponent, Carlos Flores Facussé, with 50.9 to the latter's 43.1 percent of the vote. The Nationalists captured seventy-one seats in Congress to the Liberals' fifty-five. The PINU won 1.8 percent of the vote and two congressional seats. The Christian Democrats took 1.4 percent but were shut out of Congress.

These results reinforced the impression that political development was continuing and democracy taking hold. For the first time in fifty-seven years, power had been transferred from one party to another by peaceful means. Hondurans were developing an "electoral vocation." The balloting also confirmed that the two-party system was not likely to be transformed in the foreseeable future. No matter how unhappy Hondurans were with the two major parties, they had even less faith in third parties. Between 1981 and 1989, the combined PINU/Christian Democratic vote had declined from a meager 4.1 percent to 3.2 percent.

The campaign itself was vintage Honduran: shrill in tone and devoid of content. The candidates chose to hurl insults at one another rather than to address the issues. Charges and countercharges abounded. Both Liberals and Nationalists were accused of registering foreigners on the electoral rosters. Callejas was charged with having bought dollars from the contras, and in response the Nationalists accused the Liberals of using state funds and resources in their campaign and tried to portray Flores as an extension of eight years of Liberal failure. As it became increasingly clear that the Liberals would go down in defeat, they began to cry foul. There followed a last-minute attempt to scrub the electoral rosters and allow voting through the use of temporary identification cards. As accusations and counteraccusations flew, the U.S. ambassador-designate in Washington, Cresencio Arcos, was instructed to call in the Honduran ambassador to express concern that a last-minute postponement and/or the addition of new rules would appear less than democratic. The latter passed the message on to Foreign Minister López Contreras (a National Party stalwart), who promptly leaked it. In this way, the Nationalists were able to use an expression of U.S. diplomatic concern as evidence of Liberal skullduggery.

At this point, Azcona exploded. He denounced Arcos's comments as interference in Honduras's internal affairs. There followed a barrage of anti-imperialist rhetoric that was all the more remarkable considering its source. For almost four years the Azcona government had been the United States's closest ally in the region. On 13 November the president publicly rejected the IMF-AID economic prescription for Honduras and charged that a suspension of US$70 million in U.S. aid was politically motivated: By deepening the country's economic crisis, the AID was undercutting the Liberal campaign and helping Callejas. There was an element of truth in this, but most observers dismissed Azcona's performance as a desperate attempt to manipulate nationalistic sentiment on behalf of the Liberal

Party. Nor were many impressed by subsequent charges, made in the bitter aftermath of defeat, that the CIA and the AID had infiltrated the National Electoral Tribunal and manipulated the vote to Callejas's advantage.

In fact, the Liberals had no one to blame for their defeat but themselves. They had been in office for two terms and accomplished nothing. After eight years of economic hardship, contras, corruption, and ineptitude, Hondurans were tired of the "circus." They wanted to punish the Liberals for their misuse of power. Above all, they wanted a change for the better. (Typical of the popular disgust was a February 1988 Doumont cartoon that showed rats carrying "Yo para Presidente" signs marching out of a horn of plenty labeled "Partido Liberal.") Moreover, beyond the burden of having to campaign on their record, the Liberals had made an unfortunate choice of candidates. Even within party circles, Flores Facussé was often perceived as arrogant and unscrupulous. He was a *turco* (Arab) married to a gringa, and his name (Flowers) did not inspire confidence in this machismo-oriented society. To make matters worse, the Facussé family was deeply involved in the CONADI scandal. In the words of one dissident Liberal, Flores's attitude was that he had "bought the nomination and therefore deserved it."[1] It was not an attitude that would win him many votes. In contrast, in Rafael Callejas the Nationalists had the most popular politician in the country. Whereas Flores was colorless, plain-looking, and an uninspiring speaker, Callejas was charismatic, handsome, and often brilliantly articulate. Even those who disagreed with his politics had to admit that he was a decent person who had "at least a little feeling for his countrymen."[2]

Adding to the Liberals' woes, the party had never resolved its chronic factionalism. In the aftermath of the 1985 nomination wars, there had been an effort to democratize. Leaders of the various *corrientes* (currents) had been allowed to pursue their candidacies through a primary election, but the ensuing campaign had only underlined the party's disunity. Flores won, but with only 35.5 percent of the vote he emerged in a weakened position. His enemies considered him a front man for former President Suazo, who admitted having contributed heavily to Flores's candidacy. Symptomatic of the problem was an incident during the Liberals' campaign-launching ceremony, when two of the speakers "forgot" the name of their candidate and urged the audience to "unite for victory" behind Carlos Roberto Reina (head of the M-LIDER faction). Nor did President Azcona, long a Flores rival, give him the support that was needed for a Liberal victory.[3]

Finally, the National Party had also been going through major reforms since the mid-1980s, but those changes had been much more conducive to the creation of a modern, technologically oriented, and effective political machine. Whereas in the Liberal Party democratization had occurred without modernization, in the National Party precisely the opposite was the case. After 1986, when Callejas had become president of the central committee, the party organization had been systematically remodeled. New techniques of organization and control had been introduced. The traditional, clientelistic rural *caciques* (bosses) who had dominated the party for decades had been co-opted and marginalized by a new urban elite with business and managerial skills appropriate for the 1980s. This "technification" of the apparatus enabled the Nationalists to coordinate operations and mobilize support much more effectively than when they had relied on patronage and personal loyalties alone.[4] As a result, the Nationalists "got out the vote" and the Liberals did not. Many Liberals, indeed, either voted for Callejas or stayed home rather than cast their ballots for a candidate in whom they had little confidence and even less affection.

The Cannibalization of the High Command: The Regalado Scandal and the Decapitation of the Fifth Promotion

While Hondurans were choosing their president, another kind of election was taking place, this one within the military. On 15 October the *New York Times* disclosed that senior Honduran officers had accused General Regalado of misappropriating millions of dollars in U.S. military aid. The sources claimed that for several years Regalado had been selling donated equipment to units under his command and depositing the money in a special bank account that he personally controlled. Records had been falsified to cover up the losses. The allegations caused shock waves in Tegucigalpa. Regalado denied them, claiming that such abuses were impossible because of the way U.S. military aid was delivered: in provisions rather than cash. (That, of course, did not really address the issue. No one had accused him of taking U.S. *monetary* donations.) President Azcona and the COSUFFAA backed him, as did former ambassador Briggs, who termed the press reports "very imaginative and inventive."[5] Supposedly, such theft was impossible given the strict auditing and other controls that were placed on U.S. aid.

But the charges could not be so easily dismissed. Only the previous year, Reagan administration officials had told the *Times* of their suspicions that Regalado was protecting Colombian drug traffickers living in Honduras. Regalado's half-brother, Rigoberto Regalado Lara, in jail in Miami for his own involvement in the cocaine trade, had told Honduran investigators that his supplier was a close friend of the general. Another convicted trafficker, also imprisoned in the United States, said that he had discussed drug deals with him. (As if all this were not enough, in December a Honduran investigative commission revealed that General Regalado's daughter was also in the cocaine business.)[6]

More important than the question of guilt or innocence were the political implications of the scandal. Some months earlier, Regalado had let it be known that he wanted to continue beyond his term as armed forces commander. This was difficult, first, because it required a constitutional amendment and, second, because not everyone wanted him to stay. This did not, however, inhibit him from exploring the possibilities behind the scenes. When the president of Congress publicly declared that it had been a "historical error" to limit the commander's term to three years, it became clear that resistance from civilian authorities would be minimal.[7]

Others, however, were interested in the job. By July it was clear that Regalado faced strong opposition within the military. New candidates had arisen, including Colonel Riera Lunatti, the former FUSEP commander who had held back his troops during the 1988 riot. Finding himself blocked, Regaldo retreated, expressing lack of interest in staying on—unless, of course, the COSUFFAA wished it.[8] In September his aspirations for reelection were rejected by a majority of his colleagues. But even that did not end the matter. On 5 October President Azcona submitted a request to Congress that Regalado be promoted to division general, a move that his opponents interpreted as an attempt to enhance his chances of reelection. It was at this point that Regalado's enemies in the fifth promotion made their charges to the *New York Times.*

The high command had been placed in a difficult position. It was appropriations time in Washington. U.S. military aid to Honduras was being debated in Congress. Even before the scandal broke, there had been deep concern in the COSUFFAA that aid might be cut. The Regalado affair had heightened that concern. Clearly, the general was a liability and had to go. Yet, the high command could not publicly repudiate him. The armed forces' carefully cultivated image of "granite unity" was at stake, and in any case he knew too much. In the end, the U.S. Department of Defense was asked to investigate. New measures for joint U.S.-Honduran control of military aid were established. Within the high command, a compromise was reached between Regalado and the leaders of the 6th promoción. The general would get his promotion and a measure of revenge against his enemies. Seniority would be set aside. The position of armed forces commander would go to the sixth graduating class. To make the choice palatable to the most powerful members of that faction (all of whom aspired to the post themselves), it was decided to select a noncontroversial figure. In a decision that astounded outside observers, the COSUFFAA voted for Colonel Arnulfo Cantarero López, the head of the navy, traditionally the weakest branch of the armed forces. Cantarero was almost no one's first choice. Rather, he was the lowest common denominator that could be agreed on.

In the weeks that followed, the fifth promotion was decapitated. In January it was disclosed that the last members of the class would be retired, most involuntarily. They did not, however, go quietly. On 22 February five of them, including Riera Lunatti and Núñez Montes, issued an extraordinary public statement. Rejecting official explanations of their retirement, they attacked Regalado for "irregularities." The recent violation of seniority in the selection of armed forces commander was denounced. The deposed colonels protested their forced and "premature" retirements and the campaign to ruin their reputations (all of this, allegedly, because they had refused to join Regalado's "scheme").

So much for the "granite unity" of the armed forces. The guard had been changed, but unity could not be restored. To no one's surprise, Cantarero proved to be a weak leader. The sixth promotion now began to turn inward and devour its children.

Callejas in Office:
The Pain of Adjustment

In January 1990, amidst spiraling inflation and growing scarcity of gasoline, medicine, and basic foodstuffs, Rafael Callejas was inaugurated president. Few envied him his task. The 1980s had been a lost decade in terms of economic development. Per capita income was 13 percent lower than it had been in 1980. Over the past two years, the black market rate for the lempira had soared from 2.4 to 4.5 to the dollar. The public debt was 8.7 billion lempiras, 90.1 percent of the GDP. The foreign debt was US$3.3 billion. The country had fallen US$727 million behind in its foreign repayments, with US$247 million outstanding, and had been declared ineligible for new loans. The 1989 budget deficit amounted to 12.5 percent of the GDP. Years of easy credit and unrestrained spending had failed to translate into self-sustaining economic growth. Now the moment had come to settle accounts.[9]

Callejas had few options, and none of them were good. Clearly, austerity was necessary, but at what cost? The vast majority of Hondurans already lived in abject poverty. One could not draw blood from a stone. Nevertheless, one could try. The new president was one of the most competent leaders Honduras had ever had, but he was also very conservative. He lost little time in surrounding himself with skilled technocrats, most of them of his ideological persuasion. To all appearances, this was an abrupt departure from the traditional corrupt, incompetence-riddled politics of the past. In the weeks that followed, a systematic study was made of the economic situation. In the end, it was decided that only a drastic program of structural reform could restore the country to economic health. The massive fiscal deficit that had been overstimulating imports and damaging the country's balance of payments would be slashed. Exports would be encouraged and excessive imports discouraged through a devaluation of the lempira. A more competitive, export-oriented private sector would be promoted by reducing trade protectionism.

In March a comprehensive program of reforms was pushed through Congress. Among the items in this *"Pacquetazo"* were budget cuts, public employee layoffs, increased sales and income taxes, higher fuel and public service charges, sharp tariff reductions, streamlined investment regulations, and a floating exchange rate. At the same time, monetary policy was tightened, and in June the president moved to accelerate the privatization of money-losing state enterprises. Still larger rate increases followed in August for electricity (50 percent), water (100 percent), telephone service (100 percent), and fuel (over 100 percent for the year). In December, a more efficient income tax system was introduced.

The reaction of foreign creditors was enthusiastic. No sooner was the program announced than the Bush administration agreed to release the remainder of the US$70 million in economic support funds that had been frozen. In addition, the AID agreed to grant the Honduran government US$147 million, mostly for balance of payments assistance. In June Callejas announced that a US$247.5 million bridge loan had been obtained from the United States, Japan, Venezuela, and Mexico. The funds were to be transferred to international lending institutions to cover Honduras's back interest payments. The next day the World Bank and the IMF announced that Honduras had been removed from their blacklist. The Inter-American Development Bank (IDB) followed suit shortly thereafter. During his first eight months in office, Callejas contracted over US$1.17 billion from international sources, including some US$750 million in loans and credits from the IMF, the IDB and the World Bank to be distributed over the next three years. In the process, however, he also increased the country's foreign debt to US$3.4 billion, a sum that would be difficult to service without strong economic growth.

If the structural adjustment program won the confidence of international financiers, in Honduras it was met with a firestorm of criticism. Opponents argued that the primary burden of austerity would be borne by the poor and the middle class. Even before the program was announced, the government proclaimed the imminent layoff of about 5 percent of the workers on its payroll. Since the overwhelming majority of these jobs were filled by Liberal Party supporters, the press quickly dubbed the firings the "blue broom," an allusion to the National Party's color. Critics also noted that some of these positions were refilled by nacionalistas, some of whom were given higher salaries than their predecessors. At the same time, public employee unions charged that the government was creating parallel workers' organizations to weaken opposition to Callejas's program. By May some 7,000 state jobs had been eliminated. A nationwide strike by the Honduran Association of Public Employees closed public hospitals, secondary schools, and half of government offices for a week.

The public employees' strike ended without major concessions, but it was just the beginning. On 10 June 4,000 members of the public health workers' union went on strike to protest rumored plans to privatize some health ministry services. On 26 June they were joined by 10,000 banana workers from SITRATERCO, the union at the Tela Railroad Company. SITRATERCO was the most powerful union in the country, and it was able to rally the support of unions affiliated with the CTH. Within two days some 70,000 workers, mostly on the north coast, had launched sympathy strikes. Three other federations soon joined the fray. By early July the country was virtually paralyzed. When the *Plataforma de Lucha* (the Fighting Platform), a formidable labor coalition that had taken on the task of resisting the austerity program, threatened to call a general strike, the administration saw the light and came to an agreement with the health workers.

The SITRATERCO strike was more difficult. For forty-two days it dragged on, the longest such labor action in three decades. As losses to the government and Tela mounted into the tens of millions of dollars, the administration began to fear that the company might pull out altogether. When a mediation effort stalled in early August, Callejas sent in troops to militarize the plantations and resume operations. At this point, the strike collapsed. The Plataforma de Lucha failed to deliver on its threats. Union leaders agreed to a government-sponsored accord that gave the workers a modest raise. The next day's headline in *El Tiempo* said it all: "SITRATERCO Capitulates."

Meanwhile, trouble was brewing in the countryside. In August, an "agrarian reconciliation" agreement was signed between representatives of the government, large landowners, cattlemen, and some peasant groups. The idea was to encourage cooperation between haves and have-nots so that basic grain production could be increased without threatening the agro-export sector. Honduras was in the midst of the worst food shortage in its history, the product of chronic drought, the demands of a large refugee population, and—perhaps most important—the increasing use of lands for cattle raising and export agriculture. Over a fourth of Honduras's farmlands were devoted to cattle, with most of the beef being sold abroad. That left most domestic food production in the hands of small subsistence farmers, whose lands tended to be overworked and less fertile. As a consequence Honduras, which had once been self-sufficient, had become dependent on food imports.[10]

The agrarian reconciliation was intended to placate both large landowners and peasants by pledging government assistance to both, but most of the major campesino groups denounced it as a thinly veiled attempt to undermine the agrarian reform. By now at least a third of the rural population was landless, and more than three-fourths were living in absolute poverty. Thousands of children were dying every year, mostly in the countryside, from malnutrition and diarrhea. As socioeconomic conditions worsened and desperation spread, so did the number of land recuperations and the violence that attended them. Nineteen ninety-one would be a traumatic year.

The Banana War

If 1990 marked a turning point in Honduran political leadership and economic strategy, it also promised to be a watershed in the country's relations with the outside world. In April a federation of independent banana growers, the Compañía Agrícola y Ganadera de Sula, S.A. (CAGSSA), signed a US$2.5 million contract with Fyffes, a British firm, to sell the latter bananas at US$4.40 a box. This was a much higher price than was being paid by the Tela Railroad Company (Chiquita Brands), and in addition Fyffes agreed to pay in dollars rather than lempiras. When Tela objected that it had an exclusive contract with the CAGSSA, the stage was set for a banana war. The Fyffes challenge, the most serious that the U.S. fruit companies had ever had to their privileged position, was a test case. Tela's other Honduran growers were watching, as were independent growers in Ecuador, Panama, Costa Rica, and Colombia. In the words of a Chiquita executive, "If people realize Fyffes can induce producers to break contracts, then everybody will do it."[11]

There followed a scene that could have come out of the golden days of *el pulpo:* Chiquita obtained a court order that empowered officials to confiscate 300,000 boxes of Fyffes-bound bananas, worth some US$3.6 million. Court officials, at times accompanied by armed soldiers, confiscated truckload after truckload of fruit. In one incident, a train carrying 20,000 pounds of bananas was derailed when it struck a railroad spike that someone had jammed between two lengths of rail. In another, police with automatic rifles, accompanied by two Chiquita employees and a company lawyer (who also happened to be an alternate member of the Honduran Supreme Court), burst into a hotel in Puerto Cortés looking for the Fyffes officials who had arranged the CAGSSA deal. The latter escaped, one of them literally ducking out the back door, but thereafter some Fyffes representatives began to disguise their identities and travel with bodyguards.

The whole thing was an economic and public relations disaster for Chiquita. The spectacle of the giant company bullying independent growers that had managed to get better terms from its much smaller British competitor resurrected all the old memories and resentments of the Zemurray era. Some of the seized fruit spoiled or was stolen. Most was sold for small change on the local market. All told, the cost to the company and the Honduran government was over US$1.5 million.

Under pressure from the United States, Britain, and the European Community (EC), a compromise was reached in June: For the remainder of the year the growers would sell 40 percent of their production to Fyffes and 60 percent to Chiquita, which would now have to pay in dollars. From the start of the new year to 9 April, Fyffes's share would increase to 45 percent, with Tela receiving the rest. After that, the CAGSSA would be free to negotiate sales with whomever it chose. The growers would be compensated by Chiquita for the 300,000 boxes of bananas whose export had been prohibited. The ultimate winner was Honduras. In the words of one observer, the agreement represented "liberation from the absolute dominion" of the U.S. transnationals, which had previously been able to impose their prices and conditions on local producers.[12] From now on, the latter would be free to seek independent buyers in the EC and in the markets opening in Eastern Europe.

The Honduran Military at a Crossroads

The Honduran military was also at a crossroads. For years its official raison d'être had been defense of the nation against foreign and domestic enemies. By the early 1990s, however, the dangers of war and subversion were fast disappearing. The Cold War was over and the threat of Soviet/Cuban subversion greatly reduced. The Sandinistas had been ousted. The civil war in El Salvador seemed headed toward a negotiated solution. Everywhere in Central America, elected civilian governments were in office. National agendas were undergoing sweeping changes as traditional security concerns were increasingly superseded by economic priorities.

For the armed forces, peace posed as great a threat as war. Since 1980, the U.S. Department of Defense had sent US$463 million in military aid to Honduras. Now the gravy train was drying up. In 1990 aid was slashed by almost half to US$21.3 million, the lowest level since 1981. In an ironic meeting of minds, the new commander, General Cantarero, was warned by his Sandinista counterpart, Humberto Ortega, that the United States would cast the Honduran military aside.[13] U.S. leaders now began to speak openly about the "demilitarization" of Central America. Domestic developments were also pressing for smaller and leaner armed forces. The structural adjustment program required that sacrifices be made by all sectors, including the military. In Callejas's first year, the military budget was cut by 10 percent. The institution lost its traditional access to duty-free imports. Increasingly, there was talk of salary cuts and force reductions. The president even began to speak vaguely of a need to restructure the armed forces, reorienting it toward national development (civic action, environmental management, fire fighting) and the prevention of drug trafficking.

At the same time, continuing scandals, power struggles, and human rights violations had seriously eroded the legitimacy of the institution, raising questions about its mission, its role in society, and its relationship with the civilian authorities. In late spring, these discontents found expression in a major civil-military confrontation over the issue of conscription. Outrage over the routine kidnapping of Honduran youths subject to the draft was nothing new. On 29 May, however, Liberal deputy Gustavo Alfaro introduced a bill that would have abolished mandatory universal conscription. According to the measure's supporters, the military's recruiting practices were flagrantly unconstitutional. They were discriminatory, affecting only the children of the poor and middle class, and the methods used tended to be brutal and occasionally lethal.

For the military, this was too much. For months it had felt increasingly under siege. It had blocked efforts to cut its size and close the military checkpoints scattered throughout the country, but on the budget reduction it had had to give in. Now, faced with an issue that was central to its autonomy, the high command said, in effect, "Enough." The day after Alfaro's proposal was made public, the armed forces spokesman, Colonel Oscar Flores, issued a scarcely veiled threat: "The tiger must not be corralled!" "The tiger will stay calm as long as he is not annoyed!" The offending bill was denounced as part of a "well-orchestrated campaign against the armed forces." In a news conference, General Cantarero declared that "democracy is maintained with arms, not with words or violins!" Once again invoking the specters of regional war and subversion, he warned that "the left never sleeps, and we are the only obstacles to their plans." He recalled an incident in 1904 in which the legislature had challenged the military. On that occasion, the latter had dissolved Congress and jailed a number of deputies.[14]

This was not very subtle, but it was effective. Deputies from both major parties virtually fell over one another trying to disassociate themselves from the offending legislation. The measure was thrown out by the president of Congress, who declared it unconstitutional. Subsequently Callejas, acutely aware of his dependence on the military in the wake of its forcible termination of the banana workers' strike, publicly reassured the armed forces that he was not interested in cutting their size or further reducing their budget.

But the institution faced a much more formidable threat. Throughout the year, the internal power struggles unleashed by Regalado's failed attempt to retain his position had swirled beneath the surface. The incessant conflict was eating away at the institution. At the heart of the matter was the fact that General Cantarero had never been able to consolidate his position. He had never had the backing of a majority of his colleagues in the sixth promotion. Rather, he had been elected largely because of his support from the other classes, notably the eighth, ninth, and tenth. Once in office, he had surrounded himself with allies from those promotions. Not surprisingly, this growing devolution of power within the high command had alienated the senior officers who had been passed over.

Beyond this, there was considerable unhappiness with Cantarero's management of the institution. The military was increasingly on the defensive. The budget cut in particular lent weight to the growing feeling that the general was incapable of defending the military's interests against civilian encroachment. There were those, moreover, who felt that Cantarero's style only made things worse. Many had voted for him in the expectation that he would be a conciliator. Instead, he had adopted a highly provocative approach, resorting to threats and repression that some considered unwarranted. Nor were all these threats aimed at civilians. In August, he had declared ominously that the armed forces itself had been infiltrated by subversive elements.[15]

The first indication that something was brewing—though it was not public knowledge at the time—occurred about midyear, when Cantarero discovered that Colonel Luis Alonso Discua (head of the navy and former commander of Battalion 3-16) and several other members of the sixth promotion were maneuvering to force his resignation. Of more serious concern, however, were the activities of an alleged "radical" faction led by Colonels René Fonseca, Mario Amaya, and Erick Sánchez. Both Fonseca and Amaya aspired to be commander in chief, but although the latter was more often mentioned as a possible candidate, Fonseca was the more immediate threat. He had been an influential force behind Regalado's attempt at reelection.[16] Fonseca was commander of the strategic 105th Infantry Brigade based in San Pedro Sula. He was also a liberal, who believed that social unrest was "fought not with rifles but with social justice."[17]

On 11 October it was announced that Colonel Amaya had been removed from command of the 115th Infantry Brigade and given an unspecified assignment in the joint chiefs of staff, which amounted to being "warehoused" while awaiting retirement. Sánchez received similar treatment. At the same time, Fonseca was transferred from the 105th Brigade to the much less powerful position of chief of army operations and training. Several other officers were also transferred or demoted. All this gave rise to reports that a barracks revolt had been in the offing. Cantarero, however, denied this. Such behavior, he said, was "a thing of the past." Nor did he consider these changes to be purges; rather, they were merely routine transfers.[18]

In fact, the changes were anything but routine. Cantarero had struck a heavy blow at the sixth promotion, effectively eliminating its most talented and respected leaders. And this was only the beginning. He now began planning the removal of Discua and others who had sought his ouster the previous summer.[19] This time, however, his enemies struck first. In late November, Cantarero made the mistake of traveling to Fort Leavenworth, Kansas, to receive a military honor. While he was away, the high command met in San Pedro Sula to plot his removal. A message was sent requesting his "urgent" return. On his arrival in Tegucigalpa, he was met by a delegation of his fellow officers with a letter of resignation that they demanded he sign. When he objected, they threatened him with exile and the loss of his military benefits. He thereupon acquiesced and was briefly put under house arrest. In his place as commander in chief, the COSUFFAA elected Discua.

As was traditional in such decisions, civilian participation was minimal. President Callejas had not been consulted, and he was visibly shaken. Denying that Cantarero had been planning a coup, he described the deposed leader as a disciplined and loyal officer but went on to say that these were internal military matters and had to be accepted. As if to reassure the high command of *his* loyalty, the president dismissed any ideas of introducing a military reform that would bring the institution under civilian control. Nor would he "permit" any reduction of troop levels.[20] As usual, Congress accepted the military's "recommendation" of Discua with little discussion. As had his predecessors, the new commander received the rank of general.

But the matter was not quite settled. On 6 December Honduran television viewers were treated to the local version of the "I Love Lucy" show, as Cantarero's wife went public. Denouncing both the plot leaders and Callejas as "traitors," Lucy Cantarero provided details of her husband's fall and the maneuvers that had preceded it. The next day Cantarero himself held a press conference to denounce his removal as unconstitutional and request an opportunity to address Congress. These actions broke a gentleman's agreement under which he had promised to say nothing prejudicial about the military. The request was refused. President Callejas declared that the general's dismissal was a "consummated fact" and that further investigation was useless, unnecessary, and inadvisable for the country's stability. The case was closed. Cantarero was sent into diplomatic exile.

Still, the conspiracies swirled on. Toward the end of the month General Discua declared that there was no room in the army for the "weak and the faltering." In January he drove the point home with sweeping personnel changes. Five more high-ranking colonels were transferred or relieved. One of them, Air Force Commander Roberto Mendoza Garay, had played a central role in the plot to oust Cantarero, cultivating his friendship and then at the critical moment betraying him. In October 1989 Mendoza had been the COSUFFAA's second choice for commander in chief. He had assumed that with Cantarero gone he would inherit the post. Embittered at having been passed over, he refused to accept his dismissal and launched a barracks revolt. With the help of other commanders, rebel forces seized the Hernán Acosta Mejía Air Base in Tegucigalpa and several other installations. But the revolt soon fizzled. As helicopters circled the capital, troops surrounded the installation; mediating forces were able to regain control. Subsequently, a new wave of purges was launched.

A Military Mission Redefined

This chaos did nothing to restore confidence in the institution. Toward the end of January, President Callejas sought to quell public discontent by proposing a "national debate" on the structure and role of the military. But Callejas was merely the president; Discua was commander in chief. At this point, there was little that the civilians could do to impose the kinds of changes they wanted.

This became painfully clear when the new government budget was announced. Under pressure from international lending agencies to cut spending, the administration slashed the education and health budgets. The latter was a particular sore spot. Only the previous day the government had gathered the foreign diplomatic corps to warn of a cholera epidemic that was inexorably making its way toward Honduras. According to official projections, as many as 30,000 people might require hospitalization, and there were only enough beds to accommodate 10 percent of this number. It was estimated that 630 million lempiras would be required to fight the epidemic. Now the government was actually cutting the health budget by 11 million lempiras (a little over US$2 million). Adding to the public outrage was the fact that the armed forces budget had been increased through a provision that gave the military its own dollar budget for military purchases. Although the armed forces budget was officially announced at 247.5 million lempiras, it was widely understood to be much larger.[21]

The military had become an institution without a purpose beyond self-perpetuation and self-aggrandizement. In consequence, the search for a new mission would have very different meanings for civilian and military proponents. Even as it had pulled back from the overtly political role it had played when officers occupied the Presidential Palace, the military had expanded into other areas. Under the doctrine of national security the range of jobs available to it in the state bureaucracy had been considerably broadened. In the process, entire entities—including the national telephone company, the directorates of geography and history, migration, customs, and transit, the merchant marine, the Ministry of Foreign Relations, the arms and munitions business, and others—had been converted into areas of exclusive or nearly exclusive military influence. The armed forces routinely intervened in such matters as voter registration, the setting of black-market exchange rates, and negotiations over the shipment of Salvadoran goods across Honduran territory. Over the years the military had taken on the appearance of a private business, with its own bank, a funeral parlor, insurance and real estate concerns, a car dealership, a barbed-wire company, four farms (others were planned), and investments in the clothing, shoe, and cereal industries. Now, moreover, as part of President Callejas's vision of incorporating it into the national development process, the institution was expanding even further. By 1990 military farms employed between 7,000 and 10,000 peasants and supplied 70 percent of the staple grain for the armed forces. (If things went according to plan, the military would soon be self-sufficient in staple grains.) In 1991 the military went into the cement business, purchasing one of the "privatized" factories that were being sold off.[22] In short, it had established a far-reaching economic empire that it had a strong interest in protecting.

There were now more fingers in the pie than ever. With 113 colonels and 127 lieutenant colonels, the officer corps was top-heavy with brass. Honduras had three times as many colonels and lieutenant colonels as El Salvador in an army less than half the size. The COSUFFAA itself operated as a kind of military parliament, a "floating seminar" of sixty-three officers with the commander in chief as first among equals, which meant that an otherwise vertical power structure had been made horizontal at the top. Since there was only a handful of high positions, not everyone's ambition could be accommodated. The net effect was the spread of internal conflicts to an ever-widening network of classes and factions. In May, the eighth promotion was purged of some of its senior officers to the benefit, mainly, of the tenth and twelfth. Discua was making new alliances and looking to the support of the younger generations in his bid to consolidate power.

But if civilian authorities lacked the power to put a stop to all this, they had influential foreign allies. The Bush administration was increasingly weary of the military. Ambassador Arcos had little but contempt for Discua and his cronies. He regarded them as "slugs" and "scumbags" and let them know (though in more diplomatic language) that things had to change. In a major policy statement in *Foreign Service Journal,* he served notice that

> In the past, our single-minded focus on external security threats often led us to overlook various governments' mismanagement of economic, social, and environmental policies. As Soviet policies have changed and U.S. security concerns receded, these failings are being laid bare. In the years ahead, governments that tolerate human rights abuse, reject sustainable economic and environmental policies, or permit gross inefficiency and corruption may find themselves simply cut off from U.S. assistance. Likewise, Washington will be much less patient in channeling resources to countries or sectors—such as the judiciary, armed forces, or agriculture—where past U.S. assistance has failed to produce significant improvements.
>
> The most immediate effects of change . . . will be felt by the region's armed forces. During a decade of war and confrontation, Central America's militaries swelled to a size that is simply unsustainable over the long term. . . . Momentum is growing . . . to reduce the heavy burden of military expenditures on these poor . . . countries. In the face of tight budgets and diminishing resources, they simply have no other choice. . . . The most useful assistance the U.S. government can offer is to help the armed forces . . . redefine their role in a less conflictive era. We can accomplish this through our

> military assistance, through civilian training programs, and by stressing constantly the importance of civilian control of the armed forces. One way to accomplish this is to channel military assistance through civilian authorities, rather than relying on military-to-military relationships, as we have in the past.[23]

Pressure on the military now mounted. In May 1991 a Honduran deputy took the unprecedented step of asking for a cut in the armed forces budget. The move failed, but it was just the beginning. By summer the World Bank and the International Monetary Fund had joined the campaign, making it clear that future aid to indebted nations would be conditioned on a reduction of military spending. In September PINU deputy Carlos Sosa introduced a constitutional amendment calling for the "modernization" of the armed forces, including the elimination of the post of commander in chief and the subjection of military decisions to the president of the republic. The joint chiefs of staff would be subordinate to the president, who would also preside over the COSUFFAA and appoint the secretary of defense. Appointments and promotions would be made by the president through a secretariat of national defense and public safety.

On 22 September the influential Cortés Chamber of Commerce and Industries, representing north-coast businessmen, called for a reduction of all Central American armies as a contribution to "sustained and balanced development." Among other things, the businessmen suggested that Honduras's fighter aircraft be sold and the proceeds used to pay the foreign debt. (The planes in question were the most modern in the region; they had been acquired from the United States at a reported cost of over US$120 million.) The following day the Liberal Party announced that it would submit a motion to Congress calling for the dismantling of various infantry battalions and the transfer of the soldiers to the police force. About this same time, a Gallup poll revealed that 71 percent of Hondurans felt that the civilian government should have more control over the military, and 45 percent favored a reduction in the institution's size.

The armed forces were under siege, and they reacted defensively. "Anybody making such suggestions is insulting the military forces and their honor," thundered Discua. "These people are viewing the facts with twisted interpretations." The military was not a financial burden; people should "feel honored" by their association with it. The U.S. ambassador was "meddling" in the country's internal affairs. Hondurans would never allow the "imposition of foreign ideas."[24]

Human Rights Under Callejas: Social Unrest, Military Response, and the U.S. Reaction

The military left no stone unturned in its efforts to preserve its size and budget and ensure the continued flow of U.S. aid. In June 1990, a brief flare-up of tensions in the Gulf of Fonseca gave it an opportunity to demonstrate the continued existence of a foreign threat (El Salvador). Shortly thereafter, an aborted bank robbery by Cinchonero guerrillas at Zamorano provided the occasion for an announcement that a growing presence of "seditious groups" justified increased militarization. Sporadic acts of violence continued throughout 1990-1991, with the armed forces losing few opportunities to blame the left. Few were fooled. The Cold War was rapidly winding down; the Soviet empire (and indeed the Soviet Union itself) was crumbling; the Sandinistas had been ousted; peace in El Salvador seemed just around the corner. Almost everywhere, communism had been defeated or was in retreat.

In Honduras, too, the left was beginning to come in from the cold. In May 1990 the head of the Morazanista Front for the Liberation of Honduras renounced his leadership, declaring that armed struggle had no future. The following April the Popular Revolutionary Forces (Lorenzo Zelaya) announced its readiness to abandon guerrilla warfare if the government would grant its members amnesty and guarantee their safety. In May four leaders of the Cinchoneros renounced armed struggle. In July Congress approved a general amnesty. Meanwhile, dozens of exiles were returning to the country. Although a few recalcitrants continued to engage in sporadic terrorism, by autumn 1991 all of the significant rebel groups had to some extent taken advantage of the amnesty.

The disintegration of the revolutionary left had little impact on the human rights situation. Even as many of the guerrillas were disbanding, social unrest was sharply on the rise, and the military's response was more repression. People were encouraged to inform on suspected malefactors. The extrajudicial killing of common criminals continued. Suspects detained by police were frequently tortured (the use of the *capucha,* a rubber hood placed over the head to induce suffocation, being a favorite technique). "Leftists" were subjected to threats and assassination.

One particularly notorious case involved Francisco Javier Bonilla, a former president of the Social Security Institute's employees' union, and Ramón Antonio Briceño, a student activist at the National University. In late May 1990 Bonilla was gunned down while leaving a union meeting in Tegucigalpa. A few days later the tortured body of Briceño was found in a vacant lot. The killings traumatized leftist and labor circles. Both Bonilla and Briceño had been subjected to threats and surveillance prior to their deaths, and many feared that the killings were but a prelude to a new wave of repression. Demands were issued for a special investigatory commission to include representatives from the Catholic church, Congress, the private sector, and the unions. Partly in response, President Callejas did appoint a commission, but it was composed solely of military officers. There followed a clumsy attempt to place the blame on the left. At a 26 July press conference, the military produced two prisoners who, it claimed, had been hired to kill Bonilla and Briceño by one Martín Pineda, an activist in a progressive student group. The extrajudicial confessions of the prisoners were made public and the case declared closed—notwithstanding that the "evidence" in the commission's report related only to the Bonilla murder and the alleged killers retracted their confessions as soon as they were allowed to see a judge. The military's case was completely discredited when the courts released Pineda for lack of evidence.

Another major incident involved the killing of five peasants (and the wounding of eight others) in Agua Caliente, near the Atlantic coast, in May 1991. On this occasion, some sixty peasants had occupied a piece of land claimed by Colonel Leonel Galindo during the usual spring wave of land invasions. Two days later, fifteen armed men confronted the squatters, ordering them off the property. When they refused, the gunmen opened fire. Once again, there was a nationwide outcry. The military denied that any of its members had participated in the massacre and defended Colonel Galindo's right to the disputed land. But again, its claims were not supported by the evidence. A congressional commission found that most of the assailants had been dressed in military uniforms and appeared to be a military unit.[25] The National Agrarian Institute revealed that the land had been granted to the peasant organization El Astillero in the mid-1970s but had subsequently been illegally sold to Galindo by an INA official. In a meeting involving Callejas, Discua, campesino leaders, and the INA, it was agreed that the peasants had had a right to be where they were. It was decided that in future conflicts the INA rather than the military would do whatever evicting had to be done, but whether the agreement would be adhered to remained doubtful. The INA itself was under siege, with budget cuts and a proposed reorganization threatening to gut it. The military seemed unlikely to surrender its traditional prerogative of using force, especially in the face of continuing unrest. Nor did the handling of the Galindo case inspire confidence: Though witnesses claimed that he had ordered the shootings, the military refused to prosecute. Efforts to bring him before civilian courts were frustrated when Callejas's amnesty decree was amended to include armed forces members guilty of human rights violations. (In March 1992, after much public pressure, it was announced that Galindo would be tried in a civilian court—the first officer ever to be so prosecuted.)

Continuing abuses drew continuing criticism. In June 1991 Americas Watch and Amnesty International issued reports castigating the Callejas administration for its failure to investigate past or stop current violations. As usual, the charges were dismissed as being based on "distorted" information from "unreliable" leftist sources. This time, however, the monitors had an unexpected ally. For months the State Department had been expressing its concern to the Honduran government over human rights abuses. The previous year it had even canceled the FUSEP's participation in a police training course on counterterrorism. In February 1991, moreover, its annual country report had been released. After a decade of defending the military against criticism, the DOS finally found its public voice: The report complained of "numerous" killings by the police and security forces. The military, it was said, often tried to cover up violations and failed to prosecute offenders. The prospects for improvement were limited, since the FUSEP was "still commanded by career army officers lacking police training who are inclined to condone the use of excessive force." The department even had some good words for the CODEH, admitting that it had made "a number of genuine efforts on behalf of human rights" (though this was qualified by the observation that its charges were frequently "exaggerated and ill-documented, and in some cases false").[26]

But how far was the Bush administration willing to go? It was soon put to the test. In July an eighteen-year-old student named Riccy Mabel Martínez went to the Las Tapias military base, outside Tegucigalpa, to petition for the release of her boyfriend from military service. She was last seen alive leaving the installation with Colonel Angel Castillo Maradiaga and other personnel. Shortly thereafter, she was found dead, having been tortured, raped, and horribly mutilated. Again an armed forces investigation was launched, and again there were protests. Classmates of Martínez who publicly criticized the military's handling of the case were threatened or assaulted. When thousands of students gathered in front of the Presidential Palace and the Congress to demand that the matter be turned over to civilian authorities, the high command responded by militarizing the streets of Tegucigalpa.

As usual, there was an attempted cover-up. An effort was made to place the blame on a lowly sergeant. But that ploy collapsed when the accused repudiated his confession, claiming that it had been signed under threat of torture. ("I fear for my life," he explained. "I can feel giant footsteps behind me.")[27] When a civilian judge ordered the arrests of Castillo and another officer, the FUSEP chief, Colonel Guillermo Paredes, refused to serve the warrant, declaring that the military had its own system of justice. The two men were, however, arrested and held at their military unit pending resolution of the jurisdictional dispute. That issue was resolved in the civilian court's favor in late August.

Meanwhile, the embassy plunged into the fray. Nothing better dramatized the sea change that had occurred in American policy than the performance of the U.S. ambassador during these weeks. Whereas Briggs and his staff had systematically deemphasized the issue of human rights (often ignoring it or treating human rights monitors as the enemy), Cris Arcos was active in the struggle for justice and decency. Already in disfavor with the military because of his pressure to cut its budget and manpower, he had, in addition, irritated the Honduran government with his criticisms of economic policies and corruption. (He had the quaint notion that U.S. aid should be used for the purposes for which it was intended.) Now, with the Martínez case, he would pay the consequences.

As it became clear that the military was trying to hamper the investigation, Arcos began to express his "extreme concern" over the armed forces' efforts to cover up the involvement of their personnel. By early August it was being widely reported that elements within the military and government wanted him declared persona non grata. In October, matters came to a head when it was learned that semen and urine specimens sent to the FBI for laboratory tests had been tampered with and that the military had arranged for other tests to be made at a private laboratory. The Bush administration had agreed to the FBI tests on the condition that U.S. authorities would be in sole charge of the case. The agreement had been broken, and Arcos was furious. Again, he went public, indicating his dismay and lack of confidence in the Honduran system of justice. That in turn drew the ire of President Callejas and General Discua, who accused him of meddling in the country's internal affairs. On Callejas's orders, a complaint was lodged with the State Department. Arcos was recalled to Washington for "consultations."

[Note: U.S. efforts did lead to at least a semblance of justice. In July 1993 Colonel Castillo was sentenced to sixteen years and six months for murder and rape. Sergeant Llovares received ten years and six months for rape. Whether the convicted would serve their full terms remained to be seen.]

The Pain of Adjustment (Continued)

Meanwhile, Hondurans continued to labor under the burden of austerity. Eighteen months into the Callejas administration, the structural adjustment had produced decidedly mixed results. The public debt had been reduced from 90 percent of the GDP in 1989 to 76 percent in 1990. The fiscal deficit had been cut from 7.8 percent of the GDP to 6.3 percent.[28] International lending agencies were pouring money into the country. In March 1991 the Inter-American Development Bank announced a three-year program to distribute US$700 million to Honduras. The World Bank contributed another US$20 million. In June the IMF added US$1.8 billion to be disbursed over the next three years. The expectation was that more austerity and foreign capital, together with a free market, would enable Honduras to generate enough self-sustaining growth to eventually repay its debt. Now, however, that debt was mounting. As of March, payments would be made at the devalued rate of 5.3 instead of the previous 2 lempiras to the dollar. Many feared that if the president's economic strategy failed to produce results, aid would again be cut off, leaving the country with an impossible debt and no way out.

There were other problems as well: In 1990 the GDP had fallen by 1 percent (3.8 percent per capita), the first such decline in seven years. Inflation had reached 36.4 percent. Some 10,000 public-sector jobs had been lost, and thousands more cuts could be expected. (Only about 44 percent of the workforce was now fully employed in the formal economy, while 49 percent worked in the informal sector.) Public investment had declined by 13 percent and private investment by 10 percent. Although devaluation resulted in windfall profits for national and transnational exporters, there was little evidence that these earnings were being reinvested in Honduras. Rather, capital flight continued unabated. Nor was it clear that Callejas's vaunted privatization program would have the desired results. The announcement of the intention to sell off the CONADI's bankrupt businesses had produced new corruption. Critics charged that state enterprises were being sold at bargain-basement prices to the same venal and incompetent private-sector interests that had been responsible for the CONADI and other such disasters in the first place. Nationalists wondered whether privatization might not open the door to an unacceptable degree of foreign penetration, since few Hondurans could afford to buy state entities such as the electric company, the basic grains distributor, the coffee and banana marketing agencies, and the agricultural development bank.[29]

Opposition cut across class and ideological lines. A growing number of businessmen were unhappy with the government's tight-money policies and with increased import costs, declining demand, and the prospects of foreign competition. Dozens of enterprises had closed down. Privileges long taken for granted were being threatened. The private sector was especially angry about the new taxes to which it was subject. Nor was it pleased at government moves to transfer many tax-collecting responsibilities to employers (though, as critics pointed out, this would place large sums of new capital at their disposal, creating even more opportunities for corruption).

At the same time, there was growing resentment over the military's "economic imperialism." Businessmen grumbled that colonels acquired resources illegally through bribery or the diversion of state assets and then used those resources to drive out legitimate enterprises. The activities of the Military Pension Institute were a particular sore spot. The institute was in deep financial trouble and was trying to pull itself out through an aggressive campaign of investments. In 1991, it purchased controlling stock in the formerly government-owned cement factory. There was much apprehension that it would bid on the telecommunications company if the latter was privatized as anticipated. Many entrepreneurs believed, with good reason, that the military had an unfair competitive advantage in such matters.

Workers, too, were increasingly restless. Large-scale labor agitation in 1991 was a year-round affair. Hundreds of strikes, threatened strikes, slowdowns, and demonstrations occurred. The last third of the year was spent under the threat of a general strike motivated mainly by major conflicts involving the El Mochito mine, the Tela Railroad Company, and the national electric company. The strike at El Mochito began in early October, when workers took over the mine's access routes to protest the firing of several dozen militants who had tried to organize a union. (The miners had only a *solidarista* organization, which effectively left them without representation in labor disputes.) When government troops tried to dislodge the miners, shots were fired. One person was killed and twenty-five wounded. Eventually, Callejas intervened to mediate a settlement favorable to the workers. It was agreed that the labor code would be revised to subordinate solidarity organizations to the unions. From now on, according to the president, the latter would be "the only representatives of the workers."[30] In the Tela strike, as at El Mochito, the government came down on the side of the workers, accusing company negotiators of intransigence. Again, Callejas mediated the dispute. In December a new collective agreement was signed providing for a 75 percent increase in salaries over the next three years and reinstating some three hundred workers dismissed the previous month.

In contrast, the conflict with the electrical workers' union was handled very differently. STENEE had strongly opposed the government's privatization program and the structural adjustment in general. It claimed that the administration had violated collective agreements by privatizing certain divisions within the company. It also rejected proposed rate hikes and accused the management of corruption. In response, the union's critics pointed out that the company was deeply in debt and that either rates had to be raised or workers fired. In November, the year-long conflict escalated when militants prevented nonunion maintenance workers from entering the country's largest hydroelectric installation, El Cajón. The government accused the militants of endangering the country's "fundamental infrastructure" and declared the strike illegal. Troops were deployed at power stations throughout the country. At the same time, the company fired one hundred employees, including the entire union leadership. On 17 December a parallel STENEE directorate was named to replace the previous members. The new directorate, which supported the government on every point in contention, was immediately denounced as a "phantom organization" and part of a plot to destroy the union.

The tactic was, of course, a familiar one. Only the previous year, the administration had dealt with the medical workers' and public employees' unions in similar fashion. In this case, it prevailed when the major labor federations, which had pledged solidarity with STENEE, backed down, conditioning their support on the resignation of the original directorate. On 2 January the organization's ousted president, Gladys Lanza, castigating the labor leadership for lacking "the belligerence" to continue the fight, conceded that the union was isolated and would have to retreat. Strikers were called on to accept the government's terms and return to work. Hours after negotiations collapsed, a grenade was thrown into a café in which several members of the STENEE parallel directorate were eating. Two persons were killed, and the directorate's secretary general was injured. Although the charge that the former directors were behind the attack was denied, one could not escape the impression that the working class had begun to turn on itself.

And not only workers. As the struggle for land intensified in the countryside, the number of land invasions increased, and so did the violence accompanying them. Now, however, the conflicts involved more than just owners against peasants. Increasingly, campesinos began to confront—and sometimes kill—each other. On 15 May, less than two weeks after the Agua Caliente massacre, an armed clash between the Nueva Esperanza and Unión Lempira peasant organizations left four dead and eight wounded in Santa Bárbara. On 10 September, in San Isidro Intibucá, nine agricultural workers died in fighting between members of the UNC and the FENACH. The next day the head of the National Agrarian Institute resigned, citing "serious obstacles" to the implementation of the agrarian reform and pointing to the San Isidro incident as an example of what could happen if peasant discontent was not defused.

In fact, the future of the agrarian reform was very much in doubt. In the face of growing calls for an acceleration of land distribution, Callejas had slashed the INA's 1991 budget by almost 50 percent. Rather than agrarian reform, he favored agricultural modernization. In accordance with the advice of the World Bank and the AID, legislation was proposed that would free communally held lands for sale and "development." The INA would lose its autonomy and be subordinated to the Ministry of Natural Resources, traditionally a bastion of the large landowners. In effect, the law would largely reduce the agrarian reform to a titling program for lands already repatriated.

The Economic and Political Outlook at Midterm

Callejas had taken an enormous gamble, and the results were not yet in. On the positive side, Honduras had now acquired a Triple A rating from the International Monetary Fund. Foreign aid continued to roll in. (In September, in the largest U.S. debt forgiveness ever involving a Latin American country, the United States excused US$434.6 million of Honduras's foreign debt; in December, the IDB and the AID announced new loans of US$110 million and US$17 million, respectively.) By year's end, the president was predicting that the worst was over: "The economy is stable; there is international credibility; there is economic growth of 1 or 1.2 percent this year; inflation has been reduced; and we have an optimistic outlook for 1992."[31]

Others were not so sure. Two-thirds of the workforce was now either unemployed or underemployed (mostly the latter). Some 170,000 peasant families were landless. Added to this, many Honduran economists believed that only the first stage of the structural adjustment—the stabilization period—was over. A second and more acute phase involving the total liberalization of the economy might still lie ahead. In November, Finance Minister Benjamín Villanueva acknowledged that the IMF had urged "stronger efforts" to cut the fiscal deficit. Budget forecasts predicted that the current deficit of US$250 million would grow to US$350 million in 1992, far exceeding the percentage of the GNP promised to international lenders. To reduce this figure, Villanueva announced, it would be necessary to slash thousands of more jobs from the public payroll.[32]

Time was slowly running out for the Nationalists. Though elections were still almost two years away, the presidential campaign had already begun, with preliminary skirmishing among the prevalent *candidatos* and *corrientes* in both parties. Because Callejas, who remained personally popular in spite of his economic policies, was not eligible for reelection, the National Party had the unenviable task of finding a candidate of comparable appeal in a political climate favorable to the Liberals. If the Nationalists were to win in 1993, the socioeconomic situation had to improve markedly.

Their chances were not helped by the reemergence of factional warfare. As early as the previous summer, first blood had been drawn with the removal of Supreme Court President Oswaldo Ramos Soto. Ramos was leader of the National Party's extreme right wing. He was corrupt, demagogic and enormously ambitious, with an oratorical style that resembled a series of high-pitched shrieks. He had never made a secret of his presidential aspirations. For years, "Oswaldo Viene" posters had graced the mountains and bridges of Tegucigalpa. He had close ties to the most reactionary sector of the military, whose political support he was assiduously courting. It had been he who, as rector of the National University, had incited students to attack the U.S. embassy in April 1988.[33]

Ramos Soto was the last thing the National Party—or the country—needed. He was a throwback to the corrupt, old politics of *caciquismo.* As Supreme Court president he had openly engaged in partisan politics: He had court employees organize political events on his behalf and instituted obligatory deductions from their salaries for his campaign. He openly participated in National Party political activities and appealed for support for his candidacy over television and in newspapers. All of these things were prohibited by law.

Thus it was that in May 1991 the president of Congress, Rodolfo Irías Navas, who was also a nacionalista and had presidential ambitions of his own, created a special congressional commission to investigate the situation. The group's report recommended that Congress demand the chief justice's resignation, and in August, by a vote of 107 to 7, it did. Ramos protested that he was the victim of a political maneuver. He predicted "strong opposition" to his removal and hinted that he might seek to destabilize the government, but when the legislators responded by revoking his mandate he acquiesced.

Ramos Soto's fall seemed to open the door for Irías's candidacy. Although Callejas had not taken a stand on the issue, Irías was the head of the president's MONARCA (Movimiento Nacional Callejista) political movement. As a member of the "modernization" faction of the party, he had been Callejas's choice over Ramos for the presidency of Congress. (Ramos had been given the Supreme Court post as a consolation prize.) But he was not alone in his ambitions. Among the other contenders were the president of the national bank, Ricardo Maduro, and the mayor of Tegucigalpa, Nora Gúnera de Melgar Castro. Moreover, Ramos Soto still had considerable support among the public and certain sectors of the military and the National Party. Within the latter, there remained serious rivalry between *técnicos* and *políticos,* with the latter blaming the Iríases and Maduros for the sad state of the economy and the party's loss of popular support.

The Liberals too were divided, but their conflicts seemed comparatively benign. The early leader was Carlos Roberto Reina, an old war-horse of social democratic persuasion. But he was soon challenged by former Vice President Jaime Rosenthal, owner of *El Tiempo.* Both candidates were intelligent, honorable men, but both carried considerable political baggage. Reina's brother, Jorge Arturo, had been president of the National University in the days when it had been a bastion of the extreme left, and some still held the connection against him. At the same time, many leftists now considered Reina an anachronism and were looking elsewhere for political inspiration. As for Jaime Rosenthal, he had still not been forgiven by party conservatives for his (and his newspaper's) "treasonous" criticism of the Azcona administration. If the two front-runners faltered, there were always others ready to take their places.

In short, the prospects for 1993 remained wide open and heavily dependent on the state of the economy, the smoothness of the parties' leadership selection processes, and the quality of the candidates that emerged. As of late 1991, however, the Liberals seemed to have the advantage.

The Gringos

And what of U.S.-Honduran relations? In the short run, at least, the Arcos affair marked the limits of North American intervention. For several years, the decline in Honduras's value to U.S. foreign policy had allowed Washington to more vigorously twist arms with regard to issues such as human rights, corruption, economic policy, and the size and budget of the armed forces. The problem was that beyond a certain point those pressures were a direct threat to the most powerful interest group in the country. The destruction of the Panamanian defense forces, the neutralization of the Sandinista army, and the liquidation of the contras had convinced many in the high command that the *real* goal of U.S. policy was to "pulverize" the Central American armies. The decline in U.S. military aid (almost 50 percent between 1989 and 1990) reinforced that impression even as it gradually undermined the Bush administration's bargaining power. For the Honduran armed forces, negative incentives were increasing just as the positive incentives for cooperation were decreasing. Trouble was predictable.

Yet, both sides still had an interest in maintaining the relationship. Honduras still needed massive economic assistance, and the United States was in a position to deliver it, both directly, through new aid, and indirectly, through its influence on international lending agencies and foreign governments. By the same token, General Discua and his colleagues wanted to maintain the flow of U.S. military aid, which, though greatly reduced, was far from negligible. Conversely, the United States continued to have a stake in a stable, friendly, and reasonably democratic Honduras. To push too hard or too publicly on sensitive issues such as human rights was considered counterproductive. Washington also wanted to retain use of Soto Cano (Palmerola) Air Base. The drug war had become an increasingly important part of U.S. foreign policy. Indeed, for the U.S. military it was one of the few "growth industries" left. There was talk of redefining the U.S. mission at Soto Cano and turning the installation into a regional center for antidrug operations. To do this, obviously, required the cooperation of the Hondurans.

The relationship therefore seemed destined to continue, imperfect, troubled, but essentially intact. By the year's end, the "delicate situation" between the U.S. ambassador and the Honduran government had eased. Relations were once again "normal." To many Hondurans, Arcos had even become something of a hero. Students had demonstrated in his favor. A local magazine, *Hablemos Claro,* had voted him "Man of the Year," declaring him to be a "hawk who trims the . . . military's wings." Such praise raised a few eyebrows among more jaundiced observers, who viewed the ambassador as one more in a series of would-be proconsuls, albeit a benevolent one.

Honduras 1992: Social Deterioration and Political Turmoil

The first half of the new year witnessed continued socioeconomic deterioration. Coffee prices fell to their lowest level in twenty years, leading to predictions of a drastic drop in production, increased rural unemployment, and a US$100 million shortfall in foreign exchange earnings. Banana and lumber exports declined, the latter by more than half from the previous year. Moves by the European Community to create a quota and tariff system for banana imports from Latin America threatened tens of thousands of permanent and temporary jobs. The National Association of Small and Medium-Sized Industries reported that 255 affiliated businesses would declare bankruptcy and another 1,000 would temporarily suspend operations as a result of the government's structural adjustment policies. Over 5,000 jobs would be lost.

At the same time, social decay was accelerating. By now, Honduras had developed a significant drug consumption problem of its own. Violent crime was rapidly escalating. Weapons from the former contra and FMLN armies and the greatly reduced Sandinista military were flooding the black market. The FUSEP reported almost twice as many violent deaths in 1991 as in 1990, including 549 by firearms and 324 by knife or machete.[34] A CID-Gallup poll published in September 1991 revealed that one out of ten Hondurans reported that either they or a member of their family had been the victim of a violent crime or robbery within the previous four months. The FUSEP's report for the first half of 1992 indicated that the situation was getting worse. Ironically, as Central America in general moved toward peace,

Honduras was becoming more violent (though relatively little of this was political in nature).

The Callejas administration forged ahead with its program, and these months witnessed major progress toward regional economic integration. In May a trilateral agreement was signed by Honduras, Guatemala, and El Salvador providing for common customs duties and unrestricted passage of nearly all goods and capital. The accord met with mixed reactions in Honduras, where consumers would benefit but many businessmen feared having to compete with low-priced foreign imports. Free trade meant that the comparatively backward Honduran industries would have to modernize if they were to survive. Many owners lacked the capital and technology to do so. (High interest rates made it difficult to borrow money for such purposes.) Others, unused to competition, were simply unwilling to change.

In March Congress passed the long-awaited Agricultural Modernization Law, designed to end state regulation, guarantee private property, free land for development, and provide incentives for foreign investment. The measure exempted much of the property that had been subject to expropriation under the agrarian reform. The INA lost most of its functions and autonomy. The national agricultural development bank was transformed into a commercial enterprise; no longer would it provide peasants with low-interest loans to buy land. Predictably, the measure led to an outcry: The president of the COCOCH declared that the agrarian reform was dead. Others predicted that the new law would be met with a wave of social violence.

There followed the usual round of land invasions but with a difference. On 7 May, the anniversary of the massacre at Agua Caliente, some 40,000 hectares of land were seized in ten departments. After initially taking a hard line, the INA unexpectedly adopted a conciliatory approach, agreeing to a settlement that included lands not subject to the agrarian reform. The director was abruptly fired and replaced by a staunch conservative more in line with administration policy, and the agreement was repudiated. As the stalemate dragged on, the landowners began to take matters into their own hands. On 12 June two campesinos were killed during a violent eviction in Santa Cruz de Yojoa.

As the months passed, it became apparent that the fears of the critics were justified. Growing numbers of peasant cooperatives, no longer able to obtain credit and technical assistance, were forced to sell out, often at a fraction of the value of their properties. (In July, for instance, the Lourdes Sugar Cooperative sold its land for 3 million lempiras, though the book value was over 30 million.) Elements of the law designed to prevent a land grab by rich landowners and transnationals (or at least to ensure that other lands were made available to the landless) went unenforced. Increasingly, too, military officers and National Party stalwarts began to take some of the best lands for themselves. Landlessness increased, and with it conflict within campesino organizations as some peasants opted to take what was offered and others refused to sell. In the end, those who sold were sometimes reduced to "working like slaves" on land that had once been their own.[35]

Meanwhile, foreign aid continued to flow. In April Treasury Minister Villanueva announced that Honduras had received US$2.5 billion from international lenders and foreign countries during the first three months of 1992. Some of this included forgiveness of debt arrears, but much was in the form of new loans. The Inter-American Development Bank, the World Bank, and the Central American Economic Integration Bank pledged almost US$1.18 billion. In turn, the Callejas administration continued on its neoliberal course, pushing through a new investment law designed to attract foreign capital, removing controls on the exchange rate, and increasing the price of gasoline.

How much effect this would have on the 1993 elections was still uncertain. The National Party had been hurt less than might have been supposed. A CID-Gallup poll conducted in May showed public ambivalence: For all the discontent (40 percent of the respondents felt that Callejas had accomplished nothing good), the Liberals were only a slight favorite. The president himself remained personally popular; clearly, his policies had benefited someone. By summer, however, as it became clear that Carlos Roberto Reina was the most popular precandidate, the Liberal Party began to rally around him. When he acquired the backing of Carlos Flores, it began to look as if this would be the most unified and formidable Liberal campaign since 1981.

This made it all the more imperative for the Nationalists to field a strong candidate. As the weeks passed, it became evident that Rodolfo Irías Navas had little popular support and that Oswaldo Ramos Soto did. This was a bitter pill for the "modernizers" in the party. Initially, the president's MONARCA faction responded by appearing to support the candidacy of the popular mayor of Tegucigalpa, Nora Gúnera de Melgar (widow of former President Juan Alberto Melgar Castro). Throughout the spring and early summer, Doña Nora and Oswaldo waged a bruising battle for the nomination.

Gradually, however, it became clear that it would be impossible to persuade Ramos Soto to step aside. That in turn raised the prospect of a long, bitter fratricidal struggle that might pave the way for a Liberal victory. At the same time, Melgar showed herself to be surprisingly independent of Callejas, criticizing his economic model as incapable of improving living standards. When in June a sector of the military came out in her favor, it created a flurry of alarm within the Callejas camp. The president's project, it seemed, was being threatened not only by the extreme right but by those who were ostensibly his allies.

The truth was that, for all his contributions as a modernizer, Callejas had never been able to escape his roots in the Honduran political culture. Beneath the technocratic surface of his administration, Byzantine intrigue, cronyism, corruption, and incompetence still flourished. The National Party itself remained a highly authoritarian and vertical organization. Policymaking tended to be ad hoc, much of it taking place in the president's Tuesday breakfast group or in Thursday night poker games. At times, the government's behavior had the same comic-opera quality as its predecessors. (On one occasion, for instance, it was able to get its way on a key piece of legislation by supplying free hamburgers and bringing the measure to a vote while the deputies were busy eating.)

Like many of his predecessors, moreover, Callejas was not interested in retiring from politics once his legal term was up. He was too young. He had come to love the sound of his own name, and the trappings of office and power. He intended to continue to be a factor on the political landscape; the question was how to arrange it. He could not run for reelection, but he could at least remain a major force within the National Party. Accordingly, for some time he had been negotiating behind the scenes with the *oswaldistas* to secure a share of the spoils. This was, truly, an odd couple: The erudite, handsome young president and the uncouth, rotund Ramos seemed about as compatible as oil and water. They did, however, share the traditional penchant of Honduran politicians for smoke-filled rooms. ("Let's Make a Deal" being the national pastime.) In the agreement that was finally hammered out at Callejas's home in the early morning hours of 20 July, Ramos Soto ceded half of his congressional deputies to MONARCA.[36]

Doña Nora was now discarded like an old shoe. She had, in truth, been badly used. Callejas had toyed with her, just as he had with "Frito" Irías and the other aspirants to the nomination, carefully playing them off against each other so as to prevent any one of them from attaining a concentration of power. Only Oswaldo, through sheer persistence, had survived. Melgar was, of course, outraged. Among other things, she had been betrayed by two of her closest advisers, who—as it turned out—were Callejas's spies. Though she protested, it was to no avail. When MONARCA threatened not to pay her campaign debts, she grudgingly accepted the inevitable.[37]

Meanwhile, another political campaign was unfolding. General Discua's term as commander in chief was scheduled to end in early 1993. Though he too was ineligible for reelection, this was no constraint on *his* ambition. In September 1991 he had floated a military reform proposal that would have replaced the commander in chief with a secretary of national defense and the COSUFFAA with an eight-man junta of commanders. The arrangement would have enabled Discua to become defense secretary and assume considerable control over the high command. Unfortunately for him, others aspired to be commander in chief, and there was not much support for eliminating the COSUFFAA. Most Honduran officers had spent their careers anticipating the day when they would ascend to such exalted positions, with all the opportunities for spoils that went with them. The proposal drew immediate and strong opposition. In October, Discua had to retreat, announcing that he had no plans to cut the COSUFFAA. At the end of the year, however, he was able to strengthen his hand through the annual shuffling of commands. Almost forty officers were transferred to new positions. Young officers from the tenth through thirteenth promotions (especially the twelfth) were elevated to the COSUFFAA, bypassing many of their seniors. Yet, Discua was also able to co-opt some members of his own class (the sixth), half a dozen of whom were given early promotions to brigadier general. Discua himself was raised to division general, only the fourth officer ever to achieve such rank.

In February 1992 reports began to circulate that COSUFFAA had decided to eliminate the post of commander in chief and dissolve itself in favor of a national defense council composed of the recently promoted generals and three to five other high-ranking officers. Discua rejected the reports as "absolutely false." On 22 February a communiqué was issued by a group of junior officers calling themselves the General José Trinidad Cabañas Revolutionary Movement. The group (whose membership was anonymous) accused Discua of conspiring with the National Party to politicize the armed forces. The dissidents argued that the replacement of the commander in chief by a secretary of defense appointed by the president would make the military "puppets of any political party that comes to power." They attacked Discua for manipulating the promotion system and seeking to perpetuate himself in power. They warned that he should "remember the ambition" of General Regalado, who had "wanted his term of office extended" and was stopped. They complained that officers had the same right as he to be commander in chief and charged him and the other generals with appointing members of the twelfth promotion to high positions in order to win their votes. In an ominous reference to the recent coup attempt in Venezuela, they warned that, whereas junior officers had failed there, they would not fail in Honduras.[38]

This enraged Discua, but it also forced him to back off. In late March he replied to a reporter's question that "under no circumstances" would he become secretary of defense. The reforms were postponed. Behind the scenes, however, the struggle continued. In July, there was a brief furor over remarks Discua had reportedly made concerning certain "hillbilly officers" (*oficiales de cerro*); the general was obliged to issue a public denial that bordered on an apology. Not long thereafter, rumors began to circulate that he was secretly negotiating the sale of the country's F-5E fighter planes to Chile. Again, he denied the charge, suggesting that it was intended to discredit him. In early September, too, there were unconfirmed reports that the chairman of the joint chiefs of staff, General Lázaro Avila Soleno, who was known to covet Discua's position as commander in chief, was conspiring to oust him.[39]

In the end, Discua prevailed. Whatever his liabilities, he had done a masterful job of protecting the armed forces from the ravages of the post-Cold War era. Though the institution had officially suffered major budget cuts and there had been a drastic reduction in U.S. aid, Discua had managed to compensate for those losses through a variety of measures ranging from hidden budgets to the dramatic expansion of the military's economic empire.[40] The benefits, both for specific officers and the institution as a whole, were not inconsiderable: It was through such means that the armed forces were able to avoid the reductions that their Nicaraguan and Salvadoran counterparts were experiencing while maintaining their autonomy. There was even enough money for military pensions to be increased (in some cases by 50 percent). Meanwhile, officers were increasingly taking advantage of the Agricultural Modernization Law and the government's "privatization" program to acquire lands and businesses at cut-rate prices. Not surprisingly, those who had profited from Discua's leadership were not anxious to see him go.

Added to this were the general's superb political skills. In terms of political maneuvering, he was the "military equivalent of Callejas, . . . as masterful as the politicos in betrayal, treachery, and . . . deviousness." As the former chief of intelligence, he was said to have information on many of the country's leading political and military figures that he was not above using to intimidate friends and foes alike. In the words of the U.S. ambassador,

> Discua has done nothing horrific in his plays and games. Both he and Rafa [Callejas] use the "elixir" or grease available to co-opt, suborn, remove, and minimize resistance. Both subscribe to the old saw (well applied in U.S. bureaucracies)—punish your enemies, reward the kiss-asses and most importantly destroy, eliminate, or neutralize your rivals. Discua plainly outfoxed all of his colleagues. . . . Both the Honduran political system and the military establishment with their laid-back, garden-variety chicanery were *not* prepared for the cunning, superior and masterful abilities, and enthusiasm for betrayal and manipulation that Luis Alonso Discua . . . and Rafa have brought to the game.[41]

Thus it was that in late September the COSUFFAA submitted a proposal to Congress to revoke Article 32 of the Constituent Law of the Armed Forces, which forbade the reelection of the commander in chief. The measure was passed "with the speed of light."[42] A week later, the deputies voted to give Discua another term.

Discua had won the battle, but had he won the war? Some observers did not think so. Fewer than half of the deputies had been willing to vote for him in the end, the remainder either voting against, abstaining, or absenting themselves.[43] Dissident junior officers (this time calling themselves the Career Officers' Movement) again expressed their dismay, claiming that military professionalism would now be impossible and that opportunities for career advancement would be closed off. Commenting on all this, *El Tiempo* remarked that the "greatest enemies of the armed forces are those who destabilize it from within, ensuring permanent political unrest and creating future knots of generational tension."[44]

Nevertheless, as the weeks passed there was growing concern that the traditional checks and balances within the institution were no longer functioning. In the aftermath of his reelection, Discua felt confident enough to suggest that by the year 2000 the armed forces would be in a "phase of many structural reforms." He even suggested that he might be the "commander of transition," though simple arithmetic showed that for that to occur he would have to be elected for yet another term.[45] In the short run, there would be more purges. When the year-end promotions and rotations were announced, it turned out that Discua's chief nemesis, Avila Soleno, had been "promoted" to the political administrative post of minister of defense, where he would be isolated from the chain of command. The former defense minister, Claudio Laínez, was sent into diplomatic exile as a military attaché. Taking over Avila Soleno's old job in the joint chiefs of staff (the second-most-powerful post in the armed forces) was a close Discua collaborator, Reynaldo Andino Flores.

An Ambassador Prepares to Depart (but Not Quietly)

By now, also, it was time for the U.S. ambassador to move on. Cresencio Arcos had spent most of his last year in Honduras continuing what he had begun: serving as a kind of all-purpose critic, alternately prodding and cajoling Honduran authorities to move in the directions that he wanted. As always, he was controversial. Early in 1992 he had caused an uproar by countering the official optimism on the economy and suggesting that what was preventing more progress was the growth of government bureaucracy and increased military spending. In August, he further aroused Honduran ire by declaring that "justice must not be like a viper that only bites those without shoes and leaves alone those who wear boots"—a clear allusion to the military.[46] He again emphasized the need to cut the armed forces budget as part of the government's deficit reduction strategy. The United States, he said, would continue to reduce its aid to Honduras in the years to come, perhaps even eliminating it by the turn of the century. ("It is no longer a question of handing over the fish, but rather of learning how to fish.")[47] By September calls for Arcos's removal were again being heard, but this time nothing came of them. Throughout his remaining months in office the ambassador continued to express his views, both publicly and privately, on everything from the military's expanding economic empire to electoral reform.

Nor was Arcos alone in his criticism. The State Department's annual human rights report on Honduras, released in early 1993, cited numerous instances of extrajudicial execution and political killing, arbitrary and incommunicado detention, torture and abuse of prisoners, impunity of armed forces personnel, and absence of swift and impartial justice. The Callejas administration, it said, had been unable to ensure that human rights violations would be fully investigated or that most perpetrators would be brought to justice. The criminal justice system, with its endemically corrupt, ill trained, and poorly equipped judiciary and police force, was cited as the primary obstacle. Though the armed forces played a less intrusive political role than in the past, they still operated with "considerable institutional and legal autonomy in internal security and military affairs." The military still tended to protect its own, with the result that, to date, no military personnel accused of human rights violations had been found guilty.[48] The report was not well received by Honduran authorities. Nor was their humor much improved when, in March, a Voice of America broadcast suggested that Honduras did not have organized civilian institutions or a genuine democracy. Rather than being a country with an army, the commentary said, it was more like an army with a country.

Honduras and El Salvador: Peace at Last?

In September, amidst much anxiety in Honduras, the World Court issued its long-awaited decision on the Honduras-El Salvador border dispute. Honduras was granted about two-thirds of the 168 square miles of land under contention. The court ruled that the two countries would have to share control of the Gulf of Fonseca with Nicaragua, with El Salvador receiving the islands of Meanguera and Meanguerita and Honduras receiving Tiger Island. The verdict was joyfully received in Honduras, but, even so, it created problems: Most of the inhabitants of the territories awarded to Honduras still considered themselves Salvadorans; many, indeed, were supporters of the FMLN. The thought of living in Honduras terrified them. In the words of one, who no doubt spoke for many others, "We were sold out, betrayed. Just when we were beginning to breathe a bit the air of liberty . . . we're facing the prospect of another army coming to repress us."[49] Though the court had prescribed a ninety-day transition period during which the two governments were not supposed to exert sovereignty in the zones, Honduran soldiers almost immediately began to appear, sometimes in a confrontive way, making a tense situation worse.

The question was how to incorporate these territories into Honduras and El Salvador with a minimum of conflict while protecting the legitimate interests of the inhabitants. In the months that followed, residents presented petitions to both governments demanding that the zones remain demilitarized; that the Honduran government respect landownership and grant property titles to those already in possession; that dual nationality be granted, along with free movement to both countries; that the inhabitants be permitted to create their own municipality independent of neighboring ones; and that state powers not be installed until the Honduran-Salvadoran bilateral commission had reached an accord on such matters.

The petitions were supported by local Catholic priests, who charged that the Honduran military had assassinated, tortured, robbed, and arrested inhabitants and burned their homes. But the authorities in Tegucigalpa remained adamant. In the words of Foreign Minister Mario Carías Zapata, "the question of the state and sovereignty is not under discussion. These territories are Honduran and the court has ratified it. The government will extend its presence, . . . naming auxiliary mayors, judges, and other representatives of national authority."[50] Tension in the bolsones remained high, and there was continued violence, but not so much that things seemed likely to get out of hand. Both governments appeared committed to the settlement, and it seemed likely that, with time, the situation would stabilize.

Development or Decay? The Socioeconomic and Political Outlook in Early 1993

As of March 1993 the prospects for the future were decidedly mixed. Although socioeconomic conditions had improved in some respects, they had seriously deteriorated in others. The government, of course, chose to accentuate the positive. In a series of public reports, President Callejas claimed that he had reversed the downward spiral of the economy and "prepared the way for the twenty-first century." The fiscal deficit, he announced, had been reduced to around 3 percent of the GDP; inflation had fallen from 36.4 percent in 1990 to 6.5 percent in 1992; real GDP had increased from 2.2 percent in 1991 to 4.3 percent in 1992; the exchange rate was stable; international reserves had passed the US$120 million mark; and the foreign debt had been reduced from US$3.3 billion in 1990 to US$3.1 billion. At the same time, there had been major gains in road construction and the installation of telephone lines. The president even claimed to have reduced the gap between rich and poor through increases in the minimum wage (206 percent), the extension of health and social security coverage (from 600,000 to 1 million people), the creation of over 100,000 new jobs in Tegucigalpa and San Pedro Sula, and the improvement of the purchasing power of the lower classes. Nineteen ninety-three, he predicted, would see even more progress, with economic growth projected at between 5 and 6 percent.[51]

Not everyone, of course, agreed. Some of the president's claims and projections seemed unduly optimistic. The head of the Association of Honduran Economists, while granting that some of the country's macroeconomic problems had been corrected, criticized the administration for having sacrificed the living standards of the populace. In sharp contrast to Callejas, he claimed that the number of people living in poverty had *increased* (from 68 percent of the population to 71 percent) over the past three years. Other observers pointed out that Honduras's relative economic stability was more the result of international financial support (including US$582.7 million in debt forgiveness) and economic policies in the financial sector than real growth in economic activity.[52] Coffee and banana prices remained very low, and the latter seemed likely to decline even further. In December, the European Economic Community had imposed a two-million-ton annual quota and a 20 percent tariff on Latin American banana exports, to take effect in July. They also set a punitive duty of 170 percent on any deliveries over the limit. Although the impact on Honduras was expected to be less than on some producers (only 12 percent of its exports went to Europe), it would still be substantial. Bananas not sold in Europe would have to be dumped on the world market, which would depress prices and reduce earnings. Banana lands would lose value; workers would lose jobs.[53]

Nor was this all. Throughout 1992, social and political decay had continued to worsen. By now corruption was engulfing the Callejas administration. Some of the president's closest advisers and even members of his family were implicated. Violence was spiralling out of control. San Pedro Sula had acquired the reputation of being not only the AIDS capital of Latin America but the crime capital of Honduras. During the first weeks of the new year, the city was jolted by a series of execution-style killings and bombings. "Political violence, intermingled dangerously with ordinary delinquency and seasoned with money from drug traffic, . . . had ignited a social fire that threatened the entire country."[54] Alarmed, President Callejas ordered the deployment of 2,000 troops to reinforce San Pedro's security.

Notwithstanding these problems, the political tide seemed to favor the Nationalists. In December, the National Party's president, Celim Discua, announced that the government was preparing an "enormous plan of social works . . . to win the election."[55] The following month, Callejas announced a US$500 million "social compensation" program to alleviate the hardships caused by the structural adjustment. Even Nora de Melgar did her bit, proposing a US$20 million plan to repair the capital's streets and build a half-dozen peripheral markets and three bus terminals. In combination, the rebounding economy and the promise of more jobs, schools, hospitals, roads, and other social infrastructure seemed to be making a difference. In early March a CID-Gallup poll found that Callejas was still the most popular political figure in the country. More important, Ramos Soto was now second and Doña Nora third. Carlos Roberto Reina could do no better than fourth. Although neither of the presidential candidates (Ramos Soto and Reina) could yet command a majority of the vote, the National Party had an advantage over the Liberal Party, with 47 percent to the latter's 43 percent.[56] Obviously, there was a long way to go, and the race was still very close, but the trends could not be encouraging to the Liberals.

Nor were they encouraging for political stability or democracy. Quite apart from the dolorous implications of a possible Ramos Soto victory, there was the growing problem of the armed forces. As the economic power and autonomy of the institution grew, so did public criticism and the military's contempt for civilian authority. For months Discua and his colleagues had been warning the politicians to stay out of the military's internal affairs. On 15 January the commander in chief delivered a particularly truculent speech in which he accused the army's enemies of trying to portray it as corrupt and abusive. Literally bellowing into the microphone, he warned that "politicians must not stick their noses" into military matters. On another occasion, he went even farther, threatening to use "confidential documents" to "unmask" these "enemies."[57]

Among the adversaries Discua wanted to unmask was, not surprisingly, the human rights movement. For much of the previous year the Honduran government had been engaged in an extraordinary attempt to discredit Honduran and international monitors. In September these maneuvers had led to a bizarre kidnapping of the Costa Rican minister of security, Luis Fishmán, the head of the DNI, Colonel Manuel Luna, and the bishop of Santa Rosa de Copán, Alfonso Santos. The kidnapper, Orlando Ordóñez, was a deranged former member of the Honduran army who claimed to have information about Angel Manfredo Velásquez and Saúl Godínez, the two "disappeared" whose cases had led the Inter-American Court of Human Rights to condemn the Honduran government in 1988.

Ordóñez claimed that Velásquez and Godínez were alive and that he could produce them. With the help of a Costa Rican journalist who was researching the alleged link between Honduran subversive groups and the Honduran human rights movement, he was able to arrange a meeting with Fishmán, Luna, Santos, and the Mexican ambassador to Costa Rica. At this meeting, however, Ordóñez drew a gun and demanded to be flown to Honduras with his hostages. From there, he went on to Mexico after reportedly receiving a ransom of US$100,000.[58]

Ordóñez was both an impostor and a notorious criminal. He claimed to be a former member of the Cinchoneros, from whom supposedly he had learned that Velásquez and Godínez were alive (he said that they had once been Cinchoneros also). But in fact there was no evidence to support this. There was evidence, however—and the DNI was well aware of it—that Ordóñez had engaged in drug trafficking, car robberies, and blackmail. He had spent time in the Central Penitentiary in Tegucigalpa and was currently wanted in Costa Rica for child rape and other crimes. The Honduran government had helped him settle in Costa Rica, paid him substantial sums of money, and helped hide the truth about his life-style, and its motives seem not to have been humanitarian. The relatives of Velásquez and Godínez were never told about the operation. Indeed, for some time the Callejas administration had been refusing to pay them the bulk of the money due them as a result of the judgment of the Inter-American Court.

From the evidence, then, it seems that the purpose of the scheme—at least as far as the Honduran government was concerned—was to discredit domestic and foreign human rights groups (the CODEH and Americas Watch), the Inter-American Court, and the families of the "disappeared." In this way, the government and the armed forces may have hoped to salvage their reputations and justify the continued nonpayment of compensation.[59] But the operation backfired. Rather than salvaging reputations, it undermined them. Nor was the military's image improved when it was learned that among the officers promoted at the end of the year were several (including the notorious Alexander Hernández, who now became a colonel with the police) who were linked to Battalion 3-16. Subsequently, Honduran human rights groups charged that Discua himself had once directed a renamed version of 3-16, called the Counterintelligence Battalion, and that he was placing officers linked to the group in high- and middle-level positions of the armed forces.[60]

Under other circumstances, these accusations might have been shrugged off as politically motivated. In early 1993, however, the north coast was in the grip of an unprecedented wave of violence, and there was evidence to suggest that the military was deeply involved. Moreover, some of this violence seemed aimed at discrediting the left. In late January, a terrorist cell calling itself the Group of Four and claiming to be the "military arm of the Human Rights Defense Committee" sent a communiqué to the media taking credit for an attempt on the life of Humberto Regalado's son. The effort to link the group to the CODEH was too blatant to be credible. It was quickly denounced as "psychological warfare" by Ramón Custodio, who compared it to the 1987-1988 campaign to brand leftists as "subversive."

Relations between the military and the CODEH were now moving toward a confrontation. On 29 January a local businessman, Eduardo Piña Van Tuyl, was shot down in San Pedro Sula. In the aftermath of the killing, a group purporting to be the Morazanista Front took credit, charging that Van Tuyl belonged to Battalion 3-16, but the claim did not stand up to scrutiny. By pure chance, the assassination had been witnessed by a passing journalist, Eduardo Coto, who had filmed the perpetrators as they fled. Subsequently, Coto was subjected to a campaign of intimidation. When he sought protection from *El Tiempo*, the home of the paper's manager, Yani Rosenthal, was bombed. Fearing for his life, Coto fled to Spain.

Before he left, however, Coto was able to help in the (still very tentative) identification of the assassins. The latter had made the mistake of attending the victim's funeral, where they had openly fraternized with security agents sent by General Discua. Working from Coto's verbal descriptions, a CODEH artist rendered composite sketches of the suspects. On this basis, Ramón Custodio accused three members of the armed forces of having killed Van Tuyl. The military, of course, denied it, and, indeed, this "evidence" might have been dismissed as unreliable had not another witness come forward to lend it credence. On 8 February the former DNI agent Josué Elí Zúñiga presented the editors of *El Tiempo* with information about the security forces' involvement in the Rosenthal bombing, the Van Tuyl assassination, and at least seven other unsolved murders in San Pedro Sula within the past year. Among other things, he implicated Battalion 3-16 in the killings of two STENEE leaders and linked several narcotics inspectors to a triple murder. The Van Tuyl assassination, he suggested, might have been committed by middle-level DNI agents involved in drug trafficking, but his efforts to verify this through one of his former colleagues had been blocked by DNI authorities.[61]

It was in this atmosphere of rapidly escalating scandal and siege that the decision was made to occupy Tegucigalpa. On the morning of 26 February *capitalinos* awoke to find the streets filled with armored vehicles, mobile artillery, and roaming units of camouflage-clad soldiers. For days there had been rumors of an intense power struggle within the military, and many assumed that Discua was simply moving to deter or preempt a coup. This was, as usual, denied. President Callejas himself announced that *he* had ordered the move as a "surprise" to deter "criminal violence," but he had apparently not talked to Discua. The military had its own rationale: The Morazanista Front, it seemed, was planning terrorist attacks, and the mobilization was intended to discourage them. In any event, few observers were convinced: Tanks and antiaircraft guns did not seem to be a particularly effective response to urban terrorism and common crime. The siege lasted only a weekend. All it really demonstrated was that, while the Marxists had been ousted in Nicaragua, the Marx brothers were still very much in power in Honduras.

Notes

1. Conversation with Roberto Martínez Castañeda, who has known both Flores and Callejas since childhood. I heard similar things from many other Liberals.

2. Ibid.

3. Flores Facussé to the authors.

4. Víctor Meza, *"Elecciones en Honduras: Un Intento de Interpretación,"* Boletín Informativo Honduras, Special No. 48, July 1990, pp. 7-8.

5. *New York Times,* 15 October 1989. When we spoke with him six months later, Briggs admitted that he did not know whether the charges were true but said that, if they were, it wouldn't be the first time that a Honduran commander got caught with his hand in the till." Interview, 9 April 1990.

6. *New York Times,* 15 October 1989; *Boletín Informativo Honduras,* No. 104, December 1989, p. 4.

7. *Boletín Informativo Honduras,* No. 98, June 1989, p. 1.

8. Ibid., No. 99, July 1989, p. 7; ibid., No. 102, October 1989, p. 4.

9. *Central America Report,* 23 March 1990 and 15 February 1991; Miguel Angel Funes, *"Crisis en la Decada 80 y Reestructuración de la Economía,"* Boletín Informativo Honduras, Special No. 53, March 1991.

10. *Central America Report,* 14 September 1990.

11. *Wall Street Journal,* 7 June 1990.

12. CEDOH *"El Proyecto de Callejas,"* Boletín Informativo Honduras, Special No. 55, May 1991, p. 9.

13. Cantarero to a high-ranking U.S. embassy official. Not-for-attribution.

14. *El Heraldo,* 30 and 31 May, 1 and 5 June, 12 July 1990.

15. There were also some delicate personal issues involved here that the publisher prefers that we not mention.

16. From a U.S. embassy source. Not-for-attribution.

17. *El Heraldo,* 5 February 1990.

18. Ibid., 19 October 1990.

19. Confirmed by Cantarero in ibid., 8 December 1990.

20. *El Tiempo,* 12 December 1990; *El Heraldo,* 4 December 1990.

21. *El Tiempo,* 19 December 1990; *Boletín Informativo Honduras,* No. 120, April 1991, p. 11.

22. Foreign Broadcast Information Service (FBIS), *Daily Report: Latin America,* 11 December 1990; *Boletín Informativo Honduras,* No. 132, April 1992, p. 3.

23. Cresencio Arcos, "Managing Change in Central America," *Foreign Service Journal,* Vol. 68, No. 4, April 1991, pp. 19-20.

24. *Mesoamerica,* October 1991; *Mexico and Central America Report,* 31 October 1991; FBIS, *Daily Report,* 23 October 1991.

25. It is possible that these were not active-duty military. In some instances criminals--some of them former military personnel--have worn uniforms in the expectation that this would allow them to act with impunity.

26. U.S. Department of State, *Country Reports on Human Rights Practices for 1990* (Washington, D.C.: U.S. Government Printing Office, 1991), pp. 665-666, 672.

27. FBIS, *Daily Report,* 30 July and 12 September 1991.

28. *Central America Report,* 15 February 1991; *La Tribuna,* 28 August 1991.

29. *Central America Report,* 9 August 1991; *Boletín Informativo Honduras,* No. 117, January 1991, p. 14; ibid., No. 124, August 1991, p. 10; *La Tribuna,* 28 August 1991.

30. FBIS, *Daily Report,* 3 December 1991.

31. Ibid.

32. *Mesoamerica,* December 1991.

33. Ted Briggs said that Ramos "bragged to a member of [Briggs's] staff that he had incited his students to sack our Annex." Interview, 9 April 1990.

34. CEDOH, *"La Violencia en Honduras 1991,"* Serie Cronologías, No. 11, March 1992, pp. 1-2.

35. *Central America Report,* 21 August 1992; *Boletín Informativo Honduras,* No. 137, September 1992, pp. 6, 12.

36. *La Tribuna,* 25 July 1992.

37. *La Prensa,* 26 July 1992; *Boletín Informativo Honduras,* No. 135, July 1992, pp. 8-9.

38. FBIS, *Daily Report: Latin America,* 25 February 1992.

39. Ibid., 27 July, 3 and 10 September 1992.

40. Calculating the military budget is always a challenge. If one were to believe Callejas, between 1990 and 1992 the budget had fallen from US$137 million to US$45 million in real terms (taking into account the devaluation of the lempira). But nobody believed that. Even the State Department estimated it to be around US$100 million. Ibid., 24 March 1993; *Boletín Informativo Honduras,* No. 143, March 1993, p. 2.

41. Letter to Donald Schulz, early 1993.

42. *La Prensa,* 30 September 1992.

43. *Boletín Informativo Honduras,* No. 140, December 1992, p. 7.

44. *El Tiempo,* 30 September 1992.

45. *Latin American Weekly Report,* 15 October 1992.

46. Ibid.

47. *Mesoamerica,* September 1992.

48. *El Tiempo,* 8 February 1993; *Central America Report,* 19 February 1993.

49. *Miami Herald,* 28 September 1992.

50. *Central America Report,* 11 December 1992.

51. FBIS, *Daily Report: Latin America,* 29 December 1991, 29 January and 17 February 1993.

52. *Central America Report,* 26 February 1993.

53. At this writing, the Latin Americans are appealing to an arbitration committee of the General Agreement on Tariffs and Trade. Germany and Belgium, moreover, are suing to overturn the decision in the European Court of Justice. Thus, it is still possible that these measures will be reversed or ameliorated.

54. *Boletín Informativo Honduras,* No. 142, February 1993.

55. *El Heraldo,* 21 December 1992.

56. FBIS, *Daily Report: Latin America,* 4 March 1993. Callejas scored 61 points, Ramos Soto 54, Melgar de Castro 53, and Reina 51.

57. Ibid., 11 February; *El Heraldo,* 16 January 1993.

58. The ransom was confiscated by Mexican authorities upon arrival. Costa Rica immediately began negotiating to extradite Ordóñez, but the Mexicans released him, and he quickly fled. Subsequently, he was killed by the Belize police after having kidnapped the Salvadoran vice consul in that country. *Boletín Informativo Honduras,* No. 137, September 1992, pp. 8-9; *Central America Report,* 9 October 1992 and 15 January 1993; *Mesoamerica,* October 1992.

59. See, especially, the Americas Watch communiqué in *Boletín Informativo Honduras,* No. 138, October 1992, pp. 8-9.

60. The specifics of the charges may be found in *Central America Report,* 12 February 1993; FBIS, *Daily Report: Latin America,* 4 March 1993.

61. *Boletín Informativo Honduras,* No. 142, February 1993, pp. 8-9; *Central America Report,* 12 February and 5 March 1993.

9

How Honduras Escaped Revolutionary Violence

In Honduras, the political situation is always critical but never serious.

—Folk saying

One of the most interesting questions to emerge from the Central American turmoil of the 1980s is why Honduras did not suffer the revolutionary upheaval that plagued its immediate neighbors. After all, at first glance, it seemed to be a prime candidate: Surrounded on three sides by Nicaragua, El Salvador, and Guatemala, it shared the poverty, injustice, and military domination that led to violence in those countries. Indeed, by most socioeconomic indicators it was the most underdeveloped country in the region (though it has since been displaced by Nicaragua.)[1] Why, then, was it able to remain a relative oasis of peace?

The Sources of Stability

The answer is complex. North Americans tend to assume that all Central American countries are the same, when nothing could be further from the truth. The key to Honduras's stability lies in its uniqueness—its "exceptionality," if you will. In large part this is a matter of political culture: Hondurans are less volatile and more flexible than Salvadorans, Guatemalans, and Nicaraguans. Their political system might be likened to a homeostatic mechanism with escape valves for releasing potentially dangerous discontent. Thus, the cyclical pattern of Honduran politics, with periods of reform alternating with periods of repression and sociopolitical stagnation (except in 1980s, when reform and repression were pursued simultaneously, with the reintroduction of democracy and the rise of a "national security regime" under General Alvarez). The early legalization of unions and their co-optation as legitimate participants in the political process, the introduction of agrarian reform, and the periodic experimentation with "national unity" pacts and democracy are all indicators of a political culture that has traditionally been far more sensitive to the public mood than anything witnessed, prior to the overthrow of Somoza, among Honduras's immediate neighbors.

In this respect, the agrarian reform was particularly important. Between 1962 and 1979 various Honduran governments distributed 207,433 hectares of land to 46,890 landless and land-poor peasant families. This amounted to 8 percent of the country's farmland and by 1980 had affected about 12 percent of rural families. As Mark Ruhl has pointed out, no other Central American agrarian reform accomplished nearly as much before 1979, when the Nicaraguan revolution changed the rules of the land tenure game. Whatever the limitations of the Honduran experience, one could hardly have imagined such flexibility in El Salvador or Guatemala. The very fact that peasants could organize and sometimes win disputes and recover "stolen" properties or otherwise benefit from land distribution programs co-opted many and gave hope to many others, buttressing the legitimacy of the system.[2]

But the agrarian reform in itself is not sufficient to explain the (relative) absence of revolutionary unrest. The amount of land distributed declined sharply after 1976, leading to predictions that "competitive exclusion" and high rates of population growth would produce tens of thousands of new rural families and a "militant peasantry more angry and demanding than that of the 1970s."[3] Yet, by the end of the 1980s little seemed to have changed in terms of traditional peasant passivity. Revolution was still far from the minds of the vast majority of campesinos.

Part of the reason, of course, was the continuing appeal of agrarian reform, which still offered peasants some hope of acquiring land. Though distributions had declined, they had not been halted. Titles continued to be handed out. Seasonal land invasions kept enough pressure on the authorities that the reform could not be terminated. At the same time, massive rural-to-urban migration still served as an important release for peasant discontent. By the early 1980s, moreover, large-scale land recoveries were occurring in the cities as well as the countryside. That most of these seizures were not repressed was extremely significant in helping to defuse revolutionary pressures and maintain political and social equilibrium.

Beyond this, many peasants and workers continued to look to the union movement to advance their interests. Again, the homeostatic nature of the Honduran system had enabled the poor to organize in ways that had been inconceivable in El Salvador, Guatemala, and Nicaragua prior to 1979. Not only were unions legal; as powerful sociopolitical actors, they had to be consulted with and accommodated. In the process of becoming part of the system and achieving concrete results for their members, however, they had also become important mechanisms for co-opting and controlling the working classes. They promoted a "trade union mentality" that diverted attention from more radical types of activity. In truth they were, for the most part, conservative institutions—bureaucratic bastions of privilege for a labor elite that had a vested interest in the status quo. Whatever the original intent, the primary purposes of these organizations had become self-perpetuation, self-enrichment, and growth.

The system was at once highly bureaucratized and intensely personalized. Cultural values and poverty fostered corruption. Labor leaders carved out fiefdoms, accepted bribes, and doled out favors. Clientelism and factionalism were rampant. As a result, the movement was always susceptible to government penetration and manipulation. The use of legal recognition, financial subsidies, and coercion to ensure union "moderation" were only the most obvious techniques of manipulation.[4]

As effective as these mechanisms were in contributing to political stability, however, they might well have been inadequate had it not been for the willingness of the military to return the government to civilian control in the early 1980s. This was not, of course, an entirely spontaneous or voluntary decision. The United States had to provide considerable incentives (both carrots and sticks) to effectuate "redemocratization." Moreover, this democratic restoration was always more procedural than substantive. Civilian presidents, Congress, and the courts were severely limited in their powers. The military continued to play a hegemonic role. Whether behind the scenes or in public, it was still by far the most powerful political interest group in the country.

Although the quality of Honduran democracy may have been suspect, its appearance was of crucial significance: People could now believe, rightly or wrongly, that they governed themselves. Democratization reinforced stability by legitimating political arrangements that had previously been based largely on force. Once again Hondurans had shown themselves to be more flexible than their immediate neighbors. They had embraced democracy as a preventive measure to avoid revolutionary turmoil. Salvadorans, Guatemalans, and Nicaraguans, in contrast, accepted the forms of democracy only belatedly, after civil war had broken out. It was an important difference.

There is also another, related factor that is often overlooked—namely, that Hondurans had had much more experience with democracy. They had a two-party system, which, in spite of many dictatorial interruptions, had taken root in the political psyche of the populace. The Liberal and National parties could trace their origins to the late nineteenth and early twentieth centuries. There was a tradition of political affiliation to build on. Families were known to be nacionalistas or liberales. Habitual voting patterns had been passed down from generation to generation. Nothing like this could be found in El Salvador or Guatemala, where the parties tended to be much younger and more ephemeral. The attachment was strong enough that attempts to form third parties (such as the Christian Democrats) were bound to fail, at least in the short run. And of course habitual affiliations were reinforced by clientelism and patronage. People knew that third parties could not win or deliver the benefits that the Liberals and Nationalists could provide, so they did not waste their votes. In turn, serious reformers, understanding that a third-party strategy was a dead end, usually stayed within the traditional structures.

In short, Honduran society was characterized by an elaborate network of interlocking interest groups and political organizations that mediated conflicts and channeled personal ambitions that might otherwise have proven explosive. This constant struggle within and between competing groups had long constituted the essence of Honduran politics. Loyalties were always shifting and often for sale; this enabled both military and civilian authorities to use state resources (jobs, bribes, and favors) to defuse potentially destabilizing movements before they became dangerous. At the same time, the very fact that Honduran elites were flexible enough to allow political space for so many groups made it possible for the system to co-opt important socioeconomic and political forces that were denied participation in neighboring lands.

Within this Byzantine milieu, moreover, there was a tradition of collective decisionmaking. One of the reasons that things moved so slowly in Honduras was that most public decisions had to go through a long process of consensus building. In large part this was because of the reluctance of Hondurans to confront friends and associates. The elite was very small—probably not more than 1,000 people—and it lacked the aristocratic traditions of most Central American ruling classes. Consequently, leaders of various social groups tended to be in frequent contact with one another. They interbred, shared business interests, and mingled in their leisure. When dealing with friends and relatives, they much preferred accommodation to conflict ("a deal for my friends, and the law for my enemies," as the saying goes). Consensus building enabled the individual to escape responsibility and avoid unpleasantness. He could build a collective defense, so that his actions could not be used against him by potential rivals. And while decisions might take a painfully long time to be made and implemented, this modus operandi undoubtedly contributed much to the country's stability. Thus was Hispanic volatility ameliorated by Honduran passivity, and conflict by consensus.

This brings us to one of the central paradoxes of the political culture: its ability to combine rigidity with flexibility. On the one hand, the constant maneuvering for power and spoils required coalition building. Hondurans were always making alliances, and rarely did they let political ideas stand in the way. Opportunism rather than ideology was the driving force of politics. On the other hand, the highly personalized and egocentric nature of interpersonal relations meant that coalitions, once formed, tended to be fragile. They broke up easily and often.

Hence a major source of both the country's macrostability and its constant microinstability: For even as the Hondurans' rigidities were ameliorated by their flexibility, opportunism, and passivity, these latter qualities were insufficient to maintain order—and in some respects actually contributed to disorder or "bureaucratized anarchy"—in the day-to-day workings of political parties, unions, and other alliances.

But the political system was a homeostatic mechanism in a more passive sense as well: Just as Honduran elites were flexible enough to provide escape valves for popular discontent, they were never so violent as to inspire large-scale leftist resistance. In recent years, political scientists have become increasingly aware of the critical role played by repression in the creation of revolutionary movements. Of all the factors that account for Honduras's comparative tranquility, this was surely the most important. Whatever else might be said about that country's military, it did not display the massive, often indiscriminate savagery witnessed in El Salvador, Guatemala, and Nicaragua. Human rights violations were commonplace. Assassinations and disappearances occurred, especially during the Alvarez era. But the number of dead paled in comparison with what was happening next door. In Honduras, the body count was in the low hundreds rather than the tens of thousands. Massive repression was considered neither necessary nor desirable. Consequently, there were many fewer occasions for the development of the kind of dialectical escalation of revolutionary and counterrevolutionary violence that had led to civil war on the other side of the country's various borders.[5]

This relative restraint on the part of the military and civilian elites reflected the dominant political culture. An embassy official with long experience in the country once remarked that Hondurans were more beggars and thieves than killers. Although the characterization may say as much about North American attitudes as it does about Hondurans, it contains an important element of truth: Hondurans do not have the intensity of Salvadorans; they tend to be more passive and dependent. Even their dictatorships have usually been *dictaduras blandas*—relatively mild when compared to the excesses of their neighbors. Congenial corruption rather than bloodthirsty violence is the *estilo hondureño*.

This being said, it would be an oversight to ignore the role of coercion in maintaining stability. Repression can de-escalate as well as escalate political opposition. Thus, in the mid-1970s, the Los Horcones massacre intimidated the Catholic church, leading it to pull back from its previous commitment to social activism. Subsequently, under Alvarez Martínez, violence was used early and effectively (which is to say that it was both ruthless and selective) to decapitate the nascent revolutionary movement by destroying its leadership. The insurgent organizations were crippled from their inception and were never able to build the momentum that other Central American guerrilla movements attained.

In effect, then, Honduran elites were able to combine positive and negative incentives—reform and repression—to maximize the prospects of stability. Enough force was used to decimate the revolutionary left and deter those who might otherwise have joined it, but not so much as to drive many people into its arms. At the same time, the continuing agrarian reform provided some peasants with tangible gains and others with hope; the unions did the same for both urban and rural poor; and the restoration of democracy gave all classes the feeling that they had a say in their governing—or at least that they might eventually gain one. In short, the vast majority of Hondurans still had a stake in the system, or thought that they did. Few were willing to assume the very substantial risks and costs of revolutionary activism.

Again, one must emphasize the lack of any strong, autonomous agents for radical change. The military had acted early to preempt such organizations through land reform and other measures. Labor and peasant unions had been effectively co-opted. The Christian Democratic Party—a major factor in El Salvador and Guatemala—was never able to challenge the hegemony of the Liberals and the Nationalists. The Catholic church, which had played a crucial role in revolutionary processes elsewhere, was of marginal importance. (The Honduran church had never really been able to develop into a strong indigenous institution. It was, on the whole, a conservative organization, still heavily influenced by anticommunism. Internally divided and externally dependent—only 70 of the 292 priests in the country were Hondurans—it had been easily frightened away from the struggle for social justice.)[6] In sum, the movements that had played such a crucial organizational/mobilizational role in the Salvadoran, Guatemalan, and Nicaraguan revolutions and had helped legitimate far more radical elements through their association with the revolutionary opposition were never much of a factor in Honduras.

And neither were the revolutionaries. Groups such as the Cinchoneros were never able to acquire a mass following. Hondurans were still a highly conservative people. There was little support for revolutionary change and considerable fear that what was happening in neighboring lands might spill over into their own country. Under the circumstances, association with the Sandinistas and the FMLN was a weakness rather than a strength: It discredited the left from the very beginning. Nor did it help that the Honduran movement was plagued by the same bureaucratized anarchy and incompetence that afflicted virtually all other Honduran institutions. Bereft of popular support, badly wounded by the military's counterinsurgency operations, and riven by internecine strife and factionalism, the guerrilla movement was never able to launch much more than sporadic acts of terrorism.

A few words must be said about the U.S. role in all this. Whatever else one may think about the Reagan administration's Central American policy, it must be pointed out that the United States had a great deal to do with the preservation of Honduran stability. Had it not been for U.S. enticements and pressures, elections would probably not have been held in 1980 and 1981. The perpetuation of the military dictatorship would have undermined the legitimacy of the political order, making it far more vulnerable to revolutionary turmoil. By the same token, strong North American opposition to President Suazo's attempt to remain in power in 1985 helped preserve the fragile legitimacy that had been built over the previous five years. At the same time, massive economic aid prevented the economy's collapse, while military aid considerably strengthened the armed forces' capability of maintaining order. One can criticize the Reagan administration for its contra policy and the attendant militarization of Honduras (which limited the development of democracy and diverted scarce resources from pressing socioeconomic problems), but the fact remains that without the United States Honduras might well have disintegrated into chaos.

Several other observations must also be made. There has been some debate lately over the relative merits of state-centered (or elite-centered) explanations of Honduran stability as opposed to analyses that focus on socioeconomic conditions (e.g., relative deprivation and J-curve theory).[7] The distinction is important, but a focus on one to the exclusion of the other obscures the complexity of revolutionary processes. Socioeconomic conditions create psychological propensities to act or not act, but those conditions may also be heavily influenced (positively or negatively) by state-elite policies. In Honduras, clearly, the latter played an important role in ameliorating socioeconomic conditions that might otherwise have fueled revolutionary activism. One cannot understand the whole without understanding the parts and how they interact. Moreover, the focus on state versus society misses the crucial organizational/mobilizational linkage by which the raw socioeconomic preconditions of revolution are transformed into revolutionary behavior. We have suggested that the organizational component was very weak in Honduras, but a fuller explanation must include reference to the socioeconomic conditions themselves.

One issue has to do with the nature and timing of the country's decline. Though Honduras was hardly untouched by the worsening international economic climate of the 1970s, the deterioration in living conditions was not as great as in most neighboring countries. Honduran workers did not experience the dramatic, ongoing decline in real wages that their Guatemalan, Salvadoran, and Nicaraguan counterparts had to bear. Unemployment had stabilized at less than 10 percent. The displacement of peasants by large, export-oriented plantations and cattle ranches was considerably less severe than in, say, El Salvador. Indeed, the position of the campesino may actually have improved somewhat with land reform, the slowdown of the enclosure movement, and the boom in coffee. This last, in particular, provided a safety valve for many smallholders who turned to the product in the 1970s after having been pushed into the hills in previous decades. Partially as a consequence of all this, Honduras, though ranking lower than El Salvador on most socioeconomic indicators, had a considerably smaller percentage of landless and near-landless peasants, more medium-sized farms with fairly adequate holdings, and more secure private and ejidal national holdings independent of the power of landlords. And, of course, there were also some 18,000 well-paid banana workers—about 10 percent of the rural landless—employed by United Brands and Standard Fruit. This was, in the words of Frantz Fanon, something of a "pampered proletariat," with powerful unions and ten times the average national income. There was no equivalent in El Salvador.[8]

By the late 1970s life, though hard for most Hondurans, was still relatively stable and predictable. Important social sectors had been able to maintain—and some even to improve—their modest standards of living. The real socioeconomic crunch did not come until later. By then, however, the United States had begun to step in with massive economic and military aid. "Redemocratization" was in progress, and the still small and vulnerable revolutionary movement was being ground into oblivion by General Alvarez. In short, timing was important. The lag in the onset of the socioeconomic crisis gave U.S. and Honduran authorities breathing space in which to devise and apply a strategy of preemption.

Secondly, Honduras, though very poor, had a somewhat less inequitable socioeconomic structure than its immediate neighbors. The Honduran saying "Here even the rich are poor," while untrue if taken literally, reflects a frequent perception that the differences between rich and poor are not as great and the rich are not as rich as in El Salvador or Guatemala. Although the relationship between economic inequality and political conflict is still being debated by social scientists, there seems to be enough evidence (on the agrarian structure, especially) to support a modest version of this "equality thesis"—at least as it applied to Honduran conditions in the late 1970s and early 1980s.[9] Just as important, perhaps, many Hondurans believed it to be true and considered it a factor in their country's continuing stability.

Third, even in the 1980s relative deprivation did not increase nearly as much in Honduras as it had in neighboring countries. In part this was because the economy had less distance to fall. Honduran per capita economic growth in the early 1970s was never as high as it was in El Salvador, Guatemala, and Nicaragua. Moreover, its decline began later and was never as steep or long-lasting (see TABLE 9.1). And since the fruits of economic growth were more equitably distributed, the burden of hard times fell less disproportionately on the poor. Even when real wages did decline in the 1980s, the drop was not nearly as great as in other countries.[10] In short, the J-curve effect was not nearly as pronounced here as elsewhere.[11]

Finally, it can be argued that the very fact that Honduras was the most underdeveloped and backward of the traditional five Central American countries was a source of stability. (This is one of the paradoxes of the society: In part, its strength has been a product of its weakness.) Rapid economic growth can be highly destabilizing. That Honduras was the least industrialized, urbanized, and literate of the five meant that it would also be the least affected by the destructive and potentially destabilizing side effects of modernization.[12] This was still basically an agrarian society in its culture and psychology; it was relatively uncommercialized and had a large subsistence sector. A substantial portion of the populace remained outside the formal, capitalist economy and was less affected by the unemployment, inflation, and other plagues that can ravage more sophisticated, complex, and "developed" societies.[13] The middle class remained relatively small and unorganized as an independent political actor. The urban proletariat, though growing rapidly, was still largely a displaced peasantry. It would

TABLE 9.1 Mean Annual Growth in Gross Domestic Products per Capita for El Salvador, Guatemala, Honduras, and Nicaragua, 1970-1989 (in percentages)

	El Salvador	Guatemala	Honduras	Nicaragua
1970-1974	1.8	3.2	0.6	2.0
1975-1979	0.4	2.4	1.0	-6.8
1980-1984	-5.5	-3.1	-2.4	0.2
1985-1989	-0.7	-0.7	0.1	-6.6

Source: John A. Booth, "Socioeconomic and Political Roots of National Revolts in Central America," *Latin American Research Review*, Vol. 26, No. 1 (1991), p. 39.

take years before these emerging forces acquired a political consciousness (as opposed to merely a trade union consciousness) and developed political organizations of their own—if indeed they ever did. Meanwhile, the traditional values and habits of the countryside—conservatism, dependency, passivity and fatalism—continued to suffuse the political culture, providing a bedrock of stability that had only just begun to crack under the weight of modernization.

The Shifting Equilibrium: Prospects for the Future

We have been suggesting here that the Honduran political and social order is not as weak and fragile as has been generally supposed. Weaknesses there are—one would have to be blind not to see them—but there are also countervailing sources of strength and stability. And thus far the latter have been sufficient to maintain the system in equilibrium—with North American help.

But the equation is changing. The contra war is over, and Central America is no longer a high-priority area for U.S. foreign policy. For years one of the major Honduran concerns has been what would happen when the United States lost interest. Honduran leaders have had few illusions about U.S. motives in providing them with massive aid over the past decade. Honduras has been an instrument of U.S. policy; now that policy no longer exists. What will happen?

To its credit, Washington has not abruptly severed the country's economic lifeline. U.S. aid has been reduced gradually to give the Hondurans time to put their economic house in order. Even as direct U.S. assistance has declined, aid from other sources has risen sharply. International lending agencies such as the IMF and the World Bank have opened up the floodgates. In the short run, aid per se should not be a problem—so long as the Honduran government is willing and able to meet the conditions of the lenders.

The immediate problem has been with those conditions. The Callejas administration's structural adjustment program is a classic conservative response to economic crisis, and like other plans of this kind, it has been costly. Cuts in government spending have devastated social programs and increased unemployment. Agrarian reform has been allowed to languish. Devaluation led to an initial, rapid rise of inflation (though that problem now appears to have been solved). As always in such circumstances, it is the poor—the vast majority—who have been hit the hardest. As yet, there have been no riots comparable to those in Caracas in 1989, but tension has been building. There is massive labor and peasant unrest and growing violence in both cities and countryside.[14] One cannot discount the possibility of an explosion.

Can the economy be stabilized and growth regenerated? The answer, clearly, is yes. Much has already been accomplished. Moreover, as the region's civil wars gradually disappear (assuming that present trends continue) investor confidence should grow and capital flight should diminish. Increasing foreign investment and loans may create other problems (e.g., growing indebtedness and greater foreign control over the economy), but they should spur economic growth. Development of a kind is likely to occur. Sooner or later, however, the crucial question is likely to be who is getting the benefits.

One of the lessons of the "decade of development" was that wealth generated in highly inequitable settings is distributed inequitably. The development of the 1960s helped pave the way for the revolutionary explosions of the late 1970s and early 1980s by increasing inequalities. Agricultural modernization led to growing landlessness as peasants were displaced from their subsistence holdings by larger farms raising crops and cattle for export. At the same time, rapid population growth and urbanization created a surplus labor force that could not be absorbed by the capital-intensive industrialization that was being pursued. Consequently, unemployment and underemployment spread widely through both urban and rural workforces; in the countryside malnutrition, always bad, became rampant. Meanwhile, the rich became richer and the middle class expanded as a minority of the lower class was able to achieve some upward mobility.

There is another problem here also. Alexis de Tocqueville, writing more than a century ago about the French Revolution, noted that "it was precisely in those parts of France where there had been the most improvement that popular discontent ran the highest. There, economic and social improvement had taken place . . . but still there existed the greatest amount of unrest."[15] The point, of course, is that hope is a great facilitator of revolutionary turmoil. Once people see that improvement is possible, they yearn for more. As those accustomed to suffering in silence become politicized, pent-up frustrations are released. Gradualism is rejected; only immediate and substantive gains can satisfy. When this proves impossible, the result is violence.

The irony is that, even if the Callejas/AID/IMF/World Bank strategy proves successful in putting Honduras on the road to rapid modernization, that very success is likely to contain the seeds of instability. Most probable, in view of the region's history, is a mixed pattern of development: Some people will prosper. The rich will get richer, and the poor will become poorer and much more numerous. Agrarian reform will fail to keep pace with growing rural landlessness. The flood of peasants into urban areas will lead to even more unmanageable socioeconomic conditions there. Meanwhile, appetites will be whetted as the newcomers are exposed to the comparative opulence of middle-class life-styles. As the poor gain greater access to education and political communication becomes easier, class consciousness is likely to increase. Rising expectations will occur alongside growing inequality.

In short, one should harbor no illusions about an easy future for Honduras. The socioeconomic raw materials of revolution are present and will almost certainly increase. The question is whether the stabilizing factors that have thus far been able to maintain systemic equilibrium will continue to sustain that balance. The outlook is decidedly mixed. One would have hoped for more progress in terms of political and social development. Instead, after three years of the Callejas presidency it seems that opportunities have been missed, that in certain respects Honduras has slipped backward, and that things could soon get considerably worse. The most obvious warning signs are the following:

1. The revision of the military code to permit Discua's reelection has opened the door for his indefinite continuation in office. This suggests that the checks and balances that have in recent years prevented any one individual from attaining

and consolidating control over the institution are no longer functioning—or at least are not as effective as they once were. Despite (or perhaps because of) this, continuing unrest within the armed forces could very well spark a barracks revolt.

2. The military's expanding economic empire and the development of new missions seem likely to increase its autonomy from civilian control.
3. The failure of the National Party to democratize internally has hampered the larger process of political democratization. The party remains a highly authoritarian and vertical structure. Should it fall into the hands of the wrong president it could, along with the armed forces, serve as a base for a new era of dictatorship.
4. The nomination of Oswaldo Ramos Soto has injected uncertainty into calculations about the future of democracy and political stability. Ramos Soto could be the "wrong president" just mentioned.
5. The continued escalation of social violence could draw the military further into the political arena, perhaps even providing it with a rationale for a coup.
6. Continuing high levels of corruption and human rights violations and the increase in landlessness as influential members of the National Party and the military take advantage of government policy to enrich themselves are undermining the implicit social contract on which Honduran stability rests. When powerful elites can act with impunity, there are no rules of the game. If there are no rules, then the temptation is for everyone to pursue their own interests regardless of the consequences for the country as a whole.

Suffice it to say that these present and possible future trends do not bode well for Honduras. It is probably no coincidence that the current election campaign has been marked by repeated rumors of *continuismo* (maneuvers by Callejas to remain in power). It would not be surprising if, within the next five years, the constitution were amended to allow the reelection of presidents and former presidents. Such a change would extend to the civilian power the same privilege now enjoyed by the military. It would open the door for the return of the still young and popular Rafael Callejas or perhaps enable a Ramos Soto or a Carlos Roberto Reina to stay in office indefinitely.

By the same token, these warning signs suggest that the military's traditional role of chief regulator in the homeostatic system of Honduran politics may be changing. Clearly, the high command feels threatened by the políticos and civil society. If the threat (to its autonomy, budget, force levels, business empire) grows, it may eventually choose to respond with force. There are indications that Discua himself may have political ambitions. He is well connected within the National Party (of which his brother is president) and may fancy himself another López Arellano.

Within this context, the North American role could be crucial. If declining U.S. economic and military aid will probably not be destabilizing, a reduction in Washington's political influence could be. For years the U.S.-Honduran alliance has been based on an exchange relationship in which U.S. aid has been traded (explicitly or tacitly) for certain concessions. The most obvious of these had to do with the contra presence, but it was not the only one. Among other things, the Honduran military agreed to return the government (with the exception of certain key offices and powers) to civilian control. In effect, the Reagan and Bush administrations paid the Honduran armed forces not to seize power. The question is whether the military will revert to its historical pattern of intervention as U.S. incentives for nonintervention diminish or are withdrawn.

The hope is that by that time democracy will have become ingrained in the political culture, but if that does not happen—or, worse, if the military intervenes *in spite of* a growing popular attachment to democracy—then the likely result will be political instability. One of the most important safety valves of the 1980s will have been closed off and the legitimacy of the country's political arrangements dealt a serious blow. (A related issue here concerns the willingness of *civilians* to play by the rules of democracy, especially when they lose. In the past, their commitment has been equivocal at best. If the democratizing and modernizing factions in the Liberal and National Parties prevail, then the future may be fairly bright. On the other hand, if the traditional caciques like Ramos Soto succeed in turning back the clock, then it will be something else again.)

A return to a policy of benign neglect by the United States would also free the Honduran armed forces to deal more brutally with dissidents and "subversives." Again, one cannot predict whether they would do this. The military does not have a history of massive human rights violations. But then, it has never had to deal with the kind of massive political unrest that the Salvadoran military faced in the late 1970s and early 1980s. If discontent and violence were to grow, the temptation to resort to similar methods might prove overwhelming. That, in turn, would risk setting in motion a "dialectic of revolution"—a self-intensifying, mutually destructive spiral of violence. Excessive repression could drive moderates and the uncommitted to the extreme left, heightening revolutionary violence, and intensifying the counterrevolutionary response.

Forecasting revolutions is a hazardous enterprise, much more an art than a science. There are too many intangibles. One cannot confidently predict the future behavior of the Honduran military (except, perhaps, for its seemingly limitless propensities for corruption and internal bickering). Nor can such intervening variables as economic crisis be easily forecast: A period of rapid growth and rising expectations followed by a sharp economic reversal might finally thrust Honduras onto the J-curve of revolution. But this is highly problematic. All that can be said with confidence is that the potential exists.

In the short run, however, the prospects for political stability are moderately good. The socioeconomic crisis of the initial Callejas years came not after a period of rapid growth but rather at the end of a decade of stagnation and decline. Demoralization, not rising expectations, has been the norm. Relative deprivation might increase if the economy were to deteriorate (and as of spring 1993 there are some signs of this, especially in terms of export earnings), but the fact remains that the public mood is one of pessimism and fatalism. Most people see a bleak future and no way out.

At the same time, there is a marked absence of the kind of leadership and organization that could mobilize the discontented into a viable revolutionary movement. The Honduran guerrillas have never had much popular support. With the collapse of communism in the Soviet Union and Eastern Europe, the ouster of the Sandinistas, the end of the Salvadoran civil war, and the growing crisis in Cuba, their credibility has virtually disappeared. They have lost their foreign sponsors; their sources of ideological inspiration have been badly damaged. Many of them have already given up the armed struggle. Consequently, even if popular discontent continues to grow, there is currently no way of harnessing it for revolutionary purposes. Under these circumstances, revolution is unlikely.

In short, the immediate danger comes from above, not below. It is the political and military elites, rather than the masses, who pose the greatest threat to democracy and political stability. But even there the situation is far from hopeless. Ramos Soto may not be elected, or, if elected, he may prove less destructive than we have suggested. Nor should one expect the military to overthrow the democratic system. The risks and costs—in terms of economic, political, and perhaps even military sanctions—would be considerable, and this may well be enough to deter such a move for the foreseeable future.

We remain, then, cautiously optimistic. In the medium run, the prospects for economic "development" (keeping in mind what that term means in the Honduran context) are modest but not negligible. If the present export-promotion strategy can be combined with an effective job creation program and at least some attention to social justice (land being the most crucial issue), then perhaps growth can be achieved with some degree of equity. The political culture has given Hondurans the flexibility to adapt to changing circumstances. Everything we have said about their capacity for muddling through with a combination of restraint and reform will still, hopefully, apply. In addition, the rate of population growth has finally begun to decline as urbanization and industrialization have thrust the country into the demographic transition. There remain substantial unused territories in Olancho that could help alleviate the problem of landlessness if foreign assistance and domestic resources could be mobilized to develop them. (*How* they would be developed, of course, is a crucial issue.) The threat of foreign subversion has declined. The factionalization of the small revolutionary movement continues. The traditional conservatism and passivity of the culture persist. The "habit" of democracy seems to be taking hold. If Hondurans have a long way to go—if indeed there has been some backsliding during the past year—they have still come a considerable distance. Although stability and democracy remain fragile and incomplete, a base now exists that can be built upon. If the powers that be are willing to do that, then the future could be fairly promising. If they are not, then there will be trouble.

Conclusions: The Lessons of a Nonrevolution

The United States will continue to play an important role in Honduras's future. Though the civil wars in Nicaragua and El Salvador are over, the North American military presence could continue for years. The United States has virtual carte blanche to station troops, land aircraft, and conduct war games in Honduras. With U.S. bases in Panama scheduled to close at the decade's end, the country could become one of the last U.S. military outposts in the region. Under the circumstances—especially given the recent shift in foreign policy focus toward the drug war—it is unlikely that the gringos will soon go home. In the words of one official, "Once we're out, politically it is going to be very difficult to come back into Latin America."[16]

This is not to imply that the U.S. role will remain unchanged. The days of massive military and economic aid—some US$2 billion over the past dozen years—are clearly over. (At its peak, such aid reached US$296.4 million in FY 1985; in 1994, it will be US$43.6 million. Of the latter, military aid will be only US$2.5 million, compared to US$81.1 in 1986.)[17] The U.S. presence will be reduced, but how much and in what ways are open questions. If the U.S. and Panamanian governments decide to extend U.S. base rights in Panama, then Honduras will lose much (though not all) of its value. American interest will decline accordingly.

In the past, U.S. policy toward Latin America has tended to fluctuate between active involvement and neglect. But even noninvolvement is a kind of involvement. Washington has been instrumental in moving Honduran elites toward democracy. To adopt a "hands-off" posture would be to tilt the balance of internal politics in the other direction. Whatever the United States chooses to do—or not do—will have an effect. One can only hope that it will continue to use its influence but in more constructive ways than in the past. This is more than a matter of promoting economic development: Honduras needs to move in the direction of more democratization and social reform and greater respect for human rights. The United States can make a positive contribution in all these areas if it has the will.

Within this context, the preceding analysis suggests an important lesson for both countries: namely, the value of moderation and flexibility. Hondurans have been able to escape revolution for a variety of reasons, some of which were beyond their control. Most important, however, they have shown considerable adaptability in terms of (1) a willingness to provide escape valves for social tensions that, left unattended, might have become explosive and (2) a disinclination to take measures that might have driven large numbers of people into the arms of the revolutionary left. The obvious conclusion is that if Honduras is to avoid revolutionary turmoil, this pattern must continue.

Recent shifts in U.S. policy toward more vigorous promotion of democratization and human rights are most welcome. If these changes have sometimes brought U.S. and Honduran authorities into conflict, that may be part of the price of continued stability. For all their flexibility, the Hondurans may sometimes have to be prodded into taking necessary measures or restrained from actions that might be potentially destabilizing.

The issue of land is a case in point. Neither the United States nor the Callejas administration has understood the value of agrarian reform. Current efforts by the AID and the Honduran government to deal with the crisis in the countryside have taken the form of an agricultural development program that seeks to eliminate state intervention, encourage foreign investment, and free more land for modernization. The INA has been stripped of most of its functions. The agricultural development bank no longer gives peasants low-interest loans. The agrarian reform is being reversed. The danger is that this will lead to an increase in landlessness and the concentration of property in the hands of large Honduran owners and foreign corporations producing export crops at the expense of domestic food production. The experience of Central America (including Honduras) from the 1950s to the 1970s is particularly suggestive; in political and social terms, at least, export agriculture was the problem rather than the solution.[18]

These matters are especially important in light of growing unrest in the countryside. The past few years have witnessed a marked upsurge in agrarian violence, with several massacres perpetrated by large landowners and/or members of the armed forces. Although the situation is not yet out of control, it contains the potential for violence that could eventually lead to a real insurgency. That danger should be taken seriously. Accordingly, the United States should use its influence with the Honduran government and military to ensure that (1) undue violence on the part of the authorities is avoided, (2) human rights violations are prosecuted, (3) land distribution and titling are accelerated, and (4) export agriculture (in itself a legitimate component in national development strategy) is not pursued *at the expense of* small producers and domestic food crops. How these issues are dealt with will in large part determine the prospects for rural stability.

Beyond this, it is time to recognize that a purely economic approach to the Honduran crisis is inadequate and dangerous. If the Suazo/Azcona policy was excessively political and aggravated the economic causes of the crisis, the Callejas/AID approach has failed to deal with the social consequences of economic restructuring. The recent dramatic escalation of social violence is but the most alarming indicator of the extent to which this strategy has accelerated social decay. There is a pressing need for a more balanced policy, one that combines efficiency and incentives for production and investment with a social safety net and more equitable distribution. To continue marching straight ahead, fixated solely on neoliberal economic objectives, is to risk marching off a cliff.

The implication of all this, of course, is that U.S. economic aid ought not to be allowed to continue on its downward spiral; moreover, the program should be restructured to give greater emphasis to social development. It is especially important that means be found for integrating marginalized sectors into productive activity. This includes both civilian unemployed/underemployed and demobilized military personnel. One cannot expect the COSUFFAA to cut the officer corps unless jobs are available in the civilian sector. Lacking that condition, the military is likely to continue on its current course of economic expansion as a way of preserving the well-being of its elite.

In short, if the United States wishes to remain in Honduras and avail itself of the military facilities that exist there, it will be well advised to provide more tangible benefits. Recent polls indicate that a growing number of Hondurans believe that the time has come for U.S. troops to leave. They also show that the vast majority of people are unaware of the AID's assistance programs. To continue a large-scale military presence at the same time that the economic and military benefits to Honduras are declining (or at least becoming less visible) and the social costs of a U.S.-promoted economic strategy are still painfully apparent is to ask for trouble. The Callejas/AID strategy may yet generate economic development and improve living standards. If it does not, however, the ensuing frustration and resentment may well be directed at the United States.

Finally, the United States should encourage the further development of Honduran democracy. Among other things, this means fostering civilian control over the armed forces. Here, however, it is necessary to add a word of caution: The doctrine of civilian control is predicated on the assumptions that civilian leaders are democratic and that it is the military that is the greatest threat to political stability and democracy. Neither of these premises necessarily holds in the Honduran case.

[Note: As this book goes to press, Carlos Roberto Reina has been elected president of Honduras by a margin of 52.3 percent to 40.7 percent for Oswaldo Ramos Soto. The new president pledged to move boldly against human rights abuses and public corruption, to shake up the widely reviled judicial system and impose tighter control over government spending, and to gradually reduce the military budget. Commenting on his opponent's plans, Ramos Soto predicted that if Reina tried to impose the changes that he was contemplating the military would overthrow him.]

Notes

1. By Central America, we mean the traditional "five fingers": Guatemala, El Salvador, Honduras, Nicaragua, and Costa Rica. We do not include Panama, since its history is quite different from that of the others. Similarly, newly independent, English-speaking Belize is Central American only by an accident of geography. It has much more in common with the black British Commonwealth Caribbean tradition than with Hispanic Central America.

2. J. Mark Ruhl, "Agrarian Structure and Political Stability in Honduras," *Journal of Interamerican Studies and World Affairs,* Vol. 26, No. 1, February 1984, pp. 52-56.

3. Ibid., p. 56.

4. This is not to suggest that there are no dedicated militants or that the union movement as a whole has "sold out." Strikes and land seizures are endemic. But they are accepted as legitimate—or at least semilegitimate—activities, and in this sense they have become part of the system.

5. See, especially, Donald E. Schulz, "Ten Theories in Search of Central American Reality," in *Revolution and Counterrevolution in Central America and the Caribbean,* edited by Donald E. Schulz and Douglas H. Graham (Boulder: Westview Press, 1984), pp. 27-35; also John A. Booth, "Socioeconomic and Political Roots of National Revolts in Central America," *Latin American Research Review,* Vol. 26, No. 1, 1991, pp. 33-73.

6. See, especially, Gustavo Blanco and Jaime Valverde, *Honduras: Iglesia y Cambio Social,* San José: Departamento Ecuménico de Investigaciones, 1987. The statistics on the number of priests are from *La Tribuna,* 21 August 1989.

7. See, especially, Christopher Boyer, "Keeping the People In: An Examination of Non-Revolution in Honduras," *LASA Forum,* Vol. 22, No. 2, summer 1991, pp. 1, 5-12; the exchange of letters between Boyer and Jeff Goodwin in ibid., Vol. 22, No. 4, winter 1992, pp. 3-5; and Héctor René Fonseca, "Honduras: Will the Revolution Come?" Master's thesis, U.S. Army Command and General Staff College, Fort Leavenworth, Kansas, 1983, pp. 80-87.

8. Ruhl, "Agrarian Structure," pp. 48, 57; Booth, "Socioeconomic Roots," pp. 40-48; Boyer, "Keeping the People In," pp. 6-9.

9. Ruhl, "Agrarian Structure," pp. 56-59.

10. Even during the growth years of the 1970s, real wages had decreased disproportionately in Guatemala, El Salvador, and Nicaragua. That did not happen in Honduras. Boyer, "Keeping the People In," pp. 6-7, 11; Booth, "Socioeconomic Roots," p. 42.

11. The J-curve is the sudden gap between expectations and reality produced by a cyclical economic downturn. The larger the gap, the greater the loss of confidence in the regime and the more likely the resort to revolution. See James C. Davies, "Toward a Theory of Revolution," *American Sociological Review,* Vol. 27, No. 1, February 1962, pp. 5-19.

12. See, especially, Mancur Olson, "Rapid Growth as a Destabilizing Force," *Journal of Economic History,* Vol. 23, No. 4, December 1963, pp. 529-552; and Schulz, "Ten Theories," pp. 21-23.

13. We are grateful to Philip L. Shepherd for this insight.

14. On the initial socioeconomic impact of the Callejas program, see Alcides Hernández, "El Ajuste Estructural y Sus Repercusiones Económicas y Sociales," *Boletín Informativo Honduras,* Special No. 58, December 1991.

15. Alexis de Tocqueville, *The Old Regime and the French Revolution* (Garden City: Doubleday, 1955), p. 176.

16. *Miami Herald,* 13 April 1992.

17. *Boletín Informativo Honduras,* No. 143, March 1993, p. 6; ibid., No. 147, July 1993, p. 6.

18. See, for example, William H. Durham, *Scarcity and Survival in Central America: Ecological Origins of the Soccer War* (Stanford: Stanford University Press, 1979); and Victor Bulmer-Thomas, *The Political Economy of Central America Since 1920* (Cambridge: Cambridge University Press, 1987). On the recent changes in Honduran agrarian/agricultural policy, see *Puntos de Vista,* No. 5, July 1992.

Abbreviations

AFL-CIO	American Federation of Labor-Congress of Industrial Organizations
AID	Agency for International Development
AIFLD	American Institute for Free Labor Development
ALIPO	Popular Liberal Alliance
ANACH	National Association of Honduran Peasants
APROH	Association for the Progress of Honduras
CAGSSA	Agricultural and Cattle Company of Sula, S.A.
CEDOH	Honduras Documentation Center
CGT	General Central of Workers
CIA	Central Intelligence Agency
CIAV	International Commission of Support and Verification
CNC	National Campesino Congress
CNTC	National Central of Rural Workers
COCOCH	Coordinating Council of Honduran Campesino Organizations
CODEH	Committee for the Defense of Human Rights in Honduras
COFADEH	Committee of Relatives of the Detained-Disappeared of Honduras
COMUNBANA	Multinational Banana Trading Company
CONADI	National Corporation of Industrial Development
COSUFFAA	Superior Council of the Armed Forces
CREM	Regional Military Training Center
CTH	Confederation of Honduran Workers
CUTH	Unitary Confederation of Honduran Workers
DEA	Drug Enforcement Administration
DIA	Defense Intelligence Agency
DNI	National Department of Investigations
EC	European Community
ECLA	U.N. Economic Commission for Latin America

FBI	Federal Bureau of Investigation
FCH	Federation of Honduran Peasants
FDN	Nicaraguan Democratic Force
FECORAH	Federation of Agrarian Reform Cooperatives of Honduras
FENACH	National Federation of Peasants of Honduras
FENAGH	National Federation of Agriculturalists and Cattlemen of Honduras
FITH	Independent Federation of Honduran Workers
FMLN	Farabundo Martí National Liberation Front
FUSEP	Public Security Force
FUTH	Unitary Federation of Honduran Workers
FY 77	Fiscal Year 1977
GAO	Government Accounting Office
GDP	Gross Domestic Product
GNP	Gross National Product
GOH	Government of Honduras
HONDUTEL	Honduran Telecommunications Enterprise
IDB	Inter-American Development Bank
IMF	International Monetary Fund
INA	National Agrarian Institute
M-LIDER	Liberal Democratic Revolutionary Movement
MONARCA	Callejista National Movement
NSC	National Security Council
OAS	Organization of American States
ORIT	Inter-American Regional Organization of Workers
PDRH	Honduran Revolutionary Democratic Party
PINU	Innovation and Unity Party
PRTC	Revolutionary Party of Central American Workers
RIG	Restricted Interagency Group
SITRAINA	Workers' Union of the National Agrarian Institute
SITRASFRUCO	Standard Fruit Company Workers' Union
SITRATERCO	Tela Railroad Company Workers' Union
SOUTHCOM	U.S. Southern Command

STENEE	National Electrical Energy Company Workers' Union
SUTRASFCO	Unified Syndicate of Standard Fruit Company Workers
TNE	National Electoral Tribunal
UFCO	United Fruit Company
UN	United Nations
UNC	National Peasant Union
USG	United States Government
UNO	National Opposition Union
USIA	United States Information Agency

Selected References

Acker, Alison. 1988. *Honduras: The Making of a Banana Republic.* Boston: South End Press.

Amaya Amador, Ramón. 1987. *Prisión Verde.* Tegucigalpa: Editorial Universitaria.

Americas Watch. 1986. *Human Rights in Honduras After General Alvarez.* New York.

________. 1987. *Human Rights in Honduras: Central America's "Sideshow."* New York.

________. 1989. *Honduras: Without the Will.* New York.

Anderson, Thomas P. 1981. *The War of the Dispossessed.* Lincoln: University of Nebraska Press.

________. 1982. *Politics in Central America.* New York: Praeger.

Andrews, David, and Bobbie Andrews. 1989. "Los Vendedores Ambulantes en Tegucigalpa." Unpublished manuscript.

Arancibia, Juan. 1984. *Honduras: ¿Un Estado Nacional?* Tegucigalpa: Editorial Guaymuras.

Arcos, Cresencio. 1991. "Managing Change in Central America." *Foreign Service Journal* 68:19-21.

Argueta, Mario R. 1989. *Bananos y Política: Samuel Zemurray y la Cuyamel Fruit Company en Honduras.* Tegucigalpa: Editorial Universitaria.

________. 1989. *Tiburcio Carías: Anatomía de una Epoca, 1923-1948.* Tegucigalpa: Editorial Guaymuras.

________. 1992. *Historia de los sin Historia, 1900-1948.* Tegucigalpa: Editorial Guaymuras.

Barahona, Marvin. 1989. *La Hegemonía de los Estados Unidos en Honduras, 1907-1932.* Tegucigalpa: Centro de Documentación de Honduras.

________. 1991. *Evolucíon Histórica de la Identidad Nacional.* Tegucigalpa: Editorial Guaymuras.

Bardales Bueso, Rafael. 1980. *Historia del Partido Nacional.* Tegucigalpa: Serviocopiax Editores.

Barry, Tom, and Deb Preusch. 1988. *The Soft War: The Uses and Abuses of U.S. Aid in Central America.* New York: Grove Press.

Barry, Tom, and Kent Norsworthy. 1990. *Honduras: A Country Guide.* Albuquerque: Inter-Hemispheric Education Resource Center.

Becerra, Longino. 1987. *Cuando las Tarántulas Atacan.* Tegucigalpa: Editorial Baktún.

________. 1988. *Evolución Histórica de Honduras.* Tegucigalpa: Editorial Baktún.

Benjamin, Medea. 1988. "Campesinos: Between Carrot and Stick." *NACLA Report on the Americas* 22:22-30.

Blanco, Gustavo, and Jaime Valverde. 1987. *Honduras: Iglesia y Cambio Social.* San José: Departamento Ecuménico de Investigaciones.

Blutstein, Howard I., et al. 1971. *Area Handbook for Honduras.* Washington, D.C.: U.S. Government Printing Office.

Booth, John A. 1991. "Socioeconomic and Political Roots of National Revolts in Central America." *Latin American Research Review* 26:33-73.

Boyer, Christopher. 1991. "Keeping the People In: An Examination of Non-Revolution in Honduras." *LASA Forum* 22:1, 5-12.

Brand, Charles. 1972. "Background of Capitalist Underdevelopment: Honduras to 1913." Ph.D. diss., University of Pittsburgh.

Brockett, Charles D. 1987. "Public Policy, Peasants, and Rural Development in Honduras." *Journal of Latin American Studies* 19:69-86.

________. 1988. *Land, Power, and Poverty: Agrarian Transformation and Political Conflict in Central America.* Boston: Unwin Hyman.

Buckley, Tom. 1984. *Violent Neighbors.* New York: Times Books.

Bueso, Julio Antonio. 1987. *El Subdesarrollo Hondureño.* Tegucigalpa: Editorial Universitaria.

Bulmer-Thomas, Victor. 1987. *The Political Economy of Central America Since 1920.* Cambridge: Cambridge University Press.

Burbach, Roger. 1977. "Union Busting: Castle and Cook in Honduras." *NACLA Report on the Americas* 11:40-41.

________. 1978. "Honduras: Challenging Castle and Cook." *NACLA Report on the Americas.* 12:43-45.

Caldera, Hilda. 1986. *"Las Invasiones Urbanas en Tegucigalpa."* Boletín Informativo Honduras Special No. 26.

Calix Suazo, Miguel. 1984. *Carcel de Horizontes.* Tegucigalpa: Industrias Gráficas Tulin.

Cannon, Lou. 1991. *President Reagan: The Role of a Lifetime.* New York: Simon and Schuster.

Carías, Marco Virgilio, and Víctor Meza. 1975. *Las Compañías Bananeras en Honduras: Un Poco de Historia.* Tegucigalpa: Universidad Nacional Autónoma de Honduras.

Centro de Documentación de Honduras. 1984. *"APROH: Origen, Desarrollo y Perspectivas."* Boletín Informativo Honduras Special No. 9.

________. 1987. *"25 Años de la Reforma Agraria."* Boletín Informativo Honduras Special No. 30.

________. 1991. *"El Proyecto de Callejas."* Boletín Informativo Honduras Special No. 55.

________. 1993. *"Consideraciones sobre la Ley para la Modernización y Desarrollo del Sector Agricola."* Boletín Informativo Honduras Special No. 63

Challener, Richard D. 1973. *Admirals, Generals, and American Foreign Policy, 1898-1914.* Princeton: Princeton University Press.

Colegio de Economistas de Honduras. 1993. *"Analisis del Comportamiento Económico Nacional 1990-1993."* Boletín Informativo Honduras Special No. 64.

Contreras, Carlos A. 1970. *Entre el Marasmo: Análisis de la Crisis del Partido Liberal de Honduras, 1933-1970.* Tegucigalpa: n.p.

Danby, Colin, and Richard Swedberg, comps. 1984. *Honduras: Bibliography and Research Guide.* Cambridge: Central America Information Office.

del Cid, Rafael. 1977. "Las Clases Sociales y Su Dinámica en el Agro Hondureño." *Estudios Sociales Centroamericanos* 18:119-155.

Delgado Fiallos, Aníbal. 1986. *Honduras Elecciones 85.* Tegucigalpa: Editorial Guaymuras.

Díaz Chavez, Filander. 1982. *Carías: El Ultimo Caudillo Frutero.* Tegucigalpa: Editorial Guaymuras.

Dickey, Christopher. 1985. *With the Contras.* New York: Simon and Schuster.

Dillon, Sam. 1991. *Comandos.* New York: Henry Holt.

Draper, Theodore. 1991. *A Very Thin Line.* New York: Hill and Wang.

Durham, William. 1979. *Scarcity and Survival in Central America: Ecological Origins of the Soccer War.* Stanford: Stanford University Press.

Fernández, Arturo. 1988. *Partidos Políticos y Elecciones en Honduras, 1980.* Tegucigalpa: Editorial Guaymuras.

Finney, Kenneth. 1973. Precious Metal Mining and the Modernization of Honduras: In Quest of El Dorado (1880-1990). Ph.D. diss., Tulane University.

Flores Machado, Roberto. 1988. "La Situación del Empleo en Honduras." *Cuadernos de Realidad Nacional* 3:1-12.

Flores Valeriano, Enrique. 1987. *La Explotación Bananera en Honduras.* Tegucigalpa: Editorial Universitaria.

Fonseca, Héctor René. 1983. "Honduras: Will the Revolution Come?" Master of Military Art and Science thesis, U.S. Army Command and General Staff College, Fort Leavenworth, Kansas.

Funes, Miguel Angel. 1991. *"Crisis en la Decada 80 y Reestructuración de la Economía."* Boletín Informativo Honduras Special No. 53.

Garst, Rachel, and Tom Barry. 1990. *Feeding the Crisis.* Lincoln: University of Nebraska Press.

Garvin, Glenn. 1992. *Everybody Had His Own Gringo: The CIA and the Contras.* Washington, D.C.: Brassey's Inc.

Gómez, Alfredo León. 1978. *El Escándalo del Ferrocarril.* Tegucigalpa: n.p.

Gutman, Roy. 1984. "America's Diplomatic Charade." *Foreign Policy* 56:3-23.

________. 1988. *Banana Diplomacy: The Making of American Policy in Nicaragua, 1981-1987.* New York: Simon and Schuster.

Hammond, Tony. 1991. The Role of the Honduran Armed Forces in the Transition to Democracy. Master's thesis, University of Florida.

Helms, Mary W. 1984. "The Society and Its Environment," in James D. Rudolph, ed., *Honduras: A Country Study,* Pp. 53-100. Washington, D.C.: American University Press.

Hernández, Alcides. 1983. *El Neoliberalismo en Honduras.* Tegucigalpa: Editorial Guaymuras.

________. 1991. *"El Ajuste Estructural y Sus Repercusiones Económicas y Sociales."* Boletín Informativo Honduras Special No. 58.

________. 1992. *Del Reformismo al Ajuste Estructural.* Tegucigalpa: Editorial Guaymuras.

Hernández F., Héctor. 1991. *Solidarismo y Sindicalismo en Honduras.* Tegucigalpa: FUTH.

Instituto Hondureño de Desarrollo Rural. 1980. *84 Meses de Reforma Agraria del Gobierno de las Fuerzas Armadas de Honduras.* Tegucigalpa.

Karnes, Thomas L. 1978. *Tropical Enterprise: The Standard Fruit and Steamship Company in Latin America.* Baton Rouge: Louisiana State University.

Kepner, Charles David, Jr. 1936. *Social Aspects of the Banana Industry.* New York: Columbia University Press.

Kepner, Charles David, Jr., and Jay Henry Soothill. 1963. *The Banana Empire: A Case Study of Economic Imperialism.* New York: Russell and Russell.

Kornbluh, Peter. 1987. *Nicaragua: The Price of Intervention.* Washington, D.C.: Institute for Policy Studies.

Kornbluh, Peter, and Malcolm Byrne, eds. 1993. *The Iran-Contra Scandal: The Declassified History.* New York: The New Press.

Krehm, William. 1984. *Democracies and Tyrannies of the Caribbean.* Westport, Conn.: Lawrence Hill.

LaFeber, Walter. 1983. *Inevitable Revolutions.* New York: W. W. Norton.

Laínez, Vilma, and Víctor Meza. 1973. "El Enclave Bananero en la Historia de Honduras." *Estudios Sociales Centroamericanos* 2:115-156.

Langley, Lester D. 1983. *The Banana Wars: An Inner History of American Empire, 1900-1934.* Lexington: University Press of Kentucky.

Lapper, Richard, and James Painter. 1985. *Honduras: State for Sale.* London: Latin America Bureau.

Leiva Vivas, Rafael. 1969. *Un País en Honduras.* Tegucigalpa: Imprenta Calderón.

________. 1973. *Honduras: Fuerzas Armadas, Dependencia o Desarrollo.* Tegucigalpa: n.p.

LeMoyne, James. 1988. "Testifying to Torture." *New York Times Magazine* 5 June:45-47, 62-64, 66.

Lernoux, Penny. 1980. *Cry of the People.* New York: Doubleday.

López Contreras, Carlos. 1984. *Las Negociaciones de Paz: Mi Punto de Vista.* Tegucigalpa: Imprenta Lithopress.

MacCameron, Robert. 1983. *Bananas, Labor, and Politics in Honduras: 1954-1963.* Syracuse: Syracuse University Press.

McCann, Thomas. 1976. *An American Company: The Tragedy of United Fruit.* New York: Crown.

McNeil, Frank. 1988. *War and Peace in Central America.* New York: Scribner's.

Mariñas Otero, Luis. 1987. *Honduras.* Tegucigalpa: Editorial Universitaria.

Mayer, Jane, and Doyle McManus. 1988. *Landslide: The Unmaking of the President, 1984-1988.* Boston: Houghton Mifflin.

Medina Bardales, Marel. 1993. *La Devaluación en Honduras.* Yoro: Editorial El Jamo Olanchito.

Mejía, Bohanerges, and María Elena Méndez. 1989. "Honduras: Crisis y Demandas Populares," in Leticia Salomón, ed., *Honduras: Panorama y Perspectivas,* pp. 151-200. Tegucigalpa: Centro de Documentación de Honduras.

Mejía, Medardo. 1969. *Historia de Honduras.* 6 Volumes. Tegucigalpa: Editorial Universitaria.

Menjívar, Rafael, Sui Moy La Kam, and Virginia Portuguez. 1985. "El Movimiento Campesino en Honduras," in Daniel Camacho and Rafael Menjívar, eds., *Movimientos Populares en Centroamérica.* San José: Editorial Universitaria Centroamerica.

Meza, Víctor. 1980. *Historia del Movimiento Obrero Hondureño.* Tegucigalpa: Editorial Guaymuras.

________. 1981. *Política y Sociedad.* Tegucigalpa: Editorial Guaymuras.

________. 1988. "The Military: Willing to Deal." *NACLA Report on the Americas* 22:14-21.

________. 1990. *"Elecciones en Honduras: Un Intento de Interpretación."* Boletín Informativo Honduras Special No. 48.

Millett, Richard L. 1984. "Historical Setting," in James D. Rudolph, ed., *Honduras: A Country Study*, pp. 1-52. Washington, D.C.: American University Press.

Molina Chocano, Guillermo. 1985. *Estado Liberal y Desarrollo Capitalista en Honduras.* Tegucigalpa: Editorial Universitaria.

Morris, James A. 1974. Interest Groups and Politics in Honduras. Ph.D. diss., University of New Mexico.

________. 1975. *The Honduran Plan Político de Unidad Nacional, 1971-1972: Its Origins and Demise.* El Paso: University of Texas Center for Latin American Studies.

________. 1984. *Honduras, Caudillo Politics, and Military Rulers.* Boulder: Westview Press.

Morris, James A., and Steve C. Ropp. 1977. "Corporatism and Dependent Development: A Honduran Case Study." *Latin American Research Review* 12:27-68.

Morris, James A., and Marta F. Sánchez Soler. 1977. "Factores de Poder en la Evolución Política del Campesinado Hondureño." *Estudios Sociales Centroamericanos* 16:85-103.

Murga Frassinetti, Antonio. 1975. "Concentración Industrial en Honduras." *Economía Política* 9:70-78.

________. 1985. *Enclave y Sociedad en Honduras.* Tegucigalpa: Editorial Universitaria.

Natalini de Castro, Stefanía, Maria de los Angeles Mendoza Saborío, and Joaquín Pagán Solórzano. 1985. *Significado Histórico del Gobierno del Dr. Ramón Villeda Morales.* Tegucigalpa: Editorial Universitaria.

Noé Pino, Hugo. 1992. *"Consideraciones Generales Sobre el Ajuste Estructural en Honduras."* Boletín Informativo Honduras Special No. 60.

Noé Pino, Hugo, and Andrew Thorpe. 1992. *Honduras: El Ajuste Estructural y la Reforma Agraria.* Tegucigalpa: Centro de Documentacíon de Honduras.

Noé Pino, Hugo, Andy Thorpe, and Rigoberto Sandoval Corea. 1992. *El Sector Agricola y la Modernización en Honduras.* Tegucigalpa: Centro de Documentación de Honduras.

Oquelí, Ramón. 1982. *Cronología de la Soberanía Militar.* Tegucigalpa: Centro de Estudios y Promoción del Desarrollo.

________. 1988. *Bibliografía Sociopolítica de Honduras.* Tegucigalpa: Editorial Universitaria.

Orellana, Edmundo. 1986. *La Reforma Administrativa en Honduras*. Tegucigalpa: Editorial Universitaria.

Oseguera de Ochoa, Margarita. 1987. *Honduras Hoy: Sociedad y Crisis Política*. Tegucigalpa: Centro de Documentación de Honduras.

Pan American Publicity Corporation. 1930. *Honduras*. Havana.

Pardo-Maurer, R. 1990. *The Contras, 1980-1989: A Special Kind of Politics*. New York: Praeger.

Pastor, Robert A. 1987. *Condemned to Repetition: The United States and Nicaragua*. Princeton: Princeton University Press.

Pastor, Rodolfo. 1986. "*El Ocaso de los Cacicazgos*." Boletín Informativo Honduras Special No. 21.

Paz Barnica, Edgardo. 1986. *La Política Exterior de Honduras, 1982-1986*. Madrid: Editorial Iberoamericana.

Paz, Ernesto. n.d. *Historia de los Partidos Políticos en Honduras*. Tegucigalpa: Editorial Guaymuras.

Peckenham, Nancy, and Annie Street, eds. 1985. *Honduras: Portrait of a Captive Nation*. New York: Praeger.

Posas, Mario. 1979. "Política Estatal y Estructura Agraria en Honduras (1950-1978)." *Estudios Sociales Centroamericanos* 24:37-116.

_________. 1980. *Lucha Ideológica y Organización Sindical en Honduras (1954-1965)*. Tegucigalpa: Editorial Guaymuras.

_________. 1980. "Honduras at the Crossroads." *Latin American Perspectives* 7:45-56.

_________. 1981. *Luchas del Movimiento Obrero Hondureño*. San José: Editorial Universitaria Centroamericana.

_________. 1981. *El Movimiento Campesino Hondureño*. Tegucigalpa: Editorial Guaymuras.

_________. 1981. *Conflictos Agrarios y Organización Campesina*. Tegucigalpa: Editorial Universitaria.

_________. 1987. *Breve Historia de las Organizaciones Campesinas en Honduras*. Tegucigalpa: Fundación Friedrich Ebert.

_________. 1989. "*El Movimiento Sindical Hondureño durante la Decada del Ochenta*." Boletín Informativo Honduras Special No. 44.

_________. 1989. *Modalidades del Proceso de Democratización en Honduras*. Tegucigalpa: Editorial Universitaria.

Posas, Mario, and Rafael del Cid. 1983. *La Construcción del Sector Público y del Estado Nacional de Honduras, 1876-1979*. San José: Editorial Universitaria Centroamericana.

Ronfeldt, David. 1989. *U.S. Involvement in Central America: Three Views from Honduras*. Santa Monica: RAND Corporation.

Ropp, Steve C. 1974. "The Honduran Army in the Sociopolitical Evolution of the Honduran State." *The Americas* 30:504-528.

Rosenberg, Mark B. 1983. "Honduran Scorecard: Military and Democrats in Central America." *Caribbean Review* 12:12-15, 39-42.

________. 1984. "Honduras: Bastion of Stability or Quagmire?" in Donald E. Schulz and Douglas H. Graham, eds., *Revolution and Counterrevolution in Central America and the Caribbean*, pp. 331-350. Boulder: Westview Press.

________. 1985. "The Current Situation in Honduras and U.S. Policy." Prepared Statement before the Subcommittee on Western Hemisphere Affairs, Committee on Foreign Relations, U.S. House of Representatives.

________. 1988. "Narcos and Politicos: The Politics of Drug Trafficking in Honduras." *Journal of Interamerican Studies and World Affairs* 30:143-165.

________. 1989. "Can Democracy Survive the Democrats? From Transition to Consolidation in Honduras," in John A. Booth and Mitchell A. Seligson, eds., *Elections and Democracy in Central America*, pp. 40-59. Chapel Hill: University of North Carolina Press.

Rosenberg, Mark B., and Philip L. Shepherd, eds. 1986. *Honduras Confronts Its Future*. Boulder: Lynne Rienner.

Ruben, Raúl. 1989. *Notas Sobre la Cuestión Agraria en Honduras*. San José: Universidad Libre de Amsterdam.

________. 1991. *El Problema Agrario en Honduras*. Tegucigalpa: Centro de Documentación de Honduras.

Ruben, Raúl, and Francisco Fúnez. 1993. *La Compra-Venta de Tierras de la Reforma Agraria*. Tegucigalpa: Editorial Guaymuras.

Rudolph, James D., ed. 1984. *Honduras: A Country Study*. Washington, D.C.: American University Press.

Ruhl, J. Mark. 1984. "The Economy," in James D. Rudolph, ed., *Honduras: A Country Study*, pp. 101-146. Washington, D.C.: American University Press.

________. 1984. "Agrarian Structure and Political Stability in Honduras." *Journal of Interamerican Studies and World Affairs* 26:33-67.

________. 1985. "The Honduran Agrarian Reform Under Suazo Córdova, 1982-85; An Assessment." *Inter-American Economic Affairs* 39:63-80.

Salomón, Leticia. 1982. *Militarismo y Reformismo en Honduras*. Tegucigalpa: Editorial Guaymuras.

________. 1988. *"La Doctrina de la Seguridad Nacional en Honduras."* Boletín Informativo Honduras Special No. 33.

________, ed. 1989. *Honduras: Panorama y Perspectivas*. Tegucigalpa: Centro de Documentación de Honduras.

________. 1992. *Política y Militares en Honduras.* Tegucigalpa: Centro de Documentación de Honduras.

Salomón, Leticia, and Bethenia Galo. 1985. *"El Proceso de Urbanización en la Capital de Honduras."* Boletín Informativo Honduras Special No. 19.

Schulz, Donald E. 1984. "Ten Theories in Search of Central American Reality," in Donald E. Schulz and Douglas H. Graham, eds., *Revolution and Counterrevolution in Central America and the Caribbean,* pp. 3-64. Boulder: Westview Press.

________. 1992. "How Honduras Escaped Revolutionary Violence." *Small Wars and Insurgencies* 3:90-111.

Schulz, Donald E., and Douglas H. Graham, eds. 1984. *Revolution and Counterrevolution in Central America and the Caribbean,* Boulder: Westview Press.

Scott, Peter Dale, and Jonathan Marshall. 1991. *Cocaine Politics.* Berkeley: University of California Press.

Selser, Gregorio. 1983. *Honduras: República Alquilada.* Coyoacán, Mexico: Mex-Sur Editorial.

Shaw, Royce Q. 1978. *Central America: Regional Integration and National Political Development.* Boulder: Westview Press.

Sheehan, Edward R.F. 1986. "The Country of *Nada.*" *New York Review of Books* 33:11-12, 14, 16-17.

Shepherd, Philip L. 1984. "The Tragic Course and Consequences of U.S. Policy in Honduras." *World Policy Journal* 2:109-154.

________. 1984. "Six Keys to the Understanding of Current United States-Honduran Relations." Prepared Statement before the Subcommittee on Military Installations and Facilities, U.S. House of Representatives.

________. 1987. "The Honduran Economic Crisis and U.S. Economic Assistance: A Critique of Reaganomics for Honduras." Unpublished manuscript.

________. 1988. "The Case of the Invisible Aid." *NACLA Report on the Americas* 22:31-38.

Slutzky, Daniel, and Esther Alonso. 1978. *Notas sobre las Transformaciones Recientes del Enclave Bananero en Honduras.* Tegucigalpa: Universidad Nacional Autónoma de Honduras.

________. 1980. *Empresas Transnacionales y Agricultura: El Caso del Enclave Bananero en Honduras.* Tegucigalpa: Universidad Nacional Autónoma de Honduras.

Smith, Wayne S. 1987. "Lies About Nicaragua." *Foreign Policy* 67:87-103.

Stokes, William S. 1950. *Honduras: An Area Study in Government.* Madison: University of Wisconsin Press.

Stringer, Randy. 1989. "Honduras: Toward Conflict and Agrarian Reform," in William C. Thiesenhusen, ed., *Searching for Agrarian Reform in Latin America*, pp. 358-383. Boston: Unwin Hyman.

Tojeira, José María. 1986. *Panorama Histórico de la Iglesia en Honduras*. Tegucigalpa: Centro de Documentación de Honduras.

Tower, John, Edmund Muskie, and Brent Scowcroft. 1987. *The Tower Commission Report*. New York: Times Books.

United Nations Economic Commission for Latin America. 1973. *Tenencia de la Tierra y Desarrollo Rural en Centroamérica*. San José: CEPAL.

U.S. General Accounting Office. 1985. *Providing Effective Economic Assistance to El Salvador and Honduras: A Formidable Task*. Washington, D.C.

U.S. Senate Foreign Relations Committee, Subcommittee on Terrorism, Narcotics, and International Operations. 1989. *Drugs, Law Enforcement, and Foreign Policy*. Washington, D.C.: U.S. Government Printing Office.

Vega Carballo, José Luis. 1988. "Partidos, Desarrollo Político y Conflicto Social en Honduras y Costa Rica: Un Análisis Comparativo." *Cuadernos de Realidad Nacional* 3:30-50.

Volk, Stephen. 1981. "Honduras: On the Border of War." *NACLA Report on the Americas* 15:2-37.

Walker, Ian. 1990. *"Deuda y Ajuste Estructural: El Caso de Honduras, 1980-1988."* Boletín Informativo Honduras Special No. 50.

White, Richard Alan. 1984. *The Morass: United States Intervention in Central America*. New York: Harper and Row.

Williams, Robert G. 1986. *Export Agriculture and the Crisis in Central America*. Chapel Hill: University of North Carolina Press.

Woodward, Bob. 1987. *Veil: The Secret Wars of the CIA, 1981-1987*. New York: Simon and Schuster.

Zúniga Andrade, Edgardo. 1990. *Las Modalidades de la Lluvia en Honduras*. Tegucigalpa: Editorial Guaymuras.

About the Book and Authors

Prior to the 1980s Honduras was an obscure backwater, of little public or policy concern in the United States. With the advent of the Reagan administration, however, Hondurans found themselves at the center of the U.S.-Central American imbroglio, a launching pad for the administration's contra war against the Sandinista government in Nicaragua and for counterinsurgency operations against guerrillas in El Salvador.

Placing events in the context of Honduran history, the authors provide penetrating insights into the causes of revolution in Central America and the sources of stability that enabled Honduras to escape the civil strife that consumed its neighbors. At the same time, the work offers a fascinating account of Honduran domestic politics and of the personalities, motives, and maneuvers of policymakers on both sides of the U.S.-Honduras relationship—too often a tale of intrigue, violence, and corruption.

Donald E. Schulz is associate professor of national security at the Strategic Studies Institute, U.S. Army War College. He is the co-editor of *Revolution and Counterrevolution in Central America and the Caribbean* (Westview) and has published extensively on Latin America and comparative Communism.

Deborah Sundloff Schulz, a freelance writer, has lived in Honduras for several years, where she has taught at Academia Saint Patrick and the Metropolitan School in Tegucigalpa.

Index